WEB PROGRAM DESIGN

Wei Teng and Yujun Zhang

WEB PROGRAM DESIGN

Wei Teng and Yujun Zhang

COSMOS PUBLISHING

COSMOS PUBLISHING

必睿国际文化
B-RIGHT CULTURE

Web Program Design

A Publication by Cosmos Publishing Group
Address: 1312 17th Street Unit #2023 Denver Co 80202US
Word Count (for Space of all Pages): 231 Thousand Words
ISBN: 978-1-967277-04-9

About the Author

Wei Teng was born in Anshan, Liaoning, P.R. China, in 1978. She received the master's degree from University of Science and Technology Liaoning, P.R. China. Now, she works in School of Computer Science and Software Engineering, University of Science and Technology Liaoning, her research interests include image processing, computational intelligence and big data analysis.

Yujun Zhang was born in Chaoyang, Liaoning, P.R. China, in 1977. He received the doctor's degree from University of Science and Technology Liaoning, P.R. China. Now, he works in School of Computer Science and Software Engineering, University of Science and Technology Liaoning, his research interests include Pattern Recognition & Intelligent Systems.

INTRODUCTION

ASP.NET stands as one of the mainstream technologies for web application development. This technology is simple and efficient, it is compatible with any .NET language for development. ASP.NET based on Visual Studio Community 2019 is built on the .NET Framework. It emphasizes developer productivity, and enhances system performance and scalability. LINQ technology based on Entity Framework offers a unified model for querying data across diverse data sources and formats. Additionally, the ASP.NET Ajax significantly simplifies the implementation of partial page refreshing in ASP.NET websites. Visual Studio Community 2019 can seamlessly support technologies like XHTML5, CSS3, jQuery, and Bootstrap, and provide intelligent coding of JavaScript. Furthermore, it facilitates the development of modern applications based on cloud, including internet of things and smartphones, and it enables cross-platform development and deployment across Windows, Mac, Linux, and other operating systems.

This book is primarily written around cultivating technical application skills, and it is based on the Visual Studio Community 2019 platform. It emphasizes a student-centered approach, covers fundamental knowledge and theoretical systems, highlights practicality and operational capability, and reinforces case-based teaching. Through practical training, students can deepen their understanding of theoretical knowledge. The book underscores the integration of knowledge and skills, and seamlessly incorporates key concepts into practical project development. Guided by this philosophy, the conte

Chapter 1 introducing runtime, development environment, and website configuration of ASP.NET based on Visual Studio Community 2019.

Chapter 2, according to web application development, introduces the knowledge of .NET technology mainly including core XHTML5 elements, page models, CSS3, JavaScript, popular jQuery, XML, configuration files, global application class files, Bootstrap, etc.

Chapter 3 and Chapter 4 introduce the application of ASP.NET standard controls and validation controls.

Chapter 5 introduces HTTP request, response, and state management mechanism of ASP.NET page.

Chapter 6 introduces the methods of accessing databases by using data source controls and LinQ technology. This chapter also introduces the methods of accessing XML data by using LinQ technology.

Chapter 7 introduces the technology by using data-bound controls to present data in a database.

Chapter 8 introduces the common three-tier architecture technology by taking the user management in the MyPetShop application as an example and introducing web application development methods by using ASP.NET three-layer architecture.

Chapter 9 introduces the utilization of themes, master pages, and user controls from the perspective of maintaining overall website style consistency.

Chapter 10 introduces website navigation techniques.

Chapter 11 introduces ASP.NET Ajax technology that can enhance user experience.

Chapter 12 introduces web services that are widely used on the Internet.

Chapter 13 introducing file processing on web servers.

Chapter 14 takes the MyPetShop application as a comprehensive example to introduce the entire process of developing web applications based on the ASP.NET three-tier architecture, and offers an excellent learning template.

The book encompasses numerous teaching examples. Utilizing this book can significantly boost the enthusiasm of international students for learning, alleviate their learning burden, and ultimately equip them with the ability to develop web applications by using ASP.NET 4.7, including information publishing systems, forums, message boards, chat rooms, blogs, etc.

Contents

Chapter 1 ASP.NET and Development Environment

Points:

- Understanding the page composition of ASP.NET website and the NET Framework
- Understanding the development mode of ASP.NET
- Be familiar with ASP.NET environment, Web application and virtual directory settings
- Be familiar with Visual Studio 2019
- Mastering the method of managing websites, publishing web applications and copying websites through solutions

1.1 ASP.NET Overview

ASP.NET is based on NET Framework, which calls .NET Framework class library through .NET language to realize the development of Web application.

1.1.1 Static and dynamic pages

Static pages only contain HTML elements and CSS styles, and are generally stored with the extension name: htm or. html. Static pages usually display the same content. The interpretation and execution of static pages are completely done by the browser.

Dynamic pages can contain HTML elements and CSS styles, JavaScript codes and the codes that need to be compiled and executed on the Web server. The development technology of dynamic pages also includes ASP, JSP, PHP, etc. The contents of dynamic pages are stored in the database. All dynamic pages need to be converted into static pages by the Web server before the final effect can be displayed on your browser.

On the same ASP.NET website, static pages and dynamic pages can exist at the same time. When the page contents can be updated directly through the page design without changing the database, the static pages are often used; otherwise, they are the dynamic pages. And the access speed of static pages is faster than dynamic pages.

1.1.2 .NET framework

.NET framework is a set of frameworks of Microsoft application development, which provide a consistent development model.

.NET framework has two components: Common Language Runtime (CLR) and .NET Framework class libraries.

1.1.3 The characters of .NET Framework

ASP.NET is not a program language, but a component provided by .NET Framework.

1.ASP.NET and .NET Framework are perfectly integrated

2.ASP.NET is compiled rather than interpreted

1.1.4 ASP.NET development mode

1. ASP.NET web form

The ASP.NET Web Form is a common development mode. It contains tags for page rendering such as XHTML and ASP.NET controls, and codes for handling pages and control events by using .NET language (such as C #).

2.ASP.NET MVC

ASP.NET MVC contains model, view, and controller. The model is used to implement data logical operations; the view is used to display the user interface of the applications; as an intermediate component of the model and view, the controller uses the model to obtain data and generate views through handling user interaction, and displays them on the user interface.

3.ASP.NET core

ASP.NET core is the refactored version of ASP.NET, it runs on .NET Core and .NET Framework. ASP.NET Core supports cross-platform development and deployment on Windows, Mac, Linux and other operating systems.

1.2 Visual Studio Community 2019

1.2.1 Overview of development environment

VSC 2019 provides a convenient development environment for ASP.NET website.VSC 2019 is free and it includes all of the functions and tools needed to create web applications. Web applications created

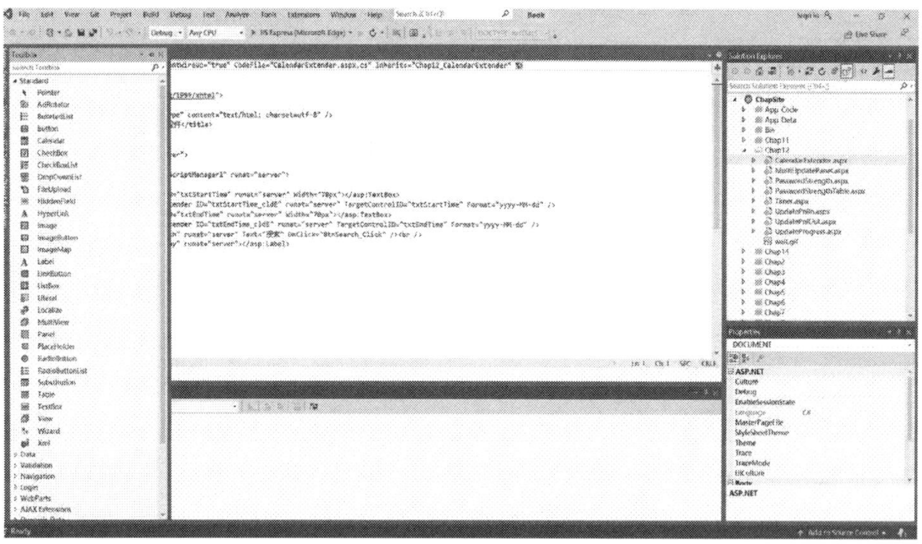

Figure 1-1 Main window interface

with VSC 2019 and the commercial editions are fully compatible with each other. Therefore, VSC 2019 is suitable for learning and website development of Small and medium-sized enterprises.

1.Toolbar

The toolbar provides some buttons that are convenient for programming.Such as the debug and run button ▶ can start the debugging and running process of the website.

When you right-click the toolbar and select the "HTML Edit Source" command in the shortcut menu, the "HTML Edit Source" button will be added into the toolbar. Among them,"Arrange the format of the whole document" button applies to the windows whose current window is" source" view."Comment Selected Lines" button applies to centralize the comments on selected lines during programming.

2.Common Windows

In the document window, there are three views of a page: "design", "split" and "source". Among them, the "design" view presents the design interface of the page; the "split" view presents the design and source codes interface of the page; the "source" view presents the source codes interface of the page.

In the "Solution Explorer" window, you can organize and manage the projects you are editing, you can create, rename, and delete folders and files.

In the "Service Explorer" window, you can open database connection and display database, etc.

In the "SQL Server Object Explorer" window, you can easily manage the database objects in the installed SQL Server instances.

In the "Error List" window, the "Errors", "Warnings", and "Messages" generated when you edit and compile codes will be displayed.

3.Common settings of "Options" in the "Tool" menu

When you select "Tool"→ "Select" command, common settings of VSC 2019 can be made in the displayed "Option" dialog box.

(1)In the "Option" dialog box, when you select "Environment "→ "Font and Color" command, the font and color for text rendering in the document window can be set.

(2)In the "Option" dialog box, you can select "Projects and Solutions" command, and select the "Always show solutions" check box in the displayed dialog box, all of the web applications in the form of solutions in the "Solution Explorer" window can be conveniently managed.

(3) In the "Option" dialog box, you can select "Text editor" → "All languages" command and select the "Line Number" check box in the displayed dialog box to facilitate the developers to quickly locate the specified line according to the line number.

(4) In the "Option" dialog box, you can select "Text editor" → "All languages" → "Tab" command, when you set the values of "Tab Sizc" and "Indent Size" in the rendered dialog box, you can change the number of characters represented by a tab and the number of characters automatically indented in each line.

1.2.2 Managing the new website established in VSC 2019 by using solution

Taking the establishment of Book solution in the folder of C:\ASPNET\Book as an example to illustrate the establishment process of the solution.

Selecting "File"→"New"→"Project" command, and opening the "Solution" in the displayed dialog box, selecting the "Blank solution" template, then input name "Book", location "c:\ASPNET", As is shown in Figure 1-2, Figure 1-3. Finally, clicking " Create " button to establish the Book solution.

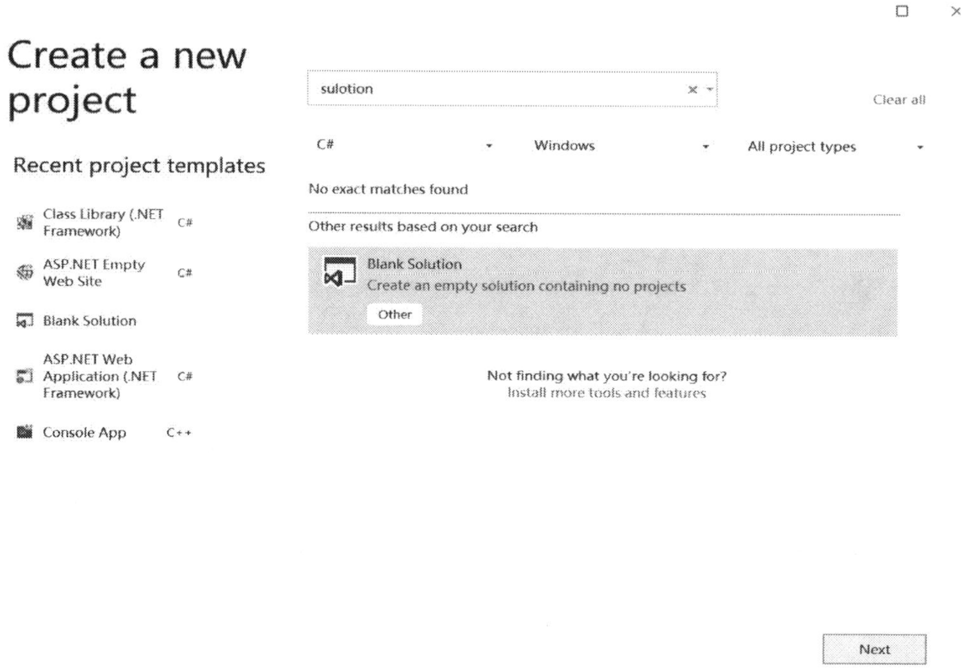

Figure 1-2 Establishing solution interface (1)

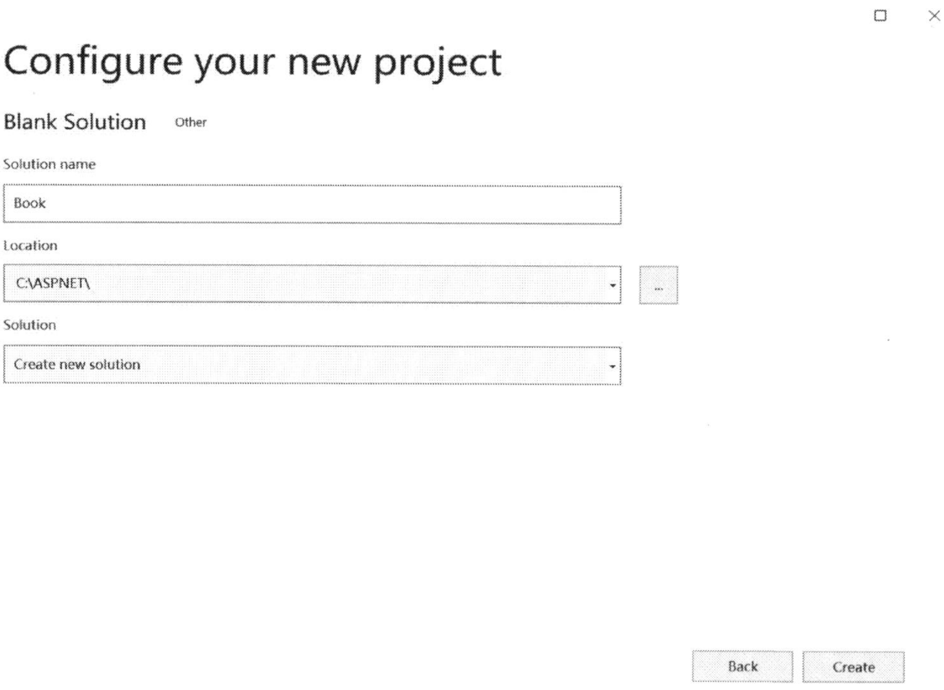

Figure 1-3 Establishing solution interface (2)

After establishing the solution, the Website can be added in it. Then we will introduce how to create a new file system Website ChapSite in the solution. The Website ChapSite is stored in the folder that is C:\ASPNET\Book\ ChapSite. The steps are as follows:

Opening the "Solution Manager" window, right-clicking "Solution Book", selecting "Add" → "New Project" command from the shortcut menu, searching "website" in the dialogue box, selecting "empty Website" template,

clicking next button, then inputting name ChapSite and location C:\ASPNET\Book, selecting .Net Framework 4.7.2, as is shown in Figure 1-4 and Figure 1-5. Clicking "Create" button, adding ChapSite website.

Figure 1-4 Adding new WebSite (1)

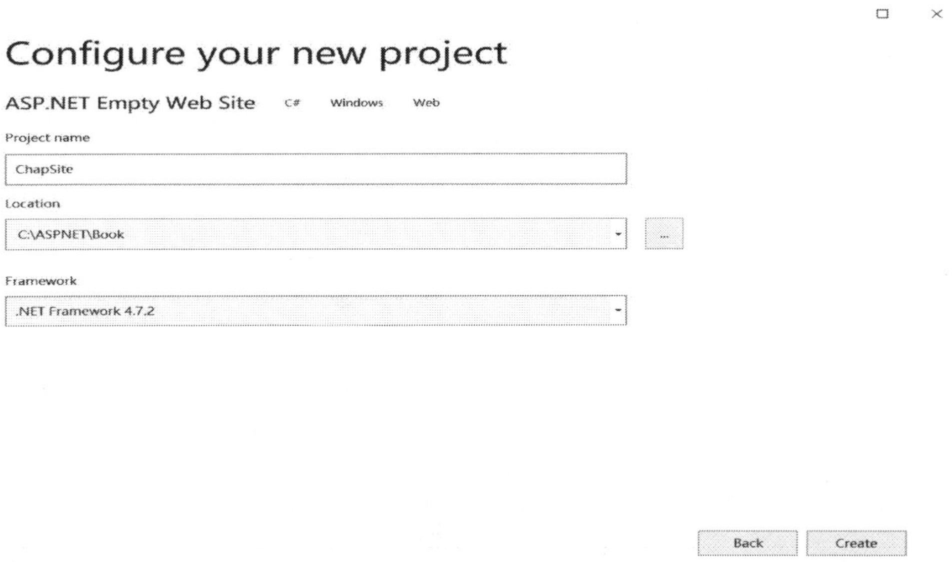

Figure 1-5 Adding new WebSite (2)

In fact, the website established in the figure belongs to "File System" website, the files of this type of website are placed in a folder on the local hard disk, or a shared location on the LAN.IIS installed independently in the operating system is not required for website development, operation and debugging, while IIS Express installed with VSC 2019 is used. We establish the new website in this book by using this type.

1.2.3 Publishing web application

After development of Web application, the application should be deployed from the development environment to the actual running environment such as Microsoft Azure or IIS etc. Microsoft Azure provides the cloud services of data base, cloud storage, artificial intelligence, CDN etc. The services of Microsoft Azure are not free, after completing the user registration, a 30 days free trial period can be provided, which can be used for the deployment test of the Web application. Web application publishing also includes "Web Deployment", "Web Deploy Package", FTP, "File System" and so on. The "File System" method is commonly used.

When publishing Web Application, you can select precompiler to compile the .cs files and code hidden pages contained in the APP_Code folder into the .dll assemble files system that is randomly named, and the compilation error is found, which makes the initial response speed of the page faster and the published website no longer contains any C # program codes.

The other compilation method of ASP.NET is dynamic compilation. If a page is accessed for the first time or is accessed after being modified and saved, the .NET environment will automatically call the compiler to compile and cache the compiled output.

The following is an example of publishing the ChapSite website through the "File System" mode. Right-clicking ChapSite website, selecting "Publish Web Application" command from the shortcut menu, the dialog box as shown in the figure 1-6 is displayed.

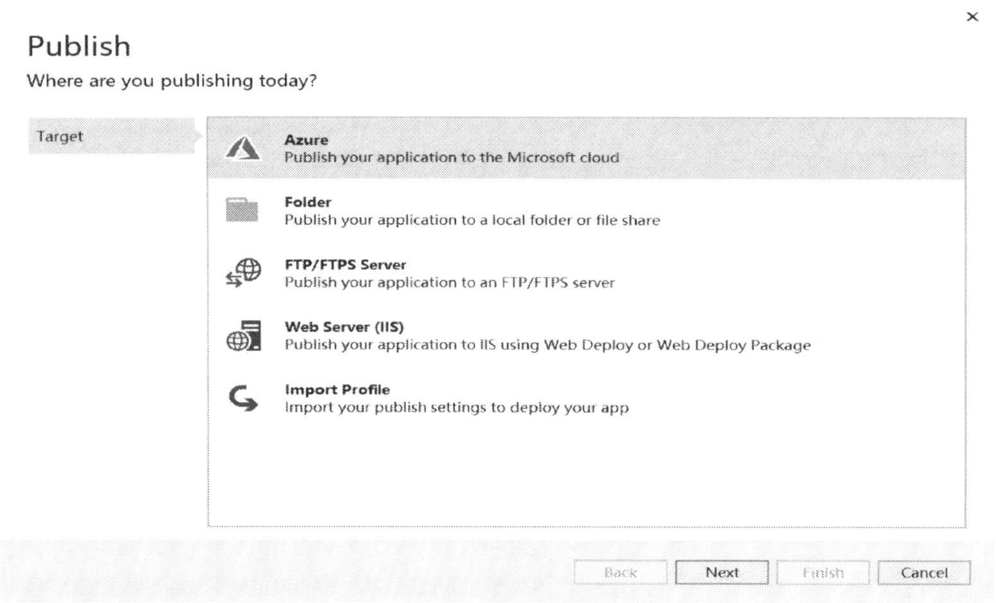

Figure 1-6 Publishing Dialog (1)

Note: If you want to start VSC 2019 to publish websites correctly through the "Publish Web Application" command, you must be an administrator.

In figure 1-6, selecting "File" command, clicking "next" button, then clicking "browse" button in the displaying dialogue box, selecting the folder "C:\ChapSitePub", the figure 1-7 is displayed.

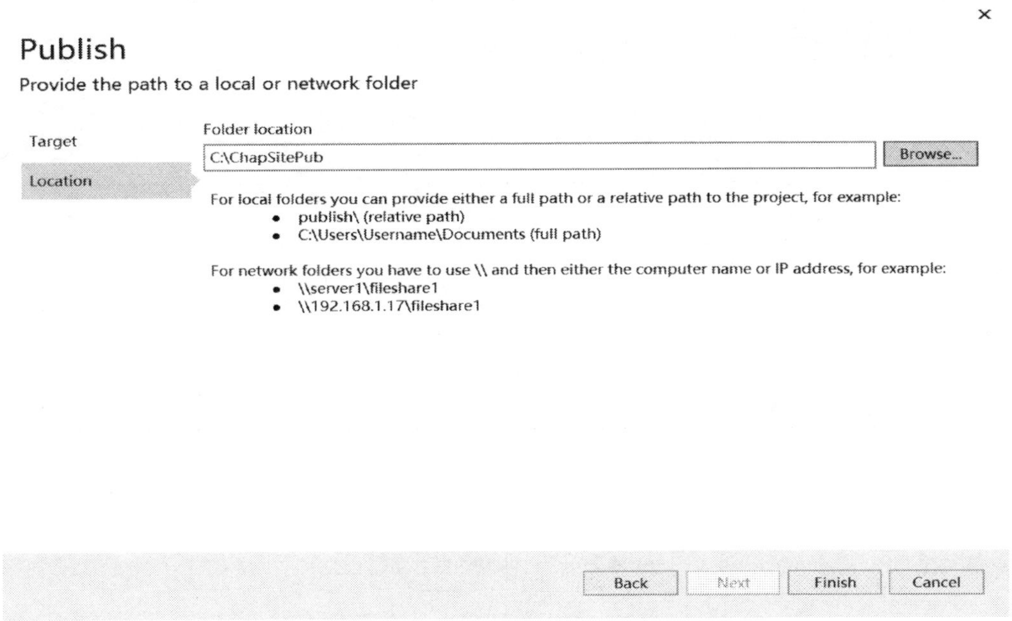

Figure 1- 7 Publishing Dialog (2)

In figure 1-7, clicking "finish" button, the dialogue box like figure 1-8 is displayed.

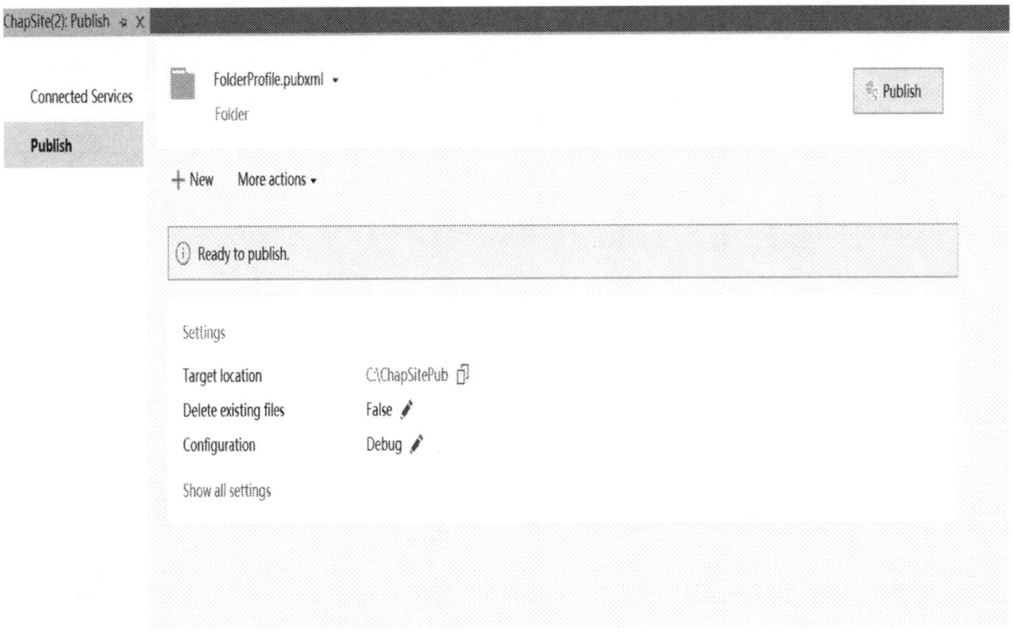

Figure 1- 8 Publishing Dialog (3)

In figure 1-8, clicking "show all settings" button, the dialog box like figure 1-9 is displayed.

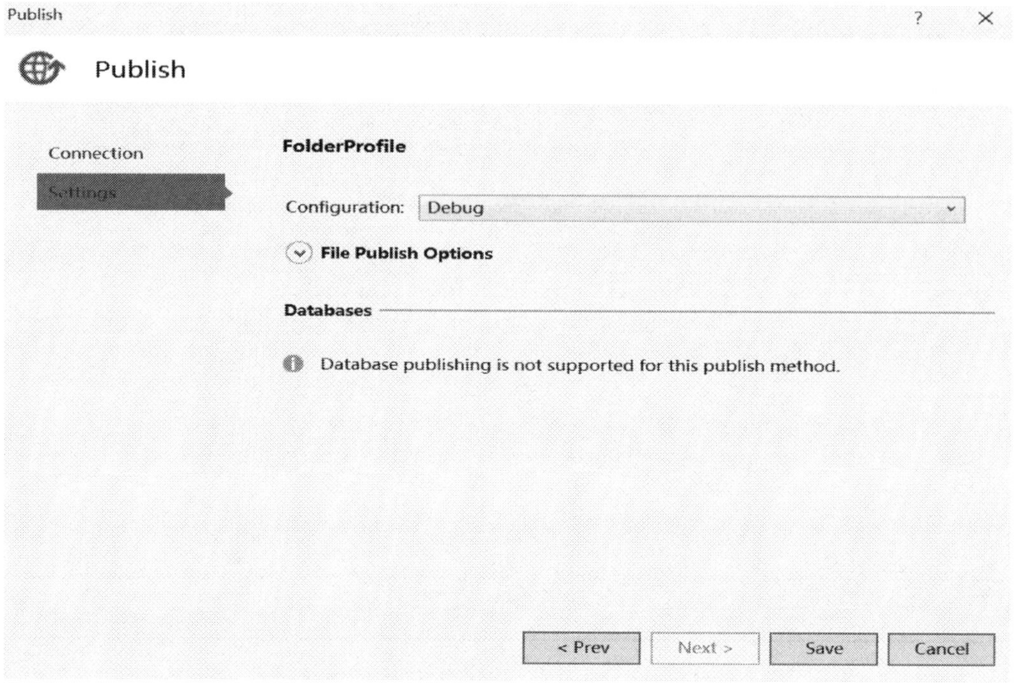

Figure 1- 9 Publishing Dialog (4)

In Figure1-9, opening "File Publish Options" list, selecting "Precompile during Publish", clicking "Save" button, then return figure 1-8, clicking "Publish" button, the ChapSite website is published. When you copy website the synchronization function is supported, and this method is commonly used to copy websites from "test server" to "commerce server".

1.2.4 Copying website

"Copying a website" essentially means you will copy files between the current website and another website. The current website will not be precompiled.

Note: In order to protect C# source codes from being stolen, you can combine "publish website" with "copy website". That is, you can publish the website on a local folder firstly, and then synchronize the files on the server website through copying website.

1.3 Summary

➢ ASP.NET Web Sites usually contain static pages and dynamic pages.

➢ The .NET Framework provides the basis for building ASP.NET websites

➢ The development modes of ASP.NET include ASP.NET Web Forms, ASP.NET MVC, ASP.NET Core, etc.

➢ IIS provides a running environment for ASP.NET, which makes it possible to run different sites on the same Web server by establishing different websites or applications.

➢ You can easily develop ASP.NET websites by using VSC 2019.

1.4 Exercises

1. Multiple-choice questions:

(1) Web application publishing does not include (　　).

A. HTTP　　B. Web deployment　　C. WebDeploy package　　D. File system

(2) (　　) statements is incorrect?

A. "Copy website" is commonly used to transfer a website from a "test server" to a "commercial server."

B. The essence of "copying a website" lies in copying files between the current website and another website.

C. "Publishing a web application" allows you to precompile the current website.

D. "Copying a website" allows you to precompile the current website.

(3) (　　) does not belong to a programming language?

A. ASP.NET　　B. Python　　C. Visual C#　　D. Java

2. Programming Questions

(1) Refer to the Book solution presented in this book, establish a new solution, and incorporate websites and folders into it.

(2) Publish the website in VSC 2019 by using the "File System" method through the "Publish Web Application" option, and then deploy it to IIS.

(3) Deploy the Web site in VSC 2019 to IIS by copying website.

(4) Register in Microsoft Arzue, and then deploy the website in VSC 2019 to Microsoft Arzue by using the "Publish Web Application" function.

Chapter 2 The File of ASP.NET Website, jQuery and Bootstrap

Points:

- Understanding the composition of ASP.NET web site
- Be familiar with the .HTM file and XHTML common elements
- Understanding the two models of Web form page: single file model and code-behind page model
- Be familiar with the definition and location of CSS style
- Be familiar with the knowledge and location of JavaScript
- Understanding the XML knowledge, be familiar with the XML document structure
- Be familiar with web.config file structure and Golbal.asax file
- Understanding Bootstrap, be familiar with the usage method of Bootstrap

2.1 .html File and XHTML5

In the web site of ASP.NET, .htm file is a static page. It does not contain any server controls, but be composed by the HTML elements. When the client browser access .html file, IIS will directly send the information to the browser without any processing, and the information will be performed by the browser to explain. XHTML5 document is used in VSC 2019 by default.

Before being recognized by the browser, all of the dynamic pages including ASP.Net elements will eventually be transformed into static pages containing corresponding XHTML elements.

2.1.1 The structure of .html file

The basic structure of .html file established in VSC 2019 is as follows:

```
<!DOCTYPE html>
<html>
<head>
<meta http-equiv="Content-Type" content="text/html; charset=utf-8"/>
  <title></title>
</head>
<body>
…
</body>
</html>
```

2.1.2 Common XHTML5 elements

The common XHTML5 elements include the following contents:

- <! DOCTYPE... > represents the declaration of document type that is HTML5.
- < HTML >... < / HTML > represents it is a HTML document, all of the other XHTML elements are between these two tabs.
- < head >... < / head > represents the header information of this document.
- <meta> represents the meta information of the document
- < title >... < / title > represents the title bar information of the browser ,it should be embedded in < head > ......< /head >.
- < style >... < / style > represents CSS style information, should be included between< head >... < /head >.
- < body >... < / body > represents document body parts.
- <header>…</header> represents the title information of the whole page.
- <aside>…</aside>represents the title information related to the content next to it.
- <section>…</section>represents the content area of the page.
- <article>…</article>represents the independent content of the page.
- <footer>…</footer>reprents the footnote information of the page.
- <nav>…</nav>represents the navigation link area of the display page.
- <h1>…</h1>reprents the first level of title, there are six levels of title in XHTML5.
- <div>…</div> represents the "layer".
- <p>…</p>represents a paragraph.
-
represents a newline.
- <hr />represents a horizontal line.
- <table>…</table>represents a table,
- < a href = "intro. HTM" > my profile < / a > represents to display hyperlink "my profile" on the browser , after clicking the hyperlink ,which will linked to intro.htm.
- < a href = "mailto:kxsg@21cn.com" > my E-mail < / a > represents to display the hyperlink "my email" on the browser, after clicking the hyperlink ,we will send mail to kxsg@21cn.com.

Some common entity symbols are shown in the table2-1

Table 2-1 The Table of Common Entity Symbols

character	Representation	character	Representation	character	Representation
The blank space		<	<	>	>
"	"	'	'	&	&
©	©	®	®	¥	¥

When you study XHTML5 elements you need not memorize, you can search some files with an extension of htm or html, you can browse the file effect in the browser firstly, then select the "View"→ "Source" command in the browser to view source codes, and understand the effect of XHTML elements.

Example 2-1 Recognizing Common XHTML Elements

This example shows the usage of common XHTML5 elements, the effect is shown as figure 2-1

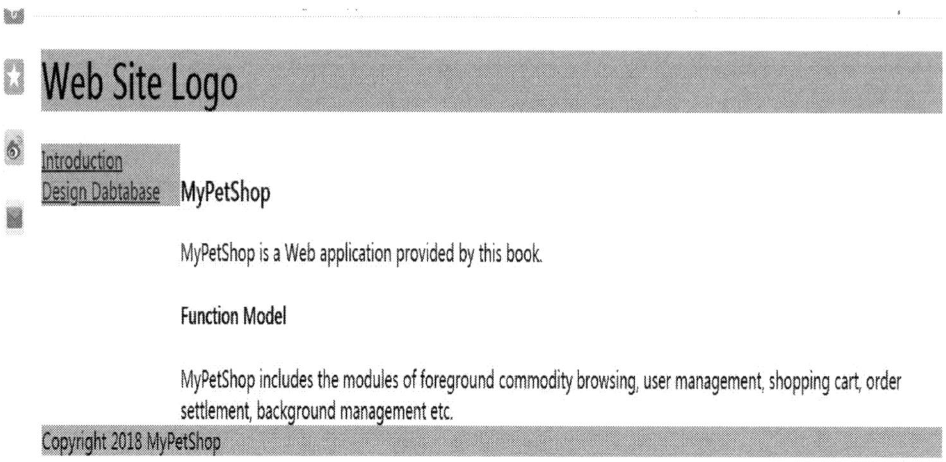

Figure 2- 1 The Browsing Effect of HTML5.html

Source Codes: HTML5.html

```
<!DOCTYPE html>
<html>
<head>
 <meta charset="utf-8" />
 <meta name="keywords" content="MyPetShop, XHTML5" />
 <meta name="description" content="XHTML5 页面示范 " />
 <meta name="author" content="ssgwcyxxd@126.com, 阿毛 " />
 <meta http-equiv="refresh" content="3" />
 <title>Recognize common XHTML5 elements</title>
 <style type="text/css">
  aside { float: left; width: 15%; }
  section { float: right; width: 85%; }
  footer { clear: both; }
 </style>
</head>
<body>
 <header>
  <h1 style="background-color: #C0C0C0">Web Site Logo</h1>
 </header>
 <aside>
  <nav style="background-color: #C0C0C0">
   <a href="Default.aspx">Introduction</a><br />
   <a href="Database.aspx">Design Dabtabase</a>
  </nav>
 </aside>
 <section>
```

```
    <h3>MyPetShop</h3>
     <article>
      MyPetShop is a Web application provided by this book.
     </article>
     <article>
       <h4>Function Model</h4>
         MyPetShop includes the modules of foreground commodity browsing, user management, shopping cart,
order settlement, background management etc.
     </article>
    </section>
    <footer style="background-color: #C0C0C0">Copyright 2018 MyPetShop</footer>
  </body>
  </html>
```

Operating Steps:

(1)Right-clicking Chap2 folder, selecting "Add"→"New Project" command in the pop-up shortcut menu, then selecting "HTML Page" template in the displayed dialog box, entering the file name HTML5, clicking "Add" button to establish the file.

(2)Inputting the source codes in the "Source" view.

Right-clicking in the "Source" view, or right-clicking HTML5.html in the "Solution Explorer", then selecting "View through Browser" command in the pop-up shortcut menu, you can browse the effect of this file.

Programme Description:

- < meta charset = utf-8" / > represent the character sets of language code is UTF-8.
- <meta name="keywords" content="MyPetShop, XHTML5" />represents that it can provide keywords " MyPetShop"and"XHTML5"for search engines.
- < meta name = "description" content = "XHTML5 demonstration" /> represents the brief introduction of the web site.
- < meta name="author" content= "ssgwcyxxd@gmail.com, A Mao" /> represents the author information.
- <meta http-equiv="refresh" content="3" />represents that the page is automatically refreshed every 3 seconds.

2.2 .aspx File

.aspx file (Web Form) is the main section in the Web site. As a fully object-oriented system, the Web form inherits from the System.Web. UI. Page class directly or indirectly.

The codes of each Web form page include two parts: one is the codes that are used to display interface and are defined in the <body> elements, including the necessary XHTML elements and the interface definition information of ASP.NET controls. The other is the c # codes containing event processing.

There are two models when C# codes are stored: simple file page model and code behind page model.

2.2.1 Simple page model

In the single page file model, the displaying interface codes and the logic processing codes (event, function etc.) are in the same .aspx file. The logic processing codes are in the <script> element. <script> element is located above the <head> element, and includes the property that is runat ="server".

Example 2-2 Simple Page Model

This example contains a TextBox, a Label, a Button control. When we input the content in the TextBox and then click "OK" Button, the content "no matter what you input, I like ASP.NET!" will display in the Label.

Source Codes: SimplePage.aspx

```
<%@ Page Language="C#" %>
<!DOCTYPE html>
<script runat="server">
  protected void BtnSubmit_Click(object sender, EventArgs e)
  {
   lblMessage.Text = "No matter what you input, I like ASP.NET!";
  }
</script>
<html xmlns="http://www.w3.org/1999/xhtml">
<head runat="server">
 <meta http-equiv="Content-Type" content="text/html; charset=utf-8" />
 <title>Be familiar with the simple page model</title>
</head>
<body>
 <form id="form1" runat="server">
  <div>
   <asp:TextBox ID="txtInput" runat="server">please enter the content</asp:TextBox>
   <asp:Label ID="lblMessage" runat="server"></asp:Label>
   <br />
   <asp:Button ID="btnSubmit" runat="server" OnClick="BtnSubmit_Click" Text="OK" />
  </div>
 </form>
</body>
</html>
```

Operating Steps:

(1) Right-clicking Chap2 folder, selecting "Add"→"New Project" command in the pop-up

shortcut menu, then selecting "Web Form" template in the displayed dialog box, entering the file name SimplePage.aspx, dose not select the checkbox "Place codes in a separate folder", then clicking "Add" button to establish the file.

(2) Adding a TextBox control, a Label control and a Button control from Toolbox onto the page in the "Design" view, then setting the properties of each control through the "Property" window. At this time, VSC 2019 will automatically generate the corresponding interface codes.

(3) Double-clicking "OK" button, then entering the content of the shadow part in the SimplePage. aspx source codes.

(4) Browse the effect of SimplePage.aspx.

Programme Description:

• Simple file page model can see the content in the <body> elements firstly when we read the codes; mainly focus on the control objects, objects'ID, and objects'event name. Then find the corresponding executive function in <script> elements through every object's event name.

• OnClick ="BtnSubmit_Click" represents that after clicking "OK" button and triggering Click event the function in the <script> elements will be executed.

2.2.2 Code behind page model

Code behind page model is suitable for multiple developers to establish the web site. It can clearly distinguish display interface and logic processing codes.

In this model, display interface codes locate in .aspx files, while logic processing codes locate in the corresponding .aspx. cs files. Unlike simple page model, .aspx file does not contain the <script> elements, but in the @ page instruction the referenced external files should be contained.

Example 2-3 Code behind page model

The function of this example is the same with example 2-2

Source Codes: CodeBehind.aspx

```
<%@ Page Language="C#" AutoEventWireup="true" CodeFile="CodeBehind.aspx.cs" Inherits="Chap2_
CodeBehind" %>
<!DOCTYPE html>
<html xmlns="http://www.w3.org/1999/xhtml">
<head runat="server">
  <meta http-equiv="Content-Type" content="text/html; charset=utf-8" />
  <title>Be familiar with the code behind page model</title>
</head>
<body>
  <form id="form1" runat="server">
    <div>
      <asp:TextBox ID="txtInput" runat="server">please enter the content</asp:TextBox>
      <asp:Label ID="lblMessage" runat="server"></asp:Label>
      <br />
```

```
    <asp:Button ID="btnSubmit" runat="server" OnClick="BtnSubmit_Click" Text="OK" />
    </div>
  </form>
</body>
</html>
```

Source Codes:CodeBehind.aspx.cs

```
using System;
public partial class Chap2_CodeBehind : System.Web.UI.Page
{
  protected void BtnSubmit_Click(object sender, EventArgs e)
  {
    lblMessage.Text = "No matter what you input, I like ASP.NET!";
  }
}
```

Operating Steps:

(1) Right-clicking Chap2 folder, selecting "Add"→"New Project" command in the pop-up shortcut menu, then selecting "Web Form" template in the displayed dialog box, entering the file name CodeBehind.aspx, selecting the checkbox "Place codes in a separate folder", then clicking "Add" button to establish the file.

(2) Adding a TextBox control, a Label control and a Button control from Toolbox onto the page in the "Design" view, then setting the properties of each control through the "Property" window. At this time, VSC 2019 will automatically generate the corresponding interface codes.

(3) Double-clicking "OK" button, then entering the content of the shadow part in the CodeBehind.aspx source codes. Right clicking the space of the document window, then selecting "deleting and sorting the content of Using" command in the pop-up shortcut menu, deleting the namespace needn't to be imported. At last, you can browse the effect of CodeBehind.aspx.

Programme Description:

• Code-behind page model can see the contents of the .aspx file when reading the codes, which mainly focus on what control objects in it, the ID value and event name of each control. Then find the corresponding executive function in the .aspx.cs file through the object's event name.

• At the beginning of CodeBehind.aspx, increasing @ Page instruction, in this instruction AutoEventWireup= "true" designates that the specified page events are automatically bound to the specified method; CodeFile = "CodeBehind.aspx.cs" specify background encoding file, and make the displaying interface associated with the background encoding file; Inherits = "chap2_CodeBehind"; specify the inherited class name, and the class is stored in the corresponding background encoding file.

• At the beginning of CodeBehind.aspx.cs,"using System;" represents to import the System namespace.

2.3. CSS Files and CSS Knowledge

XHTML elements can limit the format of the browser page, but the control ability is not strong, such as we should modify the web pages one by one if we want an unified style. CSS (Cascading Style Sheet) is the element style rule used in the web pages, which has been accepted by all kinds of browsers. On the base of XHTML, CSS provides the function of precise position and redefining the XHTML element properties. A CSS file can be applied to multiple XHTML documents. when we want to change multiple XHTML page style at the same time, we only need to modify the CSS style file. CSS includes CSS1、CSS2 and CSS3.

2.3.1 Define CSS3 styles

Each CSS style has two main parts: the selector (such as p) and the statement (such as color: blue). The statement is composed by a attribute (color) and its value (blue). According to the different usage of the style, there are different CSS3 selectors.

1. *selector

*selector is applied to all of the elements in a page and is often used for global setting.

such as* { font-family: Arial; }

2. Element selector

The name of the element selector is the XHTML element name, which is used to redefine the attributes of the specified XHTML element. For example, for all of the paragraphs between<p>and</p>, the CSS3 style with the text alignment format that is center is:

p { text-align: center; }

3. Attribute selector

As is shown in Table 2-2, the attribute selector selects elements according to their attributes or attribute values.

Table2-2 CSS3 Attribute selector

CSS3 style	Explaination
[attr]{...}	Select the element of the attr attribute
[attr=val]{...}	Select the element whose attr attribute value is val
[attr~=val]{...}	Select the element that contains the val in the attr attribute (must be spaced with spaces)
[attr|=val]{...}	Select the element in the attr attribute whose value starts with the val (must be spaced with underline)
[attr^=val]{...}	Select the element in the attr attribute whose value starts with the val
[attr$=val]{...}	Select the element in the attr attribute whose value ends with the val
[attr*=val]{...}	Select the element that contains the val in the attr attribute

4. Class selector

Class selector can be applied to different XHTML elements or the subset of some XHTML elements (such as it can be applied to the part of the paragraphs, but not all the paragraphs). The "." would be added in front of the selector when the style is defined. For example, the class selector which is used to set the CSS3 style with red color is as follows:

.intro { color: #FF0000; }

In the page, we take the method that class = "class name" to call the selector, such as:

<p class = "intro">

5. id selector

id selector is applied to the XHTML elements'attributes which are determined by the id value, and is often used to set the attribute in the single XHTML element. The "#" should be added in front of the selector(id name) when it is defined. Such as we want to set the background color of the defined layer <div id = "menubar">... </ div> to be green, the CSS3 style are:

#menubar { background-color: #008000; }

2.3.2 The location of CSS3 styles

The CSS3 style can be placed in the different positions, include inline with XHTML elements, locating in the <style>elements of the page and locating in the external style sheets (CSS files).

Note: Inline style is the most priority, the second is the CSS style of the page, and the last is the external style sheet.

1. Inline style

When we want to define attributes for a single element and don't want to reuse the style, we can use the inline style. The inline style should be defined in the attribute that is style of the XHTML elements. For example:

<p style="text-align: center; color: #FFFF00;">

During operation, you can directly select the style attribute in the corresponding "attribute" window of the XHTML element to set it. After setting, the style will be automatically generated.

2. Page style

When we want to set style for the elements of a particular page, we can define the style in the <style> element of the <head> element. We can use different selectors according to need.

Example 2-4 Applying page style

Source Codes:Interior.aspx

```
<%@ Page Language="C#" AutoEventWireup="true" CodeFile="Interior.aspx.cs" Inherits="Chap2_Interior
" %>
<!DOCTYPE html>
<html xmlns="http://www.w3.org/1999/xhtml">
<head runat="server">
  <meta http-equiv="Content-Type" content="text/html; charset=utf-8" />
  <title>Apply page style</title>
  <style type="text/css">
    * { font-family: 隶书 ; }
    [title~=attr] { color: #000080; }
    [title*=attribute] { color: #800080; }
    p { color: #008000; }
    .classTest { color: #800000; }
    #divTest { color: #808000; }
  </style>
```

```
</head>
<body>
  <form id="form1" runat="server">
    <p>the style based on element selector</p>
    <p title="attr Test">the style based on[attr~=val] attribute selector</p>
    <p title="attributeTest">the style based on[attr*=val] attribute selector </p>
    <p class="classTest">the style based on class selector</p>
    <div id="divTest">the style based on id selector</div>
  </form>
</body>
</html>
```

Operating Steps:

(1) Creating Interior.aspx file in Chap2 folder.

(2) Entering "the style based on element selector" "the style based on [attr~=val] attribute selector" "the style based on[attr*=val] attribute selector" "the style based on class selector" in the "design" view through paragraph mode. In the div layer which is established after double clicking Div in the HTML tab of the toolbox, entering "the style based on id selector", you can set the attributes of each element referring the source codes.

(3) Selecting "View"→"Manage styles" command, clicking "New style" button in the rendered window, then entering selector name of * in the rendered dialog box, then setting font, clicking "OK" button to establish * selector. The other selectors can be established similarly. At last, the effect of Interior.aspx can be browsed.

3. External style sheets

The external style sheet is often applied to the entire site, and is stored in a separate .css file. Using the <link> element can link a style sheet with a web page. An external style sheet can be linked to multiple pages, so that you can easily manage the displaying style of the entire site.

Example 2-5 External style sheet

Source Codes:Exterior.css

```
* { font-family: Times New Roman; }
[title~=attr] { color: #000080; }
[title*=attribute] { color: #800080; }
p { color: #008000; }
.classTest { color: #800000; }
#divTest { color: #808000; }
```

Operating Steps:

(1) Right-clicking Style folder, selecting "Add"→"New Project" command in the pop-up shortcut menu, then selecting "Style sheet" template in the displayed dialog box, entering the file name: Exterior.css,

then clicking "Add" button to establish the file.

Entering the content of the shadow part in the Exterior.css document window.

Source Codes:Exterior.aspx

```
<%@ Page Language="C#" AutoEventWireup="true" CodeFile="Exterior.aspx.cs" Inherits="Chap2_ExtEri-
or" %>
<!DOCTYPE html>
<html xmlns="http://www.w3.org/1999/xhtml">
<head runat="server">
  <meta http-equiv="Content-Type" content="text/html; charset=utf-8" />
  <title>Apply external style sheet </title>
  <link href="../Styles/Exterior.css" rel="stylesheet" type="text/css" />
</head>
<body>
  <form id="form1" runat="server">
    <p>Calling the style based on element selector in Exterior.css</p>
    <p title="attr Test">Calling the style based on [attr~=val] attribute selector in Exterior.css </p>
    <p title="attributeTest">Calling the style based on [attr*=val] attribute selector in Exterior.css </p>
    <p class="classTest">Calling the style based on class selector in Exterior.css </p>
    <div id="divTest">Calling the style based on id selector in Exterior.css</div>
  </form>
</body>
</html>
```

Operating Steps:

(1) Creating Exterior.aspx file in Chap2 folder.

(2) In "Design" view, entering the content referring source codes and setting the attributes of each element.

(3) Selecting "Format"→"Attach Style Sheets" command, selecting Exterior.css file in Styles folder in the rendered dialog box. At this time, <link href="../Styles/Exterior.css" rel="stylesheet" type="text/css" /> will automatically be added in Exterior.aspx, "..", indicating the folder above the current folder. Then you can see the effect through browsing Exterior.aspx.

2.4 .js File and JavaScript

JavaScript is developed by NetScape. It is an interpreting language based on object and event driven. As a script language that can be directly embedded into the XHTML page, it don't need be interpreted by the Web server browser to realize dynamic Web page processing. At present, all of the browsers support JavaScript.

The typical JavaScript applications include: creating dynamic text in XHTML; corresponding client events; reading and changing the content of XHTML elements; verifying client data; detecting the visitor's browser, and loading the corresponding page according to the browser; creating the cookies;

closing the browser window; displaying the time on the page.

2.4.1 The location of JavaScript codes

There are usually three forms of location of JavaScript codes, that are in the<head>element, in the <body>element, and in a separate. js file.

1. In the <head> element

The JavaScript codes in the <head> element are included between the <script> and </script>, the codes usually store JavaScript functions, which will be executed only when they are called.

Example 2-6 Be familiar with the JavaScript code in <head>element

Source Codes:HeadJS.aspx

```
<%@ Page Language="C#" AutoEventWireup="true" CodeFile="HeadJS.aspx.cs" Inherits="Chap2_
HeadJS" %>
<!DOCTYPE html>
<html xmlns="http://www.w3.org/1999/xhtml">
<head runat="server">
  <meta http-equiv="Content-Type" content="text/html; charset=utf-8" />
  <title>Be familiar with &lt;head&gt;the JavaScript codes in elements</title>
  <script>
    function message() {
      alert("in\<head\> element");
    }
  </script>
</head>
<body onload="message()">
  <form id="form1" runat="server">
  </form>
</body>
</html>
```

Operating Steps:

(1) Creating HeadJS.aspx file in Chap2 folder.

(2) In "Source" view, entering the content of the shadow part. At last, browsing the HeadJS.aspx to see the effect.

Programme Description:

When the page executes the <body>element, the message() function is called after the load event is triggered, and finally the message "in the <head> element" is displayed on the browser.

Note: In JavaScript, objects and functions are named with the first character being a lowercase letter.

2. In the <body> element

Be similar with <head> element, the JavaScript codes in the<body> element are also included in the <script> element. However, the JavaScript codes need to be executed when the storing page is loaded.

Example 2-7 Be familiar with the JavaScript code in <body>element

Source Codes:BodyJS.aspx

```
<%@ Page Language="C#"AutoEventWireup="true"CodeFile="BodyJS.aspx.cs" Inherits="Chap2_BodyJS
" %>
<!DOCTYPE html>
<html xmlns="http://www.w3.org/1999/xhtml">
<head runat="server">
 <meta http-equiv="Content-Type" content="text/html; charset=utf-8" />
 <title>Be familiar &lt;body&gt;the JavaScript codes in elements</title>
</head>
<body>
 <form id="form1" runat="server">
  <div>
   <script>
    document.write("in&lt;body&gt;element");
   </script>
  </div>
 </form>
</body>
</html>
```

Programme Description:

Executing document.write() function when the page is loaded, outputting the XHTML text "in <body> element". The browser displays the effect that is "in the<body>element".

Note: In XHTML, "<" is expressed through "<" and ">" is expressed through ">".

3.In a separate .js file

The separate .js file is often used when several pages need to invoke the same JavaScript codes. Usually we put all of the .js files in the same script folder in order to manage them easily. The src attribute value should be added in the <script> element when we call the external JavaScript file.

Example 2-8 The separate .js file

Source Codes:FileJS.aspx

```
<%@ Page Language="C#" AutoEventWireup="true" CodeFile="FileJS.aspx.cs"
Inherits="Chap2_FileJS"%>
<!DOCTYPE html>
<html xmlns="http://www.w3.org/1999/xhtml">
<head runat="server">
 <meta http-equiv="Content-Type" content="text/html; charset=utf-8" />
 <title>Apply the separate.js file</title>
 <script src="../Scripts/FileJS.js"></script>
</head>
```

```
<body onload="message()">
  <form id="form1" runat="server">
  </form>
</body>
</html>
Source Codes: FileJS.js
function message() {
  alert("JavaScript codes in FileJS.js file!");
}
```

Operating Steps:

(1) Right-clicking Scripts folder, selecting "Add"→"New Project" command in the pop-up shortcut menu, then selecting "JavaScript" template in the displayed dialog box, entering the file name: FileJS.js, then clicking "Add" button to establish the file, then entering the content of source file in the document window.

(2) Creating FileJS.aspx in Chap2 folder, entering the content of the shadow part. Browsing FileJS. aspx to see the effect.

Programme Description:

In the FileJS. aspx file, the src attribute of the shadow part means the location of a separate .js file; when the web page executes the <body> element, the message () function is called after triggering the load event.

2.4.2 JavaScript application examples

Example 2-9 Realizing the dynamic changing effect of the picture

This example displays a mouse picture on the page firstly. When the mouse pointer points to the picture, another mouse picture is displayed. After removing the mouse pointer, the original mouse picture is displayed again to achieve the effect of changing the picture.

Source Codes:ChangeImg.aspx

```
<%@ Page Language="C#" AutoEventWireup="true" CodeFile="ChangeImg.aspx.cs"
 Inherits="Chap2_ChangeImg" %>
<!DOCTYPE html>
<html xmlns="http://www.w3.org/1999/xhtml">
<head runat="server">
  <meta http-equiv="Content-Type" content="text/html; charset=utf-8" />
  <title>Realize the dynamic changing effect of the picture</title>
  <script>
    function mouseOver() {
      document.getElementById("mouse").src = "../Images/mouseOver.jpg";
    }
```

```
    function mouseOut() {
      document.getElementById("mouse").src = "../Images/mouseOut.jpg";
    }
  </script>
</head>
<body>
  <form id="form1" runat="server">
    <div>
      <a href="http://www.sina.com" target="_blank">
        <img id="mouse" border="0" alt="visit sina!" src="../Images/mouseOut.jpg" onmouseover="mouseOver()"
 onmouseout="mouseOut()" />
      </a>
    </div>
  </form>
</body>
</html>
```

Programme Description:

mouseOut jpg is displayed after the page is loaded. GetElementById () returns the XHTML element with the specified id. When the mouse pointer points to the picture, the mouseOver event is triggered, and then the mouseOver() function is called to display mouseOver.jpg. When the mouse pointer moves away, the mouseOut event is triggered, and then the mouseOut() function is called to display mouseOut. jpg. After clicking the picture, www.sina.com will be linked.

Example 2-10 A simple clock

This example displays a digital clock on the page, in which the time data come from the client.

Source Codes:Timer.aspx

```
<%@Page Language="C#" AutoEventWireup="true" CodeFile="Timer.aspx.cs"
 Inherits="Chap2_Timer" %>
<!DOCTYPE html>
<html xmlns="http://www.w3.org/1999/xhtml">
<head runat="server">
  <meta http-equiv="Content-Type" content="text/html; charset=utf-8" />
  <title>A simple clock</title>
  <script>
    function startTimer() {
      var today = new Date();
      var h = today.getHours();
      var m = today.getMinutes();
      var s = today.getSeconds();
      m = checkTime(m);
```

```
    s = checkTime(s);
      document.getElementById("divTimer").innerHTML = h + ":" + m + ":" + s;
      setTimeout("startTimer()", 1000);
    }
    //checkTime(i)
    function checkTime(i) {
      if (i < 10) {
        i = "0" + i;
      }
      return i;
    }
  </script>
</head>
<body onload="startTimer()">
  <form id="form1" runat="server">
    <div id="divTimer"></div>
  </form>
</body>
</html>
```

Programme Description:

When the page is loaded, the load event of the<body>element is triggered, and the custom startTimer() function is executed. The function calls itself repeatedly after 1 second and displays the current system time on the divTimer of the div layer continuously. The time data comes from the client.

2.5. jQuery

jQuery was created by John Resig in 2006. As an excellent JavaScript framework, it makes the users access and manage XHTML elements, set the CSS style of XHTML elements, handle the events of XHTML elements, realize the animation effects of XHTML elements, and provide Ajax interaction for the website conveniently by providing the JavaScript library. It supports XHTML5 and CSS3. jQuery mobile can be easily used for web application development of mobile phone and tablet computer. Now most browsers support jQuery.

In VSC 2019, we can install jQuery through NuGet package manager conveniently. After installation, the latest JavaScript library provided by jQuery will be automatically added in the scripts folder under the root folder of the website.

In VSC 2019, in order to use the JavaScript library provided by jQuery, you need to add a corresponding reference in the <head> element of the page. The example codes are as follows:

```
<script src="../Scripts/jquery-3.6.0.min.js"></script>
```

jquery-3.6.0.min.js should be changed according to the actual jQuery version number. The route should be determined by the location of the page.

2.5.1 jQuery basic grammar

The basic syntax format of jQuery is: $(selector).action(). Selector is used to select browser objects (such as window object which represents browser window; document object, which represents XHTML document, etc.) and XHTML elements; action () performs specific operations on the selected object by calling defined methods of jQuery or editing custom methods.

Table 2-3 shows the commonly used jQuery selectors for selecting XHTML elements.

Table 2-3 Custom jQuery selectors

Selector	Example	Element meaning
*selector	$("*")	Select all of the elements
element selector	$("p")	Select all of the <p> elements
attribute selector	$("[attr]")	Select all of the elements with attr
	$("[attr ='val']")	Select all of the elements whose value of attr is val
	$("[attr!='val']")	Select all of the elements whose value of attr is not val
class selector	$(".intro")	Select the elements that class="intro"
id selector	$("#menubar")	Select the elements that id="menubar"
first selector	$("p:first")	Select the first<p> element
contains selector	$(":contains('W3C')")	Select all of the elements containing the specified string "W3C"

The common jQuery methods are shown in Table 2-4

Table 2-4 Custom jQuery methods

Method	Meaning
attr()	Set or return the properties and values of the selected element
bind()	Add event codes to the selected element
click()	Trigger or bind the function to the click event of the selected element
css()	Set or return the style of the selected element
fadeIn()	Gradually change the transparency of the selected element from hidden to visible
fadeOut()	Gradually change the opacity of the selected element from hidden to visible
fadeToggle()	Switch the selected element between hidden and visible
hide()	Hide the selected elements
jQuery.ajax()	Execute asynchronous HTTP (Ajax) requests, which is often used to realize the local refreshment of the page
load()	Trigger or bind the function to the load event of the selected element
mouseout()	Trigger or bind the function to the mouseout event of the selected element
mouseover()	Trigger or bind the function to the mouseover event of the selected element
ready()	Trigger the ready event when the HTML document is ready, and then execute the defined function
text()	Set or return the contents of the selected element

2.5.2 jQuery Application examples

Example 2-11 Managing XHTML elements by using jQuery

Source Codes:ManageXhtml.aspx

```
<%@ Page Language="C#" AutoEventWireup="true" CodeFile="ManageXhtml.aspx.cs"
Inherits="Chap2_ManageXhtml" %>
<!DOCTYPE html>
<html xmlns="http://www.w3.org/1999/xhtml">
<head runat="server">
  <meta http-equiv="Content-Type" content="text/html; charset=utf-8" />
  <title>Manage XHTML elements by using jQuery</title>
  <script src="../Scripts/jquery-3.2.1.min.js"></script>
  <script type="text/javascript">
    $(document).ready(function () {
      $("#hide").click(function () {
        $("#effect").hide();
      });
      $("#show").click(function () {
        $("#effect").show();
      });
      $(".flip").click(function () {
        $("#effect").fadeToggle();
      });
      $("#chgText").click(function () {
        $("#effect").text("My contents are changed!");
      });
      $("#chgCss").click(function () {
        $("*").css({ "background-color": "yellow", "font-family": " 隶书 " });
      });
    });
  </script>
</head>
<body>
  <form id="form1" runat="server">
    <div style="text-align: center">
      <span id="hide">Hide</span>
      <span id="show" style="color: #008080">Show</span>
      <span class="flip">Fade in or out</span>
      <span id="chgText" style="color: #008080">Change contents</span>
      <span id="chgCss">Change style</span>
    </div>
    <div id="effect" style="background-color: #DCDCDC">Click "Hide" and I will disappear; Click "Show"
and I will come back.,Click "Fade in or out" and I will fade in or out.</div>
  </form>
</body>
</html>
```

Operating Steps:

(1) Installing the jQuery by using NuGet software package in ChapSite web site.

(2) Creating ManageXhtml.aspx in Chap2 folder. Entering the contents of shadow part in "Source" view, the value of style attribute can be set through "Attribute" window.

(3) Browsing ManageXhtml.aspx to test.

Programme Description:

When the page document is ready, the ready event is triggered to execute the custom function codes, including:

(1) Setting the click event codes of the element whose ID is "hide", that will hide the element whose ID is "effect".

(2) Setting the click event codes of the element whose ID is "show", that will show the element whose ID is "effect".

(3) Setting the click event codes of the element whose class is "flip", that will fade in or out the element whose ID is "effect".

(4) Setting the click event codes of the element whose ID is "chgText", that will change the rendering text of the element whose ID is "effect" to "my text has been changed!".

(5) Setting the click event codes of the element whose ID is "chgCss", that will change the background color of all of the elements to yellow and the font to official script.

Example 2-12 Realizing a timer by using jQuery whose data come from the server

This example uses jQuery and JavaScript to implement a clock,
where the time data comes from the server.

Source Codes:Ajax.aspx

```
<%@ Page Language="C#" AutoEventWireup="true" CodeFile="Ajax.aspx.cs" Inherits="Ajax" %>
```

Source Codes:Ajax.aspx.cs

```
<%@ Page Language="C#" AutoEventWireup="true" CodeFile="Ajax.aspx.cs" Inherits="Ajax" %>
using System;
public partial class Ajax : System.Web.UI.Page
{
 protected void Page_Load(object sender, EventArgs e)
 {
   //Output the system time of the current server. This value will be passed to the datetime
variable in //TimerJQuery.aspx
   Response.Write(DateTime.Now);
 }
}
Source Codes:TimerJQuery.aspx
<%@ Page Language="C#" AutoEventWireup="true" CodeFile="TimerJQuery.aspx.cs" Inherits="Chap2_
TimerJQuery" %>
<!DOCTYPE html>
```

```
<html xmlns="http://www.w3.org/1999/xhtml">
<head runat="server">
  <meta http-equiv="Content-Type" content="text/html; charset=utf-8" />
  <title>Realize a timer by using jQuery whose time data comes from the server</title>
  <script src="../Scripts/jquery-3.2.1.min.js"></script>
  <%-- refresh() function refreshes the divMsg of the div layer locally at an interval of 500 milliseconds.
Where $. ajax() calls the ajax() method of jQuery to execute asynchronous requests --%>
  <script type="text/javascript">
    function refresh() {
      $.ajax({
        url: "Ajax.aspx", //Send the page address of the asynchronous request
        cache: false, //Do not cache pages that is requested asynchronously
        success: function (datetime) {
//Set the rendering content of divMsg of the div layer to be the system time output by the server
          $("#divMsg").text(datetime);
          }
      });
      setTimeout("refresh()", 500); //Calling the custom refresh() function repeatedly after 500 milliseconds
    }
  </script>
</head>
<body onload="refresh()">
  <form id="form1" runat="server">
    <div id="divMsg"></div>
  </form>
</body>
</html>
```

Operating Steps:

(1) Creating Ajax.aspx in Chap2 folder, keeping @ Page command line and deleting the other contents in "Source" view .

(2) Creating Ajax.aspx.cs in Chap2 folder, entering the contents of shadow part.

(3) Creating TimerJQuery.aspx in Chap2 folder, entering the contents of shadow part in "Source" view.

(4) Browsing TimerJQuery.aspx to see the effect.

Programme Description:

When the page is loaded, the load event in the <body> element is triggered and the custom refresh() function is executed. This function sends asynchronous requests through Ajax.aspx. When Ajax.aspx is successfully executed, the system time of the current server will be sent to"datetime" of TimerJQuery. aspx, then the time will be displayed on the divMsg of div layer. The refresh() function calls itself repeatedly every 500 milliseconds to realize the local refreshment of divmsg in div layer and present the changing system time on the server.

2.6 .XML file and XML general knowledge

In ASP.NET web site, .XML files are often used to solve the problem of data exchange of cross-platform. In fact, this format has become the standard format of internet data exchange.

XML (eXtensible Markup Language) is a kind of extensible Markup Language, which can define the corresponding semantic Markup according to the actual needs. Compared with XHTML, XHTML is designed to display data, while XML is designed to transport and store data.

Example 2-13 The menu for breakfast of XML format

This example describes a breakfast menu, including the name of the food, price, description, quantity of heat, etc.

Source Codes:Breakfast.xml

```
<?xml version="1.0" encoding="utf-8" ?>
<!-- Breakfast menu -->
<breakfast_menu>
 <food>
  <name>Soybean Milk</name>
  <price>¥2.0</price>
  <description>Rich nutrition and low energy</description>
  <calories>40</calories>
 </food>
 <food>
  <name>Deep-fried Dough Sticks</name>
  <price>¥3.0</price>
  <description>Very delicious, a lot of grease</description>
  <calories>300</calories>
 </food>
</breakfast_menu>
```

Operating Steps:

(1) Right-clicking Chap2 folder, selecting "Add"→"New Project" command in the pop-up shortcut menu, then selecting "XML file" template in the displayed dialog box, entering the file name: Breakfast. xml, then clicking "Add" button to establish the file, then entering all of the contents.

(2) Right-clicking Breakfast.xml in the "Solution Explorer" window, and selecting "View in Browser" in the pop-up shortcut menu to browse the effect.

Programme Description:

<? xml... ?> is the XML declaration including the version and encoding attribute.

<! --... --> represents an notation.

<breakfast_menu> represents the root element; a root element must be included and be unique in a.xml file.

<food>... </ food> describes a kind of breakfast by using the child elements. All of the child

elements <food> constitute the brotherhood.

2.7 Web.config

The configuration file of web site is an XML format file, which is used to store configuration information. They can be in multiple folders on the website, and form a certain hierarchical relationship. The top-level configuration file in a website is Web.config in the root file of the website, and the next layer is Web.config located in the sub folder of the root folder. The Web.config under the root folder of the web site applies to the whole site, while the Web.config in the sub-folder is often used to store the authorization information of the folder.

The basic structure of Web.config file is shown as follows:

```
<? The XML version = "1.0" encoding = "utf-8"?>
<configuration>
 <configSections>
......
</configSections>
......
</ configuration>
```

<configuration>represents the root element of the file. According to the different configuration requirements, multiple child elements included in the <configuration> can be defined. The configuration elements in the actual project mainly are:

<appSettings> configuration of custom application.

<authentication>-- configuration for authentication.

<pages>-- the specific configuration that is used for page. For example, when you need to use the controls contained in the AjaxControlToolkit package in the page, you can set them through the child element<controls>.

<sessionState>-- configuration for session state.

2.8 Global.asax

Global.asax file (global application file) is an optional file that contains the codes that responds to application-level and session-level events. It must be stored in the root folder, each site only can contain one Global.asax file, and the codes in Global.asax will be executed firstly.

The methods of handling typical events in Global.asax file are shown as follows:

Application_Start()——the codes that are executed when Web application is started.

Application_End()——the codes that are executed when Web application is closed.

Application_Error()——the codes that are executed when the errors of Web application aren't handled.

Session_Start()——the codes that are executed when an user accesses the Web application to start a new session.

Session_End()——the codes that are executed when an user ends the session.

2.9 Bootstrap

At present, Bootstrap has become the main web front design and development framework, and be supported by all of the mainstream browsers. It is based on the technology of HTML5, CSS3, JavaScript and jQuery, and has preset the style of HTML elements, global CSS and extensible class selector, including reusable components and some custom jQuery plugin.

Bootstrap takes the mobile devices as the design idea, and fully reflects the responsive design idea. During the specific operations, the corresponding design is implemented by setting the name attribute value of <meta> element as the viewpoint, The sample codes are as follows:

```
<meta name="viewport" content="width=device-width, initial-scale=1.0" />
```

In VSC 2019, Bootstrap can be easily installed through the NuGet package manager. The specific operations are as follows: selecting "web site"→ "manage NuGet package"command, then selecting "browse" tag in the rendered window, searching Bootstrap and then install it. After installation, the latest CSS style and JavaScript library provided by Bootstap will be added in Content folder and Scripts folder under the root folder of the site automatically.

In VSC 2019, if you want to use CSS style and JavaScript library provided by Bootstrap, the CSS style sheet

and the corresponding .js file should be added in <head> element of the page. The sample codes are as follows:

```
<link href="../Content/bootstrap.min.css" rel="stylesheet" type="text/css" />
<script  src="../Scripts/bootstrap.min.js"> </script>
```

Example 2-14 Designing the form through Bootstrap

Source Codes:FormBootStrap.aspx

```
<%@ Page Language="C#" AutoEventWireup="true" CodeFile="FormBootstrap.aspx.cs" Inherits=
"Chap2_FormBootstrap" %>
<!DOCTYPE html>
<html xmlns="http://www.w3.org/1999/xhtml">
<head runat="server">
  <meta http-equiv="Content-Type" content="text/html; charset=utf-8" />
  <meta name="viewport" content="width=device-width, initial-scale=1.0" />
  <title>Design the form through Bootstrap</title>
  <link href="../Content/bootstrap.min.css" rel="stylesheet" type="text/css" />
  <script src="../Scripts/jquery-3.2.1.min.js"></script>
  <script src="../Scripts/bootstrap.min.js"></script>
</head>
<body>
  <form id="form1" runat="server">
    <div class="form-group">
```

```
      <label for="inputEmail">E-mail:</label>
      <input type="email" class="form-control" id="inputEmail" placeholder="Please enter the address
of E-mail" />
    </div>
    <div class="form-group">
      <label for="inputPassword">Password:</label>
      <input type="password" class="form-control" id="inputPassword" placeholder="Please enter the
password" />
    </div>
    <div class="checkbox">
      <label>
        <input type="checkbox" />
        Remember me     </label>
    </div>
    <asp:Button ID="btnSubmit" CssClass="btn btn-default" runat="server" Text="Submit" />
  </form>
</body>
</html>*/
```

Operating Steps:

(1) Installing Bootstrap through the NuGet package manager in ChapSite web site.

(2) Creating FormBootStrap.aspx in Chap2 folder, entering source codes except for automatically generated codes in "Source" view, the attribute value of each XHTML element can also be set through "Attribute" window.

(3) Browsing FormBootStrap.aspx, changing the width of the browse window, experiencing the effect of responsive design.

Programme Description:

The definition of CSS class selectors such as form-group, form-control, checkbox, and "btn default" are included in the bootstrap.min.css file.

Note: XHTML elements call the CSS class selector through the attribute of class, while the ASP. NET controls through the attribute of CssClass.

2.10 Summary

- The content of any. aspx file must be converted to XHTML before it can be viewed in the browser.
- Most software companies adopt the code behind page model when developing Web applications.
- CCS style can keep a uniform style for all of the websites.
- JavaScript provides dynamic function for static pages.
- JQuery can easily control and manage XHTML elements.
- XML has become the standard format for Internet data exchange.

➢ Web.config is used to store the configuration information of the Web application.

➢ The Global.asax file is used to contain codes that respond to application level and session level events.

➢ Bootstrap is the mainstream framework for front-end design and development of Web applications, which takes mobile devices firstly as the design concept and fully reflects the responsive design idea.

2.11 Exercises

1.Short-answer Questions

(1) Describe the uses of CSS3 briefly.

(2) Why the JacaScript is required when you develop a ASP.NET web site?

(3) Provide examples to demonstrate the function of jQuery.

(4) Describe the features and functions of Web.config file briefly.

(5) Describe the features and functions of Global.asax file briefly.

2.Programming Questions

(1) Establish and debug all of the instances in this chapter.

(2) Establish an external style sheets to control multiple pages.

(3) Realize a Clock whose time data comes from the client by using jQuery.

(4) Establish a XML file containing student information.

(5) Establish a web site navigation by using Bootstrap.

Chapter 3 ASP.NET Standard Controls

Points:

- Understanding the ASP.NET page event handling process
- Understanding the HTML server controls
- Be familiar with ASP.NET standard controls
- Mastering various controls application

3.1 The Overview of ASP.NET Page Event Handling

3.1.1 ASP.NET page events

Only when we are familiar with ASP.NET page event handling process, we can understand the execution order of the codes. Common page process events are as follows:

- Page.PreInit: We can determine whether to deal with this page for the first time, create dynamic control, set theme properties dynamically, and read configuration file attributes etc through the attribute IsPostBack.
- Page.Init: Initiating control attributes.
- Page.Load: Reading and updating the control attributes.
- Control event: Dealing with the specific event, such as the click event of Button control.

The order of event processing is Page.PreInit, Page.Init, Page.Load, and control events. When the click event is triggered, the page will be processed back and forth. When the change event is triggered, the event information will be stored in the client's buffer temporarily, until we give information to the server the next time; the information will be sent to the server with other information. If we want to let the server response to the change event immediately, we need to set the attribute AutoPostBack to be true.

3.1.2 The attribute IsPostBack

When the control event is triggered, Page.Load event will be triggered before the control event. If you do not want to perform the codes of the Page.Load event when perform the codes of the control event, you can set the attributes Page.IsPostBack. When users access to the web page for the first time, the attribute IsPostBack will return false, otherwise, it is true.

Example 3-1 Applying IsPostBack attribute

In this example, when the page is loaded for the first time, "the page load for the first time!" will be displayed on the page. When the button is clicked, "Click event code executed!" will be shown.

Source Codes: IsPostBack.aspx

```
<%@ Page Language="C#" AutoEventWireup="true" CodeFile="IsPostBack.aspx.cs" Inherits=
"Chap3_IsPostBack" %>
<!DOCTYPE html>
<html xmlns="http://www.w3.org/1999/xhtml">
<head runat="server">
  <meta http-equiv="Content-Type" content="text/html; charset=utf-8" />
  <title>Apply IsPostBack attribute </title>
</head>
<body>
  <form id="form1" runat="server">
    <div>
      <asp:Button ID="btnSubmit" runat="server" Text="Submit" OnClick="BtnSubmit_Click" />
    </div>
  </form>
</body>
</html>
```

Source Codes: IsPostBack.aspx.cs

```
using System;
public partial class Chap3_IsPostBack : System.Web.UI.Page
{
  protected void Page_Load(object sender, EventArgs e)
  {
    if (!IsPostBack)
    {
      Response.Write("The page is loaded for the first time!");
    }
  }
  protected void BtnSubmit_Click(object sender, EventArgs e)
  {
    Response.Write("Excecute the codes of click event!");
  }
}
```

Program description:

When the button is clicked, the page will be processed back and forth: firstly Page_Load event will be triggered; the codes of Page_Load() method will be executed; but because "! IsPostBack" is false, so we do not perform "Response. Write" ("page is loaded for the first time!"), then handling the codes of Click event, "Codes of Click event are executed!" is shown.

3.2 Summary of ASP.NET Server Controls

ASP.NET provides two types of server controls: HTML server controls and Web server controls.

3.2.1 Introduction of HTML server controls

HTML server controls realize the transition from the XHTML element to server controls. At the same time, every HTML server control has a corresponding XHTML element. After transformation, the Web form can access the XHTML elements (HTML server controls), and realize the program of HTML server controls at the server.

To convert XHTML elements to HTML server controls, you can find the XHTML elements in the "Source" view and add the attribute "runat=" server ". Such as, XHTML element is:

```
<input id = "inputName" type = "button" value = "button" />
```

If it is converted to HTML server control, it will be:

```
<input id = "inputName" type = "button" value = "button" runat= "server" />
```

3.2.2 Introduction of Web server controls

Creating Web form by using Web server controls can describe the function of page elements, features, operat-ion mode and behavior, etc. For different browsers, XHTML output may be different.

According to the different functions, the controls are classified into standard control, data control, validation control, navigation control, login control, WebParts control, AJAX Extensions control, dynamic data control and user custom control etc.

- Standard control: In addition to button, text box, drop-down list box and the other control that are commonly used in Web form, there are also some special controls, such as calendar.
- Data control: It is used to connect and access the database, display database data, etc.
- Validation control: It is used to validate the information entered by the user, such as the value should be within the specified range.
- Navigation control: It is used to navigate website.
- AJAX extension control: It is used to update the local information of the page without going back and forth to the whole page.
- Dynamic data control: It is used to create dynamic data pages.
- User custom control: It is used to expand system functions, such as maintaining the unified style of the website.

3.3 Common ASP.NET Standard Controls

ASP.NET standard controls provide the basic functions creating the Web form. These controls have some co-mmon attributes, as shown in table 3-1.

Table 3-1 Common attribute sheet for web server controls

Attribute name	**Description**	**Attribute name**	**Description**
AccessKey	The keyboard shortcuts of the control	Font	The control's font attribute
Attributes	All of the attribute setting of the control	Height	The height of the control
BackColor	The background color of the control	ID	Programme identifier of the control
BoderWidth	The border width of the control	Tab Index	Control index of the order
BoderStyle	The border style of the control	Text	Text displayed on the control
CssClass	The CSS class name of the control	Tool Tip	The displayed text when the mouse hovers over the control
CssStyle	The style of the control	Visible	Whether the control is displayed on the page
Enabled	Whether to enable the Web server control	Width	The width of the control

3.3.1 Label control

Label control is used to display text on the page, and specify the content displayed by the control through the Text Attribute to dynamically modify the displayed text on the server. The syntax is as follows:

```
<asp:Label ID = "Label1" runat = "server" Text = "Label"> </ asp:Label>
```

There is a very useful attribute that is AssociatedControlID in Lable control. The Label control can be associated with another server control on the form by setting its value.

Example 3-2 Activating specific text boxes through keyboard shortcuts

As is shown in figure 3-1, when pressing the ALT + N, the text box to the right of the user name will be activated; when pressing the ALT + P, the text box to the right of the password will be activated .

Figure 3-1 The Browsing Effect of Lable.aspx

Source Codes: Lable.aspx

```
<%@ Page Language="C#" AutoEventWireup="true" CodeFile="Label.aspx.cs" Inherits=
"Chap3_Label" %>
<!DOCTYPE html>
<html xmlns="http://www.w3.org/1999/xhtml">
<head runat="server">
 <meta http-equiv="Content-Type" content="text/html; charset=utf-8" />
 <title>To activate specific text boxes through keyboard shortcuts </title>
</head>
<body>
```

```
    <form id="form1" runat="server">
      <div>
        <asp:Label ID="lblName" runat="server" AccessKey="N" AssociatedControlID="txtName"
Text="User Name(N):"></asp:Label>
        <asp:TextBox ID="txtName" runat="server"></asp:TextBox><br />
        <asp:Label ID="lblPassword" runat="server" AccessKey="M" AssociatedControlID="txtPassword"
Text="Password(M):"></asp:Label>
        <asp:TextBox ID="txtPassword" runat="server"></asp:TextBox>
      </div>
    </form>
</body>
</html>
```

Operating Steps:

Creating Lable.aspx in Chap3 folder, adding two Label controls and two TextBox controls to complete the

the page layout. Setting the attributes of each control referencing source program. Browsing Lable. aspx and testing it.

3.3.2 TextBox control

TextBox control is used to display or input data. The syntax is as follows:

`<asp:TextBox ID = "TextBox1" runat = "server"> </ asp:TextBox>`

The practical attributes, methods and events are shown in Table 3-2

Table 3-2 Table of attributes, methods and events of TextBox control

TextMode attribute	The value "SingleLine" represents single-line textbox; Value "Password" represent passwordbox, which will show the special characters such as "*"; Value "MultiLine" represents MultiLine textbox.
AutoPostBack attribute	The "true" show that when the content of the textbox is changed and the focus is moved out of the textbox, the TextChanged event will be triggered, and this will cause the page back and forth.
AutoCompleteType attribute	Annotate complete types automatically, such as E-mail can complete the mail list automatically.
Focus()	Set focus on a textbox.
TextChanged event	The event will be triggered when change the content of the textbox and the focus leaving the textbox.

Example 3-3 The comprehensive application of TextBox control

As is shown in figure 3-2, when the page is loaded, the focus will locate on the Textbox on the right of the user name textbox automatically; When we input the user name and remove the focus out of

Textbox, the TextChanged event will be triggered to determine whether the user name is available; if the name is available, the Lable control lblValidate will show tick, else it will show "User name has been occupied!". The textbox on the right of password shows that it is the password box; the Textbox on the right of E-mail has the function of auto-completion.

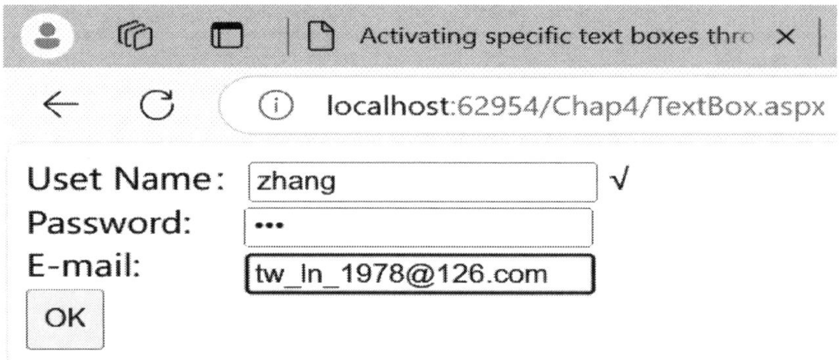

Figure 3-2 The Browsing Effect of TextBox.aspx

Source Codes: TextBox.aspx

```
<%@ Page Language="C#" AutoEventWireup="true" CodeFile="TextBox.aspx.cs"
Inherits="Chap3_TextBox" %>
<!DOCTYPE html>
<html xmlns="http://www.w3.org/1999/xhtml">
<head runat="server">
  <meta http-equiv="Content-Type" content="text/html; charset=utf-8" />
  <title>The comprehensive application of TextBox control</title>
</head>
<body>
  <form id="form1" runat="server">
    <div>
        User name:<asp:TextBox ID="txtName" runat="server" AutoPostBack="True"
        OnTextChanged="TxtName_TextChanged" Width="150px"></asp:TextBox>
        <asp:Label ID="lblValidate" runat="server"></asp:Label><br />
      Password:<asp:TextBox ID="txtPassword" runat="server" TextMode="Password"
Style="position:
       relative; left: 16px" Width="150px"></asp:TextBox><br />
      E-mail:<asp:TextBox ID="txtMail" runat="server" AutoCompleteType="Email" Style="position:
      relative; left: 16px" Width="150px"></asp:TextBox><br />
      <asp:Button ID="btnSubmit" runat="server" Text="OK" OnClick="btnSubmit_Click"
Height="32px" />
    </div>
  </form>
</body>
</html>
```

Source Codes: TextBox.aspx.cs

```
using System;
public partial class Chap3_TextBox:System.Web.UI.Page
{
 protected void Page_Load(object sender, EventArgs e)
 {
  txtName.Focus();
 }
 protected void TxtName_TextChanged(object sender, EventArgs e)
 {
  if (txtName.Text == "leaf")
  {
   lblValidate.Text = "User name has been occupied!!";
  }
  else
  {
   lblValidate.Text = "√";
  }
 }
}
```

Operating Steps:

(1) Creating TextBox.aspx in Chap3 folder, adding one Label control, three TextBox controls and one Button control. Setting the attributes of each control referencing source program.

(2) Double clicking txtName control in "Design" view of TextBox.aspx, TextBox.aspx.cs will be opened automatically in VSC 2019. Entering the contents of shadow part.

(3) Browsing TextBox.aspx, the interface shown in Figure 3-2 is displayed, entering the information and testing it.

Program description:

The attribute value of Style of TextBox control in TextBox.aspx is the style codes automatically generated by VSC 2019 after using the "Position" command under the "Format" menu to adjust the position of the TextBox control in the "Design" view.

When the page is loaded, the Page.Load event is triggered to execute the codes of Page_ Load () method, and focus on the TextBox to the right of the user name.

In this example, the user legitimacy is judged by comparing with the fixed user name leaf. In actual, you need to connect to the database and compare with the user name saved in the database.

You need to enter Email address and click OK firstly, then enter the information again to see the effect of automatically completing the Email list.

3.3.3 Button control, LinkButton control and ImageButton control

There are three types of button in a Web form, that are Button, LinkButton and ImageButton.

They have the same functions, but they are different in appearance. Button presents traditional Button appearance; LinkButton presents hyperlink appearance; ImageButton presents graphic appearance whose image is set by ImageUrl attribute. The defined syntax format is as follows:

<asp:Button ID = " Button1 " runat = "server" Text = "Button" />

<asp:LinkButton ID = "LinkButton1" runat = "server"> LinkButton </ asp:LinkButton>

<asp:ImageButton ID = "ImageButton1" runat = "server" ImageUrl = "~ / Images/map. jpg" />

The practical attributes and events are shown in Table 3-3

Table 3-3 Table of practical attributes and events of Button

Attribute and Event	Description
PostBackUrl attribute	Setting the path of targetpage for cross page submission
Click event	Being triggered when the button is clicked to execute codes at server
ClientClick event	Being triggered when the button is clicked to execute codes at client

XHTML element <a> and LinkButton control can both render hyperlink, but the methods of setting link are different. In <a> element, the jump can be set through href attribute, such as: <a href = "www.21cn.com"> Link to aliyun</ a>.

While in LinkButton we should set attribute PostBackUrl or input the codes in the Click event by using the method Redirect () of object Response, such as:

Response. Redirect (" http://www.aliyun.com ");

Example 3-4 Executing client scripts by using Button control

Executing the client scripts after clicking the Button control, you need to use ClientClick event and JavaScript. As is shown in Figure 3-3 and Figure 3-4, this example can pop up confirmation dialog box before deleting data, then clicking "OK" button to delete the data.

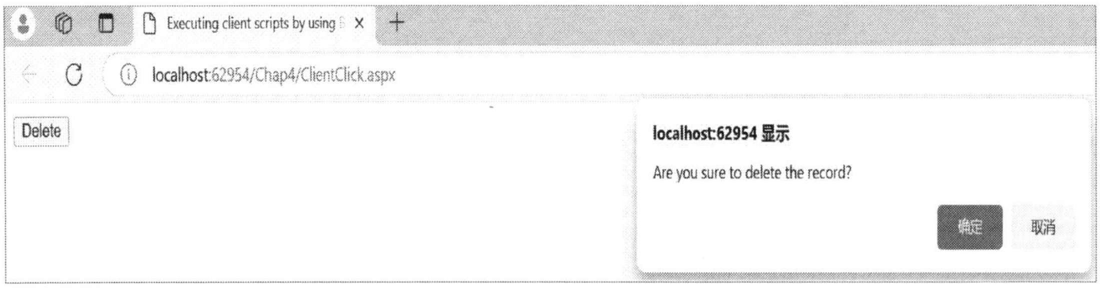

Figure 3-3 The Browsing Effect (1) of ClientClick.aspx

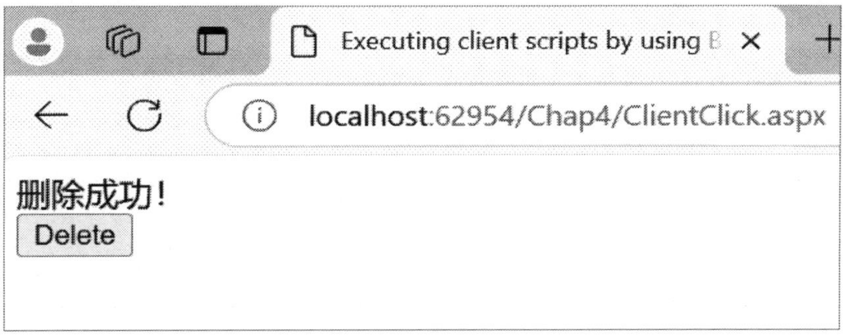

Figure 3-4 The Browsing Effect (2) of ClientClick.aspx

Source Codes: ClientClick.aspx

```
<%@ Page Language="C#" AutoEventWireup="true" CodeFile="ClientClick.aspx.cs"
Inherits="Chap3_ClientClick" %>
<!DOCTYPE html>
<html xmlns="http://www.w3.org/1999/xhtml">
<head runat="server">
 <meta http-equiv="Content-Type" content="text/html; charset=utf-8" />
 <title>Executing client scripts by using Button control</title>
</head>
<body>
 <form id="form1" runat="server">
  <div>
   <asp:Button ID="btnDelete" runat="server" Text="Delete" OnClick="BtnDelete_Click"
OnClientClick="return confirm('Are you sure to delete the record?')" />
  </div>
 </form>
</body>
</html>
```

Source Codes: ClientClick.aspx.cs

```
using System;
public partial class Chap3_ClientClick:System.Web.UI.Page
{
 protected void BtnDelete_Click(object sender, EventArgs e)
 {
  Response.Write("Delete success!");
 }
}
```

Operating Steps:

(1) Creating ClientClick.aspx in Chap3 folder, adding one Button control and setting the attributes,

entering the contents of the shadow part of ClientClick.aspx in "Attribute" window or "Source" view.

(2) Double clicking Button control, entering the contents of the shadow part of ClientClick.aspx.

(3) Browsing ClientClick.aspx, the interface shown in Figure 3-3 is displayed, clicking "OK" button, the interface shown in Figure 3-4 is displayed.

Program description:

In figure 3-3, when we click "Delete" button, ClientClick event is triggered, JavaScript codes "return confirm ('Are you sure to delete records?')" is executed, and confirmation dialog is popped. If you click "OK" button, the Click event is triggered, and deletion operation (only information is output here, and the actual operation needs to connect to the database) is performed. If you click "Cancel" button, the click event will no longer be triggered, and the program run over.

3.3.4 DropDownList control

DropDownList control allow users to choose one item from the predefined drop-down list. The syntax format that is defined is as follows

<asp:DropDownList ID = "DropDownList1" runat = "server"> </ asp:DropDownList>

Practical attributes and events are shown in Table 3-4

Table 3-4 Table of practical attributes and events of DropDownList

Attribute \ Event	Description
DataSource attribute	Using the data source.
DataTextField attribute	An item corresponding to the data source, all of the contents of the item will be displayed in the drop-down list.
DataValueField attribute	An item of a data source, designating the value of each selected item in the drop-down list.
Items attribute	The sets of all the options in the list, we often add items by using Add () method , delete all of items by using clear () method.
SelectedItem attribute	The current selected item.
SelectedValue attribute	The attribute value of the current selected item.
SelectedIndexChanged attribute	Being triggered when selecting an item of drop-down list.
DataBind() method	Bounding data source.

In DropDownList control, there are three types of adding item method. The first is to set the items directly in the attribute window.

The second is to add items by using the method Items.Add() of DropDownList control, such as:

ddCity. Items. Add (new ListItem (" zhejiang ", "zhejiang"));

The third is to set the data source through the DataSource attribute, and then display data through the DataBind () method. If you want to use this method, you should connect to the data base.

Example 3-5 Realizing linkage drop-down list

Linkage of drop-down list is very common in the actual engineering projects. For example in order to query a class schedule, the linkage drop-down list such as "school year - semester - branch - class" is needed.

This example takes the linkage of date as an example, that is shown as Figure 3-5: to display system date, when we change the year or month, the corresponding number of days per month will be changed along with them.

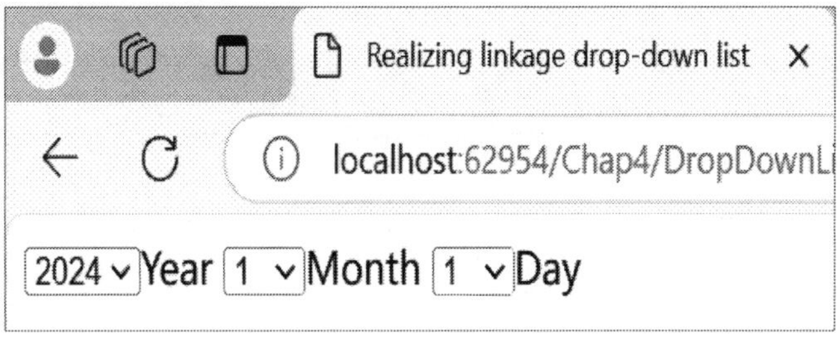

Figure 3-5 The Browsing Effect of DropDownList.aspx

Source Codes: DropDownList.aspx

```
<%@ Page Language="C#" AutoEventWireup="true" CodeFile="DropDownList.aspx.cs"
Inherits="Chap3_DropDownList" %>
<!DOCTYPE html>
<html xmlns="http://www.w3.org/1999/xhtml">
<head runat="server">
<meta http-equiv="Content-Type" content="text/html; charset=utf-8"/>
   <title>realize linkage drop-down list</title>
</head>
<body>
   <form id="form1" runat="server">
      <div>
         <asp:DropDownList ID="ddlyear" runat="server" AutoPostBack="True"
OnSelectedIndexChanged="ddlyear_SelectedIndexChanged">
         </asp:DropDownList>
         year
         <asp:DropDownList ID="ddlmonth" runat="server" AutoPostBack="True">
         </asp:DropDownList>
 month
         <asp:DropDownList ID="ddlday" runat="server">
         </asp:DropDownList>
         day</div>
   </form>
</body>
</html>
```

Source Codes: DropDownList.aspx.cs

```
using System;
using System.Web.UI.WebControls;
public partial class Chap3_DropDownList:System.Web.UI.Page
{
   protected void Page_Load(object sender, EventArgs e)
   {if (!IsPostBack)
      {
         BindYear();
         BindMonth();
         BindDay();
      }
   }
   protected void BindYear()
   {
      ddlyear.Items.Clear();
      int startYear = DateTime.Now.Year - 10;
      int currentYear = DateTime.Now.Year;
      for (int
i = startYear; i <= currentYear; i++)
      {
         ddlyear.Items.Add(new ListItem(i.ToString()));
      }
      ddlyear.SelectedValue = currentYear.ToString();
   }
   protected void BindMonth()
   {
      ddlmonth.Items.Clear();
      for (int i = 1; i <= 12; i++)
         ddlmonth.Items.Add(i.ToString());
   }
   protected void BindDay()
   {
      ddlday.Items.Clear();
      string year = ddlyear.SelectedValue;
      string month = ddlmonth.SelectedValue;
      int days = DateTime.DaysInMonth(int.Parse(year), int.Parse(month));
      for (int i = 1; i <= days; i++)
         ddlday.Items.Add(i.ToString());
   }
   protected void ddlyear_SelectedIndexChanged(object sender, EventArgs e)
   {
      BindDay();
   }
   protected void ddlmonth_SelectedIndexChanged(object sender, EventArgs e)
   {
      BindDay();
   }
}
```

Operating Steps:

(1) Creating DropDownList.aspx in Chap3 folder, adding three DropDownList controls and setting the attributes of each control referencing the source program.

(2) wwCreating DropDownList.aspx.cs file. At last, Browsing DropDownList.aspx and testing it.

Program description:

When the program is running, Page.Load event is triggered firstly, codes of Page_Load() method is executed, binding data including year, month, and day to three DropDownList controls. When we change year or month, the SelectedIndexChanged event of corresponding control will be triggered to perform the page back and forth, and the corresponding number of day is bound to the ddlDay.

3.3.5 LlistBox control

DropDownList control and ListBox control all allow the user to choose the item from a list. The difference is that the list of DropDownList control will be hidden before the user select the item, while the list of ListBox is visible, and we can choose several items at the same time. The syntax format defined is as follows:

<asp:ListBox ID = "ListBox1" runat = "server"> </ asp:ListBox>

The attribute, method and event of ListBox control are similar to DropDownList control. However, a practical attribute is added that is SelectionMode, the value Multiple shows that you can select several items.

Example 3-6 Moving items between ListBox controls

As is shown in Figure 3-6, when we select the items in the list box on the left, then click the button, the corresponding items will be moved to the list box on the right.

Figure 3-6 The Browsing Effect of ListBox.aspx

Source Codes: ListBox.aspx

```
<%@ Page Language="C#" AutoEventWireup="true" CodeFile="ListBox.aspx.cs"
Inherits="Chap3_ListBox" %>
<!DOCTYPE html>

<html xmlns="http://www.w3.org/1999/xhtml">
<head runat="server">
```

```
<meta http-equiv="Content-Type" content="text/html; charset=utf-8"/>
  <title>To move items between ListBox controls</title>
</head>
<body>
  <form id="form1" runat="server">
    <div>
      <asp:ListBox ID="lstLeft" runat="server" SelectionMode="Multiple">
        <asp:ListItem>hunan</asp:ListItem>
        <asp:ListItem>shanghai</asp:ListItem>
        <asp:ListItem>beijing</asp:ListItem>
        <asp:ListItem></asp:ListItem>
        <asp:ListItem>jiangxi</asp:ListItem>
      </asp:ListBox>
      <asp:Button ID="btMove" runat="server" OnClick="btMove_Click" Text="&gt;" />
      <asp:ListBox ID="lstRight" runat="server" SelectionMode="Multiple"></asp:ListBox>
    </div>
  </form>
</body>
</html>
```

Source Codes: ListBox.aspx.cs

```
using System;
public partial class Chap3_ListBox : System.Web.UI.Page
{
  protected void Page_Load(object sender, EventArgs e)
  {

  }
  protected void btMove_Click(object sender, EventArgs e)
  {
    for (int i = 0; i <lstLeft.Items.Count; i++)
    { if (lstLeft.Items[i].Selected)
      {
        lstRight.Items.Add(lstLeft.Items[i]);
        lstLeft.Items.Remove(lstLeft.Items[i]);
        i--;
      }
}
  }
}
```

Operating Steps:

(1) Creating ListBox.aspx in Chap3 folder, adding two ListBox controls and a Button control, and setting the attributes of each control referencing the source program.

(2) Creating ListBox.aspx.cs file. At last, browsing ListBox.aspx and testing it.

3.3.6 CheckBox control and CheckBoxList control

CheckBox control and CheckBoxList control all can provide users with "true/false", "yes/no" or "on/off". If you need multiple choice, you can use multiple CheckBoxs or a single CheckBoxList, but generally we use the CheckBoxList. The defined syntax format is as follows:

```
<asp:CheckBox ID = "CheckBox1" runat = "server" />
<asp:CheckBoxList ID = "CheckBoxList1" runat = "server"> </ asp:CheckBoxList>
```

Note: The attribute which is used to decided whether the CheckBox is selected is Checked, while the attribute is selected for the CheckBoxList control to determine whether the items in the list are selected.

In the engineering projects, we usually set the attribute AutoPostBack of the CheckBoxList to be false. And do not use CheckBoxList event itself to submit data to the server, but often cooperate with the event of the Button control.

Example 3-7 The application of CheckBoxList

As is shown in Figure 3-7, when we choose the personal preference and click the submit button, the information of the selected item will be displayed.

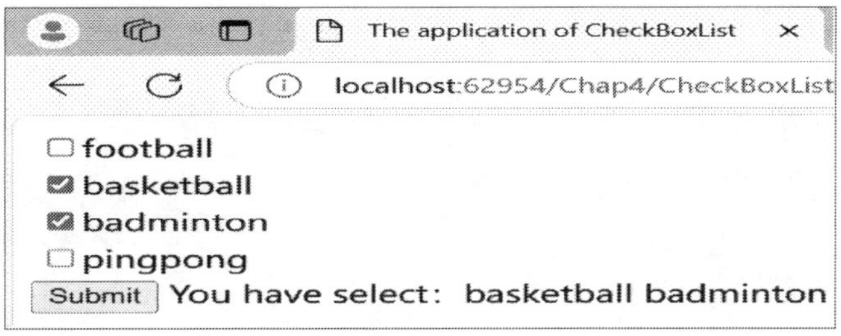

Figure 3-7 The Browsing Effect of CheckBoxList.aspx

Source Codes: CheckBoxList.aspx

```
<%@ Page Language="C#" AutoEventWireup="true" CodeFile="CheckBoxList.aspx.cs"
Inherits="Chap3_CheckBoxList" %>
<!DOCTYPE html>
<html xmlns="http://www.w3.org/1999/xhtml">
<head runat="server">
<meta http-equiv="Content-Type" content="text/html; charset=utf-8"/>
  <title>The application of CheckBoxList</title>
</head>
```

```
<body>
  <form id="form1" runat="server">
    <div>
      <asp:CheckBoxList ID="chkSport" runat="server">
        <asp:ListItem>football</asp:ListItem>
        <asp:ListItem Value="basketball"></asp:ListItem>
        <asp:ListItem>badminton</asp:ListItem>
        <asp:ListItem>pingpong</asp:ListItem>
      </asp:CheckBoxList>
      <br />
      <asp:Button ID="btnSubmit" runat="server" OnClick="btnSubmit_Click" Text="Submit" />
      <asp:Label ID="lblMsg" runat="server"></asp:Label>
    </div>
  </form>
</body>
</html>
```

Source Codes: ListBox.aspx.cs

```
using System;
using System.Web.UI.WebControls;
public partial class Chap3_CheckBoxList : System.Web.UI.Page
{
  protected void btnSubmit_Click(object sender, EventArgs e)
  {
    lblMsg.Text = "You have chosed:";
    foreach (ListItem listItem in chkSport.Items)
    {
      if (listItem.Selected)
        lblMsg.Text = lblMsg.Text + listItem.Text+" ";
    }
  }
}
```

Operating Steps:

(1) Creating CheckBoxList.aspx in Chap3 folder, adding a CheckBoxList control, a Button control and a Label control, and setting the attributes of each control referencing the source program.

(2) Creating CheckBoxList.aspx.cs file. At last, browsing CheckBoxList.aspx and testing it.

3.3.7 RadioButton control and RadioButtonList control

RadioButton control and RadioButtonList control usually are used to choose one of the several options. The individual RadioButton can only provide to choose a single item, but we can group several RadioButtons by setting the attribute GroupName of each RadioButton the same name. The defined syntax format of RadioButton is as follows:

<asp:RadioButton ID = "RadioButton1 runat =" server "GroupName" = "group" />

The defined syntax format of RadioButtonList is as follows:

The <asp:RadioButtonList ID = "RadioButtonList1 runat =" server ">"

<asp:ListItem> male</ asp:male ListItem>

<asp:ListItem> women </ asp:ListItem>

</ asp:RadioButtonList>

Note: The attribute which is used to decided whether the RadioButton is selected is Checked, while the attribute is SelectedItem for the RadioButtonList control to determine whether the items in the list are selected.

3.3.8 Image control and ImageMap control

The Image control is used to display images on the Web form. You can use the ImageUrl attribute to specify an image source file during interface design or programming. In practical project, it is always bound with data source, and display images according to the data source information. The defined syntax format is as follows:

<asp:Image ID = "Image1" runat = "server" ImageUrl = "~ / Images/map.jpg" />

Note: The Image control does not contain the Click event. If you want to use Click event, you can use ImageButton control instead of the Image control.

The ImageMap control can be used to display the image, but also can realize image links. The image can be divided into hot spots of different shapes, and be linked to different pages. In the practical engineering projects, it is always used for navigation, map, etc. As is shown in Figure 3-8, hot spots are set by attribute HotSpot, the area is divided into CircleHotSpot, and PolygonHotSpot RectangleHotSpot and every region is linked to the designated URL by attribute NavigateUrl.

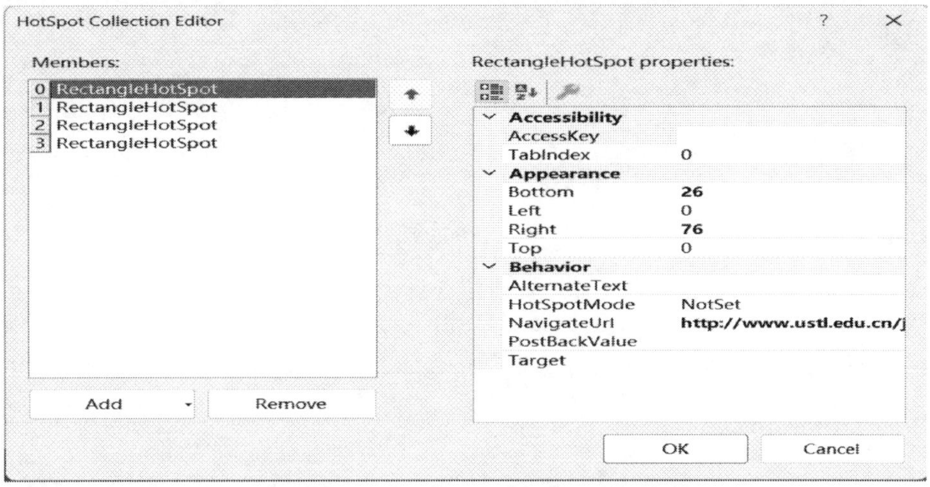

Figure 3-8 Setting HotSpots Attribute

Example 3-8 Designing the navigation by using ImageMap control

As is shown in Figure 3-9, the navigation bar is a picture. After we set the hot spots, clicking the different regions, these regions will be linked to the different web pages.

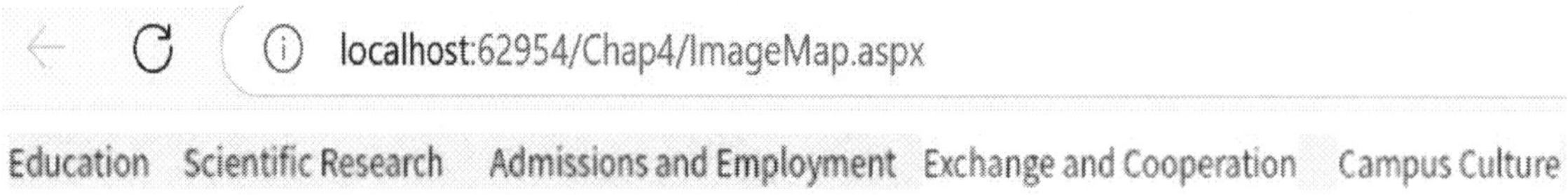

Figure 3-9 The Browsing Effect of ImageMap.aspx

Source Codes: ImageMap.aspx

```
<%@ Page Language="C#" AutoEventWireup="true" CodeFile="ImageMap.aspx.cs"
Inherits="Chap3_ImageMap" %>
<!DOCTYPE html>
<html xmlns="http://www.w3.org/1999/xhtml">
<head runat="server">
<meta http-equiv="Content-Type" content="text/html; charset=utf-8"/>
  <title>Design the navigation by using ImageMap control</title>
</head>
<body>
  <form id="form1" runat="server">
    <div>
      <asp:ImageMap ID="imapnav" runat="server" ImageUrl="~/Images/map.jpg">
        <asp:RectangleHotSpot Bottom="26" NavigateUrl="http://www.163.com" Right="76" />
        <asp:RectangleHotSpot Bottom="26" Left="72" NavigateUrl="http://www.sina.com"
Right="141" />
        <asp:RectangleHotSpot Bottom="26" Left="143" Right="214" />
        <asp:RectangleHotSpot Bottom="26" Left="216" Right="287" />
      </asp:ImageMap>
    </div>
  </form>
</body>
</html>
```

Operating Steps:

Creating ImageMap.aspx in Chap3 folder, adding an ImageMap control, setting ImageUrl attribute and HotSpots attribute, then dividing it into several rectangular hot spots, setting the NavigateUrl attribute of different regions, browsing ImageMap.aspx, and clicking different regions to test.

3.3.9 HyperLink control

HyperLink control is used to create linkage on the page, and it is different from the <a> element, that is it can be bound with the data source. The defined syntax format is as follows:

```
<asp:the HyperLink ID = "HyperLink1" runat = "server" Target = "_blank">
  </ asp:the HyperLink>
```

Target attribute is very important to the HyperLink control, whose values are usually _blank and _self. _blank determines to display the link page in a new window, and _self decides to display the link page in the original window.

Note: The HyperLink control does not include the Click event. If we want to use the Click event, we should take the LinkButton control instead of it.

The usage of the ImageUrl attribute can link to an image. When we set the Text and ImageUrl attributes at the same time, ImageUrl is preferred. If we can't find the image, the content of the Text will be displayed.

The size of the image which is displayed after setting ImageUrl in the HyperLink directly is not adjusted. If you want to change the size, you should use the Image control.

Example 3-9 Combining the HyperLink control with the Image control

This example implements the different effect between the image size displayed in the page and the actual image.

Source Codes: HyperLink.aspx

```
<%@ Page Language="C#" AutoEventWireup="true" CodeFile="HyperLink.aspx.cs"
Inherits="Chap3_HyperLink" %>
<!DOCTYPE html>
<html xmlns="http://www.w3.org/1999/xhtml">
<head runat="server">
  <meta http-equiv="Content-Type" content="text/html; charset=utf-8" />
  <title>Combining the HyperLink control with the Image control</title>
</head>
<body>
  <form id="form1" runat="server">
    <div>
      <asp:HyperLink ID="hlkMouse" runat="server" NavigateUrl="http://www.21cn.com">
     <asp:Image ID="imgMouse" runat="server" ImageUrl="~/Images/mouseOut.jpg" Width="50" />
      </asp:HyperLink>
    </div>
  </form>
</body>
</html>
```

Operating Steps:

Establishing HyperLink.aspx in Chap3 folder, adding an HyperLink control, inserting an Image control between <asp:HyperLink> and </asp:HyperLink> in "Source" view, and setting the attributes of each control referencing the source program. At last, browsing the HyperLink.aspx to test.

3.3.10 Table control

Table control is used to dynamically create a table on a Web form. It is a container control. While the table established through clicking "Table"→ "Insert a table" command is usually used for page layout and corresponding XHTML elements<table>, Table object created through Table control is composed of row (TableRow) objects, and TableRow objects are made of cell (TableCell) objects. The syntax format defined is as follows:

```
<asp:Table ID = "Table1" runat = "server" GridLines => "Both"
  <asp:TableRow runat = "server">
<asp:TableCell runat = "server"> student id </ asp:TableCell>
<asp:TableCell runat = "server"> name </ asp:TableCell>
<asp:TableCell runat = "server"> score </ asp:TableCell>
</ asp:TableRow>
</ asp:Table>
```

Note: Using attribute Rows to add rows to the table object; using attribute Cells to add cells to the TableRow object; using attribute Controls to add controls to the TableCell object.

Example 3-10 Creating table dynamically

As is shown in Figure 3-10, the simple interfaces of score entry on the page is essentially a form that is generated dynamically.

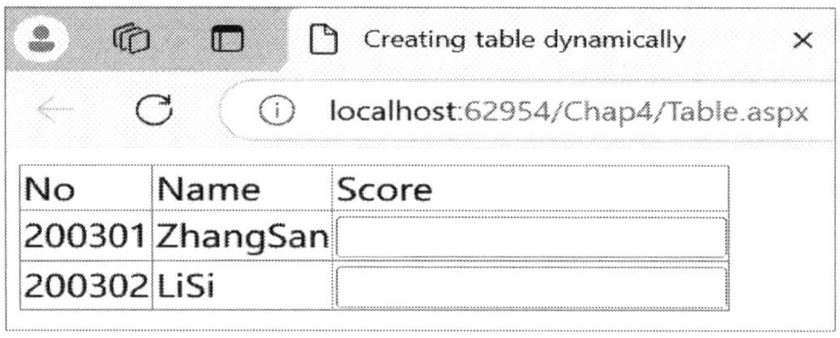

Figure 3-10 The Browsing Effect of Table.aspx

Source Codes: Table.aspx

```
<%@ Page Language="C#" AutoEventWireup="true" CodeFile="Table.aspx.cs"
Inherits="Chap3_Table" %>
<!DOCTYPE html>
<html xmlns="http://www.w3.org/1999/xhtml">
<head runat="server">
<meta http-equiv="Content-Type" content="text/html; charset=utf-8"/>
   <title>Create table dynamically</title>
</head>
<body>
   <form id="form1" runat="server">
      <div>
         <asp:Table ID="tblScore" runat="server" GridLines="Both">
```

```
            <asp:TableRow runat="server">
                <asp:TableCell runat="server">No</asp:TableCell>
                <asp:TableCell runat="server">Name</asp:TableCell>
                <asp:TableCell runat="server">Score</asp:TableCell>
            </asp:TableRow>
        </asp:Table>
    </div>
  </form>
</body>
</html>
```

Source Codes: Table.aspx.cs

```
using System;
using System.Web.UI.WebControls;
public partial class Chap3_Table : System.Web.UI.Page
{
    protected void Page_Load(object sender, EventArgs e)
    {
        string[] name = { "zhangsan", "lisi" };
        string[] number = {"202001","202002" };
        for (int i = 1; i <= 2; i++) {
            TableRow row = new TableRow();
            TableCell cellNumber = new TableCell();
            TableCell cellName = new TableCell();
            TableCell cellInput = new TableCell();
            cellNumber.Text = number[i - 1];
            cellName.Text = name[i - 1];
            TextBox txtInput = new TextBox();
            cellInput.Controls.Add(txtInput);
            row.Cells.Add(cellNumber);
            row.Cells.Add(cellName);
            row.Cells.Add(cellInput);
            tblScore.Rows.Add(row);
        }
    }
}
```

Operating Steps:

(1) Creating Table.aspx in Chap3 folder, adding one Table control, then adding a TableRow on the dialog in which setting attribute Rows, then adding three TableCells on the dialog in which setting attribute Cells of TableRow, and setting the value of attribute Text of TableCell to be "No" "Name" "Score".

(2) Creating Table.aspx.cs. At last, browsing Table.aspx and testing it.

3.3.11 Panel control and PlaceHolder control

Panel control and PlaceHolder control are all the container controls. They are usually used to dynamically build controls and they can display different contents under different conditions at the same page. When we use the Panel control, the advantage is that you only need to load a page to render different content.

The syntax format defined of Panel control is as follows:

<asp:Panel ID = "Panel1" runat = "server"> </ asp:Panel>

The syntax format defined of PlaceHolder control is as follows:

The <asp:PlaceHolder ID = "PlaceHolder1" runat = "server"> </ asp:PlaceHolder>

Example 3-11 Realizing simple registration page by using Panel

As is shown in Figure 3-11, entering the user name, clicking the "Next" button, the interface as Figure 3-12 is shown, then entering the name, telephone and other information, clicking the "Next" button, the interface as Figure 3-13 is shown. By creating three Panel controls, you can easily present different contents corresponding to the three steps

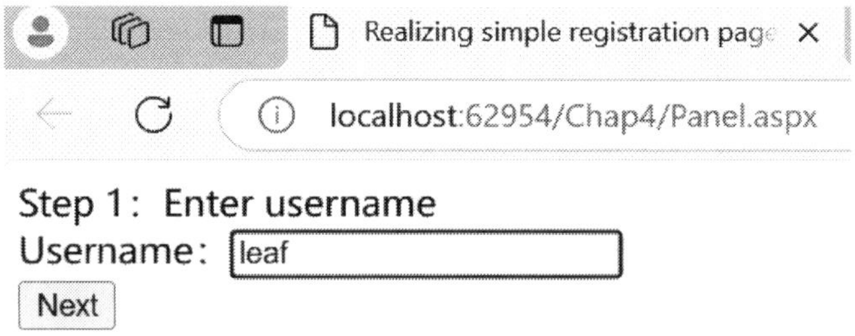

Figure 3-11 The Browsing Effect(1)

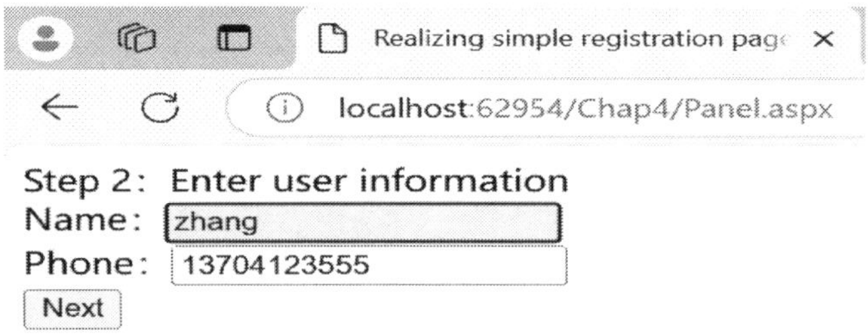

Figure 3-12 The Browsing Effect (2)

Figure 3-13 The Browsing Effect (3)

Source Codes: Panel.aspx

```
<%@ Page Language="C#" AutoEventWireup="true" CodeFile="Panel.aspx.cs"
Inherits="Chap3_Panel" %>
<!DOCTYPE html>
<html xmlns="http://www.w3.org/1999/xhtml">
<head runat="server">
<meta http-equiv="Content-Type" content="text/html; charset=utf-8"/>
  <title>Realizing simple registration page by using Panel</title>
</head>
<body>
  <form id="form1" runat="server">
    <div>
      <asp:Panel ID="pnlStep1" runat="server" style="margin-bottom: 0px">
        step1:Input username<br /> user name<asp:TextBox ID="txtUser"
             runat="server"></asp:TextBox>
        <br />
        <asp:Button ID="btnStep1" runat="server" OnClick="btnStep1_Click" Text="Next" />
      </asp:Panel>
    </div>
    <asp:Panel ID="pnlStep2" runat="server">
      step2:Input user information<br /> Name:<asp:TextBox ID="txtName"
           runat="server"></asp:TextBox>
      <br />
      Tele:<asp:TextBox ID="txtTelephone" runat="server"></asp:TextBox>
      <br />
      <asp:Button ID="btnStep2" runat="server" OnClick="btnStep2_Click" Text="Next" />
    </asp:Panel>
    <asp:Panel ID="pnlStep3" runat="server">
      step3:please ensure your information<br />
      <asp:Label ID="lblMsg" runat="server"></asp:Label>
      <br />
      <asp:Button ID="btnStep3" runat="server" Text="Ok" />
    </asp:Panel>
  </form>
</body>
</html>
```

Source Codes: Panel.aspx.cs

```
using System;
using System.Web.UI.WebControls;
public partial class Chap4_Panel : System.Web.UI.Page
```

```
{
    protected void Page_Load(object sender, EventArgs e)
    {
        if (!IsPostBack)
        {
            pnlStep1.Visible = true;
            pnlStep2.Visible = false;
            pnlStep3.Visible = false;
                }
    }
    protected void btnStep1_Click(object sender, EventArgs e)
    {
        pnlStep1.Visible = false;
        pnlStep2.Visible = true;
        pnlStep3.Visible = false;

    }
    protected void btnStep2_Click(object sender, EventArgs e)
    {
    pnlStep1.Visible = false;
    pnlStep2.Visible = false;
    pnlStep3.Visible = true;
    lblMsg.Text = "user name:" + txtUser.Text + "<br/>name:" + txtName.Text + "<br/>telephone:" +
  txtTelephone.Text;
    }
}
```

Operating Steps:

(1) Creating Panel.aspx in Chap3 folder, adding three Panel controls, adding the other controls in each Panel control, and setting the attributes of each control referencing the source program.

(2) Creating Panel.aspx.cs. At last, browsing Panel.aspx, entering the information and testing.

Program description:

When the page loads, the Page_Load event is triggered, and the codes of Page_Load() method are executed firstly; setting the pnlStep1 to be visible, while the other two Panel controls are set to be invisible.

Example 3-12 Adding controls dynamically by using PlaceHolder

PlaceHolder control play a role as placeholders on the Web form, and you can dynamically add the required controls to it. As is shown in Figure 3-14, the "Submit" button and text box displayed on the page are dynamically generated when the page is loaded. As is shown in Figure 3-15, clicking "Submit" button to output the information. As is shown in Figure 3-16, clicking the "Acquire" button to get and output the information entered in the text box.

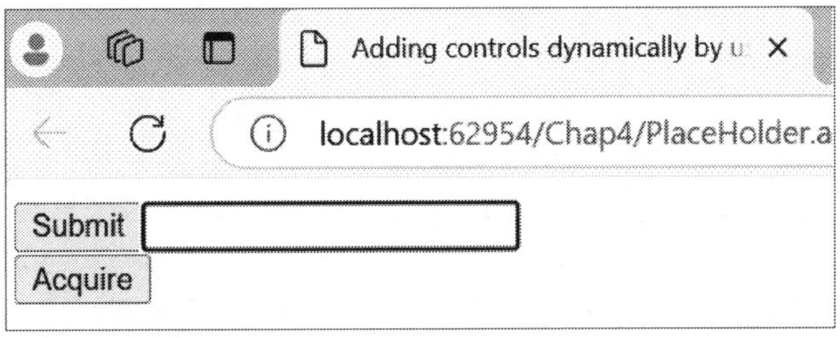

Figure 3-14 The Browsing Effect (1)

Figure 3-15 The Browsing Effect (2)

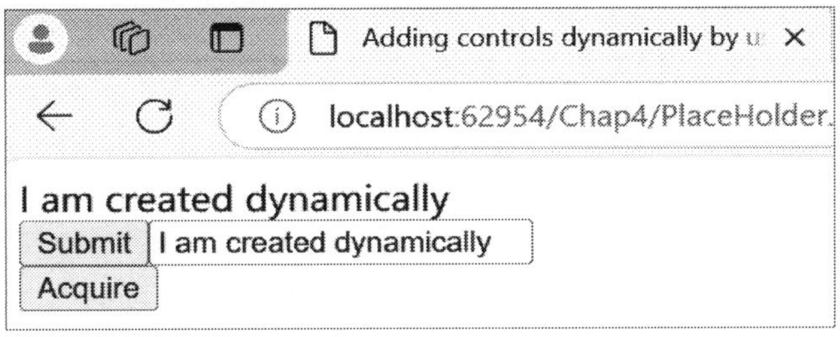

Figure 3-16 The Browsing Effect (3)

Source Codes: PlaceHolder.aspx

```
<%@ Page Language="C#" AutoEventWireup="true" CodeFile="PlaceHolder.aspx.cs" I
nherits="Chap3_PlaceHolder" %>
<!DOCTYPE html>
<html xmlns="http://www.w3.org/1999/xhtml">
<head runat="server">
  <meta http-equiv="Content-Type" content="text/html; charset=utf-8" />
  <title>Adding controls dynamically by using PlaceHolder</title>
</head>
<body>
  <form id="form1" runat="server">
    <div>
      <asp:PlaceHolder ID="plhTest" runat="server"></asp:PlaceHolder>
      <br />
      <asp:Button ID="btnAcquire" runat="server" Text="Get" OnClick="BtnAcquire_Click" />
    </div>
  </form>
</body>
</html>
```

Source Codes: PlaceHolder.aspx.cs

```
using System;
using System.Web.UI.WebControls;
public partial class Chap4_PlaceHolder : System.Web.UI.Page
{
 protected void Page_Load(object sender, EventArgs e)
 {
  Button btnSubmit = new Button();
  btnSubmit.ID = "btnSubmit";
  btnSubmit.Text = "OK";
  btnSubmit.Click += new EventHandler(BtnSubmit_Click);
  plhTest.Controls.Add(btnSubmit);
  TextBox txtInput = new TextBox();
  txtInput.ID = "txtInput";
  plhTest.Controls.Add(txtInput);
 }
 protected void BtnSubmit_Click(object sender, EventArgs e)
 {
  Response.Write("Trigger the Click event of 'OK' button!");
 }
 protected void BtnAcquire_Click(object sender, EventArgs e)
 {
  TextBox txtInput = (TextBox)plhTest.FindControl("txtInput");
  Response.Write(txtInput.Text);
 }
}
```

Operating Steps:

(1) Creating PlaceHolder.aspx in Chap3 folder, adding one PlaceHolder control and one Button control, and setting the attributes of each control referencing the source program.

(2) Creating PlaceHolder.aspx.cs. At last, browsing PlaceHolder.aspx, entering the information and testing.

Program description:

When the page loads, the Page_Load event is triggered, the codes of Page_Load() method are executed, and a Button control and a TextBox control are created dynamically. Executing the codes of BtnSubmit_Click() method according to registered events.

3.4 Summary

➢ If you want to understand event processing flow of ASP.NET page, you need to be clear about the triggered order of Page_ PreInit, Page_ Init, Page_ load and the control event.

➢ The IsPostBack attribute is often used to determine whether or not to execute the corresponding codes during page round-trip.

- You can convert XHTML elements into HTML server controls by adding "runat="Server".
- Web server standard controls are the basis for building Web forms.

3.5 Exercises

1. Multiple Choice Questions

(1) Which of the following controls dosen't belong to Web serve controls (   )

A.Table   B.Input   C.AdRotator   D.Calendar

(2) Which of the following controls can't correspond to the mouse-click event (   )

A.ImageButton   B.ImageMap   C.Image   D.LinkButton

(3) Which properties allow client scripts to be executed after clicking a Button type control(   )

A.OnClientClick   B.OnClick   C.OnCommandClick   D.OnClientCommand

(4) Which of the following controls dosen't belong to container controls (   )

A.Panel   B.CheckBox   C.Table   D.PlaceHolder

2. Programming Questions

(1) Establish and debug all of the instances in this chapter.

(2) Implement a simple calculator. When receiving two numbers as input, the calculator can calculate their sum, difference, and other operations.

(3) Create an interconnected dropdown list with "Academic Year - Semester - College - Teacher", and automatically generate a table when selecting "Teacher" as the final option.

(4) Create a user registration page by using the Panel contro. The registration interface includes fields for user name, password, full name, gender, date of birth, phone, email, interests, and hobbies, etc.

(5) Implement a test page containing multiple-choice questions by using the PlaceHolder control, where the question information is contained in an array.

Chapter 4 The Validation of ASP.NET Form

Points:

- Understanding the validation of the client and server
- Mastering the usage of ASP.NET validation controls

4.1 The Overview of The Form Validation

Validation is usually used to develop a set of rules for the collected data. Validation does not guarantee the truth of the input data, it can only represent that the data meet some rules, such as "text box must input data", "the format of the input data must be the E-mail address", etc.

Form validation is divided into two forms: server validation and client validation. Server validation refers to send all of the information input by users to the Web server for validation; Client validation refers to validate the data by using JavaScript before the data is sent to the server. Client validation can quickly respond to users. However, the JavaScript scripts will be exposed to users, which will bring security risks. Server validation is relatively safe, but the response speed is slow

The form validation of ASP.NET uses the implicit validation method supported by jQuery by default. The configuration steps are as follows:

(1)Using NuGet to install jQuery.

(2)Establish Global.asax file (global application class file), and the source codes that are added to the Application_Start() method are as follows:

```
ScriptResourceDefinition scriptResDef = new ScriptResourceDefinition();
scriptResDef.Path = "~/Scripts/jquery-3.2.1.min.js";
ScriptManager.ScriptResourceMapping.AddDefinition("jquery", scriptResDef);
```

ASP.NET form validation can also choose disable implicit validation, Adding the configuration codes in the <configuration> element of the Web.config file are as follows:

```
<appSettings>
  <add key="ValidationSettings:UnobtrusiveValidationMode" value="None"/>
</appSettings>
```

To be sure if all of the controls of the page pass the verification by judging the value of the attribute, IsValid. "True" represents all of the controls pass the verification, while "false" represents some controls of your page don't pass the validation.

4.2 The Server Validation Controls of ASP.NET

ASP.NET have six validation controls, that are RequiredFieldValidator, CompareValidator, RangeValidator, RegularExpressionValidator, CustomValidator and ValidationSummary. Except ValidationSummary control, the other five controls have some common attributes, which are shown in Table 4-1.

Table 4-1 Table of common attributes

Attribute	Description
ControlToValidate	Specify the ID of the control to be validated.
Display	Specify the display mode of the validation controls on the page. Value "Static" indicates the validation controls always occupy the page space; Value "Dynamic" indicates the validation controls occupy page space only when they display validation error message; Value "None" indicates validation error messages are shown in ValidationSummary.
EnableClientScript	Set whether to enable client authentication, and the default value is true.
ErrorMessage	Set the error messages which are displayed in the ValidationSummary control, and the Text attribute will replace it if the value is empty.
SetFocusOnError	When validation is invalid, determine whether to focus on the validation controls.
Text	Set the display information of the validation control.
ValidationGroup	Set the group name of validation controls.

In order to ensure the response speed, we general set the value of attribute EnableClientScript of validation controls to be true. When the value of the control designated by attribute ControlToValidate is changed and the focus was removed, the validation will be implemented at client. The JavaScript codes for validation are not developed by developers, but generated by the system. If the value of EnableClientScript is set to be false, the validation will be implemented when the page has a round-trip time. The validation is fully implemented at server at this time.

If the value of CausesValidation is "false", that represent the validation does not be performed.

In order to set multiple rules for a control, we can let multiple validation controls work together. At this time, the attribute ControlToValidate of the validation controls should be the same.

If you want to provide group validation function of different controls on the same page, you can set the attribute ValidationGroup of the same group controls to be the same group name.

4.2.1 RequiredFieldValidator control

RequiredFieldValidator is usually use to validate some information that must be input, such as user name, password, etc. When you fill in the form on the page, you can often see that some text boxes are followed by an *, which is the effect of this validation control. The defined syntax format is as follows:

```
<asp:RequiredFieldValidator ID = "RequiredFieldValidator1" runat = "server" ControlToValidate =
"TextBox1" ErrorMessage = "RequiredFieldValidator">
</ asp:RequiredFieldValidator>
```

There is a very useful attribute InitialValue which is used to specify the initial text of the validated control. If the value of the InitialValue is set, the validation will pass only when the value is entered in the validated control and it is different from the value of InitialValue.

Example 4-1 Prohibiting empty data and changing the initial value simultaneously

As is shown in Figure 4-1 to Figure 4-3, When the content of the text box on the right of the user name is changed and the focus is removed, the client validation is performed. If the content is still the initial value of the original text box, then shows "it is not the same with the initial value"; If the content is empty, then the red * is shown.

Figure 4-1 The Browsing Effect of Require.aspx (1)

Figure 4-2 The Browsing Effect of Require.aspx (2)

Figure 4-3 The Browsing Effect of Require.aspx (3)

Source Codes: Require.aspx

```
<%@ Page Language="C#" AutoEventWireup="true" CodeFile="Require.aspx.cs"
Inherits="Chap4_Require" %>
<!DOCTYPE html>
<html xmlns="http://www.w3.org/1999/xhtml">
<head runat="server">
  <meta http-equiv="Content-Type" content="text/html; charset=utf-8" />
  <title> Prohibiting empty data and changing the initial value at the same time </title>
</head>
<body>
<form id="form1" runat="server">
  <div>
    User Name: <asp:TextBox ID="txtName" runat="server">Your Name</asp:TextBox>
    <asp:RequiredFieldValidator ID="rfvName1" runat="server"
ControlToValidate="txtName">*</asp:RequiredFieldValidator>
    <asp:RequiredFieldValidator ID="rfvName2" runat="server" ControlToValidate="txtName"
InitialValue="Your Name">it is not the same with the initial value!</asp:RequiredFieldValidator>
  </div>
</form>
</body>
</html>
```

Operating Steps:

Creating Require.aspx in Chap4 folder, adding one TextBox control and two RequiredFieldValidator controls, and setting the attributes of each control referencing the source program. At last, browsing Require.aspx and testing it.

Program description:

rfvNamel ensures that the user name must be input, while rfvNaqme2 ensures that user name that is input must be different from the initial value.

4.2.2 CompareValidator control

CompareValidator control is usually use to compare the value of a control and another control. If the two values are equal, the verification is passed. This control also can be used to compare the value of a control and a specified value. If the result of the comparison is true, the verification is passed. The defined syntax format is as follows:

```
<asp:CompareValidator ID="CompareValidator1" runat="server"
 ControlToCompare="TextBox2" ControlToValidate="TextBox1"
 ErrorMessage="CompareValidator">
</asp:CompareValidator>
```

The practical attribute sheet of CompareValidator control is shown as Table 4-2

Table 4-2 The practical attribute sheet of CompareValidator control

Attribute	Description
ControlToCompare	Specify the control ID comparing with the validated control
Operator	Set the operator, including: Equal, NotEqual, GreaterThan, GreaterThanEqual, LessThan, LessThanEqual and DataTypeCheck.
Type	Set data types.
ValueToCompare	Designate the value which will compare with the validated controls.

Example 4-2 The application of CompareValidator control

As is shown in Figure 4-4 and Figure 4-5, validating the consistence of Password text box and confirming password text box; testing whether the validation value of answer text box is "A"; testing whether the validated data type of the amount text box is Currency.

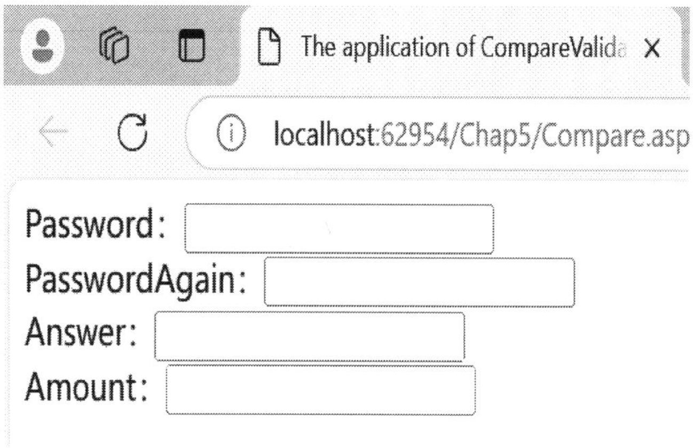

Figure 4-4 The Browsing Effect of Compare.aspx (1)

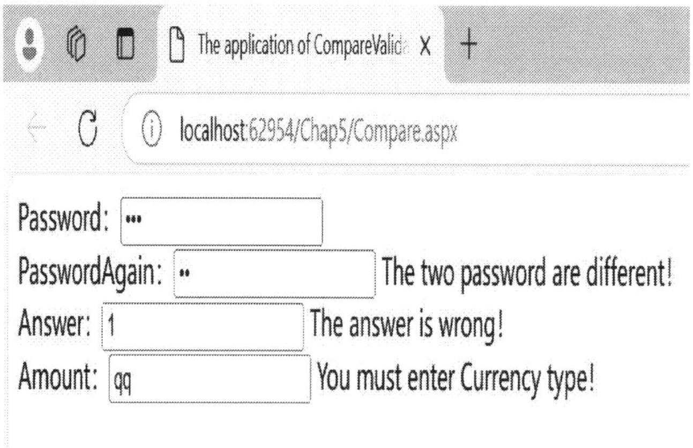

Figure 4-5 The Browsing Effect of Compare.aspx (2)

Source Codes: Compare.aspx

```
<%@ Page Language="C#" AutoEventWireup="true" CodeFile="Compare.aspx.cs"
Inherits="Chap4_Compare" %>
<!DOCTYPE html>
<html xmlns="http://www.w3.org/1999/xhtml">
<head runat="server">
<meta http-equiv="Content-Type" content="text/html; charset=utf-8"/>
  <title>The application of CompareValidator control </title>
</head>
<body>
  <form id="form1" runat="server">
    <div>
      Password:<asp:TextBox ID="txtPassword" runat="server"
      TextMode="Password"></asp:TextBox>
      <br />
      <br />
      PasswordAgain:<asp:TextBox ID="txtPaswordAgain" runat="server"
      TextMode="Password"></asp:TextBox>
      <asp:CompareValidator ID="cvPassword" runat="server" ControlToCompare="txtPassword"
      ControlToValidate="txtPaswordAgain" ErrorMessage="The two passwords are not the
      same!"></asp:CompareValidator>
      <br />
      <br />
      Answer:<asp:TextBox ID="txtAnswer" runat="server"></asp:TextBox>
      <asp:CompareValidator ID="cvAnswer" runat="server" ControlToValidate="txtAnswer"
      ErrorMessage="the answer is wrong!" ValueToCompare="A"></asp:CompareValidator>
      <br />
      <br />
      Amount:<asp:TextBox ID="txtAmount" runat="server"></asp:TextBox>
      <asp:CompareValidator ID="cvAmount" runat="server" ControlToValidate="txtAmount"
      ErrorMessage="you must input currency type!" Operator="DataTypeCheck"
      Type="Currency"></asp:CompareValidator>
      <br />
      <br />
      <asp:Button ID="btnButton" runat="server" OnClick="btnButton_Click" Text="OK" />
    </div>
  </form>
</body>
</html>
```

Operating Steps:

Creating Compare.aspx in Chap4 folder, adding four TextBox controls and three CompareValidator controls, and setting the attributes of each control referencing the source program. At last, browsing Compare.aspx and testing it.

4.2.3 RangeValidator control

RangeValidator control is usually used to validate whether the input values are within the specified range. The defined syntax format is as follows:

```
<asp:RangeValidator ID="RangeValidator1" runat="server"
   ControlToValidate="TextBox4" ErrorMessage="RangeValidator"
   MaximumValue="30" MinimumValue="10" Type="Integer">
</asp:RangeValidator>
```

In order to verify whether the input value is within the specified range, the attributes that are MaximumValue and MinimumValue are provided, which correspond to the maximum and minimum values of the validation range respectively.

Example 4-3 The application of RangeValidator control

As is shown in Figure 4-6 and Figure 4-7, requiring that the value of grade Text box is between 0 ~ 100; the value of Date text box is between 2019-1-1 and 2018-1-1.

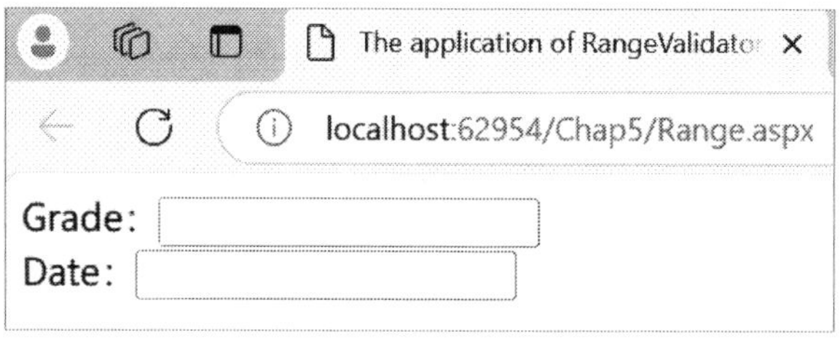

Figure 4-6 The Browsing Effect of Range.aspx(1)

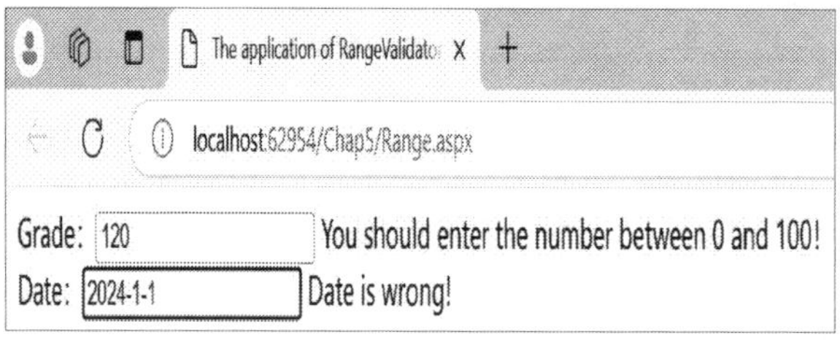

Figure 4-7 The Browsing Effect of Range.aspx (2)

Source Codes: Range.aspx

```
<%@ Page Language="C#" AutoEventWireup="true" CodeFile="Range.aspx.cs"
Inherits="Chap4_Range" %>
<!DOCTYPE html>
<html xmlns="http://www.w3.org/1999/xhtml">
<head runat="server">
<meta http-equiv="Content-Type" content="text/html; charset=utf-8"/>
   <title>The application of RangeValidator control</title>
</head>
<body>
   <form id="form1" runat="server">
```

```
<div>
    Grade:<asp:TextBox ID="txtGrade" runat="server"></asp:TextBox>
    <asp:RangeValidator ID="rvGrade" runat="server" ControlToValidate="txtGrade"
    ErrorMessage="you should input the integer btween 0 and 100!" MaximumValue="100"
    MinimumValue="0" Type="Double"></asp:RangeValidator>
    <br />
    <br />
    Date:<asp:TextBox ID="txtDate" runat="server"></asp:TextBox>
    <asp:RangeValidator ID="rvDate" runat="server" ControlToValidate="txtDate"
    ErrorMessage="The date is wrong!" MaximumValue="2018-1-1" MinimumValue="2019-1-1"
    Type="Date"></asp:RangeValidator>
    <br />
    <br />
    <asp:Button ID="Button1" runat="server" OnClick="Button1_Click" Text="OK" />
  </div>
 </form>
</body>
</html>
```

Operating Steps:

Creating Range.aspx in Chap4 folder, adding two TextBox controls and two RangeValidator controls, and setting the attributes of each control referencing the source program. At last, browsing Range.aspx and testing it.

4.2.4 RegularExpressionValidator control

RegularExpressionValidator control is usually used to validate whether the input values match the definition of a regular expression, and usually is used to validate the phone number, postal codes, E-mail, etc. The defined syntax format is as follows:

```
<asp:RegularExpressionValidator ID="RegularExpressionValidator1" runat="server"
    ErrorMessage="RegularExpressionValidator">
</asp:RegularExpressionValidator>
```

The attribute ValidationExpression of RegularExpressionValidator control is used to determine the regular expression required for validation. As is shown in Figure 4-8

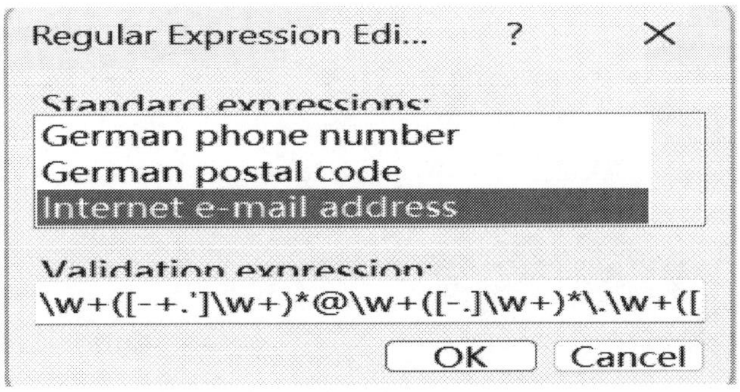

Figure 4-8 Setting ValidationExpression attribute

Example 4-4 Validating Email address

As is shown in Figure 4-9 and Figure 4-10, when the Email address entered does not conform to the rules, clicking "Submit" and "Email address error!" will be displayed. Otherwise, "Verification passed!" will be displayed.

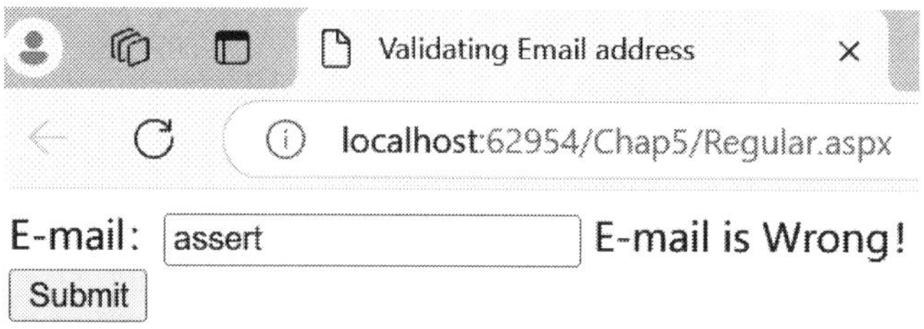

Figure 4-9 The Browsing Effect of Regular.aspx (1)

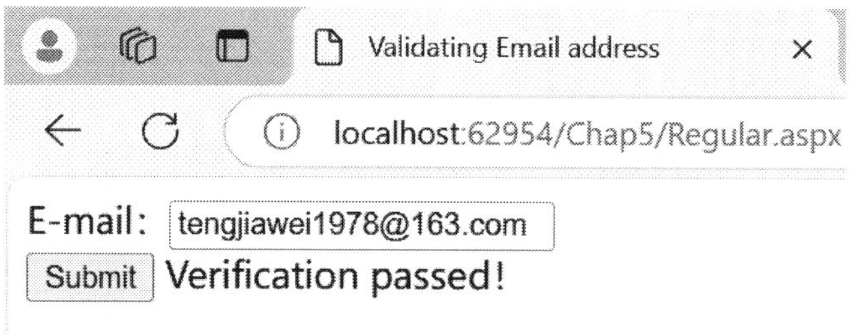

Figure 4-10 The Browsing Effect of Regular.aspx (2)

Source Codes: Regular.aspx

```
<%@ Page Language="C#" AutoEventWireup="true" CodeFile="Regular.aspx.cs"
Inherits="Chap4_Regular" %>
<!DOCTYPE html>
<html xmlns="http://www.w3.org/1999/xhtml">
<head runat="server">
<meta http-equiv="Content-Type" content="text/html; charset=utf-8"/>
  <title>Validating Email address</title>
</head>
<body>
  <form id="form1" runat="server">
    <div>
      E_mail:<asp:TextBox ID="txtMail" runat="server"></asp:TextBox>
      <asp:RegularExpressionValidator ID="revMail" runat="server" ControlToValidate="txtMail"
      ErrorMessage="Email address error!"
     ValidationExpression="\w+([-+.']\w+)*@\w+([-.]\w+)*\.\w+([-.]\w+)*"></asp:RegularExpr
      essionValidator>
      <br />
      <asp:Button ID="Button1" runat="server" OnClick="Button1_Click" Text="OK" />
```

```
        <asp:Label ID="lblMsg" runat="server"></asp:Label>
      </div>
   </form>
</body>
</html>
```

Source Codes: Regular.aspx.cs

```
using System;
using System.Web.UI;

public partial class Chap5_Regular : System.Web.UI.Page
{
   protected void Button1_Click(object sender, EventArgs e)
   {
      if (Page.IsValid)
         lblMsg.Text = "Verification passed!";
   }
}
```

Operating Steps:

(1) Creating Regular.aspx in Chap4 folder, and adding one TextBox control, one Button control, one Label control and one RegularExpressionValidator control. As is shown in Figure 4-8, setting the attribute ValidationExpression of RegularExpressionValidator control to be "Internet Email address", and setting the attributes of another controls referencing the source program.

(2) Creating Regular.aspx.cs. At last, browsing Regular.aspx and testing it.

Note: Each validation control has attribute IsValid. If there are multiple validation controls on a page, only when the property of the IsValid of all the validation controls are true, the attribute Page. IsValid is true.

4.2.5 CustomValidator control

When validation controls that ASP.NET provide cannot satisfy the actual needs, we can consider to define validation functions, then we can access to the functions through the CustomValidator control. The defined syntax format is as follows:

<asp:CustomValidator ID="CustomValidator1" runat="server"

ControlToValidate="TextBox1" ErrorMessage="CustomValidator">

</asp:CustomValidator>

During the validation of the CustomValidator control, if the client validation is used, you need to set the value of attribute ClientValidationFunction to be the validation function name at the client, and to set the value of attribute EnableClientScript to be true. If you want to use the server validation, the validation should be triggered by the ServerValidate event. No matter what validation methods we use, we can determine whether the control pass validation by judging the attribute IsValid of CustomValidator control.

Example 4-5 The validation of entering an even number

As is shown in Figure 4-11 and Figure 4-12, entering an integer, after clicking "Submit" button, we can judge the number and return the validation result. The specific implementation forms include client verification, server verification and mixed verification.

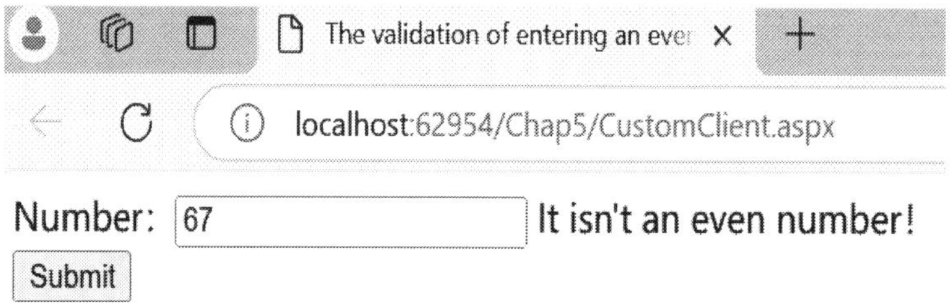

Figure 4-11 The Browsing Effect ofCustomClient.aspx (1)

Figure 4-11 The Browsing Effect of CustomClient.aspx (2)

1.The validation at client

Source Codes: CustomClient.aspx

```
<%@ Page Language="C#" AutoEventWireup="true" CodeFile="CustomClient.aspx.cs"
Inherits="Chap4_CustomClient" %>
<!DOCTYPE html>
<html xmlns="http://www.w3.org/1999/xhtml">
<head runat="server">
<meta http-equiv="Content-Type" content="text/html; charset=utf-8"/>
  <title>The validation of entering an even number</title>
  <script>
    function clientValidate(source, args)
    {
      if ((args.Value % 2) == 0)
        args.IsValid = true;
      else
        args.IsValid = false;
```

```
        }
    </script>
</head>
<body>
    <form id="form1" runat="server">
        <div>
            Number:<asp:TextBox ID="txtInput" runat="server"></asp:TextBox>
            <asp:CustomValidator ID="cvInput" runat="server" ControlToValidate="txtInput"
                ErrorMessage="the number isn't the even!"
                ClientValidationFunction="clientValidate"></asp:CustomValidator>
            <br />
            <asp:Button ID="btnSubmit" runat="server" Text="OK" OnClick="btnSubmit_Click" />
            <asp:Label ID="lblMsg" runat="server"></asp:Label>
        </div>
    </form>
</body>
</html>
```

Source Codes: CustomClient.aspx.cs

```
using System;
using System.Web.UI;
public partial class Chap4_CustomClient : System.Web.UI.Page
{
    protected void btnSubmit_Click(object sender, EventArgs e)
    {
        if (Page.IsValid)
            lblMsg.Text = "the validation is passed!";
    }
}
```

Operating Steps:

(1) Creating CustomClient.aspx in Chap4 folder, adding one TextBox control, one Button control, one Label control and one CustomValidator control, and setting the attributes of each control referencing the source program.

(2) Entering the codes of the shadow part in "Source" view of CustomClient.aspx

(3) Creating CustomClient.aspx.cs. At last, browsing CustomClient.aspx and testing it.

Program description:

The source in the ClientValidate() function represents the reference of the CustomValidator control; Args.Value indicates to obtain the value of the validated control; If the verification is successful, args. IsValid will be set to be true, otherwise it will be set to be false.

2.The validation at server

Source Codes: CustomServer.aspx

```
<%@ Page Language="C#" AutoEventWireup="true" CodeFile="CustomServer.aspx.cs"
Inherits="Chap4_CustomServer" %>
<!DOCTYPE html>
<html xmlns="http://www.w3.org/1999/xhtml">
<head runat="server">
<meta http-equiv="Content-Type" content="text/html; charset=utf-8"/>
  <title>The validation of entering an even number</title>
</head>
<body>
  <form id="form1" runat="server">
    <div>
      Number:<asp:TextBox ID="txtInput" runat="server"></asp:TextBox>
      <asp:CustomValidator ID="cvInput" runat="server" ControlToValidate="txtInput"
      ErrorMessage="the number isn't even"
      OnServerValidate="cvInput_serverValidation"></asp:CustomValidator>
      <br />
      <asp:Button ID="Button1" runat="server" Text="OK" OnClick="Button1_Click" />
      <asp:Label ID="lblMsg" runat="server"></asp:Label>
    </div>
  </form>
</body>
</html>
```

Source Codes: CustomServer.aspx.cs

```
using System;
using System.Web.UI;
using System.Web.UI.WebControls;
public partial class Chap4_CustomServer : System.Web.UI.Page
{
 protected void cvInput_serverValidation(object source,ServerValidateEventArgs args)
  {
    int value = int.Parse(args.Value);
    if ((value % 2) == 0)
      args.IsValid = true;
    else
      args.IsValid = false;
  }
  protected void Button1_Click(object sender, EventArgs e)
  {
    if (Page.IsValid)
      lblMsg.Text = "the validation is succeed!";
}
}
```

Program description:

After clicking "OK" button, the ServerValidate event of cvInput is triggered firstly, then the click event of btnSubmit is triggered.

3.The mix validation

The essence of mix validation is to combine the validationg at client and the validation at server. During implementation, you should not only set the value of the ClientValidationFunction attribute, but also write the codes of ServerValidate event.

4.2.6 ValidationSummary control

ValidationSummary control is used to summarize the error messages of other validation controls, that is, it is used to summarize the value of attribute ErrorMessage of other validation controls. The defined syntax format is as follows:

<asp:ValidationSummary ID = "ValidationSummary1 runat = "server"/>

Attribute DisplayMode of ValidationSummary control is used to specify the display format. The values are BulletList, List and SingleParagraph. Attribute ShowMessageBox is used to specify whether the error messages are displayed on a pop-up message box. Attribute ShowSummary is used to specify whether the summary of error messages is used.

Example 4-6 Comprehensive application of the validation control

As is shown in Figure 4-13, the text box which is used to enter user name uses RequiredFieldValidator control; the text boxes which are used to enter the password and confirm password use the RequiredFieldValidator control to prevent the user from leaking information. Meantime, the CompareValidator control is used to validate if the entered values are consistent; the text box which is used to enter the phone number uses the RegularExpressionValidator control, when the information format user enters is not 0573-83642378, the validation error message will be produced; the text box which is used to enter the id uses the CustomValidator control, when the format of birth contained in id is invalid, the validation error message is generated. Placing the ValidationSummary control which is used to summarize all of the validation error messages. When the validation error messages of the validation controls appeared, the focus will be positioned on the text box where validation error messages appear.

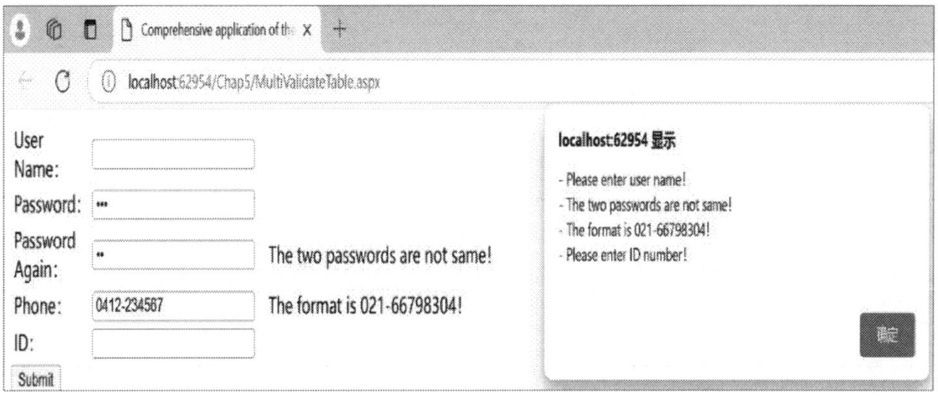

Figure 4-13 The Browsing Effect of MultiValidte.aspx

Source Codes: MultiValidte.aspx

```
<%@ Page Language="C#" AutoEventWireup="true" CodeFile="MultiValidte.aspx.cs"
 Inherits="Chap4_MultiValidte" %>
<!DOCTYPE html>
<html xmlns="http://www.w3.org/1999/xhtml">
<head runat="server">
<meta http-equiv="Content-Type" content="text/html; charset=utf-8"/>
  <title>Comprehensive application of the validation control</title>
</head>
<body>
  <form id="form1" runat="server">
    <div>
      user name:<asp:TextBox ID="txtName" runat="server"></asp:TextBox>
      <asp:RequiredFieldValidator ID="rfvName" runat="server" ControlToValidate="txtName"
          ErrorMessage="please input the user name!"
          SetFocusOnError="True"></asp:RequiredFieldValidator>
      <br />
      PassWord:<asp:TextBox ID="txtPassword" runat="server"
     TextMode="Password"></asp:TextBox>
      <asp:RequiredFieldValidator ID="rfvPassword" runat="server"
    ControlToValidate="txtPassword" ErrorMessage="please input the password!"
    SetFocusOnError="True">*</asp:RequiredFieldValidator>
      <br />
      PassWordAgain:<asp:TextBox ID="txtPasswordAgain" runat="server"
     TextMode="Password"></asp:TextBox>
    <asp:RequiredFieldValidator ID="rfvPasswordAgain" runat="server"
     ControlToValidate="txtPasswordAgain" ErrorMessage="please input the password again!"
     SetFocusOnError="True">*</asp:RequiredFieldValidator>
    <asp:CompareValidator ID="cvPassword" runat="server" ControlToCompare="txtPassword"
     ControlToValidate="txtPasswordAgain" ErrorMessage="the two passwords are not the same!"
     SetFocusOnError="True"></asp:CompareValidator>
      <br />
     Telephone:<asp:TextBox ID="txtPhone" runat="server" Height="23px"
      Width="188px"></asp:TextBox>
    <asp:RequiredFieldValidator ID="rfvTelephone" runat="server"
   ControlToValidate="txtPhone" ErrorMessage="please input the No!"
      SetFocusOnError="True">*</asp:RequiredFieldValidator>
      <asp:RegularExpressionValidator ID="rfvPhone" runat="server"
     ControlToValidate="txtPhone" ErrorMessage="please input the correct format!"
     SetFocusOnError="True"
     ValidationExpression="(\(\d{3}\)|\d{3}-)?\d{8}"></asp:RegularExpressionValidator>
      <br />
      ID:<asp:TextBox ID="txtID" runat="server" Width="188px"></asp:TextBox>
```

```
            <asp:RequiredFieldValidator ID="rfvID" runat="server" ControlToValidate="txtID"
            EnableTheming="True" ErrorMessage="please input ID!"
            SetFocusOnError="True"></asp:RequiredFieldValidator>
            <asp:CustomValidator ID="cvID" runat="server" ControlToValidate="txtID"
            ErrorMessage="the ID is Wrong!" SetFocusOnError="True"
            OnServerValidate="cvInput_serverValidate"></asp:CustomValidator>
            <br />
            <asp:Button ID="Button1" runat="server" Text="Button" OnClick="Button1_Click" />
            <asp:Label ID="Label1" runat="server"></asp:Label>
            <asp:ValidationSummary ID="ValidationSummary1" runat="server"
            ShowMessageBox="True" ShowSummary="False" />
        </div>
    </form>
</body>
</html>
```

Source Codes: MultiValidte.aspx.cs

```
using System;
using System.Web.UI;
using System.Web.UI.WebControls;
public partial class Chap4_MultiValidte : System.Web.UI.Page
{ protected void cvInput_serverValidate(object source, ServerValidateEventArgs args)
  {
    string strID = args.Value;
    args.IsValid = true;
    try
    {
            DateTime.Parse(strID.Substring(6, 4) + "-" + strID.Substring(10, 2) + "-" + strID.
             Substring(12, 2));
    }
    catch { args.IsValid = false; }
  }
   protected void Button1_Click(object sender, EventArgs e)
  {
    Label1.Text = " ";
    if (Page.IsValid)
      Label1.Text = "validation is passed!";
  }
}
```

Operating Steps:

(1) Creating MultiValidte.aspx in Chap4 folder, adding five TextBox controls, five

RequiredFieldValidator controls, one CompareValidator control, one RegularExpressionValidator control, one CustomValidator control, one ValidationSummary control, one Button control, one Label control, and setting the attributes of each control referencing the source program.

(2) Creating MultiValidte.aspx.cs. At last, browsing MultiValidte.aspx and testing it.

Program description:

If there are other validation controls in the page which don't pass the validation, the event ServerValidate of CustomValidator control will not be triggered after clicking "OK" button.

Since the value of attribute ShowMessageBox of ValidationSummary control is true and the value of ShowSummary is false, the summary of validation error messages is not displayed on the page, but in the form of dialog box.

Because the values of SetFocusError of all the validation controls are set to be true, so if a validation control dose not pass the verification, the cursor will be positioned to the corresponding text box.

4.3 Summary

➢ In form verification, it is often necessary to use both client and server side validation.

➢ ASP.NET validation controls provide the validations of "necessary input", comparison, the scope, regular expressions, and custom, and summarize the error message of other validation controls.

➢ To achieve a certain effect of verification, the actual usage of the same control may use multiple validation controls.

4.4 Exercises

1. True or False Questions

(1) If JavaScript is disable on the client, validation must be done in server format. (　　)

(2) Server verification is used to ensure faster response time for users. (　　)

(3) To perform client validation, the value of the EnableClientScript property of the validation control must be set true. (　　)

(4) The CompareValidator control cannot be used to validate data types. (　　)

(5) When using the CompareValidator control, the values of the ControlToCompare and ValueToCompare properties can be set simultaneously. (　　)

(6) The ServerValidate event of the CustomValidator control can only be used after all of the other validation controls on the page have passed validation.(　　)

2. Programming Questions

(1) Establish and debug all of the instances in this chapter.

(2) Design your own interface and use the ValidationGroup property to implement group validation for the same page.

Chapter 5 HTTP Request, Response and State Management

Points:

- Mastering the application of the HttpRequest object
- Mastering the application of the HttpResponse object
- Mastering the application of the HttpServerUtility object, and understanding the different methods of page redirection
- Mastering the application submitted across pages, understanding ViewState, HiddenField, and grasping
- the application of Cookie, Session, Application

5.1 HTTP Request

ASP.NET can control the request data well through the attribute Request of Page class, such as accessing the browser information at client, query string, Cookies, etc. In fact, the value of attribute Request of Page class is an object of HttpRequest class. It packs the HTTP Request information. The data sets of the HttpRequest class that are accessed usually are shown in Table 5-1

Table 5-1 Table of data sets of HttpRequest class

Data sets	Descirption
QueryString	Read the data submitted by the user from the query string
Cookies	Get the cookie data from the client
ServerVariables	Get the environment variable information of the server or client
Browser	Get browser information of client

When using the HttpRequest object, it is often called through the attribute Request of the Page class. Therefore, the syntax format for obtaining the Browser data sets of the HttpRequest class is often written as Request. Browser.

1. QueryString data sets

The query string obtained by using the QueryString data sets refers to the variables and values that follow the URL. They are marked with "?" interval from URL, and different variables are separated by "&".

Example 5-1 Passing data information between pages by using QueryString

As is shown in Figure 5-1 and Figure 5-2, when the link of QueryString1.aspx is clicked, the page is redirected to QueryString2.aspx, and the query string from QueryString1.aspx will be displayed on the page of QueryString2.aspx.

Figure 5-1 The Browsing Effect of QueryString1.aspx

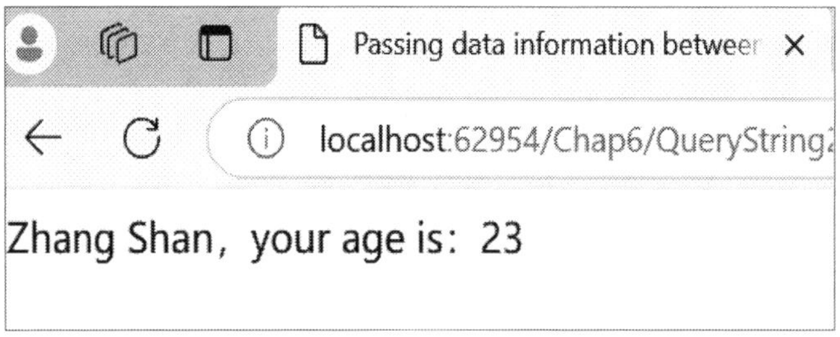

Figure 5-2 The Effect of Query string

Source Codes: QueryString1.aspx

```
<%@ Page Language="C#" AutoEventWireup="true" CodeFile="QueryString1.aspx.cs"
Inherits="Chap5_QueryString1" %>
<!DOCTYPE html>
<html xmlns="http://www.w3.org/1999/xhtml">
<head runat="server">
<meta http-equiv="Content-Type" content="text/html; charset=utf-8"/>
  <title> To transfer data information between pages by using QueryString </title>
</head>
<body>
  <form id="form1" runat="server">
    <div>
      <asp:HyperLink ID="hlkQueryString" runat="server"
NavigateUrl="~/Chap6/QueryString2.aspx?username=zhangsan&age=23">Transform the string to
QueryString2.aspx!</asp:HyperLink>
    </div>
  </form>
</body>
</html>
```

Source Codes: QueryString2.aspx

```
<%@ Page Language="C#" AutoEventWireup="true" CodeFile="QueryString2.aspx.cs"
Inherits="Chap5_QueryString2" %>
<!DOCTYPE html>
<html xmlns="http://www.w3.org/1999/xhtml">
<head runat="server">
<meta http-equiv="Content-Type" content="text/html; charset=utf-8"/>
  <title>To transfer data information between pages by using QueryString</title>
</head>
<body>
  <form id="form1" runat="server">
    <div>
      <asp:Label ID="lblMsg" runat="server"></asp:Label>
    </div>
  </form>
</body>
</html>
```

Source Codes: QueryString2.aspx.cs

```
using System;
public partial class Chap5_QueryString2 : System.Web.UI.Page
{
  protected void Page_Load(object sender, EventArgs e)
  { lblMsg.Text = Request.QueryString["username"] + ",your age: " + Request.QueryString["age"];

  }
}
```

2. ServerVariables data sets

By using the ServerVariables data sets, you can easily obtain the environment variable information of the server or client, such as the IP address of the client. The syntax format is: Request. ServerVariables ["environment variable name "]. The custom environment variable are shown in Table 5-2.

Table 5-2 The table of custom environment variable

Environment variable name	Description
LOCAL_ADDR	IP address of server
PATH_TRANSLATED	The physical root of the current page on the server
REMOTE_ADDR	IP address of client
REMOTE_HOST	Computer name of client
SERVER_NAME	Computer name of server
SERVER_PORT	The port number of the server

3.Browser data sets

The Browser data sets are used to return the user's browser type, version and other information, so that the different pages can be written according to the different browsers. The syntax format is: Request. Browser ["Browser features name "]. The common browser property names are shown in Table 5-3.

Table 5-3 The table of common browser property name

Name	Description
Browser	The browser type
Version	The browser version
MajorVersion	The browser major version
MinorVersion	The browser minor version
Cookies	Logical value, true indicates that cookies are supported
JavaScript	Logical value, true indicates that JavaScript are supported
ActiveXControls	Logical value, true indicates that ActiveXControls are supported

Example 5-2 Returning the information of server and client by using ServerVariables and Browser

As is shown in Figure 5-3, this example uses ServerVariables and Browser to return some information of the server and client.

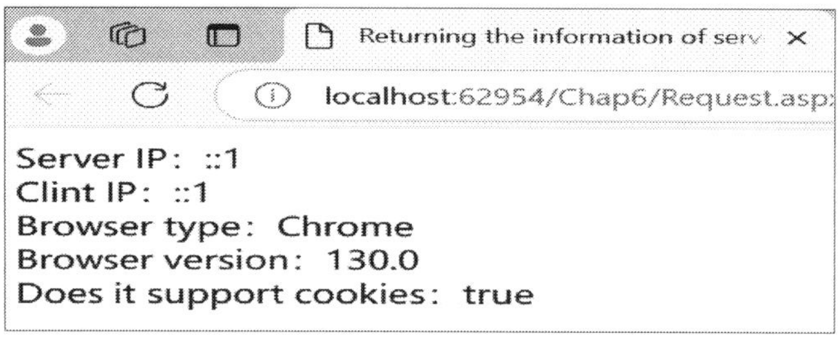

Figure 5-3 The Effect of Request.aspx

Source Codes: Request.aspx

```
<%@ Page Language="C#" AutoEventWireup="true" CodeFile="Request.aspx.cs"
Inherits="Chap5_Request" %>
<!DOCTYPE html>

<html xmlns="http://www.w3.org/1999/xhtml">
<head runat="server">
<meta http-equiv="Content-Type" content="text/html; charset=utf-8"/>
    <title> To return the information of server and client by using ServerVariables and Browser </title>
</head>
```

```
<body>
  <form id="form1" runat="server">
    <div>
      <asp:Label ID="lblMsg" runat="server"></asp:Label>
    </div>
  </form>
</body>
</html>
```

Source Codes: Request.aspx.cs

```
using System;
public partial class Chap5_Request : System.Web.UI.Page
{
  protected void Page_Load(object sender, EventArgs e)
  {
    lblMsg.Text = "server IP:" + Request.ServerVariables["LOCAL_ADDR"] + "<br/>";
    lblMsg.Text += "client IP:" + Request.ServerVariables["REMOTE_ADDR"] + "<br/>";
    lblMsg.Text+="browser type:"+Request.Browser["Browser"] + "<br/>";
    lblMsg.Text+="browser version"+Request.Browser["Version"] + "<br/>";
    lblMsg.Text += "cookies:" + Request.Browser["Cookies"];
  }
}
```

Note: This example is viewed in VSC 2019, so IP address of server and client are all local addresses. "::1" represents the local address of IPv6. After you have published the web to the web server of IIS 7.5, you will see the different address when you visit the page from another client.

5.2 HTTP Response

ASP.NET can control the output content and method well through the attribute Response of the Page class, such as page redirection, Cookie saving, etc. In fact, the value of attribute Response of the Page class is an instance object of the HttpResponse class. The common attributes and methods are shown in Table 5-4.

Table 5-4 The table of common attributes and methods of HttpResponse class

Member	Description
Cookies	Add or modify the Cookies of client
AppendToLog()	Add custom log information to the IIS log file
End()	Stop executing the web page
Redirect()	Page redirection, data is transfered between different web pages through query string of URL
Write()	Output the information on the web page

Example 5-3 Outputing XHTML text by using Write() method

The Write() method can output not only prompt information and variable values, but also XHTML text or JavaScript scripts. As is shown in Figure 5-4, the page information is output by the Write() method.

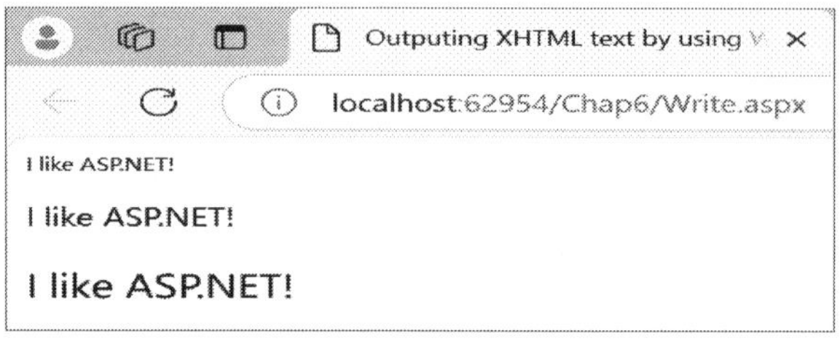

Figure 5-4 The Effect of Write.aspx

Source Codes: Write.aspx

```
<%@ Page Language="C#" AutoEventWireup="true" CodeFile="Write.aspx.cs"
Inherits="Chap5_Write" %>
<!DOCTYPE html>
<html xmlns="http://www.w3.org/1999/xhtml">
<head runat="server">
<meta http-equiv="Content-Type" content="text/html; charset=utf-8"/>
  <title>To output XHTML text by using Write() method</title>
</head>
<body>
  <form id="form1" runat="server">
    <div>
    </div>
  </form>
</body>
</html>
```

Source Codes: Write.aspx.cs

```
using System;
public partial class Chap5_Write : System.Web.UI.Page
{
  protected void Page_Load(object sender, EventArgs e)
  {
    for (int i = 10; i <= 18; i += 4)
      Response.Write("<p style=\"font-size:" + i.ToString() + "px\">I like asp.net!</p>");
  }
}
```

Program description:

The XHTML text output to the browser after the for loop is executed is as follows:

<p style="font-size:10px">I like asp.net!</p>

<p style="font-size:14px">I like asp.net!</p>

<p style="font-size:18px">I like asp.net!</p>

The output of "" "requires the escape character "\", that is, it must be written as "\" in the source program.

Example 5-4 Redirecting the web page by using Redirect() method

As is shown in Figure 5-5 and Figure 5-6, after selecting "Teacher" and clicking "Submit" button, the page is redirected to the teacher page Teacher.aspx.

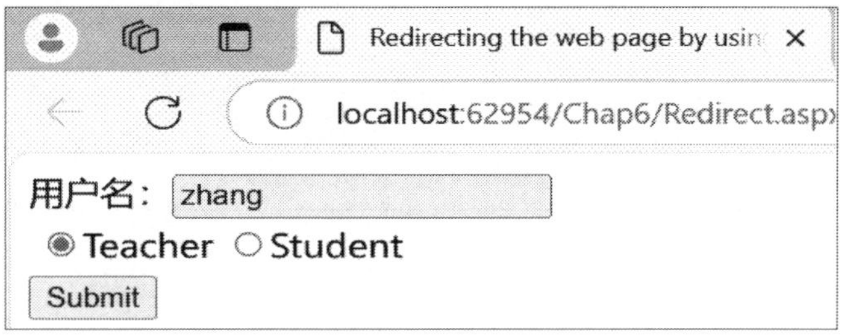

Figure 5-5 The Effect of Redirect.aspx

Figure 5-6 The Effect of Redirecting to The Teacher Page

Source Codes: Redirect.aspx

```
<%@ Page Language="C#" AutoEventWireup="true" CodeFile="Redirect.aspx.cs"
Inherits="Chap5_Redirect" %>
<!DOCTYPE html>
<html xmlns="http://www.w3.org/1999/xhtml">
<head runat="server">
<meta http-equiv="Content-Type" content="text/html; charset=utf-8"/>
   <title>To Redirect the web page by using Redirect() method</title>
</head>
<body>
```

```
    <form id="form1" runat="server">
        <div>
            username:<asp:TextBox ID="txtName" runat="server"></asp:TextBox>
            <br />
            <asp:RadioButtonList ID="rdoltstaus" runat="server" RepeatDirection="Horizontal">
                <asp:ListItem Value="Teacher"></asp:ListItem>
                <asp:ListItem Value="Student"></asp:ListItem>
            </asp:RadioButtonList>
            <br />
            <asp:Button ID="btnSubmit" runat="server" OnClick="btnSubmit_Click" Text="OK" />
        </div>
    </form>
</body>
</html>
```

Source Codes: Redirect.aspx.cs

```
using System;
public partial class Chap5_Redirect : System.Web.UI.Page
{
    protected void btnSubmit_Click(object sender, EventArgs e)
    {
        if (rdoltstaus.SelectedValue == "Teacher")
            Response.Redirect("~/Chap5/Teacher.aspx?name=" + txtName.Text);
        else
            Response.Redirect("~/Chap5/Student.aspx?name=" + txtName.Text);
    }
}
```

Source Codes: Teacher.aspx

```
<%@ Page Language="C#" AutoEventWireup="true" CodeFile="Teacher.aspx.cs"
Inherits="Chap5_Teacher" %>
<!DOCTYPE html>
<html xmlns="http://www.w3.org/1999/xhtml">
<head runat="server">
<meta http-equiv="Content-Type" content="text/html; charset=utf-8"/>
    <title>To Redirect the web page by using Redirect() method</title>
```

```
</head>
<body>
  <form id="form1" runat="server">
    <div>
      <asp:Label ID="lblMsg" runat="server"></asp:Label>
    </div>
  </form>
</body>
</html>
```

Source Codes: Teacher.aspx.cs

```
using System;
public partial class Chap5_Teacher : System.Web.UI.Page
{
  protected void Page_Load(object sender, EventArgs e)
  {
    lblMsg.Text = Request.QueryString["name"] + "teacher, Welcom!";

  }
}
```

5.3 HttpServerUtility

In ASP.NET, the attribute Server of the Page class encapsulates some operations at server, such as converting XHTML element tags into character entities, obtaining the physical path of the page, and so on. In fact, the value of attribute Server of the Page class is an instance object of the HttpServerUtility class. The custom attributes and methods are shown as Table 5-5.

Table 5-5 The table of custom attributes and methods of HttpServerUtility class

Attribute andmethod	Description
ScriptTimeOut attribute	Set the maximum time of page execution, in seconds.
Execute() method	Stop executing the current page, go to execute the new page, return to the original page after execution, and continue executing subsequent statements.
HtmlEncode() method	Convert XHTML element tags in string to character entities, such as "<" to&lt.
MapPath() method	Get the physical path of the page.
Transfer() method	Stop executing the current page, go to execute the new page, and do not return to the original page after execution.
UrlEncode() method	Convert some special characters in the string to URL encoding, such as "/" to "% 2f", and space to "+".

The difference among Response. Redirect(), Server. Execute() and Server. Transfer() is:

(1) Although Redirect() method is executed on the server, the redirection actually occurs on the client, and we can see the address change in the browser address bar. While the redirection of Execute() and Transfer() methods actually occur on the server, we can't see the address change in the browser address bar.

(2) Redirect() and Transfer() methods do not return to the original web page after they perform the new web page; while the Execute() method will return to the original page after it performs the new web page.

(3) Redirect() method can redirect to the different pages of the same web site, and can also redirect to the pages of the other web sites; while the Execute() and Transfer() methods can only redirect to the different pages of the same web site.

(4) The state management uses the form of query string when the Redirect() method transfers data between the different web pages; while the state management modes of the Execute() and Transfer() methods are the same with the Button submission method across the web page.

Example 5-5 Using HttpServerUtility object

As is shown in Figure 5-7, Server.HtmlEncode() method is usually used to output the XHTML elements on the web page. Server.UrlEncode() method is usually used to handle the URL address, such as the space is included in the address. In this example, after clicking the link of Student.aspx, the interface as the Figure 5-8 is shown, the information behind the "zhang" will be lost. When clicking the link of Student.aspx(UrlEncode), the interface as the Figure 5-9 is shown, the information behind "zhang" will not be lost because the Server.UrlEncode() method is used.

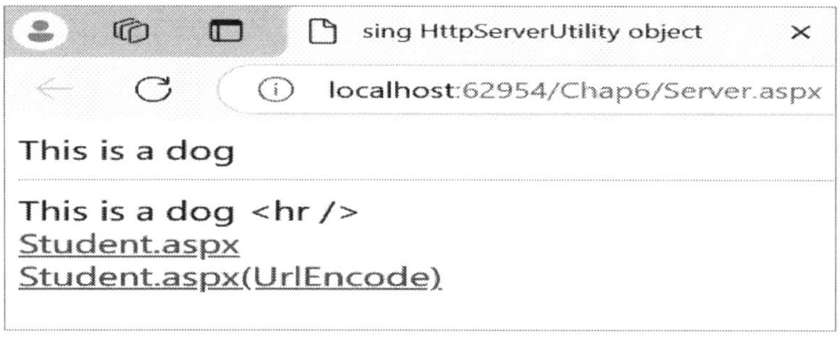

Figure 5-7 The Effect of Server.aspx

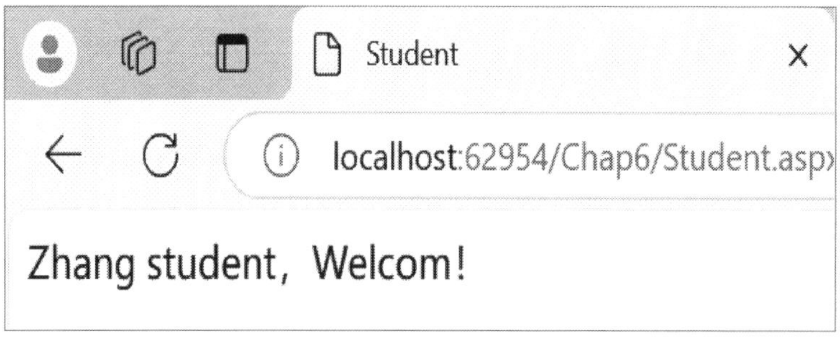

Figure 5-8 The Effect without using UrlEncode()

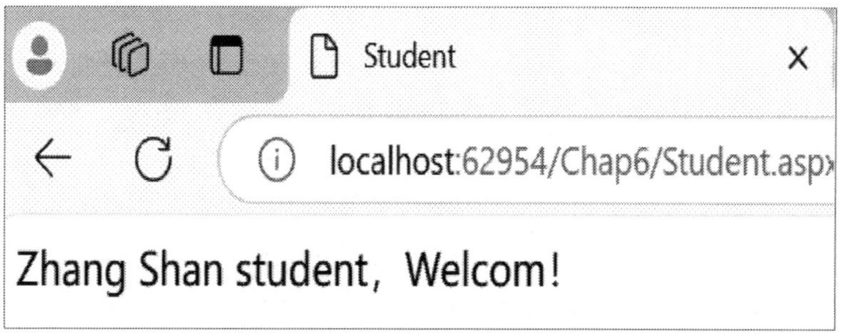

Figure 5-9 The Effect by using UrlEncode()

Source Codes: Server.aspx

```
<%@ Page Language="C#" AutoEventWireup="true" CodeFile="Server.aspx.cs"
Inherits="Chap5_Server" %>
<!DOCTYPE html>
<html xmlns="http://www.w3.org/1999/xhtml">
<head runat="server">
<meta http-equiv="Content-Type" content="text/html; charset=utf-8"/>
    <title>To use HttpServerUtility object </title>
</head>
<body>
    <form id="form1" runat="server">
        <div>
        </div>
    </form>
</body>
</html>
```

Source Codes: Server.aspx.cs

```
using System;
public partial class Chap5_Server : System.Web.UI.Page
{
    protected void Page_Load(object sender, EventArgs e)
    {
        Response.Write("This is a dog<hr/>");
        Response.Write(Server.HtmlEncode("This is a dog<hr/>") + "<br/>");
        Response.Write("<a href=Student.aspx?name=zhang san>Student.aspx</a><br/>");
        Response.Write("<a href=Student.aspx?name="+Server.UrlEncode("zhang san")+
">Student.aspx(UrlEncode)</a> ");

    }
}
```

5.4 Submission Across the Pages

To implement page redirection, the <a> element, HyperLink control, Response.Redirect(), Server. Execute () and Server.Transfer() methods can be used in ASP.NET. To achieve cross page submission by using Button control is another way to achieve page redirection.

You need to set the value of attribute PostBackUrl of the Button type control on the source page to the path of the target page. On the target page, you need to add the @ PreviousPageType directive at the top of the page, and set the value of attribute VirtualPath to be the path of the source page.

There are two ways to access the data in the source page on the target page: one is to use PreviousPage.FindControl () method to access the controls on the source page; the other is that you can define public attributes on the source page firstly, then you can use "PreviousPage.attribute Name" on the target page to obtain the data in the source page.

Note: If it is submission across the pages, the value of attribute IsCrossPagePostBack should be true; if the Server.Execute() or Server.Tranfer() method is called, the value of attribute IsCrossPagePostBack should be false.

Example 5-6 Using the technology of submission across pages

As is shown in Figure 5-10 and Figure 5-11, after entering the user name and password in Cross1. aspx, clicking "Submit" button to redirect to Cross2.aspx through the technology of submission across pages and display the data information entered in Cross1.aspx.

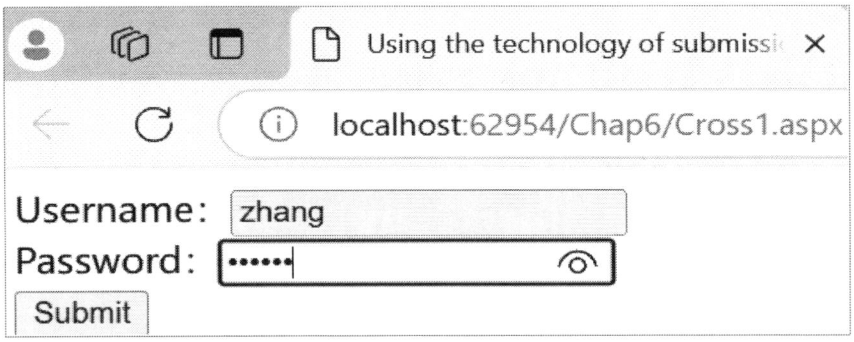

Figure 5-10 The Effect of Cross1.aspx

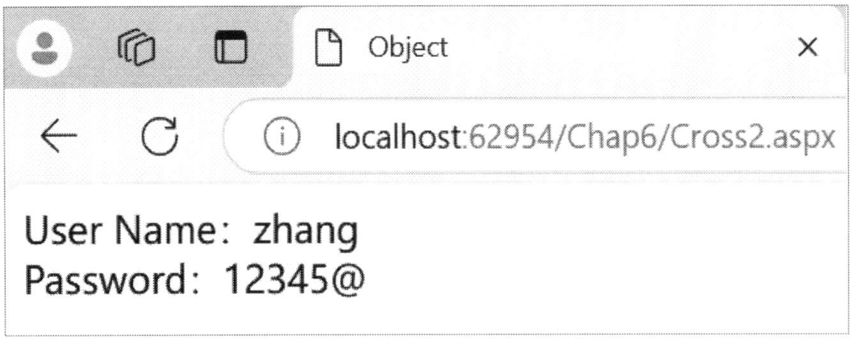

Figure 5-11 The Effect Displaying the Submission Information

Source Codes: Cross1.aspx

```
<%@ Page Language="C#" AutoEventWireup="true" CodeFile="Cross1.aspx.cs"
Inherits="Chap5_Cross1" %>
<!DOCTYPE html>
<html xmlns="http://www.w3.org/1999/xhtml">
<head runat="server">
<meta http-equiv="Content-Type" content="text/html; charset=utf-8"/>
  <title>To use the technology of submission across pages</title>
</head>
<body>
  <form id="form1" runat="server">
    <div>
      username:<asp:TextBox ID="txtName" runat="server"></asp:TextBox>
      <br />
      password:<asp:TextBox ID="txtPassword" runat="server"
     TextMode="Password"></asp:TextBox>
      <br />
      <asp:Button ID="btnSubmit" runat="server" PostBackUrl="~/Chap5/Cross2.aspx"
      Text="OK" />
    </div>
  </form>
</body>
</html>
```

Source Codes: Cross1.aspx.cs

```
public partial class Chap5_Cross1 : System.Web.UI.Page
{
  public string Name {
    get { return txtName.Text; }
  }
}
```

Source Codes: Cross2.aspx

```
<%@ Page Language="C#" AutoEventWireup="true" CodeFile="Cross2.aspx.cs"
Inherits="Chap5_Cross2" %>
<%@ PreviousPageType VirtualPath="~/Chap5/Cross1.aspx" %>
<!DOCTYPE html>
<html xmlns="http://www.w3.org/1999/xhtml">
<head runat="server">
<meta http-equiv="Content-Type" content="text/html; charset=utf-8"/>
  <title>To use the technology of submission across pages</title>
</head>
<body>
```

```
    <form id="form1" runat="server">
      <div>
        <asp:Label ID="lblMsg" runat="server"></asp:Label>
      </div>
    </form>
  </body>
</html>
```

Source Codes: Cross2.aspx.cs

```
using System;
using System.Web.UI.WebControls;
public partial class Chap5_Cross2 : System.Web.UI.Page
{
  protected void Page_Load(object sender, EventArgs e)
  {
    if (PreviousPage.IsCrossPagePostBack)
    { lblMsg.Text = "user name: " + PreviousPage.Name + "<br/>";
      TextBox txtPassword = (TextBox)PreviousPage.FindControl("txtPassword");
      lblMsg.Text += "password: " + txtPassword.Text;
    }

  }
}
```

Operating Steps:

(1) Creating Cross1.aspx in Chap5 folder, adding two TextBox controls and one Button control, and setting the attributes of each control referencing the source program.

(2) CreatingCross1.aspx.cs in Chap5 folder.

(3) Creating Cross2.aspx, adding one Lable control, and entering the codes of shadow part in "Source" view.

(4) Creating Cross2.aspx.cs. At last, browsing Cross1.aspx and testing it.

5.5 State Management

When we implement page redirection and submission across the pages, some data needs to be transferred from one page to another, which is actually a part of state management. In this section, we will describes other forms of state management.

State management of ASP.NET can be divided into state management on the client and state management on the server. The state management on the client is to keep the information on the client. When the client sends the request to the server, the state information will be sent to the server. The implementation can select ViewState, ControlState, HiddenField, Cookies and the query string, but the

ControlState can only be used for the state management of custom controls. The state management on the server is that the state information is kept on the server. The implementation is available in the Session state, Application state or database support. The state management on the client does not consume memory resources on the server, but it is easy to leak data information. The state management on the server will consume the server memory resources, but it has high security.

5.5.1 ViewState

ViewState is used to maintain the state of the Web form itself. When a user requests an ASP.NET page, ASP NET encapsulates ViewState as one or several hidden form fields and transfers them to the client. When the user submits the page again, the ViewState will also be submitted to the server. In this way, subsequent requests can obtain the state of the last request.

If you want to view the ViewState form intuitively, you can browse the ASP.NET page on the client, and select "View"→ "Source" comand on the browser.

ViewState should be disabled for pages and controls that do not have to maintain state. Setting the value of attribute EnableViewState to be false to disable ViewState.

5.5.2 HiddenField control

HiddenField is used to maintain its own form state. It will not be displayed on the user's browser, but it's attributes can be set like a set of standard controls. The members of HiddenField mainly include attribute Value and ValueChanged event.

Note: To trigger ValueChanged event, we should set the value of EnableViewState of HiddenField control to be False.

5.5.3 Cookie

Cookie is a small piece of the text information to be saved in the hard disk or the memory on the client, such as the corresponding information of web site, client and session. A typical use is to save whether the user has logged in or not through cookies

Cookie is associated with the website, and not links to the specific web page. When the user visit different sites, each site may send a Cookie to the user's browser, and then the browser will store all the cookies, respectively.

You can modify the Cookie Settings and be disable cookies on the client. When the user wants to reuse the Cookie after he close it, he can add the following statements in the<system.web> element of Web.config file:

<sessionState cookieless="AutoDetect">

<sessionState cookieless="UseUri">

Cookie text file is stored in "%userprofile%\AppData\Roaming\Microsoft\ Windows\Cookies" folder in Windows 7.

ASP.NET provides System.Web.HttpCookie class to process cookies. The common attributes are Value and Expires.Value is used to get and set the value of cookie, and Expires is used to set expiration time of cookie. Each cookie will have a period of validity. When the user access a web site, the browser will delete the expired cookies automatically. If the period of validity of Cookie don't be set, the Cookie will not be stored in hard disk file, otherwise, it will be seen as a part of the user's session information. When you close the browser, Cookie will be discarded.

There are two methods to establish Cookie. The first method is to use Response.Cookies data set, such as:

```
Response.Cookies["Name"].Value="zhang san";
```

The second method is to create HttpCookie object firstly and set the attribute, then add information by using Response.Cookies.Add() method, such as:

```
HttpCookie cookie = new HttpCookie("Name");
cookie.Value = "zhang san";
cookie.Expires = DateTime.Now.AddDays(1);
Response.Cookies.Add(cookie);
```

If you want to get the value of Cookie, you should use the Request.Cookies data set, such as:

```
String strName=Request.Cookies.["Name"].Value;
```

Example 5-7 Restricting web page access by using Cookie

As is shown in Figure 5-12, when the user access Cookie.aspx, if there are the user information in the Cookie, the welcome message will be displayed, else the page will be redirected to CookieLogin. aspx. That means when there are not user information in Cookie, you will not access Cookie.aspx. As is shown in Figure 5-13, entering user name and password, after clicking "Submit" button, user name will be entered Cookie.

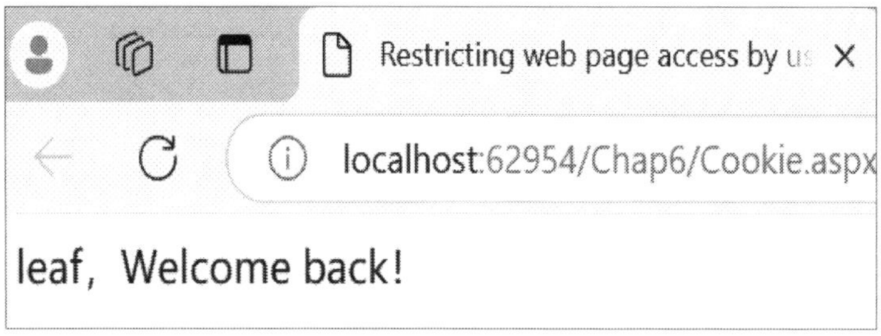

Figure 5-12 The Effect of Cookie.aspx

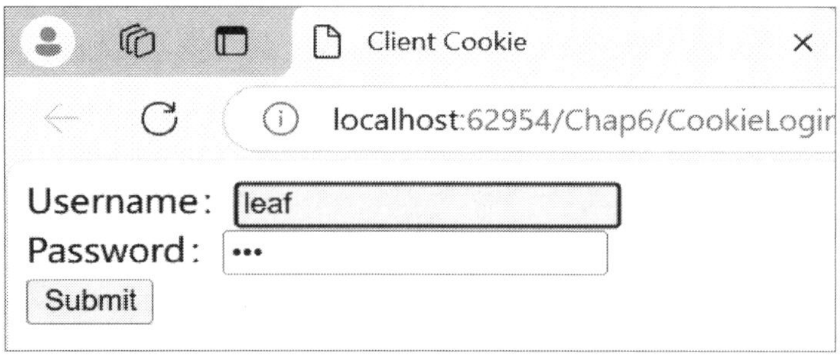

Figure 5-13 The Effect of CookieLogin.aspx

Source Codes: Cookie.aspx

```
<%@ Page Language="C#" AutoEventWireup="true" CodeFile="Cookie.aspx.cs"
Inherits="Chap5_Cookie" %>
<!DOCTYPE html>
<html xmlns="http://www.w3.org/1999/xhtml">
<head runat="server">
<meta http-equiv="Content-Type" content="text/html; charset=utf-8"/>
  <title>To restrict web page access by using Cookie</title>
</head>
<body>
  <form id="form1" runat="server">
    <div>
      <asp:Label ID="lblMsg" runat="server"></asp:Label>
    </div>
  </form>
</body>
</html>
```

Source Codes: Cookie.aspx.cs

```
using System;
public partial class Chap5_Cookie : System.Web.UI.Page
{
  protected void Page_Load(object sender, EventArgs e)
  {
    if (Request.Cookies["Name"] != null)
      lblMsg.Text = Request.Cookies["Name"].Value + ", WelCome back!";
    else
      Response.Redirect("~/Chap5/CookieLogin.aspx");
  }
}
```

Source Codes: CookieLogin.aspx

```
<%@ Page Language="C#" AutoEventWireup="true" CodeFile="CookieLogin.aspx.cs"
Inherits="Chap5_CookieLogin" %>
<!DOCTYPE html>
<html xmlns="http://www.w3.org/1999/xhtml">
<head runat="server">
<meta http-equiv="Content-Type" content="text/html; charset=utf-8"/>
  <title>To restrict web page access by using Cookie</title>
</head>
```

```
<body>
  <form id="form1" runat="server">
    <div>
      username:<asp:TextBox ID="txtName" runat="server"></asp:TextBox>
      <br />
      password:<asp:TextBox ID="txtPassword" runat="server"></asp:TextBox>
      <br />
      <asp:Button ID="btnSubmit" runat="server" OnClick="btnSubmit_Click" Text="OK" />
    </div>
  </form>
</body>
</html>
```

Source Codes: CookieLogin.aspx.cs

```
using System;
using System.Web;
public partial class Chap5_CookieLogin : System.Web.UI.Page
{
  protected void btnSubmit_Click(object sender, EventArgs e)
  {
    if (txtName.Text == "zhang san" && txtPassword.Text == "111")
    {
      HttpCookie cookie = new HttpCookie("Name");
      cookie.Value = "zhang san";
      cookie.Expires = DateTime.Now.AddDays(1);
      Response.Cookies.Add(cookie);
    }
  }
}
```

Program description:

Browsing Cookie.aspx firstly, because there isn't user name in Cookie. The page is redirected to CookieLogin.aspx, after entering user name and password. Clicking "OK" button, user name will be entered Cookie, closing browser. When you open browser again, you will browse the welcome message.

5.5.4 Session

Session is also called session state, the typical applications of which include user information storage, information transferring among multiple web pages, shopping cart, etc. The session occurs on the server, and only can provide the services for the current user. Session begins with accessing the site at last time. When reaching the setting time of Session and no accessing, the session will be finished automatically. If the same user accessed the same page again after closing the browser during browsing the web page, the server will create a new Session for that user.

ASP.NET use an unique Session ID to identify each session on the server. If the client supports Cookie, Session ID will be saved to the corresponding Cookie; else Session ID will be added to URL.

Note: Whether session ID is saved in Cookie or URL, it is both in clear text. If session ID needs to be protected, HTTPS communication can be considered.

Session is implemented through System.Web.Httpsessionstate class. When we use it, the instance of Httpsessionstate class can be accessed through attribute Session of Page class directly. The common attributes and methods are shown in Table5-6.

Table 5-6 The table of common attributes and methods of Httpsessionstate class

Attribute and methods	Description
Contents attribute	Get the reference of the object of the current session state
Mode attribute	Get the mode of the current session state
SessionID attribute	Get the unique identity of the session
TimeOut attribute	Get or set the duration of session state, (minutes). The default value is 20 minutes
Abandon() method	Cancel the current session
Remove() method	Delete the items from the session state set

The methods of being closely related to Session is Session_ Start() method and Session_ End() method of Global class, and the codes of implementing the methods are all in Global.asax file. The codes in Session_ Start() method will be executed automatically when a new session starts, while the codes in Session_ End() method will be executed automatically when a session stops.

Note: Only when the sessionstate mode in the Web.config file is set to be InProc, the codes of Session_End() can be executed. If the session mode is set to be StateServer or SQLServer, the codes of Session_ End() will not be executed.

There are two types of assignment of Session state, such as:

Session["Name"]="zhang san";

Session.Contents["Name"]="zhang san";

Note: The name used by Session are not case sensitive, so do not use case to distinguish different Session variables. In ASP.NET, Session has many storage methods, such as it may be specified through the attribute mode of <sessionState> element in Web.config. There are five enumeration values to choose, that are Off, InProc, StateServer, SQLServer and Custom. In actual engineering projects, StateServer is generally selected, while SQL server is often selected for the large websites.

Example 5-8 Restricting page accessing by using Session

This example is similar with example 5-7, while it is applicable when the client has disabled Cookie.

As is shown in Figure 5-14 and Figure 5-15, it can restrict to access Session.aspx, that is if you want to access the page, you should pass the login authentication firstly.

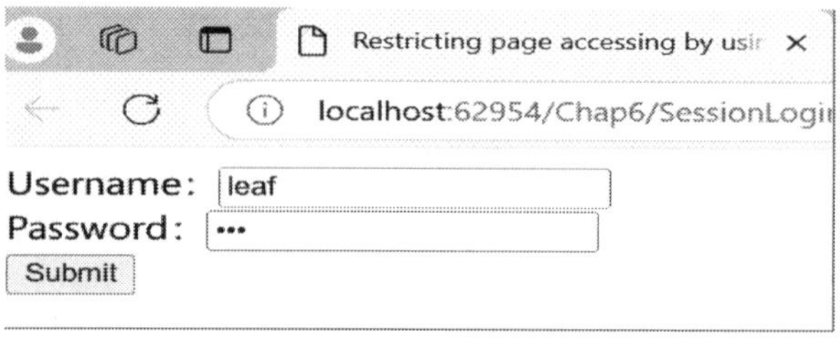

Figure 5-14 The Effect of SessionLogin.aspx

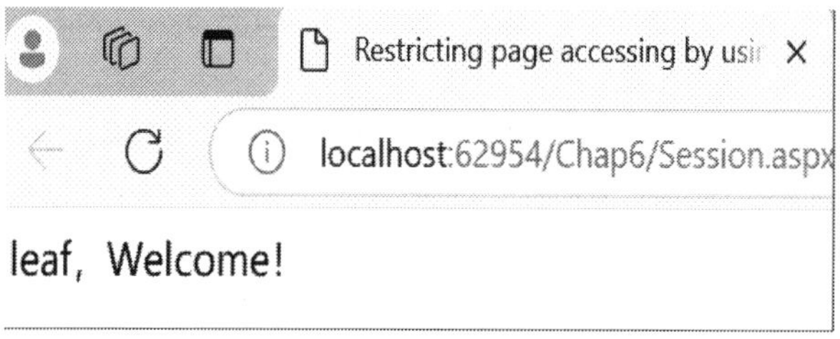

Figure 5-15 The Effect of Session.aspx

Source Codes: Session.aspx

```
<%@ Page Language="C#" AutoEventWireup="true" CodeFile="Session.aspx.cs"
Inherits="Chap5_Session" %>
<!DOCTYPE html>
<html xmlns="http://www.w3.org/1999/xhtml">
<head runat="server">
  <meta http-equiv="Content-Type" content="text/html; charset=utf-8" />
  <title>To restrict page accessing by using Session </title>
</head>
<body>
  <form id="form1" runat="server">
    <div>
      <asp:Label ID="lblMsg" runat="server"></asp:Label>
    </div>
  </form>
</body>
</html>
```

Source Codes: Session.aspx.cs

```
using System;
public partial class Chap5_Session : System.Web.UI.Page
{
  protected void Page_Load(object sender, EventArgs e)
  {
    if (Session["Name"] != null)
```

```
    {
     lblMsg.Text = Session["Name"] + "Welcome!";
    }
   else
    {
     Response.Redirect("~/Chap5/SessionLogin.aspx");
    }
  }
}
```

Source Codes: SessionLogin.aspx

```
<%@ Page Language="C#" AutoEventWireup="true" CodeFile="SessionLogin.aspx.cs"
Inherits="Chap6_SessionLogin" %>
<!DOCTYPE html>
<html xmlns="http://www.w3.org/1999/xhtml">
<head runat="server">
  <meta http-equiv="Content-Type" content="text/html; charset=utf-8" />
  <title>To establish Session</title>
</head>
<body>
  <form id="form1" runat="server">
    <div>
      User Name: <asp:TextBox ID="txtName" runat="server"></asp:TextBox><br />
      Password: <asp:TextBox ID="txtPassword" runat="server"
TextMode="Password"></asp:TextBox><br />
      <asp:Button ID="btnSubmit" runat="server" OnClick="BtnSubmit_Click" Text="OK" />
    </div>
  </form>
</body>
</html>
```

Source Codes: Session.aspx.cs

```
using System;
public partial class Chap5_SessionLogin : System.Web.UI.Page
{
  protected void BtnSubmit_Click(object sender, EventArgs e)
  {
    if (txtName.Text == "leaf" && txtPassword.Text == "111")
    {
      Session["Name"] = "leaf";
    }
  }
}
```

Program description:

When the user directly accesses Session.aspx, the state value of session ["Name"] will be judged. If it is empty, it will be redirected to SessionLogin.aspx, else the welcome message will be displayed.

In SessionLogin.aspx, after the user logs in successfully, the state value of Session ["Name"] will be established. At this time, testing whether the state value of Session ["Name"] exists, you should directly change the address in the browser that is used to browse SessionLogin.aspx to access Session.aspx.

5.5.5 Application

Application is different from the Session state of the single user. It is applied to all of the users. So, the Application state can be understood as a common global variable, and all of the visitors can access this variable in this website. Application exists at runtime, and can be released when the site is closed. Therefore, if you want to store the state data, the data should be stored in the database.

Application is implemented by System.Web.HttpApplicationState class. If you want to modify the state value of Application, you should call Application.Lock() method to lock Application state, and after modifying the value, you can call Application.Unlock() method to unlock the state. Being closely related to Application is Application_Start() method, Application_End() method and Application_Error() method of the Global class, and all of these methods are included in Global. asax file.

Example 5-9 Counting the online people number of website

As is shown in Figure 5-16, the online people number will be displayed on the page. If you want to implement this function, you should consider three aspects: initializing the counter; when an user accesses the web site, the counter should be added 1; when an user leaves the site, the counter minus 1. Using the Application_Start() event to initialize the counter and defining the Application state in the event code. Using Session_Start ()event to increase the count when users visit the web site, and increasing the Application state in the event codes. Using Session_End() event to reduce count when users leave the site, and reduce the state values of Application in the event codes.

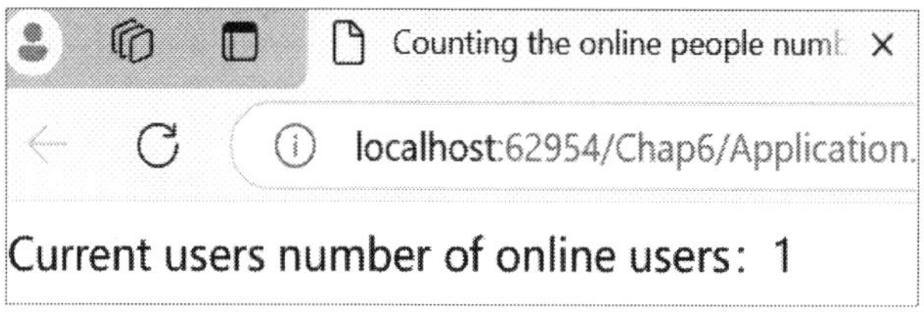

Figure 5-16 The Effect of Application.aspx

Source Codes: Global.asax

```
<%@ Application Language="C#" %>
<script runat="server">
    void Application_Start(object sender, EventArgs e)

    {
      Application["visitnumber"] = 0;
    }
    void Session_Start(object sender, EventArgs e)
    {
```

```
        if (Application["visitnumber"] != null)
          { Application.Lock();
             Application["visitnumber"] = (int)Application["visitnumber"] + 1;
          Application.UnLock();
        }
    }
    void Session_End(object sender, EventArgs e)
    {
       if (Application["visitnumber"] != null)
       {  Application.Lock();
          Application["visitnumber"] = (int)Application["visitnumber"]-1;
          Application.UnLock();
       }
    }
</script>
```

Source Codes: Application.aspx

```
<%@ Page Language="C#" AutoEventWireup="true" CodeFile="Application.aspx.cs"
Inherits="Chap5_Application" %>
<!DOCTYPE html>
<html xmlns="http://www.w3.org/1999/xhtml">
<head runat="server">
<meta http-equiv="Content-Type" content="text/html; charset=utf-8"/>
  <title>To count the online people number of website</title>
</head>
<body>
  <form id="form1" runat="server">
     <div>
        The current people number:<asp:Label ID="lblMsg" runat="server"></asp:Label>
     </div>
  </form>
</body>
</html>
```

Source Codes: Application.aspx.cs

```
using System;
public partial class Chap5_Application : System.Web.UI.Page
{
  protected void Page_Load(object sender, EventArgs e)
  {
     lblMsg.Text = Application["visitnumber"].ToString();
  }
}
```

Program description:

Application.aspx can be visited by using multiple browsers or computers at the same time. If you want to test it by using multiple computers, you should deploy the website to IIS 7.5 firstly.

5.6 Summary

➢ HttpRequest provides QueryString, ServerVariables, Browser, Cookies and other data sets to access data for different purposes.

➢ HttpResponse provides the functions such as outputting XHTML text, JavaScript scripts, and Cookies.

➢ In order to effectively prevent SQL scripts injection, the HtmlEncode() method of the HttpServerUtility object is often used. The object also provides practical methods such as UrlEncode() and MapPath().

➢ Page redirection can take multiple forms, such as <a> elements, HyperLink, Response. Redirect(), Server. Execute(), Server.Transfer() and submission across pages of Button type controls. You should pay attention to their differences when using them.

➢ State management is divided into two forms: on client and on server. Cookies and query strings are mostly used on the client, while Session, Application and data base are used on the server. Among them, Session corresponds to a single user, while Application corresponds to all of the users.

5.7 Exercises

1. Multiple Choice Questions

(1) Which of the following controls can't be used to redirect a page ( ).

A.LinkButton control B.HttpResponse.Redirect() method

C.Image control D.HttpServerUtility.Transfer() method

(2) Which of the following objects can retrieve the information submitted from the browser on client( ).

A. HttpReuest B.HttpResponse C.HttpSessionState D.HttpApplication

(3) What is the biggest difference between Session state and Cookie state ( ).

A.Different storage location B.Different type C.Different life cycles D.Different capacities

(4) What is the effective duration of the Session state by default( ).

A.30 seconds B.10 minutes C.20 minutes D.30 minutes

2.True or False Questions

(1) The value of IsCrossPagePostBack property can determine if the submission belong to cross pages.( )

(2) Application state can be modified by all of the visitors of this web site.( )

(3) ViewState can not be kept when HTML control is used.( )

(4) Session can be shared by different pages in the same session.( )

(5) ViewState can be shared among different pages of web site.( )

(6) When the window is closed, Session_End() method is executed immediately.( )

3. Programming Questions

(1) Create and debug all of the instances in this chapter.

(2) Create a page which can display the visitor's IP: When the IP start from 218.25, the welcome information is displayed, else illegal visitor is displayed, and the visit is ended.

(3) Design a page that prompts customers to register their name, gender, and other relevant information when they visit firstly, and subsequently save this information in a cookie. When the users subsequently visit, a message such as "Welcome, this is your the xxth visit to our site!" is displayed.

(4) Develop a simple chat room that displays the speaker's name, the content of their message, the time of posting, the total number of visitors, and the current number of online users.

(5) Develop two pages: the first page allows users to enter their username, which is then saved in the Session. The second page retrieves this Session information and displays a welcome message. If a user accesses the second page without logging in on the first page, the page will redirect them back to the first page. Additionally, the Session state should be saved separately to both StateServer and SQLServer.

Chapter 6 Data Access

Points:

- Understanding how to access data
- Mastering the method of managing database
- Mastering the LINQ query expressions
- Mastering the method of data access by using data source control
- Implementing the data access management by using LINQ to SQL and LINQ to XMLns

6.1 Summary of Data Access

NET Framework provides multiple ways to access database. In ASP.NET 1.x, ADO.NET is mainly used to access data. This technology is still supported in ASP.NET based on VSC 2019. ADO.NET provides the objects for database connection, data query, data inserting, data updating, and data deletion. It mainly includes the following five objects:

- Connection object: It is used to connect data base.
- Command object: It is used to execute the SQL commands for the data base.
- DataReader object: It is used to return read-only data from the database.
- DataAdapter object: It is used to return data from the database, and fill into the object of DataSet, also ensure that the data in the DataSet object is consistent with the data in the database.
- DataSet object: It can be regarded as the database in memory. After DataAdapter object transfers the data in the data base to this object, various data operations can be performed, at last, the updated data are reflected to the database by using the DataAdapter object.

The five objects provide two ways to read the database: one is to use Connection object, Command object and DataReader object. This method can only read the database; the second is to use Connection object, Command object, DataAdapter object and DataSet object. This method can implement various operations for the data base.

In ASP NET 2.0, a variety of data source controls and data binding controls have been added. The data source controls encapsulate all of the functions of acquiring and processing data, mainly including data source connection, acquiring and managing data by using the SQL statements, such as Select, Update, Delete and Insert. Data binding controls can display data through multiple methods. If data source control and data binding control are used together, you can read the database by setting relevant attributes almost without writing any codes.

In ASP NET 3.5, a new technology LINQ is introduced. This technology makes the data access operations fully integrated with .NET language, realizing the function of accessing the database through .NET language. ASP.NET 4.0 further extends this technology, and adds the data access method that is LINQ to Entities .

VSC 2019 provides LINQ to SQL tool to access data by using LINQ technology. However, this tool is considered as a single component in VSC 2019, and it can only be installed after being manually selected.

6.2 Establishing SQL Server Express Database

SQL Server 2019 Express (SSE) is the free version developed by Microsoft, and it is applicable to database development of medium-sized enterprises and learning purposes.

SQL Server 2019 Express LocalDB is a lighter version than SSE, which aims to use the database without configuration during web application development. Localdb is mainly applicable to the development environment. When the web application containing localdb database is published to IIS 7.5, the connection string used to access the database need to be changed, while the established database need not to be changed.

1. Connection string

Connection string includes the corresponding information of accessing database, which is stored in the <connectionstrings> element of the Web.config file, and it needs to be configured according to different types of database instances and different authentication forms.

In database management system, the type of database instance include SQL Server instance, SQLEXPRESS instance and LocalDB instance. Different instance type will determine the value of Data Source attribute in the connection string. For example, to access the SQLEXPRESS instance, you need to set the value of the Data Source attribute to be ". \ SQLEXPRESS "; to access the LocalDB instance, you should set the value of Data Source attribute to be "(LocalDB)\MSSQLLocalDB".

SQL Server database authentication has two modes, that are Windows authentication and SQL Server authentication. Windows authentication connects SQL Server through the users of Windows operating system, which is commonly used in local network; while SQL Server authentication connects SQL Server through the users registered in SQL Server, which is commonly used in Internet.

2. MyPetShop database

This book uses a database whose name is MyPetShop including shopping cart, commodity classification, user, order, commodity, supplier and other data tables as an sample database. The steps to establish MyPetShop database are as follows:

(1) In VSC 2019, opening MyPetShop.sql file under Sql folder of source program package of this book. The SQL toolbar as Figure 6-1 will be shown.

Figure 6-1 SQL Toolbar

(2) Clicking  button, selecting the local server that is MSSQLLocalDB in the rendered dialog, then clicking "connect" button to connect LocalDB database server.

(3) Clicking  button, executing SQL statements in MyPetShop.sql file to establish MyPetShop database, which includes CartItem, Category, Customer, Order, OrderItem, Product, Supplier and other tables and the some sample data, also includes a store procedure that is CategoryInsert.

Note: The database established in VSC 2019 belongs to the LocalDB database instance by default, and the sort rule is SQL_ Latin1_ General_ CP1_ CI_ As. In order to support Chinese information processing, the parameter COLLATE Chinese_PRC_CS_AS can be specified when using the statement CREATE DATABASE to establish the database, where CS is case sensitive, and AS means distinguishing accents.

The connecting string which is used to access MyPetShop database is as follows:

<add name="MyPetShopConnectionString"
ConnectionString="DataSource=(LocalDB)\MSSQLLocalDB;
AttachDbFilename=|DataDirectory|\MyPetShop.mdf;
Integrated Security="True";
SettingsObjectName="MyPetShop.DAL.Properties.Settings"
SettingsPropertyName="MyPetShopConnectionString"
Provider="System.Data.SqlClient />

6.3 Accessing Data by Using Data Source Control

To realize the function of data access from different data sources, ASP.NET based on VSC 2019 provides multiple different data source controls, that are EntityDataSource, LinqDataSource, ObjectDataSource, SiteMapDataSource, SqlDataSource, and XmlDataSource. EntityDataSource is used to access data based on the entity data model; LinqDataSource is used to access the database by using LINQ technology; ObjectDataSource is used to access database through business logic layer in the multi tier Web application architecture; SiteMapDataSource is used to access the Web.sitemap file of XML format; SqlDataSource is used to access Access, SQL Server, SQL Server Express, Oracle, ODBC data sources, and OLEDB data source; XmlDataSource is used to access XML data sources with the "hierarchical data" attribute.

Whatever data source interaction, the data source provides an unified basic program model. Various events defined through data source control can realize the data operations including Select, Update, Delete, and Insert etc. The data source control also provides the event before and after data operations, such as: there is the Insert() method when the data inserting operation is implemented. The Inserting event before the data inserting operation is implemented and the Inserted event after the data inserting operation is implemented.

Example 6-1 Displaying the data of the table by using LinqDataSource

As is shown in Figure 6-2, the data of Category table is displayed by using LinqDataSource and GridView controls.

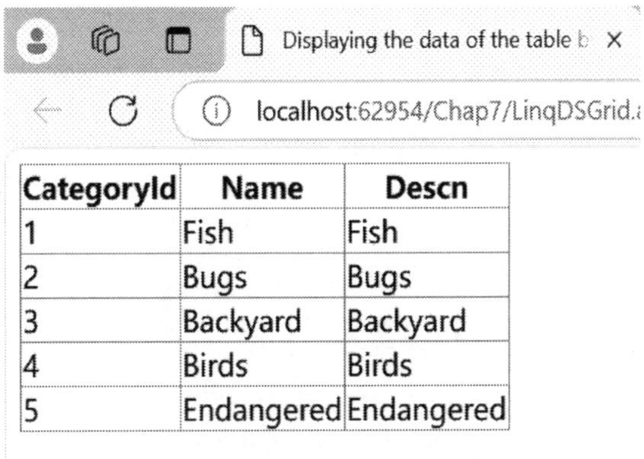

CategoryId	Name	Descn
1	Fish	Fish
2	Bugs	Bugs
3	Backyard	Backyard
4	Birds	Birds
5	Endangered	Endangered

Figure 6-2 The Effect of Application.aspx

Source Codes: LinqDSGrid.aspx

```
<%@ Page Language="C#" AutoEventWireup="true" CodeFile="LinqDSGrid.aspx.cs"
Inherits="Chap6_LinqDSGrid" %>
<!DOCTYPE html>
<html xmlns="http://www.w3.org/1999/xhtml">
<head runat="server">
 <meta http-equiv="Content-Type" content="text/html; charset=utf-8" />
 <title>To display the data of the table by using LinqDataSource</title>
</head>
<body>
 <form id="form1" runat="server">
  <div>
   <asp:GridView ID="gvCategory" runat="server" AutoGenerateColumns="False"
   DataKeyNames="CategoryId" DataSourceID="ldsCategory">
    <Columns>
     <asp:BoundField DataField="CategoryId" HeaderText="CategoryId" InsertVisible="False"
     ReadOnly="True" SortExpression="CategoryId" />
     <asp:BoundField DataField="Name" HeaderText="Name" SortExpression="Name" />
     <asp:BoundField DataField="Descn" HeaderText="Descn" SortExpression="Descn" />
    </Columns>
   </asp:GridView>
   <asp:LinqDataSource ID="ldsCategory" runat="server"
ContextTypeName="MyPetShopDataContext" TableName="Category">
   </asp:LinqDataSource>
  </div>
 </form>
</body>
</html>
```

Operating Steps:

(1) Right clicking App_Code folder, selecting "Add"→ "Add new item" command in the pop-up

shortcut menu, then selecting "LINQ to SQL class" template in the the rendered dialog, entering the file name MyPetShop.dbml, and clicking "Add" button to establish the file.

(2) Double clicking MyPetShop.dbml in "Solution Explorer" window, "Server Explorer" window appears, expanding the table, and dragging all of the data tables to the left window of the "Object Relationship Designer" in MyPetShop.dbml. VSC 2019 will create the related classes automatically.

(3) Creating LinqDSGrid.aspx in Chap6 folder. Adding one LinqDataSource control and one GridView control, and setting the values of attribute ID to be ldsCategory and gvCategory respectively.

(4) Clicking the smart tag of ldsCategory control, selecting "Configure Data Source" command, the dialog shown as Figure 6-3 is rendered, selecting MyPetShopDataContext. Clicking "Next" button, the dialog of "Configure Data Selection" shown as Figure 6-4 is rendered. In Figure 6-4, you can select the data table to query, and set the group form of data. Clicking "Where" button to configure the query term, and clicking "OrderBy" button to configure the sort method of query results. At last, clicking "Finish" button to finish the configuration of data source. The corresponding codes will generated automatically.

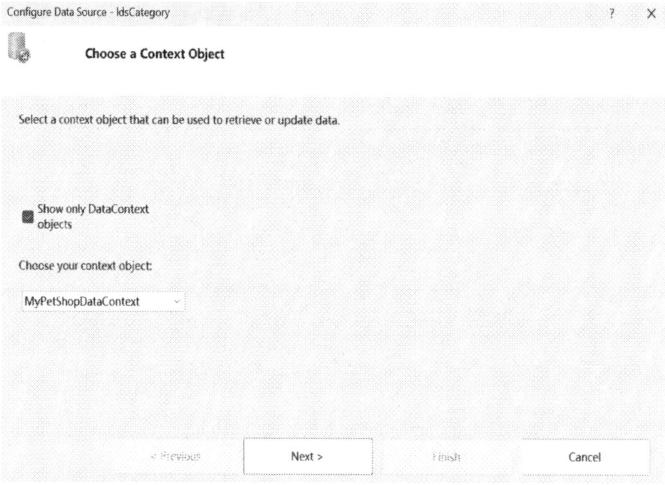

Figure 6-3 The Dialog of "Select DataContext Object"

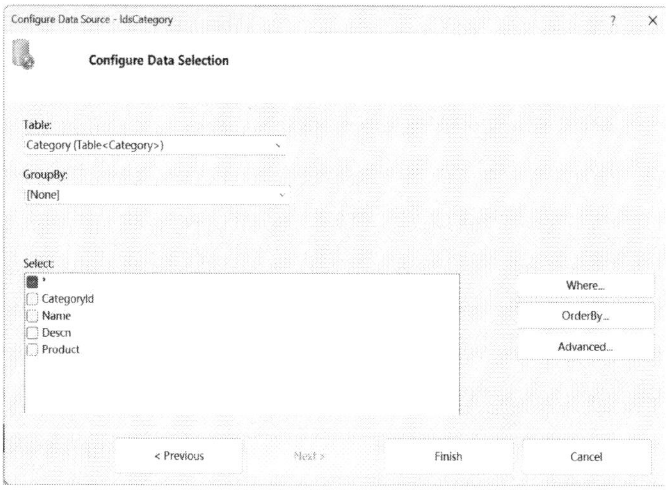

Figure 6-4 The Dialog of "Configure Data Selection"

(5) Clicking the smart tag of gvCategory control, selecting ldsCategory in drop down list box of "Select Data Source". VSC 2019 will create the related source codes automatically.

(6) Browsing LinqDSGrid.aspx to see the effect.

6.4 Accessing Data by Using LINQ

LINQ is integrated into .Net Framework. It provides an unified syntax to realize the query and management of multiple data sources. It is related to the programming languages supported by .NET, that makes data query and data management are embedded into the codes of the programming languages and makes full use of intelligent prompts of VSC 2019 and the compiler can check the syntax errors in query expressions.

According to the different data sources you visit, LINQ types can be divided into LINQ to Objects, LINQ to XML, and LINQ to ADO.NET. Among them, LINQ to ADO.NET can also be divided into LINQ to DataSet, LINQ to SQL and LINQ to Entities. In practical, LINQ to Objects is used to process the data of set type such as array and list; LINQ to XML is used to process the data of XML type; LINQ to DataSet is used to process the data of DataSet type; LINQ to SQL is used to process the data of SQL Server data base type; LINQ to Entities is used to process the data of entity type.

6.4.1 LINQ query expression

LINQ query expression realizes how to access the database. The hidden variables with the keyword var are often used to store the returned data. The variable var can not specify the data type explicitly, but the compiler can infer the type of the variable according to its expression.

LINQ query expression includes eight basic clauses, the functions of them are as follows:

- from clause——Specify the data source and the range of variables of query operation.
- select clause——Specify the type and presentation of query results
- where clause——Specify the logical condition of the filter operation.
- group clause——Group query results.
- orderby clause——Sort the query results.
- join clause——Join data sources of multiple query operations.
- let clause——Create a range variable that stores the result of a subexpression in a query expression.
- into clause——Provide a temporary identifier that can be referenced in a join, group, or select clauses.

Query expression must start with from clause and end with select clause or group clause, it can include one or more from, where, orderby, group, join, let clauses between the two clauses.

6.4.2 The summary of LINQ to SQL

LINQ to SQL provides a object model for the relation database, that means the relation databases is mapped to class objects. The mapping relationship between SQL Server database and LINQ to SQL objects is shown in Table 6-1.

Table 6-1 Mapping relationship table between database and object

SQL Server object	LINQ to SQL object
SQL Server Database	DataContext Class
Table	Entity class
Attribute	Attribute
Foreign key relationship	Relation
Storage procedure	Method

In VSC 2019, the mapping relationship between SQL Server database and LINQ to SQL objects can be created automatically.

In example6-1, when VSC 2019 establishes MyPetShop.dbml file, the MyPetShop.dbml.layout and MyPetShop.designer.cs files are established at the same time. Among them, MyPetShop.dbml defines the framework of MyPetShop database. MyPetShop.dbml.layout defines the layout of each table. MyPetShop.designer.cs defines the classes which are automatically generated, including: one is the classes corresponding to MyPetShop database, which is derived from DataContext class and is named after MyPetShopDataContext; the second is the entity classes with the table name of each table in MyPetShop databaseas as the class name.

The entity class describes the mapping relationship between TableAttribute class and the data tables through the attribute Name of this class. The following example shows that the Category entity class to be created is mapped to the Category table in MyPetShop:

[TableAttribute(Name= "dbo.Category")]

The attributes of the entity class are mapped to the attributes of the database table through the ColumnAttribute class. The following example shows the corresponding information of attribute CategoryId to be created. This attribute is mapped to the attribute CategoryId in Category table.

[ColumnAttribute(Storage= "CategoryId", AutoSync=AutoSync.OnInsert,
DbType= "Int NOT NULL IEDNTITY",IsPrimaryKey=true, IsDbGenerated=true)]

In the entity class, the relationship of foreign key among database tables is mapped through the AssociationAttribute class. The following example shows that the created relationship of Category_Product realizes that the attribute CategoryId in the Category table is used as the mapping of foreign keys in the Product table.

[AssociationAttribute(Name= "Category_Product",Storage= "_Product",
ThisKey= "CategoryId", otherKey= "CategoryId")]
[AssociationAttribute(Name= "Category_Product",Storage= "_Category",
ThisKey= "CategoryId", otherKey= "CategoryId",IsForeignKey=true)]

In the MyPetShopDataContext class, the storage procedure in the database is mapped to the corresponding method through the FunctionAttribute class, and the parameters in the storage procedure are mapped to the parameters of the corresponding method through the ParameterAttribute class. The following example shows that the created CategoryInsert() method is mapped to CategoryInsert storage procedure in the database.

[FunctionAttribute(Name= "dbo.CategoryInsert")]
Public int CategoryInsert(
[ParameterAttribute(Name= "Name",DbType= "VarChar(80)")] string name,

[ParameterAttribute(Name= "Descn",DbType= "VarChar(255)")] string descn)

6.4.3 Querying data by using LINQ to SQL

1. Projecting

Project can let us to select the attributes. A new object is created after project, and the object is usually anonymous.

Example 6-2 Implementing projection by using LINQ to SQL

This example will create the anonymous object with ProductID, CategoryID and Name attributes.

Source Codes: BtnProject_Click() in LinqSqlQuery.aspx.cs

```
protected void BtnProject_Click(object sender, EventArgs e)
 {
  MyPetShopDataContext db = new MyPetShopDataContext();
  var products = from r in db.Product
              select new
              {
               r.ProductId,
               r.CategoryId,
               r.Name
              };
  gvProduct.DataSource = products;
  gvProduct.DataBind();
 }
```

2. Selecting

Project implements the filtering of records, which is completed by the where clause.

Example 6-3 Implementing selection by using LINQ to SQL

This example will select the records of UnitCost>20.

Source Codes: BtnSelect_Click() in LinqSqlQuery.aspx.cs

```
protected void BtnSelect_Click(object sender, EventArgs e)
 {
  MyPetShopDataContext db = new MyPetShopDataContext();
  var products = from r in db.Product
              where r.UnitCost> 20
              select r;
  gvProduct.DataSource = products;
  gvProduct.DataBind();
 }
```

3. Sorting

Example 6-4 Implementing sorting by using LINQ to SQL

This example implements the descending order of the price by using orderby clause.

Source Codes: BtnOrder_Click() in LinqSqlQuery.aspx.cs

```
protected void BtnOrder_Click(object sender, EventArgs e)
 {
MyPetShopDataContext db = new MyPetShopDataContext();
var results = from r in db.Product
            orderby r.UnitCost descending
            select r;
  gvProduct.DataSource = results;
  gvProduct.DataBind();
}
```

4. Grouping

Group uses group... by clause. The grouped result set will be in the form of a set. Each element in the outer set includes a key value and a set of elements grouped according to the key value. Therefore, to access the elements in the grouped result set, you must use nested loop statements. The outer loop is used to iterate over each element in the outer set (i.e., each group), and the inner loop is used to iterate over the elements in the inner set (i.e., the elements in each group).

To reference the result of the grouping operation, you can use the into clause to create an identifier for the further query.

Example 6-5 Implementing grouping by using LINQ to SQL

This example implements grouping according to CategoryId, and displays the set whose value of CategoryId is 5.

Source Codes: BtnGroup_Click() in LinqSqlQuery.aspx.cs

```
protected void BtnGroup_Click(object sender, EventArgs e)
{
MyPetShopDataContext db = new MyPetShopDataContext();
 var results = from r in db.Product
            group r by r.CategoryId;
  foreach (var g in results)
  {
   if (g.Key == 5)
   {
    var results2 = from r in g
             select r;
```

```
            gvProduct.DataSource = results2;
            gvProduct.DataBind();
        }
    }
}
```

5. Polymerizing

Polymerize mainly involves Count(), Max(), Min(), Average() and other methods. When using these methods, the parameter often uses Lambda expression. The syntax format of lambda expression is as follows:

(input parameter) => {block}

"input parameter" may be null, one or more. When entering a parameter, the ellipsis can be used; " =>" is called Lambda operator, and is read as goes to; block represents the result of lambda expression.

When applying Lambda expression to the methods of Max(), Min(), Average(), the compiler will automatically infer the data type of the input parameter.

Example 6-6 To implement Polymerizing by using LINQ to SQL

This example counts the number of each group in groups, the maximum, minimum and average of ListPrice according to CategoryId .

Source Codes: BtnPolymerize_Click() in LinqSqlQuery.aspx.cs

```
protected void BtnPolymerize_Click(object sender, EventArgs e)
{
MyPetShopDataContext db = new MyPetShopDataContext();
 var results = from r in db.Product
              group r by r.CategoryId into g
              select new
              {
               Key = g.Key,
               Count = g.Count(),
               MaxPrice = g.Max(p => p.ListPrice),
               MinPrice = g.Min(p => p.ListPrice),
               AvgPrice = g.Average(p => p.ListPrice)
              };
   gvProduct.DataSource = results;
   gvProduct.DataBind();
}
```

6.Joining

Multi-table join query uses the join clause. But the multi-table constrained by foreign key can implement query directly through the form of the reference object, of course, also can use the join clause.

Example 6-7 Joining the direct quotation object by using LINQ to SQL

This example queries the classification name of the product through the direct quotation object.

Source Codes: BtnQuote_Click() in LinqSqlQuery.aspx.cs

```
protected void BtnQuote_Click(object sender, EventArgs e)
{
  MyPetShopDataContext db = new MyPetShopDataContext();
  var results = from r in db.Product
          select new
          {
           r.ProductId,
           r.CategoryId,
           CategoryName = r.Category.Name
          };
  gvProduct.DataSource = results;
  gvProduct.DataBind();
}
```

Example 6-8 Implementing join by using LINQ to SQL

This example implements the function that is the same with example 6-7. It is mainly applicable to join two tables without foreign key association.

Source Codes: BtnJoin_Click() in LinqSqlQuery.aspx.cs

```
protected void BtnJoin_Click(object sender, EventArgs e)
{
  MyPetShopDataContext db = new MyPetShopDataContext();
  var results = from product in db.Product
          join category in db.Category on product.CategoryId equals category.CategoryId
          select new
          {
           product.ProductId,
           product.CategoryId,
           CategoryName = category.Name
          };
  gvProduct.DataSource = results;
  gvProduct.DataBind();
}
```

7.Fuzzy querying

Fuzzy query need to call System.Data.Linq.SqlClient.SqlMethods.Like() method.

Example 6-9 Implementing fuzzy query by using LINQ to SQL

This example queries the product whose name includes fly.

Source Codes: BtnFuzzy_Click() in LinqSqlQuery.aspx.cs

```
protected void BtnFuzzy_Click(object sender, EventArgs e)
{
  MyPetShopDataContext db = new MyPetShopDataContext();
  var results = from r in db.Product
          where System.Data.Linq.SqlClient.SqlMethods.Like(r.Name, "%fly%")
          select r;
  gvProduct.DataSource = results;
  gvProduct.DataBind();
}
```

6.4.4 Managing data by using LINQ to SQL

1. Inserting data

The InsertAllOnSubmit() method and InsertOnSubmit () method are all used to insert the data. The former is used to insert a set of entity objects; the latter is used to insert a single entity.

Example 6-10 Inserting data by using LINQ to SQL

This example will get the value of the attribute Name and Descn through the Textbox, then insert the value into the Category table. Because the Category table has set the attribute CategoryID to be an identification, so the value will automatically increase. Then the value of attribute CategoryID dose not need to be inserted when we insert data.

Source Codes: BtnInsert_Click() in LinqSqlManageData.aspx.cs

```
protected void BtnInsert_Click(object sender, EventArgs e)
{
  Category category = new Category();
  category.Name = txtName.Text;
  category.Descn = txtDescn.Text;
  db.Category.InsertOnSubmit(category);
  db.SubmitChanges();
  Bind();
}
```

Source Codes: Bind() in LinqSqlManageData.aspx.cs

```
protected void Bind()
{
  var results = from r in db.Category
          select r;
  gvCategory.DataSource = results;
  gvCategory.DataBind();
}
```

2. Updating data

We need to find the updated data according to some information, such as the modification of personal information need to be authenticated in advance, then get the personal information according to the identification.

Example 6-11 Updating data by using LINQ to SQL

This example will directly obtain the data according to the input CategoryID, then update the data again. The value of the CategoryID cannot be updated because it is identification.

Source Codes: BtnUpdate_Click() in LinqSqlManageData.aspx.cs

```
protected void BtnUpdate_Click(object sender, EventArgs e)
{
  var results = from r in db.Category
          where r.CategoryId == int.Parse(txtCategoryId.Text)
          select r;
  if (results != null)
  {
   foreach (Category r in results)
   {
    r.Name = txtName.Text;
    r.Descn = txtDescn.Text;
   }
   db.SubmitChanges();
   Bind();
  }
}
```

3.Deleting data

DeleteAllOnSubmit () method is used to delete the entity set and DeleteOnSubmit () method is used to delete a single entity.

Example 6-12 Deleting data by using LINQ to SQL

This example will delete the data according to the input CategoryID.

Source Codes: BtnDelete_Click() in LinqSqlManageData.aspx.cs

```
protected void BtnDelete_Click(object sender, EventArgs e)
 {
  var results = from r in db.Category
           where r.CategoryId == int.Parse(txtCategoryId.Text)
           select r;
  db.Category.DeleteAllOnSubmit(results);
  db.SubmitChanges();
  Bind();
 }
```

4.Storage procedure

To use the the storage procedure defined in original SQL Server. The storage procedure need to be dragged into O/R designer window when we establish MyPetShop.dbml. The VSC 2019 will automatically create the method corresponding to the storage procedure. We just call the methods of the object during using storage procedure.

Example 6-13 Calling the storage procedure by using LINQ to SQL

This example inserts data by using storage procedures. The storage procedure CategoryInsert should be established at first in MyPetShop database, then corresponding CategoryInsert() method is generated in MyPetShop.dbml.

Source Codes: Storage procedure CategoryInsert

```
CREATE PROCEDURE CategoryInsert
 (
 @Name varchar(80),
 @Descn varchar(255)
 )
AS
 INSERT INTO Category(Name,Descn) VALUES (@Name,@Descn);
 RETURN
```

Source Codes: BtnProcedure_Click() in LinqSqlManageData.aspx.cs

```
protected void BtnProcedure_Click(object sender, EventArgs e)
  {
    db.CategoryInsert(txtName.Text.ToString(), txtDescn.Text.ToString());
    Bind();
 }
```

6.4.5 The overview of LINQ to XML

LINQ to XML can handle data with XML structure in .NET programming language. To provide a new object model of XML document and support LINQ query expressions. To save the document with XML structure into memory, you can easily realize query, insertion, updating, deletion and other operations.

- XDocument class: It is used to manipulate XML document. An XML document can be established by calling Save() method.
- XDeclaration class: It is used to manipulate the statement in an XML document, including version, coding, etc.
- XComment class: It is used to manipulate the comment in an XML document.
- XAttribute class: It is used to manipulate the attribute of an XML element, and it is a name/value pair.
- XElement class: It is used to manipulate the elements in the XML document, which contains child

elements with any multistage. The element name can be obtained through attribute Name; the element value can be obtained through the attribute Value. The XML document can be imported into memory through the Load() method, and the XElement instance is created; the XElement instance is stored into XML documents through Save () method; the Attribute of the element is obtained through the Attribute() method; Remove() method is used to delete an element; ReplaceNodes() method is used to replace the element content; SetAttributeValue () method is used to set attribute values of the elements.

6.4.6 Managing XML document by using the LINQ to XML

1. Creating an XML document

If you want to create an XML document, you should mainly use the XDocument object. Adding the XML document statement, elements and comments into the XDocument object according to the format of the XML document; then you can use the Save() method to save the content to the Web server disk. Note that the Save() method must use the physical path.

Example 6-14 Creating an XML document by using LINQ to XML

This example will create an XML document BookLinq. Xml, which is shown as Figure 6-5

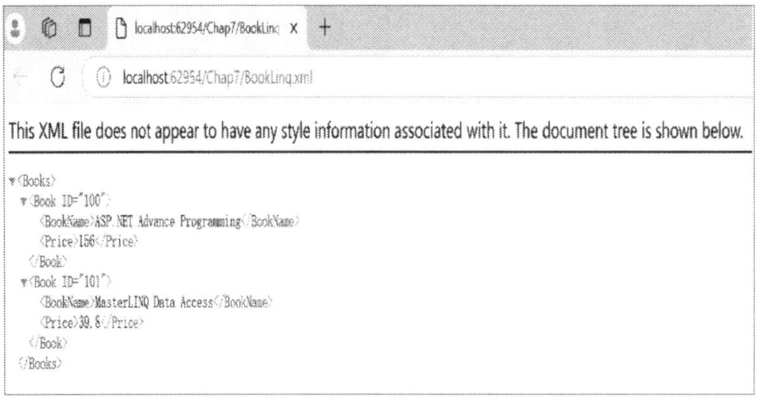

Figure 6-5 The Effect of BookLinq.xml

Source Codes: BtnCreate_Click() in LinqXml.aspx.cs

```
protected void BtnCreate_Click(object sender, EventArgs e)
{
  string xmlFilePath = Server.MapPath("~/Chap6/BookLinq.xml");
  XDocument doc = new XDocument
   (
     new XDeclaration("1.0", "utf-8", "yes"),
     new XComment("Book example "),
     new XElement("Books",
      new XElement("Book",
       new XAttribute("ID", "100"),
       new XElement("BookName", "ASP.NET "),
       new XElement("Price", 156)
            ),
      new XElement("Book",
       new XAttribute("ID", "101"),
       new XElement("BookName", " LINQ "),
       new XElement("Price", 39.8)
            ),
      new XElement("Book",
       new XAttribute("ID", "102"),
       new XElement("BookName", "ASP.NET teaching"),
       new XElement("Price", 42.6)
            )
            )
   );
  doc.Save(xmlFilePath);
  Response.Redirect("~/Chap7/BookLinq.xml");
}
```

2. Querying XML documents

You can easily read XML documents by using LINQ query expressions, query the root element, query elements of the designated name, query elements of the designated attribute, query sub-elements of designated element, and so on.

Example 6-15 Querying the elements of the designated attribute by using LINQ to XML

This example will query the element whose value of BookName element is "ASP.NET ", and finally the attribute value of the element, BookName of the next level sub-elements and the Price are all output.

Source Codes: BtnQuery_Click() in LinqXml.aspx.cs

```
protected void BtnQuery_Click(object sender, EventArgs e)
 {
  string xmlFilePath = Server.MapPath("~/Chap6/BookLinq.xml");
  XElement els = XElement.Load(xmlFilePath);
  var elements = from el in els.Elements("Book")
            where (string)el.Element("BookName") == "ASP.NET"
            select el;
  foreach (XElement el in elements)
  {
   Response.Write(el.Name + "ID:" + el.Attribute("ID").Value + "<br />");
   Response.Write("BookName:" + el.Element("BookName").Value + "<br />");
   Response.Write("Price:" + el.Element("Price").Value);
  }
 }
```

3. Inserting elements

If you want to insert some elements, an XElement instance need to be established firstly, and the corresponding contents should be added; then add the elements into the upper level elements by using the Add() method; finally save the content to the XML document by using the Save() method.

Example 6-16 Inserting the element by using LINQ to XML

This example inserts a new element into the BookLinq.xml document.

Source Codes: BtnInsert_Click() in LinqXml.aspx.cs

```
protected void BtnInsert_Click(object sender, EventArgs e)
 {
  string xmlFilePath = Server.MapPath("~/Chap6/BookLinq.xml");
  XElement els = XElement.Load(xmlFilePath);
  XElement el = new XElement
   ("Book",
    new XAttribute("ID", "104"),
    new XElement("BookName", "C# Advanced programming"),
    new XElement("Price", 119.8)
   );
els.Add(el);
els.Save(xmlFilePath);
  Response.Redirect("~/Chap6/BookLinq.xml");
 }
```

4. Updating elements

To update the element, you should search the element according to the keywords firstly, then set the value of the attribute by using the SetAttribute () method, and update the contents of the element by using ReplaceNodes () method. Finally you should save the element into the XML document by using the Save() method.

Example 6-17 Updating the element by using LINQ to XML

This example will update the element content whose attribute ID is 101.

Source Codes: BtnUpdate_Click() in LinqXml.aspx.cs

```
protected void BtnUpdate_Click(object sender, EventArgs e)
{
  string xmlFilePath = Server.MapPath("~/Chap6/BookLinq.xml");
  XElement els = XElement.Load(xmlFilePath);
  var elements = from el in els.Elements("Book")
             where el.Attribute("ID").Value == "101"
             select el;
  foreach (XElement el in elements)
  {
    el.SetAttributeValue("ID", "106");
    el.ReplaceNodes
     (
      new XElement("BookName", "Master LINQ Data Access based on C#"),
      new XElement("Price", 45.9)
     );
  }
  els.Save(xmlFilePath);
  Response.Redirect("~/Chap6/BookLinq.xml");
}
```

5. Deleting elements

If you want to delete the elements, you should search the element according to the keyword firstly, then delete the element by using the Remove() method, and finally save the element into XML documents by using the Save () method.

Example 6-18 Deleting the element by using LINQ to XML

This example will delete the element whose attribute ID is 102.

Source Codes: BtnDelete_Click() in LinqXml.aspx.cs

```
protected void BtnDelete_Click(object sender, EventArgs e)
{
  string xmlFilePath = Server.MapPath("~/Chap6/BookLinq.xml");
```

```
        XElement els = XElement.Load(xmlFilePath);
        var elements = from el in els.Elements("Book")
                where el.Attribute("ID").Value == "102"
                select el;
        foreach (XElement el in elements)
        {
          el.Remove();
        }
        els.Save(xmlFilePath);
        Response.Redirect("~/Chap6/BookLinq.xml");
    }
}
```

6.5 Summary

➢ LINQ technology is fully integrated with the programming language, and the data in it is treated as an object, which conforms to the development of data access technology.

➢ LINQ implements data query, insertion, deletion, updation and other operations very succinctly.

➢ You should fully understand that LINQ technology can meet any data access requirements, which is also the main technology for data access of Microsoft.

6.6 Exercises

1. True or False Questions

(1) After configuration, the LocalDB database instance can be accessed by using the method accessing the SQLEXPRESS database instance.( )

(2) The connection string are the same when you access LocalDB database instance and SQLEXPRESS database instance .( )

(3) The anonymous object can be established by using the value of LINQ expression.( )

(4) The value of a LINQ expression must specify a data type.( )

(5) After grouping by using the group clause in a LINQ query, the resulting set maintains the same structure as the original set.()

(6) Database established in VSC 2019 can be managed through Server Resource Manager.( )

2. Programming Questions

(1) Create and debug all of the instances in this chapter.

(2) Design a query page by using LinQ to SQL to search for the products containing the character "c" in their names and prices within 50 yuan.

(3) Implement the previous task by using the "Standard Query Operator" method of LinQ.

(4) Implement the previous task by using stored procedures.

(5) Design a back-end management page by using LinQ to SQL to add, delete, modify products.

(6) Add, search, delete, modify XML elements by using LinQ to XML according to the value input in the textbox.

Chapter 7 Data Binding

Points:

- Mastering the binding of ListControl class control and data source
- Mastering the binding of GridView control and data source
- Mastering the binding of DetailsView control and data source

7.1 Summary of Data Binding

Data source control and LINQ technology realize data access, and data binding control is required to display the accessed data. Figure 7-1 shows the inheritance hierarchy of corresponding classes of data bound controls.

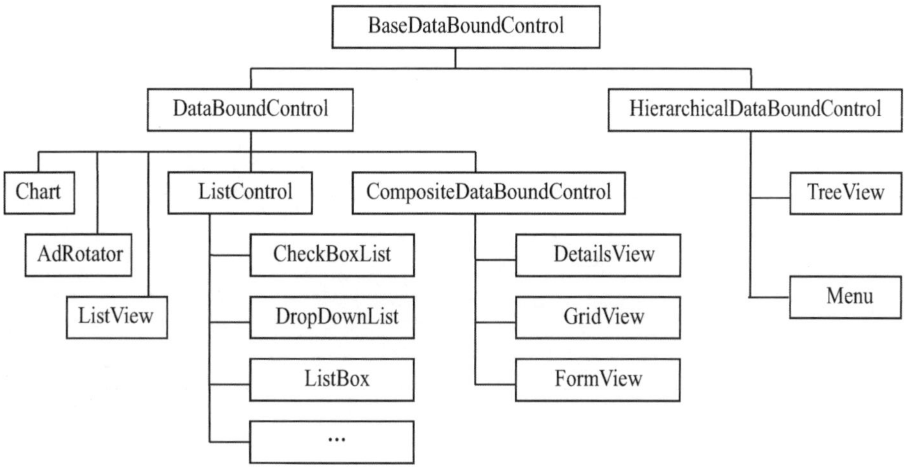

Figure 7-1 The Inheritance Hierarchy of Corresponding Classes of Data Bound Controls

If data bound controls are combined with the data source controls to display data, the attribute DataSourceID should be set by ID of data source control; if data bound controls are combined with LINQ technology, the attribute values of DataSource should be set with LINQ query result, and the DataBind() method should be called to display data.

7.2 ListControl Class Controls

This section mainly describes how to display database data in ListControl class controls.

In ListControl class controls, the attributes related to displaying database data mainly include:

AppendDataBoundItem, DataSourceID, DataSource, DataTextField, and DataValueField. Among them, AppendDataBoundItem is used to make data bound items appended to the list item of static statement. The field bound by DataTextField is used to display the list items; the field bound by DataValueField is used to set the value of the list items.

Example 7-1 Displaying data by combing DropDownList with LINQ

As is shown in Figure7-2 and Figure7-3, the value of Name field of the table Category will be displayed in DropDownList control, while the values of the list items correspond to the field value of CategoryId.

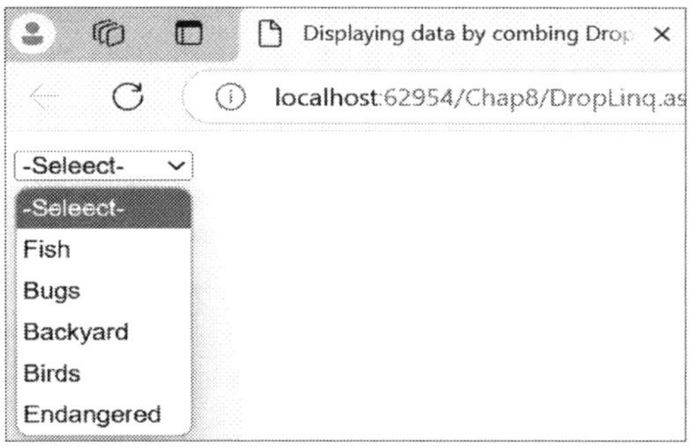

Figure 7-2 The Effect of DropLinq.aspx (1)

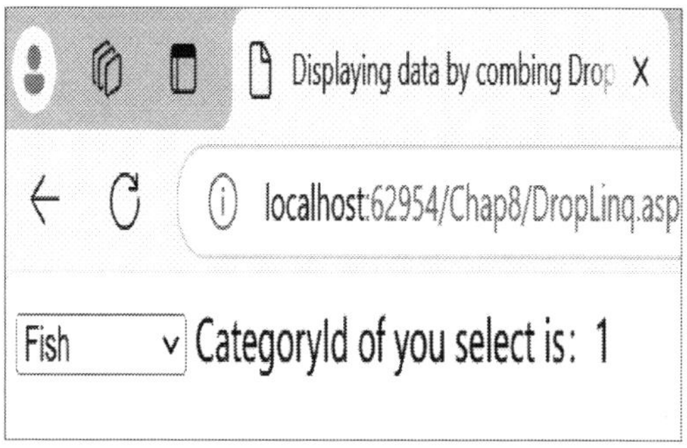

Figure7-3 The Effect of DropLinq.aspx (2)

Source Codes: DropLinq.aspx

```
<%@ Page Language="C#" AutoEventWireup="true" CodeFile="DropLinq.aspx.cs"
Inherits="Chap7_DropLinq" %>
<!DOCTYPE html>
<html xmlns="http://www.w3.org/1999/xhtml">
<head runat="server">
  <meta http-equiv="Content-Type" content="text/html; charset=utf-8" />
  <title>To display data in combination with DropDownList and LINQ</title>
</head>
<body>
  <form id="form1" runat="server">
    <div>
      <asp:DropDownList ID="ddlCategory" runat="server" AppendDataBoundItems="True"
AutoPostBack="True" DataTextField="Name" DataValueField="CategoryId"
 OnSelectedIndexChanged="DdlCategory_SelectedIndexChanged">
        <asp:ListItem>-Select-</asp:ListItem>
      </asp:DropDownList>
      <asp:Label ID="lblMsg" runat="server"></asp:Label>
    </div>
  </form>
</body>
</html>
```

Source Codes: DropLinq.aspx.cs

```
using System;
using System.Linq;
public partial class Chap8_DropLinq : System.Web.UI.Page
{
 protected void Page_Load(object sender, EventArgs e)
 {
  if (!IsPostBack)
  {
   MyPetShopDataContext db = new MyPetShopDataContext();
   var results = from r in db.Category
          select r;
   ddlCategory.DataSource = results;
   ddlCategory.DataBind();
  }
 }
 protected void DdlCategory_SelectedIndexChanged(object sender, EventArgs e)
 {
  lblMsg.Text = " CategoryId you have selected is: " + ddlCategory.SelectedValue;
 }
}
```

Operating Steps:

(1) Creating DropLinq.aspx in Chap7 folder, and adding one DropDownList control and one Label control. As is shown in Figure7-4, setting the attribute Items of DropDownList control. Setting the other attributes referencing the source program.

(2) Creating DropLinq.aspx.cs. At last, browsing DropLinq.aspx and testing it.

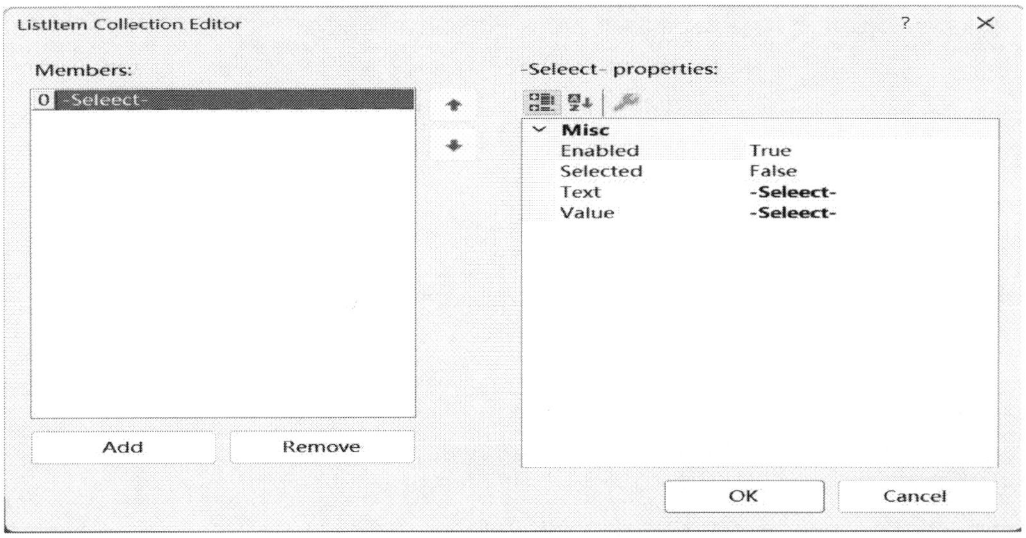

Figure 7-4 Setting the Attribute Items

Program description:

Page.Load event is triggered when the page is loaded, and the codes of Page_ Load() method is executed. If it is loaded for the first time, the Category table is queried by using LINQ technology, and then the query results are bound to the ddlCategory control. When a list item is selected, the SelectedIndexChanged event is triggered, the corresponding event processing codes are executed, and the value of the CategoryId field of the selected list item is displayed.

Example 7-2 Filling the text of ListBox according to the selected items

As is shown in Figure7-5, when the category name of the product corresponding to the radio button is selected, the names of all of the products in this category will be displayed in the list box.

Figure 7-5 The Browsing Effect of QueryString1.aspx

Source Codes: RdoListLinq.aspx

```
<%@ Page Language="C#" AutoEventWireup="true" CodeFile="RdoListLinq.aspx.cs"
 Inherits="Chap7_RdoListLinq" %>
<!DOCTYPE html>
<html xmlns="http://www.w3.org/1999/xhtml">
<head runat="server">
  <meta http-equiv="Content-Type" content="text/html; charset=utf-8" />
  <title>To fill the text of ListBox according to the selected items </title>
</head>
<body>
<form id="form1" runat="server">
  <div>
    <asp:RadioButtonList ID="rdoltCategory" runat="server" AutoPostBack="True"
DataTextField="Name" DataValueField="CategoryId"
OnSelectedIndexChanged="RdoltCategory_SelectedIndexChanged"RepeatDirection="Horizontal">
    </asp:RadioButtonList>
    <asp:ListBox ID="lstProduct" runat="server" DataTextField="Name"
DataValueField="ProductId"></asp:ListBox>
  </div>
</form>
</body>
</html>
```

Source Codes: RdoListLinq.aspx.cs

```
using System;
using System.Linq;
public partial class Chap7_RdoListLinq : System.Web.UI.Page
{
  MyPetShopDataContext db = new MyPetShopDataContext();
  protected void Page_Load(object sender, EventArgs e)
  {
    if (!IsPostBack)
    {
      var results = from r in db.Category
                    select r;
      rdoltCategory.DataSource = results;
      rdoltCategory.DataBind();
    }
  }
  protected void RdoltCategory_SelectedIndexChanged(object sender, EventArgs e)
  {
    var results = from r in db.Product
                  where r.CategoryId == int.Parse(rdoltCategory.SelectedValue)
                  select r;
    lstProduct.DataSource = results;
    lstProduct.DataBind();
  }
}
```

7.3 GridView Control

GridView control is used to display the data of two-dimension table, and it can realize the functions of data binding, paging, sorting, selection, updating, deleting etc.

7.3.1 Paging and sorting

In order to implement paging, we need to set the value of attribute AllowPaging to be true. Paging effect can be set in the set of the attribute PagerSettings, such as the attribute Mode for the paging, the attribute FirstPageImageUrl of button image URL for the "first page", etc. To realize the sorting, we need to set attribute AllowSorting to be true.

Example 7-3 Realizing the data paging and data sorting in GridView

As is shown in Figure7-6, the sorting function according to this field can be realized when clicking the field in the title bar. After selecting the number of records displayed on each page, the user can change the number of records displayed in the GridView and display the current page number and total pages at the same time.

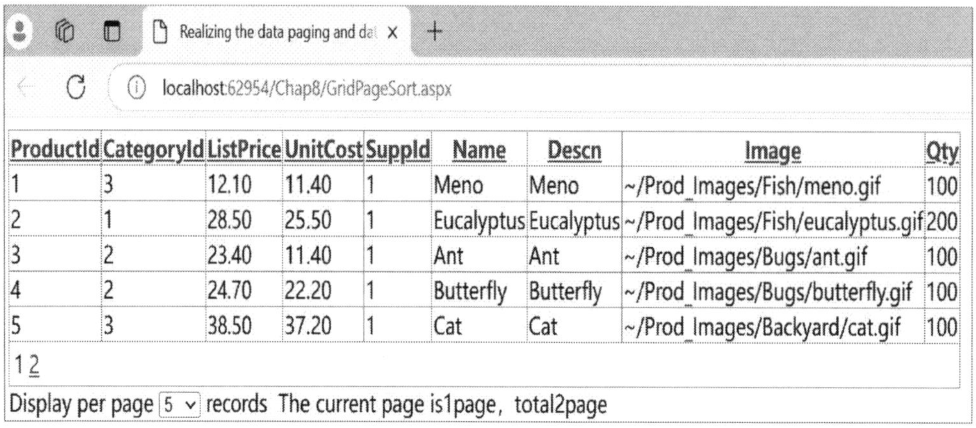

ProductId	CategoryId	ListPrice	UnitCost	SuppId	Name	Descn	Image	Qty
1	3	12.10	11.40	1	Meno	Meno	~/Prod_Images/Fish/meno.gif	100
2	1	28.50	25.50	1	Eucalyptus	Eucalyptus	~/Prod_Images/Fish/eucalyptus.gif	200
3	2	23.40	11.40	1	Ant	Ant	~/Prod_Images/Bugs/ant.gif	100
4	2	24.70	22.20	1	Butterfly	Butterfly	~/Prod_Images/Bugs/butterfly.gif	100
5	3	38.50	37.20	1	Cat	Cat	~/Prod_Images/Backyard/cat.gif	100
1 2								

Display per page 5 records The current page is1page, total2page

Figure 7-6 The Browsing Effect of GridPageSort.aspx

Source Codes: GridPageSort..aspx

```
<%@ Page Language="C#" AutoEventWireup="true" CodeFile="GridPageSort.aspx.cs"
Inherits="Chap7_GridPageSort" %>
<!DOCTYPE html>
<html xmlns="http://www.w3.org/1999/xhtml">
<head runat="server">
  <meta http-equiv="Content-Type" content="text/html; charset=utf-8" />
  <title>To realize the data paging and data sorting in GridView </title>
</head>
<body>
  <form id="form1" runat="server">
    <div>
      <asp:GridView ID="gvProduct" runat="server" AllowPaging="True" AllowSorting="True"
 AutoGenerateColumns="False" DataKeyNames="ProductId" DataSourceID="ldsProduct" PageSize="5"
 OnRowDataBound="GvProduct_RowDataBound">
        <Columns>
          <asp:BoundField DataField="ProductId" HeaderText="ProductId" InsertVisible="False" ReadOnly="True"
 SortExpression="ProductId" />
          <asp:BoundField DataField="CategoryId" HeaderText="CategoryId" SortExpression="CategoryId" />
        <asp:BoundField DataField="ListPrice" HeaderText="ListPrice" SortExpression="ListPrice" />
        <asp:BoundField DataField="UnitCost" HeaderText="UnitCost" SortExpression="UnitCost" />
        <asp:BoundField DataField="SuppId" HeaderText="SuppId" SortExpression="SuppId" />
        <asp:BoundField DataField="Name" HeaderText="Name" SortExpression="Name" />
        <asp:BoundField DataField="Descn" HeaderText="Descn" SortExpression="Descn" />
        <asp:BoundField DataField="Image" HeaderText="Image" SortExpression="Image" />
      <asp:BoundField DataField="Qty" HeaderText="Qty" SortExpression="Qty" />
      </Columns>
      </asp:GridView>
    <asp:LinqDataSource ID="ldsProduct" runat="server" ContextTypeName="MyPetShopDataContext"
TableName="Product"></asp:LinqDataSource>
```

```
    Each page shows
    <asp:DropDownList ID="ddlPageSize" runat="server" AutoPostBack="True"
OnSelectedIndexChanged="DdlPageSize_SelectedIndexChanged">
      <asp:ListItem>5</asp:ListItem>
      <asp:ListItem>10</asp:ListItem>
    </asp:DropDownList>
     records  <asp:Label ID="lblMsg" runat="server"></asp:Label>
    </div>
  </form>
</body>
</html>
```

Source Codes: GridPageSort.aspx.cs

```
using System;
using System.Web.UI.WebControls;
public partial class Chap7_GridPageSort : System.Web.UI.Page
{
  protected void DdlPageSize_SelectedIndexChanged(object sender, EventArgs e)
  {
    gvProduct.PageSize = int.Parse(ddlPageSize.SelectedValue);
    gvProduct.DataBind();
  }
  protected void GvProduct_RowDataBound(object sender, GridViewRowEventArgs e)
  {
  lblMsg.Text = "The current page is:" + (gvProduct.PageIndex + 1).ToString() + " Total pages is:" +
(gvProduct.PageCount).ToString();
  }
}
```

Operating Steps:

(1) Creating GridPageSort.aspx in Chap7 folder, adding one GridView control, one DropDownList control, one Label control and one LinqDataSource control, and setting the values of attribute ID of each control referencing the source program.

(2) Configuring the data source of LinqDataSource control to be Product table.

(3) Setting the values of attributes AllowPaging, AllowSorting, DtataSourceID, and PageSize of GridView control, and the values of attributes of other controls referencing the source program.

(4) Creating GridPageSort.aspx.cs. At last, browsing GridPageSort.aspx and testing it.

Program description:

When a page is loaded, the GridView will display the results according to the displaying number which is set on each page.

After the user selects the displaying number of each page, the SelectedIndexChanged event is triggered, the value of the attribute PageSize of the GridView control is changed after executing the corresponding event processing codes, and then the data is bound again.

The event RowDataBound of GridView is triggered after binding data of the rows, so the event will be triggered when we change the displaying number of the current page or each page. At this time, the value of the attribute PageIndex of GridView which is obtained is the number of current page, but the number of PageIndex starts from 0; the value of attribute PageCount which is obtained is the total number of pages.

7.3.2 Customizing data bound columns

GridView provides developers with flexible functions of column customization, such as adding check column boxes, displaying image columns, etc. You need to set the value of attribute AutoGenerateColumns to be False. In fact, each column of the GridView is the DataControlField class, and derives the different type of sub classes from the class. Different types of data bound columns in the GridView are shown in Table7-1.

Table 7-1 The corresponding table of different types of data bound columns in the GridView

Type	Description
BoundField	Be used to display common text content. The attribute DataField is used to set data column names which are bound; Attribute HeaderText is used to set header column names, such as the original English field name is transformed to Chinese name.
CheckBoxField	Be used to display data of Boolean type.
CommandField	Be used to create a command button. Attribute ShowEditButton, ShowDeleteButton, ShowCancelButton and ShowSelectButton are used to set whether to display the corresponding type of button.
ImageField	Be used to display image columns. Attribute DataImageUrlField is used to set data column binding image path; Attribute DataImageUrlFormatString is used to set the format of the URL of each image in the picture column.
HyperLinkField	Be used to show hyperlinks. The data columns Attribute DataTextField binding will display as the hyperlink text; the data column Attribute DataNavigateUrlFields binding will serve as the URL of hyperlinks.
ButtonField	Define button columns, unlike CommandField column: the button defined by ButtonField have no direct relation with the GridView, so the corresponding operation can be customized.
TemplateField	Customize data column in the form of a template.
ImageField	Be used to display image columns. Attribute DataImageUrlField is used to set data column binding image path; Attribute DataImageUrlFormatString is used to set the format of the URL of each image in the picture column.

Example 7-4 Customizing data bound columns of GridView

As is shown in Figure7-7, the GridView displays the part of the data of the Product table, including the header information in Chinese. ImageField column is used to display the images.

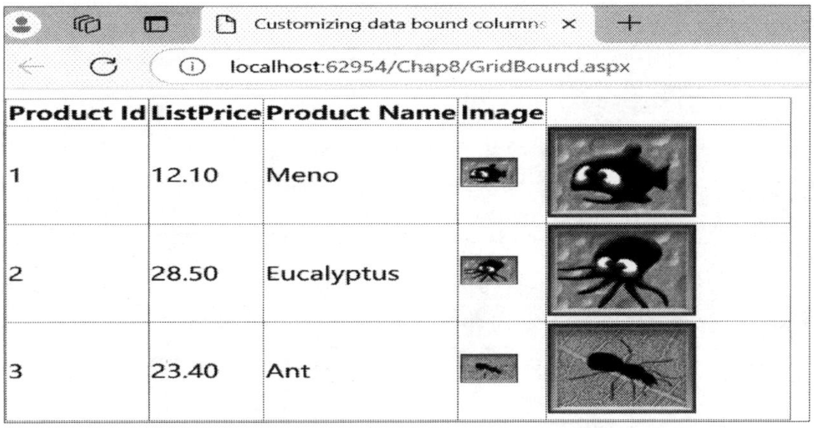

Figure 7-7 The Browsing Effect of GridBound.aspx

Source Codes: GridBound.aspx

```
<%@ Page Language="C#" AutoEventWireup="true" CodeFile="GridBound.aspx.cs"
Inherits="Chap7_GridBound" %>
<!DOCTYPE html>
<html xmlns="http://www.w3.org/1999/xhtml">
<head runat="server">
  <meta http-equiv="Content-Type" content="text/html; charset=utf-8" />
  <title>To Customize data bound columns of GridView</title>
</head>
<body>
  <form id="form1" runat="server">
    <div>
      <asp:GridView ID="gvProduct" runat="server" AutoGenerateColumns="False"
 DataSourceID="ldsProduct">
        <Columns>
          <asp:BoundField DataField="ProductId" HeaderText="ProductId" />
          <asp:BoundField DataField="ListPrice" HeaderText="ListPrice" />
          <asp:BoundField DataField="Name" HeaderText="Name" />
          <asp:ImageField DataImageUrlField="Image" HeaderText="Image">
            <ControlStyle Height="25px" Width="35px" />
          </asp:ImageField>
            <asp:ImageField DataImageUrlField="Image">
            </asp:ImageField>
        </Columns>
      </asp:GridView>
      <asp:LinqDataSource ID="ldsProduct" runat="server" ContextTypeName="MyPetShopDataCo
ntext" TableName="Product">
      </asp:LinqDataSource>
    </div>
  </form>
</body>
</html>
```

Operating Steps:

(1) Creating GridBound.aspx in Chap7 folder, adding one GridView control, one DropDownList control, and setting the values of attribute ID of each control referencing the source program.

(2) Configuring the data source of LinqDataSource control to be Product table.

(3) Setting the value of attribute DataSourceID of GridView. As is shown in Figure 7-8, setting the value of attribute Columns. In Figure7-8, you can add different types of columns according to the need, then set the attributes of the added columns respectively. At last, browsing the effect of GridBound.aspx.

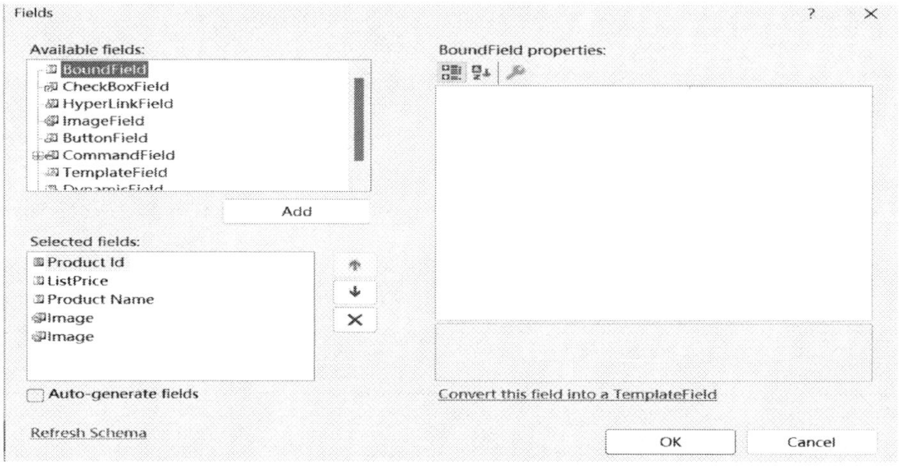

Figure 7-8 Setting the Value of Attribute Columens

Program description:

This example uses the field Image of the Product table to store the path corresponding to the images. At this time, in order to display images in the GridView, you just need to set the value of the attribute DataImageUrlField of ImageField column to be the field name that is Image, but if only the file name of the image is stored, the attribute DataImageUrlFormatString need to be used. For example, supposing that the images are stored in Images folder under the root folder of the web site uniformly, the file name of the image is stored in field Image. If you want to display the images correctly, the corresponding attributes should be set as follows:

```
<asp:ImageField DataImageUrlField = "Image" the HeaderText = "Image"
DataImageUrlFormatString = "~ \ img \ {0}">
</ asp:ImageField>
```

When the page is browsed, {0} will be instead of field Image set by attribute DataImageUrlField.

7.3.3 Using template field

In practical engineering, only using standard fields can not meet the requirements, such as entering the data in the form of DropDownList in GridView, validating the data when editing the fields. All of these problems can be solved by using template field.

When creating the TemplateField, the different templates need to be provided according to the different states and locations, as is shown in Figure 7-9. The description of the different templates is shown in Table7-2.

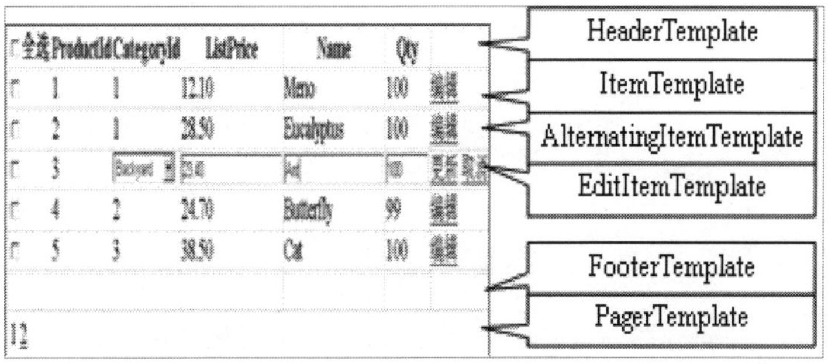

Figure 7-9 The Various Types of Templates

Table 7-2 The different types of template description table in TemplateField

The template	description
AlternatingItemTemplate	To designate displaying content for the alternate item
EditItemTemplate	To designate displaying content for the editing item
EmptyDataTemplate	To designate displaying content for the empty data item
FooterTemplate	To designate displaying content for the footnote
HeaderTemplate	To designate displaying content for the header
ItemTemplate	To designate displaying content for the TemplateField column
PagerTemplate	To designate displaying content for the page number

AlternatingItemTemplate should be used with ItemTemplate. If AlternatingItemTemplate is not set, all of data rows of GridView will be displayed with ItemTemplate; if AlternatingItemTemplate is set, the odd data rows of the GridView will be displayed with ItemTemplate, and the even data rows will be displayed with AlternatingItemTemplate.

Different data binding methods Eval() and Bind() are often used when adding content to different types of templates. Eval () is used for one-way binding (read only), while Bind () is used for two-way binding (renewable). When you use all of these methods, they should be embedded in the <% #... %>. In fact, in .aspx file, you can also bind variables, sets, expressions, etc. through<% #...%>. For example, if name is a public variable defined in .aspx.cs file, after using<% # name%>in the .aspx file and calling Page. DataBind() method in .aspx.cs file, the value of name variable can be displayed on the browsing page.

Example 7-5 Applying template columns of GridView

As is shown in Figure7-10, CheckBox field and CategoryID field are both the template fields.

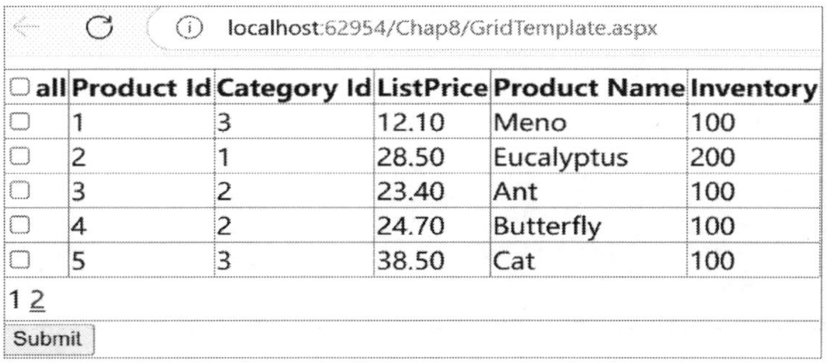

Figure7-10 The Browsing Effect of GridTemplate.aspx

Source Codes: GridTemplate.aspx

```
<%@ Page Language="C#" AutoEventWireup="true" CodeFile="GridTemplate.aspx.cs"
Inherits="Chap7_GridTemplate" %>
<!DOCTYPE html>
<html xmlns="http://www.w3.org/1999/xhtml">
<head runat="server">
  <meta http-equiv="Content-Type" content="text/html; charset=utf-8" />
  <title> To Apply template fields of GridView</title>
</head>
<body>
  <form id="form1" runat="server">
    <div>
<asp:GridView ID="gvProduct" runat="server" AllowPaging="True"AutoGenerateColumns="False"
DataKeyNames="ProductId" DataSourceID="ldsProduct" PageSize="5">
        <Columns>
          <asp:TemplateField>
            <ItemTemplate>
              <asp:CheckBox ID="chkItem" runat="server" />
            </ItemTemplate>
            <HeaderTemplate>
              <asp:CheckBox ID="chkAll" runat="server" AutoPostBack="True" Text="ChkAll"
OnCheckedChanged="ChkAll_CheckedChanged" />
            </HeaderTemplate>
          </asp:TemplateField>
          <asp:BoundField DataField="ProductId" HeaderText="ProductId" InsertVisible="False"
ReadOnly="True" />
          <asp:TemplateField HeaderText="ProductId">
            <ItemTemplate>
              <asp:Label ID="lblCategoryId" runat="server" Text='<%#
Bind("CategoryId") %>'></asp:Label>
            </ItemTemplate>
            <EditItemTemplate>
              <asp:DropDownList ID="ddlCategory" runat="server" DataSourceID="ldsCategory"
DataTextField="Name" DataValueField="CategoryId" SelectedValue='<%# Bind("CategoryId") %>'>
               </asp:DropDownList>
               <asp:LinqDataSource ID="ldsCategory" runat="server"
ContextTypeName="MyPetShopDataContext" TableName="Category">
               </asp:LinqDataSource>
            </EditItemTemplate>
          </asp:TemplateField>
          <asp:BoundField DataField="ListPrice" HeaderText="ListPrice" />
          <asp:BoundField DataField="Name" HeaderText="Name" />
          <asp:BoundField DataField="Qty" HeaderText="Qty" />
          <asp:CommandField ShowEditButton="True" />
        </Columns>
```

```
    </asp:GridView>
    <asp:LinqDataSource ID="ldsProduct" runat="server" ContextTypeName="MyPetShopDataContext"
EnableUpdate="True" TableName="Product">
    </asp:LinqDataSource>
    <asp:Button ID="btnSubmit" runat="server" Text="OK" OnClick="BtnSubmit_Click" />
    <asp:Label ID="lblProductId" runat="server"></asp:Label>
   </div>
  </form>
</body>
</html>
```

Source Codes: GridTemplate .aspx.cs

```
using System;
using System.Web.UI.WebControls;
public partial class Chap7_GridTemplate : System.Web.UI.Page
{
 protected void ChkAll_CheckedChanged(object sender, EventArgs e)
 {
  CheckBox chkAll = (CheckBox)sender;
  foreach (GridViewRow gvRow in gvProduct.Rows)
  {
   CheckBox chkItem = (CheckBox)gvRow.FindControl("chkItem");
   chkItem.Checked = chkAll.Checked;
  }
 }
 protected void BtnSubmit_Click(object sender, EventArgs e)
 {
  lblProductId.Text = "The ProductId you select is: ";
  foreach (GridViewRow gvRow in gvProduct.Rows)
  {
   CheckBox chkItem = (CheckBox)gvRow.FindControl("chkItem");
   if (chkItem.Checked)
   {
    lblProductId.Text += gvRow.Cells[1].Text + ", ";
   }
  }
 }
}
```

Operating Steps:

(1) Creating GridTemplate.aspx in Chap7 folder, adding one GridView control, one LinqDataSource control, one Button control and one Label control, and setting the values of attribute ID of each control referencing the source program.

(2) Configuring the data source of LinqDataSource control to be Product table, then setting the value of attribute EnableUpdate to be true and binding to the GridView.

(3) In the dialog box of the GridView, setting Columns attribute, adding a column of CommandField with editing, updating and canceling and a column of TemplatField, adjusting the field location of TemplatField, then converting the CategoryId to TemplatField.

(4) Clicking the smart tag of GridView, selecting "Edit Template"→ "Column[0]", the interface as shown in the Figure 7-11 is presented. Adding one CheckBox control in the content field of ItemTemplate and HeaderTemplate separately, and setting the attributes of each control referencing the source program.

(5) Selecting "Column[2]-ProductId" option, the interface as shown in the Figure 7-12 is presented. In the content field of ItemTemplate, the attribute ID of Label control is set. In the content field of EditItemTemplate, the original TextBox control is deleted, adding one DropDownList control and one LinqDataSource control, and setting the values of attribute ID of each control referencing the source program. Configuring the data source of LinqDataSource control to be Category table and binding to DropDownList control. The data field displayed on DropDownList control is Name, and the data field of value is CategoryId. Clicking the smart tag of DropDownList control, and selecting "Edit DataBindings" option, as shown in the Figure 7-13 is presented. In Figure 7-13, the custom binding code expression that is Bind("CategoryId") is entered, which binds the attribute SelectedValue to CategoryId, clicking "OK" button to complete the binding.

(6) Creating GridTemplate.aspx.cs. At last, browsing the GridTemplate.aspx and testing it.

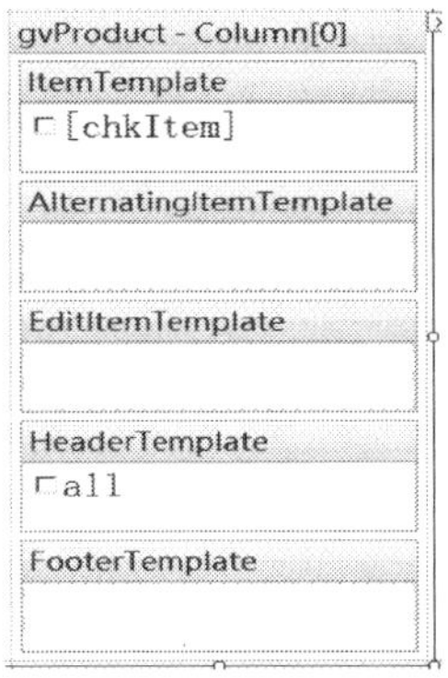

Figure7-11 The Edition Interface of "Column[0]" Template

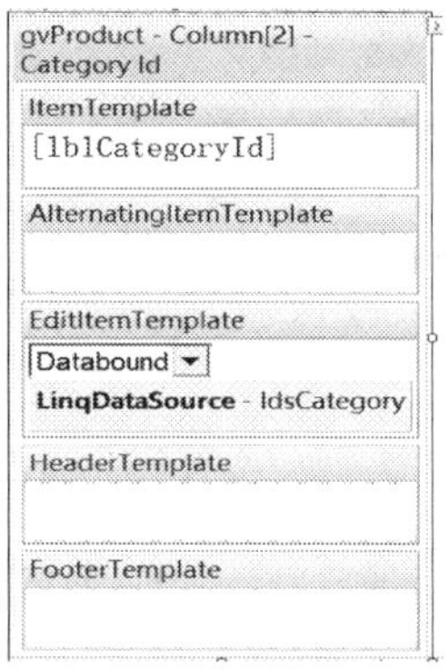

Figure7-12 The Edition Interface of "Column[2]" Template

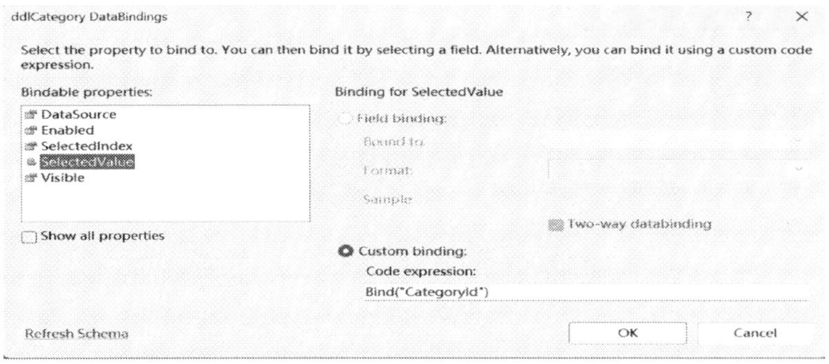

Figure7-13 The Interface of Edit DataBindings

Program description:

ChkAll_ CheckedChanged() method sets the state of all check boxes in the data row of GridView to the same state as the check boxes in the header row of GridView.BtnSubmit_ Click () method gets the numbers of all of the selected goods.

You cannot directly access the controls of each template in the template field. You need to use the FindControl() method to find them in the GridViewRow object of the GridView control to access these controls.

7.3.4 Editing and deleting data by using GridView

Clicking the smart tag of the GridView, and selecting "Enable Edit" and "Enable Delete" options to provide the functions of data editing and data deletion. Of course, the data source control bound to the GridView should also provide the functions of updating and deletion. At this time, when the user clicks "Delete" hyperlink button, the system will delete the data of the table without any prompts, that can lead to errors. We can solve this problem by adding JavaScript codes.

Example 7-6 Adding prompts of the client for the "delete" hyperlink button in GridView

As is shown in Figure7-14, when the user clicks the "Delete" button to delete a row of data, the system will give a prompt for the user to confirm.

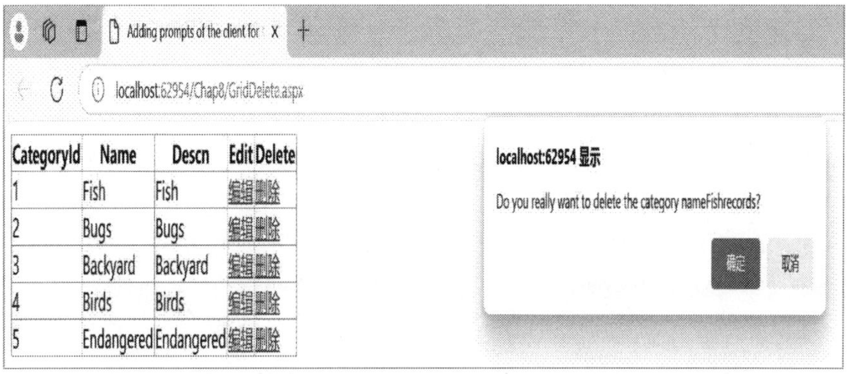

Figure7-14 The Browsing Effect of GridTemplate.aspx

Source Codes: GridDelete.aspx

```
<%@ Page Language="C#" AutoEventWireup="true" CodeFile="GridDelete.aspx.cs"
Inherits="Chap7_GridDelete" %>
<!DOCTYPE html>
<html xmlns="http://www.w3.org/1999/xhtml">
<head runat="server">
  <meta http-equiv="Content-Type" content="text/html; charset=utf-8" />
  <title>To add prompts of the client for the "delete" hyperlink button in GridView</title>
</head>
<body>
```

```
    <form id="form1" runat="server">
     <div>
       <asp:GridView ID="gvCategory" runat="server" AutoGenerateColumns="False"
DataKeyNames="CategoryId" DataSourceID="ldsCategory"
 OnRowDataBound="GvCategory_RowDataBound">
         <Columns>
           <asp:BoundField DataField="CategoryId" HeaderText="CategoryId" InsertVisible="False"
ReadOnly="True" />
           <asp:BoundField DataField="Name" HeaderText="Name" />
           <asp:BoundField DataField="Descn" HeaderText="Descn" />
           <asp:CommandField ShowEditButton="True" HeaderText="Edit" />
           <asp:CommandField HeaderText="Delete" ShowDeleteButton="True" />
         </Columns>
       </asp:GridView>
       <asp:LinqDataSource ID="ldsCategory" runat="server"
ContextTypeName="MyPetShopDataContext" EnableDelete="True" EnableUpdate="True"
TableName="Category">
       </asp:LinqDataSource>
     </div>
    </form>
</body>
</html>
```

Source Codes: GridDelete.aspx.cs

```
using System.Web.UI.WebControls;
public partial class Chap7_GridDelete : System.Web.UI.Page
{
  protected void GvCategory_RowDataBound(object sender, GridViewRowEventArgs e)
  {
    if (e.Row.RowType == DataControlRowType.DataRow)
    {
      try
      {
        LinkButton lnkbtnDelete = (LinkButton)e.Row.Cells[4].Controls[0];
        lnkbtnDelete.OnClientClick = "return confirm('Do you want to delete the name of Category " +
  e.Row.Cells[1].Text + " record?');";
      }
      catch
      {
      }
    }
  }
}
```

Operating Steps:

(1) Creating GridDelete.aspx in Chap7 folder, adding one GridView control and one LinqDataSource control, and setting the values of attribute ID of each control referencing the source program.

(2) Configuring the data source of LinqDataSource control to be Category table, then setting the value of attribute EnableUpdate and EnableDelete to be true and binding to the GridView.

(3) In the dialog box of the GridView, setting Columns attribute, and adding two columns of CommandField, one of them includes "Edit, Update and Cancel", and the other includes "Delete"

(4) Creating GridDelete.aspx.cs. At last, browsing the GridDelete.aspx and testing it.

Program description:

The CategoryId field in the Category table is the primary key. This information is contained in the attribute DataKeyNames of the GridView. The CategoryId field has been set as an identifier. The value of this field will be generated automatically and cannot be edited. Therefore, the binding column corresponding to this field should be set as InsertVisible="False" and ReadOnly="True".

The RowDataBound event of GridView is triggered when data is bound to rows respectively. Because after the "Edit" hyperlink button is clicked, "Delete" button will not exist. At this time, "Delete" button object will not be able to be accessed, so the operation in the catch block will be executed when the user clicks the "Edit "button by using the "try... catch" structure. The e.Row in the events codes can return the row object of the "Delete" button. RowType is used to determine the row type in the GridView, whose values include DataRow, Footer, Header, EmptyDataRow, Pager (navigation) and the Separator. The Cells collection returns all of the cell objects in the specified row, and the Controls collection returns all of the control objects in the specified cell.

Example 7-7 Updating data by combining GridView with independent pages

As is shown in Figure7-15 and Figure7-16, after the user clicks the "Update" hyperlink, the data corresponding to the row will be updated in another separate page.

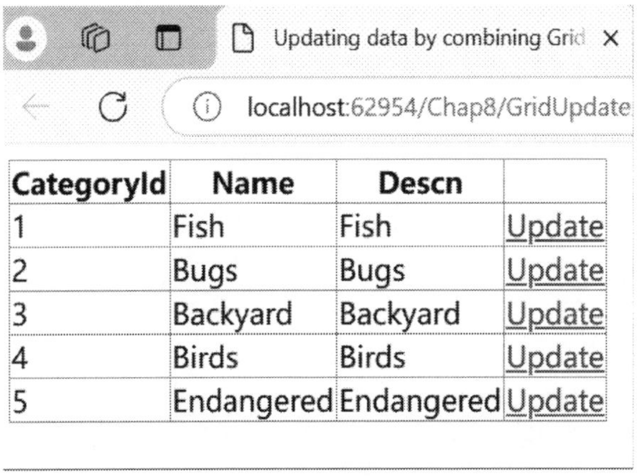

Figure7-15 The Browsing Effect of GridUpdate.aspx

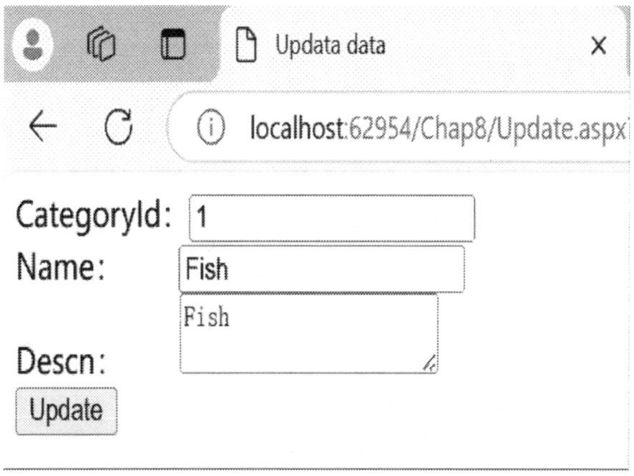

Figure 7-16 The Updating Data Interface of Independent page

Source Codes: GridUpdate.aspx

```
<%@ Page Language="C#" AutoEventWireup="true" CodeFile="GridUpdate.aspx.cs"
Inherits="Chap7_GridUpdate" %>
<!DOCTYPE html>
<html xmlns="http://www.w3.org/1999/xhtml">
<head runat="server">
  <meta http-equiv="Content-Type" content="text/html; charset=utf-8" />
  <title>To update data by combining GridView and independent pages </title>
</head>
<body>
  <form id="form1" runat="server">
    <div>
      <asp:GridView ID="gvCategory" runat="server" AutoGenerateColumns="False">
        <Columns>
          <asp:BoundField DataField="CategoryId" HeaderText="CategoryId" />
          <asp:BoundField DataField="Name" HeaderText="Name" />
          <asp:BoundField DataField="Descn" HeaderText="Descn" />
          <asp:HyperLinkField DataNavigateUrlFields="CategoryId"
DataNavigateUrlFormatString="~/Chap8/Update.aspx?CategoryId={0}" Text="Update" />
        </Columns>
      </asp:GridView>
    </div>
  </form>
</body>
</html>
```

Source Codes: GridUpdate.aspx.cs

```
using System;
using System.Linq;
public partial class Chap8_GridUpdate : System.Web.UI.Page
{
  protected void Page_Load(object sender, EventArgs e)
  {
    MyPetShopDataContext db = new MyPetShopDataContext();
    var results = from r in db.Category
              select r;
    gvCategory.DataSource = results;
    gvCategory.DataBind();
  }
}
```

Source Codes: Update.aspx

```
<%@ Page Language="C#" AutoEventWireup="true" CodeFile="Update.aspx.cs"
Inherits="Chap7_Update" %>
<!DOCTYPE html>
<html xmlns="http://www.w3.org/1999/xhtml">
<head runat="server">
  <meta http-equiv="Content-Type" content="text/html; charset=utf-8" />
  <title>To update data</title>
</head>
<body>
  <form id="form1" runat="server">
    <div>
      CategoryId: <asp:TextBox ID="txtCategoryId" runat="server"></asp:TextBox><br />
      Name: <asp:TextBox ID="txtName" runat="server"></asp:TextBox><br />
Descn: <asp:TextBox ID="txtDescn" runat="server" TextMode="MultiLine"></asp:TextBox><br />
      <asp:Button ID="btnUpdate" runat="server" Text="Update" OnClick="BtnUpdate_Click" />
    </div>
  </form>
</body>
</html>
```

Source Codes: Update.aspx.cs

```
using System;
using System.Linq;
public partial class Chap7_Update : System.Web.UI.Page
{
  protected void Page_Load(object sender, EventArgs e)
  {
    if (!IsPostBack & Request.QueryString["CategoryId"] != null)
    {
      int categoryId = int.Parse(Request.QueryString["CategoryId"]);
      MyPetShopDataContext db = new MyPetShopDataContext();
      var category = (from r in db.Category
                where r.CategoryId == categoryId
                select r).First();
      txtCategoryId.ReadOnly = true;
      txtCategoryId.Text = category.CategoryId.ToString();
      txtName.Text = category.Name;
      txtDescn.Text = category.Descn;
    }
  }
```

```
protected void BtnUpdate_Click(object sender, EventArgs e)
{
  MyPetShopDataContext db = new MyPetShopDataContext();
  var category = (from r in db.Category
            where r.CategoryId == int.Parse(txtCategoryId.Text)
            select r).First();
  category.Name = txtName.Text;
  category.Descn = txtDescn.Text;
  db.SubmitChanges();
  Response.Redirect("~/Chap7/GridUpdate.aspx");
 }
}
```

Operating Steps:

(1) Creating GridUpdate.aspx in Chap7 folder, adding one GridView control, and setting the values of attribute ID and attribute AutoGenerateColumns referencing the source program separately.

(2) In the dialog box of the GridView setting Columns attribute, adding three columns of CommandField and one column of HyperLink Field, and setting the attributes of each filed referencing the source program.

(3) Creating GridUpdate.aspx.cs.

(4) Creating Update.aspx in Chap7 folder, adding all of the controls and setting the values of each control referencing the source program .

(5) Creating Update.aspx.cs. At last, browsing the GridUpdate.aspx and testing it.

Program description:

When GridUpdate.aspx is loaded for the first time, LINQ technology is used to query the Category table and bind the results to gvCategory. The value of attribute DataNavigateUrlFormatString of the HyperLinkField field determines the format of the target URL, where {0} will be replaced by the field value corresponding to DataNavigateUrlFields during page is browsed. Therefore, if you click the "Update" link in the row where the value of CategoryId is 13, the page will jump to~/Chap7/Update.aspx?CategoryId=13, where {0} has been replaced by the value of CategoryId.

When Update.aspx is loaded for the first time and the value of CategoryId in the query string is not empty, LINQ technology is used to query the record to be updated according to the value of CategoryId in the query string, then the values of each field in the record are displayed in the corresponding text box. After the user updates the data and clicks the "Update" button, LINQ technology is used to query the records to be updated according to the value of CategoryId in the txtCategoryId, then update the corresponding attributes according to the values in the txtName and txtDescn text boxes, and finally submit the updated results to the database for saving.

7.3.5 Displaying master/detail table

The situation of displaying the main/sub table often corresponds to the "one-to-many" relationship of the database. Such as a kind of classification of the product perhaps has multiple products, and a vendor can supply multiple products. In database, this situation should let user design multiple tables. If multiple tables should be displayed, the synchronization problems of the tables is involved. For example, if the category table of the products is displayed through one GridView, then when you select the category of a certain product, the other GridView will display all of the products included in this product category synchronously.

The master/detail table can be displayed on the same page or on the different pages according to actual needs.

Example 7-8 Displaying main/sub table on the same page

As is shown in Figure7-17, when clicking the "select" hyperlink button, the "sub table" will display all of the products contained in the different product categories in the "main table".

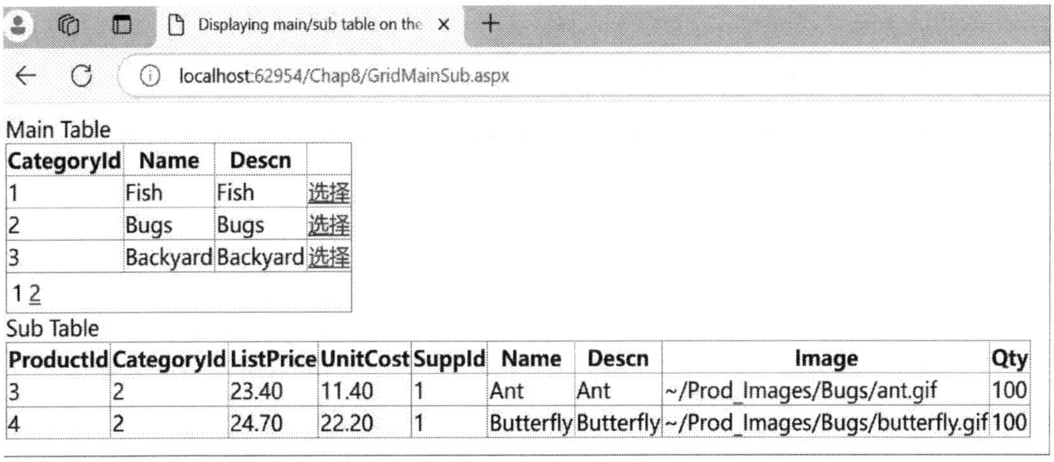

Figure 7-17 The Browsing Effect of GridMainSub.aspx

Source Codes: GridMainSub.aspx

```
<%@ Page Language="C#" AutoEventWireup="true" CodeFile="GridMainSub.aspx.cs"
Inherits="Chap7_GridMainSub" %>
<!DOCTYPE html>
<html xmlns="http://www.w3.org/1999/xhtml">
<head runat="server">
  <meta http-equiv="Content-Type" content="text/html; charset=utf-8" />
  <title>To display main/sub table on the same page </title>
</head>
<body>
  <form id="form1" runat="server">
    <div>
     Main Table
    <asp:GridView ID="gvCategory" runat="server" AllowPaging="True"AutoGenerateColumns="False"
 DataKeyNames="CategoryId" DataSourceID="ldsCategory" PageSize="3">
```

```
        <Columns>
          <asp:BoundField DataField="CategoryId" HeaderText="CategoryId" InsertVisible="False"
ReadOnly="True" />
          <asp:BoundField DataField="Name" HeaderText="Name" />
          <asp:BoundField DataField="Descn" HeaderText="Descn" />
          <asp:CommandField ShowSelectButton="True" />
        </Columns>
      </asp:GridView>
        Sub Table
      <asp:GridView ID="gvProduct" runat="server" AutoGenerateColumns="False"
DataKeyNames="ProductId" DataSourceID="ldsProduct">
        <Columns>
          <asp:BoundField DataField="ProductId" HeaderText="ProductId" />
          <asp:BoundField DataField="CategoryId" HeaderText="CategoryId" />
          <asp:BoundField DataField="ListPrice" HeaderText="ListPrice" />
          <asp:BoundField DataField="UnitCost" HeaderText="UnitCost" />
          <asp:BoundField DataField="SuppId" HeaderText="SuppId" />
          <asp:BoundField DataField="Name" HeaderText="Name" />
          <asp:BoundField DataField="Descn" HeaderText="Descn" />
          <asp:BoundField DataField="Image" HeaderText="Image" />
          <asp:BoundField DataField="Qty" HeaderText="Qty" />
        </Columns>
      </asp:GridView>
        <asp:LinqDataSource ID="ldsCategory" runat="server"
ContextTypeName="MyPetShopDataContext" TableName="Category">
        </asp:LinqDataSource>
        <asp:LinqDataSource ID="ldsProduct" runat="server" ContextTypeName="MyPetShopDataContext"
TableName="Product" Where="CategoryId == @CategoryId">
          <WhereParameters>
            <asp:ControlParameter ControlID="gvCategory" DefaultValue="1" Name="CategoryId"
PropertyName="SelectedValue" Type="Int32" />
          </WhereParameters>
        </asp:LinqDataSource>
      </div>
    </form>
</body>
</html>
```

Operating Steps:

(1) CreatingGridMainSub.aspx in Chap7 folder, adding one GridView control and one LinkDataSource control, and setting the values of attribute ID referencing the source program separately.

(2) Configuring the data source of LinqDataSource control to be Category table and binding to the gvCategory control, and clicking the smart tag of gvCategory control, selecting "Enable selected content"

option. The other attributes of gvCategory control can be set referencing the source program.

(3) Configuring the data source of ldsProduct control to be Product table, where expression can be set as Figure7-18. After finishing the configuration, ldsProduct control is bound to gvProduct control. At last, browsing the GridMainSub.aspx and testing it.

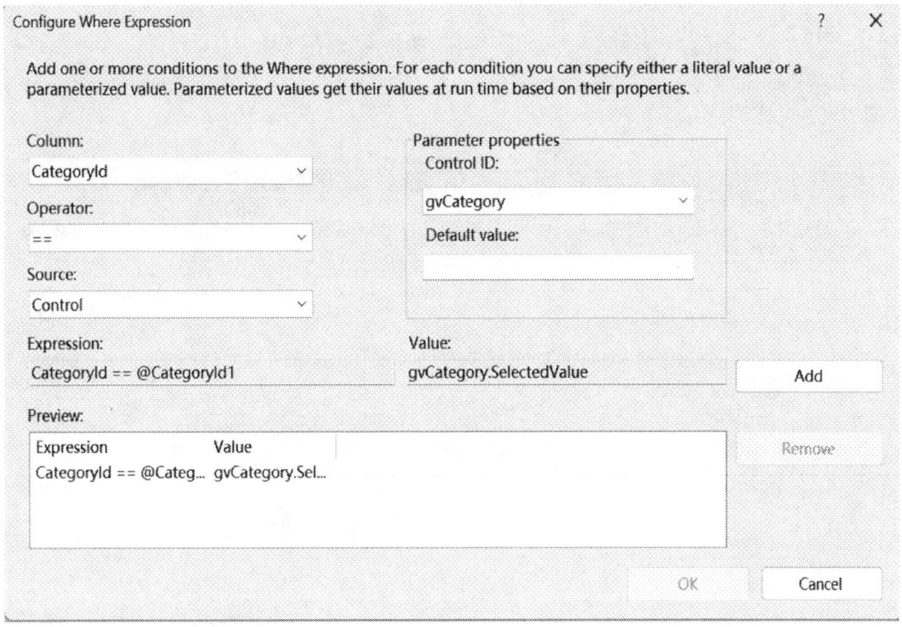

Figure 7-18 "Confirgure Where Expression" Dialog Box of ldsProduct Control

Program description:

When you click the "Select" link, the attribute gvCategory.SelectedValue returns the value of the primary key CategoryId corresponding to the selected row, and then passes this value to the parameter @ CategoryId of the query statement in ldsProduct.

Example 7-9 Displaying main/sub table on the different pages

As is shown in Figure7-19 and Figure7-20, when clicking the link in CategoryId field, the other page will display all of the products contained in the product category.

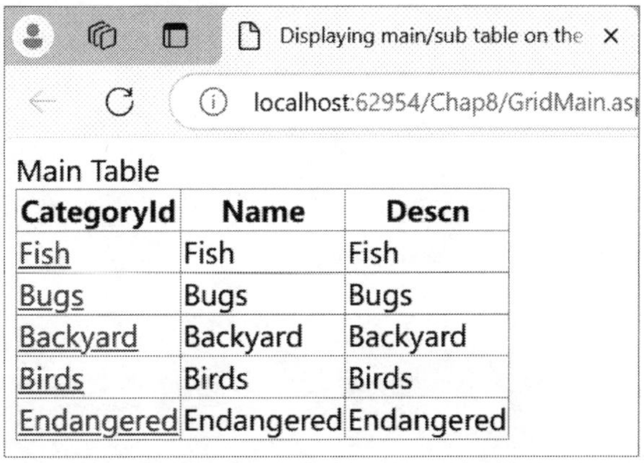

Figure 7-19 Displaying Main/Sub Table on The Different Pages (1)

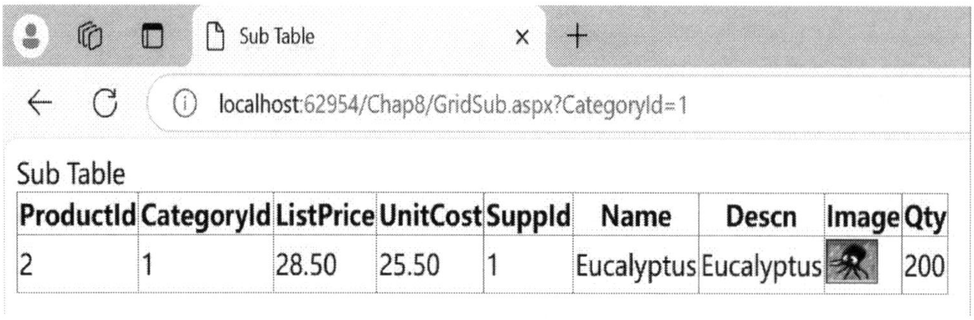

Figure 7-20 Displaying Main/Sub Table on The Different Pages (2)

Source Codes: GridMain.aspx

```
<%@ Page Language="C#" AutoEventWireup="true" CodeFile="GridMain.aspx.cs"
Inherits="Chap7_GridMain" %>
<!DOCTYPE html>
<html xmlns="http://www.w3.org/1999/xhtml">
<head runat="server">
  <meta http-equiv="Content-Type" content="text/html; charset=utf-8" />
  <title>To display main/sub table on the different pages</title>
</head>
<body>
  <form id="form1" runat="server">
    <div>
      Main Table
  <asp:GridView ID="gvCategory" runat="server" AutoGenerateColumns="false">
    <Columns>
      <asp:HyperLinkField DataNavigateUrlFields="CategoryId" DataNavigateUrlFormatString="~/
Chap8/GridSub.aspx?CategoryId={0}" DataTextField="Name"
 HeaderText="CategoryId" />
      <asp:BoundField DataField="Name" HeaderText="Name" />
      <asp:BoundField DataField="Descn" HeaderText="Descn" />
    </Columns>
  </asp:GridView>
    </div>
  </form>
</body>
</html>
```

Source Codes: GridMain.aspx.cs

```
using System;
using System.Linq;
public partial class Chap7_GridMain : System.Web.UI.Page
{
  protected void Page_Load(object sender, EventArgs e)
```

```
    {
      if (!IsPostBack)
      {
        MyPetShopDataContext db = new MyPetShopDataContext();
        var results = from r in db.Category
                      select r;
        gvCategory.DataSource = results;
        gvCategory.DataBind();
      }
    }
}
```

Source Codes: GridSub.aspx

```
<%@ Page Language="C#" AutoEventWireup="true" CodeFile="GridSub.aspx.cs"
Inherits="Chap7_GridSub" %>
<!DOCTYPE html>
<html xmlns="http://www.w3.org/1999/xhtml">
<head runat="server">
  <meta http-equiv="Content-Type" content="text/html; charset=utf-8" />
  <title>Sub Table</title>
</head>
<body>
  <form id="form1" runat="server">
    <div>
      Sub Table
    <asp:GridView ID="gvProduct" runat="server" AutoGenerateColumns="false">
      <Columns>
        <asp:BoundField DataField="ProductId" HeaderText="ProductId" />
        <asp:BoundField DataField="CategoryId" HeaderText="CategoryId" />
        <asp:BoundField DataField="ListPrice" HeaderText="ListPrice" />
        <asp:BoundField DataField="UnitCost" HeaderText="UnitCost" />
        <asp:BoundField DataField="SuppId" HeaderText="SuppId" />
        <asp:BoundField DataField="Name" HeaderText="Name" />
        <asp:BoundField DataField="Descn" HeaderText="Descn" />
        <asp:ImageField DataImageUrlField="Image" HeaderText="Image">
          <ControlStyle Height="25px" Width="35px" />
        </asp:ImageField>
        <asp:BoundField DataField="Qty" HeaderText="Qty" />
      </Columns>
    </asp:GridView>
    </div>
  </form>
</body>
</html>
```

Source Codes: GridSub.aspx.cs

```
using System;
using System.Linq;
public partial class Chap7_GridSub : System.Web.UI.Page
{
 protected void Page_Load(object sender, EventArgs e)
 {
   MyPetShopDataContext db = new MyPetShopDataContext();
   var results = from r in db.Product
           where r.CategoryId == int.Parse(Request.QueryString
["CategoryId"])
           select r;
   gvProduct.DataSource = results;
   gvProduct.DataBind();
 }
}
```

Operating Steps:

(1) Creating GridMain.aspx in Chap7 folder, adding one GridView control, and setting the values of attribute ID and attribute AutoGenerateColumns referencing the source program separately.

(2) In the dialog box of gvCategory control, setting attribute Columns, adding one column of HyperLinkField and two columns of BoundField, and setting the attributes of each filed referencing the source program.

(3) Creating GridMaine.aspx.cs.

(4) Creating GridSub.aspx in Chap7 folder, adding one GridView control, and setting the values of attribute ID and attribute AutoGenerateColumns referencing the source program separately.

(5) In the dialog box of gvProduct control, setting attribute Columns, adding eight columns of BoundField and one column of ImageField, and setting the attributes of each filed referencing the source program.

(6) Creating GridSub.aspx.cs. At last, browsing the GridMain.aspx and testing it.

Program description:

When clicking the link in the "Main Table" page, the corresponding query string is passed to the "Sub Table" page, and then the Product table is queried by using LINQ technology according to the value of CategoryId, and the query results are bound to gvProduct for displaying.

7.4 DetailsView Control

DetailsView control displays and operates the single record from data source in the form of table, and the table only contains two data columns. One is used to display each field name row by row, and the other is used to display the data value of the corresponding field name. DetailsView also increases the function of data insertion.

Example 7-10 Managing data by combining the GridView with DetailsView

As is shown in Figure7-21, after clicking "Details" hyperlink button in the GridView, in the DetailsView, the details of the record corresponding to the row where the "Details" link is located are displayed, then the record will be edited, deleted, and established in the DetailsView according to your needs.

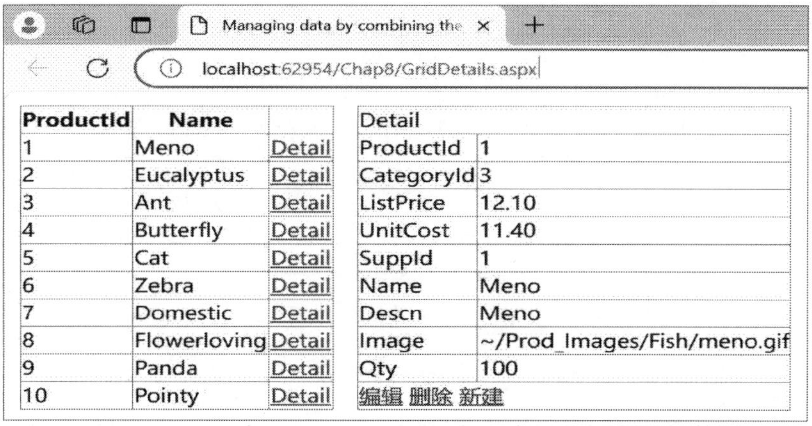

Figure 7-21 The Browsing Effect of GridDetails.aspx

Source Codes: GridDetails.aspx

```
<%@ Page Language="C#" AutoEventWireup="true" CodeFile="GridDetails.aspx.cs"
Inherits="Chap7_GridDetails" %>
<!DOCTYPE html>
<html xmlns="http://www.w3.org/1999/xhtml">
<head runat="server">
 <meta http-equiv="Content-Type" content="text/html; charset=utf-8" />
 <title>To manage data combining the GridView and DetailsView </title>
 <style type="text/css">
  .tdStyle {
   width: 244px;
  }
 </style>
</head>
<body>
 <form id="form1" runat="server">
  <div>
   <table>
    <tr>
     <td class="tdStyle">
      <asp:GridView ID="gvProduct" runat="server" AutoGenerateColumns="False"
DataKeyNames="ProductId" DataSourceID="ldsGrid">
       <Columns>
```

```
                <asp:BoundField DataField="ProductId" HeaderText="ProductId" />
                <asp:BoundField DataField="Name" HeaderText="Name" />
                <asp:CommandField SelectText="Details" ShowSelectButton="True" />
              </Columns>

            </asp:GridView>
          </td>
          <td>
            <asp:DetailsView ID="dvProduct" runat="server" AutoGenerateRows="False"
DataKeyNames="ProductId" DataSourceID="ldsDetails" HeaderText="Details"
OnItemDeleted="DvProduct_ItemDeleted" OnItemInserted="DvProduct_ItemInserted">
              <Fields>
                <asp:BoundField DataField="ProductId" HeaderText="ProductId" InsertVisible="false" />
                <asp:BoundField DataField="CategoryId" HeaderText="CategoryId" />
                <asp:BoundField DataField="ListPrice" HeaderText="ListPrice" />
                <asp:BoundField DataField="UnitCost" HeaderText="UnitCost" />
                <asp:BoundField DataField="SuppId" HeaderText="SuppId" />
                <asp:BoundField DataField="Name" HeaderText="Name" />
                <asp:BoundField DataField="Descn" HeaderText="Descn" />
                <asp:BoundField DataField="Image" HeaderText="Image" />
                <asp:BoundField DataField="Qty" HeaderText="Qty" />
                <asp:CommandField ShowDeleteButton="True" ShowEditButton="True"
ShowInsertButton="True" />
              </Fields>
            </asp:DetailsView>
          </td>
        </tr>
      </table>
    <asp:LinqDataSource ID="ldsGrid" runat="server" ContextTypeName="MyPetShopDataContext"
TableName="Product"></asp:LinqDataSource>
      <asp:LinqDataSource ID="ldsDetails" runat="server" ContextTypeName="MyPetShopDataCon
text"
 EnableDelete="True" EnableInsert="True" EnableUpdate="True" TableName="Product"
Where="ProductId == @ProductId">
        <WhereParameters>
          <asp:ControlParameter ControlID="gvProduct" DefaultValue="1" Name="ProductId"
PropertyName="SelectedValue" Type="Int32" />
        </WhereParameters>
      </asp:LinqDataSource>
    </div>
  </form>
</body>
</html>
```

Source Codes: GridDetails.aspx.cs

```
using System.Web.UI.WebControls;
public partial class Chap7_GridDetails : System.Web.UI.Page
{
 protected void DvProduct_ItemDeleted(object sender, DetailsViewDeletedEventArgs e)
 {
  gvProduct.DataBind();
 }
 protected void DvProduct_ItemInserted(object sender, DetailsViewInsertedEventArgs e)
 {
  gvProduct.DataBind();
 }
}
```

Operating Steps:

(1) Creating GridDetails.aspx in Chap7 folder. Inserting a table with 1 row and 2 columns for the page layout, and adding one GridView control and o ne DetailsView control in two cells separately. Adding two LinqDataSource controls outside the table, and setting the values of attribute ID referencing the source program separately.

(2) Configuring the data source of ldsGrid control to be Product table and binding to the gvProduct control, and selecting "Enable selected content" option of gvProduct. Deleting the other bound fields in the dialog box that is used to set the attribute Columns of gvProduct, only the Name field and ProductId field are kept.

(3) Configuring the data source of ldsDetails control to be Product table, where expression can be set as Figure7-22. After finishing the configuration, ldsDetails control is bound to dvProduct control. Clicking the smart tag of DetailsView, and selecting "Enable Insert", "Enable Delete" and "Enable Edit" option.

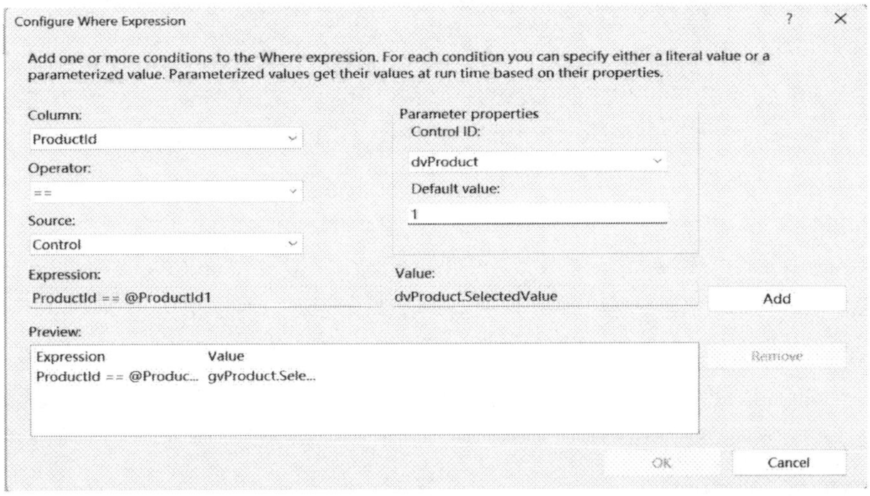

Figure 7-22 "Confirgure Where Expression" Dialog Box of ldsDetails Control

(4) Creating GridDetails.aspx.cs. At last, browsing the GridDetailsb.aspx and testing it.

Program description:

The ItemDeleted event is triggered after the record is deleted. At this time, the data in gvProduct needs to be refreshed again. The ItemInserted event is triggered after the record is inserted. At this time, the data in gvProduct needs to be refreshed again.

7.5 Summary

- ListControl class: providing the form of displaying data in a list;
- GridView: providing the form of displaying data in two-dimensional tables;
- DetailsView: providing the form of displaying data in a single record.
- ListView: displaying multiple records.
- DataList: a kind of data list control that completely uses the templates.
- FormView: displaying a single record that is completely realized through the template.

7.6 Exercises

1. True or False Questions

(1) If you want to display the value of LoginName by using <%#LoginName%>, you must call the Page.DataBind() method.(　　)

(2) GridView control has the built-in insertion function.(　　)

(3) Any type of controls can be used in the column of template.(　　)

(4) The binding method of template column must be the format of <%Eval("Name")%> or <%Bind("Name")%> .(　　)

(5) DetailsView can display multiple records simultaneously through setting .(　　)

2. Multiple Choice Questions

(1) If you want to display the "Previous page" and "Next page" navigation bars in GridView control, the Mode property within the PageSettings property set should be set to (　　).

A.Numeric　　B.NextPrevious　　C.NextPrev　　D.Previous page, Next Page

(2) If you want to implement sorting function in the GridView control after customizing data columns, in addition to setting the AllowSorting property of the GridView to be True, you should also configure the (　　) property.

A.SortExpression　　B.Sort　　C.SortField　　D.DataFieldText

(3) When displaying main-sub table data by using the GridView and DetailsView, if refreshing the GridView necessarily when inserting a record in the DetailsView, the DataBind() method in the GridView should be placed in the(　　) even codes.

A.ItemInserting of GridView　　B.ItemInserted of GridView　　C.ItemInserting of DetailsView

D.ItemInserted of DetailsView

3. Programming Questions

(1) Create and debug all of the instances in this chapter.

(2) Use the combination of GridView and DetailsView controls to display the Product table on

different pages. The DetailsView should support operations such as insertion, editing, and deletion, and include a drop-down list box for selecting foreign key data during data insertion.

(3) The FormView control is used to display and edit records in the Order table that meet custom-defined conditions.

(4) The ListView control is used to display and edit data from Product table, and it also provides the pagination function at the same time (combining it with the DataPager control).

Chapter 8 Three-Layer Framework of ASP.NET

Points:

- Understanding three-layer framework of ASP.NET and be able to use it skillfully
- Understanding and mastering the user management method based on three-layer framework of ASP.NET

8.1 Summary of Three-layer Framework of ASP.NET

Web forms contain. aspx files for interface displaying codes and. aspx.cs files for event handling codes. In essence, the Web form is a typical two-layer framework. This framework adopts the way that the user interface directly interacts with the database, and carries out business logic processing and other work at the same time. It is characterized by high data access rate and low complexity of Web application development. While the two-layer framework also has the characteristics of high coupling, poor system scalability and is not conducive to the division of labor and cooperation of the project team, so usually, an intermediate layer is added to the two-layer framework to realize business logic processing, and forming a three-layer framework.

As is shown in Figure 8-1, Web application program is divided into three layers when you use three-layer framework of ASP.NET: Web, BLL and DAL.

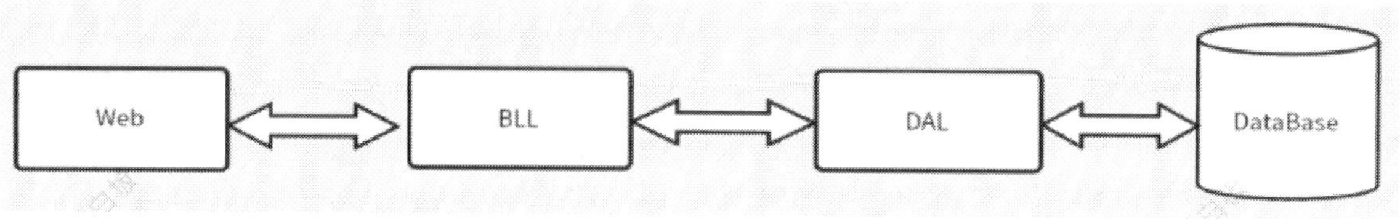

Figure 8-1 Three-layer Framework of ASP.NET

According to Web applications developed through different technologies of data access, ASP.NET three-layer framework has different members. For example, if you use Connection, Command, DataReader, DataAdapter, and DataSet objects in ADO.NET to operate the database, the business entity project Model and database access general project DBUtility, etc will be added. If you use LINQ to SQL technology to operate the database, because LINQ to SQL has encapsulated some operations such as data searching, insertion, updating and deletion, only Web, BLL and DAL are required.

8.2 Building Three-layer Framework of ASP.NET

This section takes MyPetShop as an example to illustrate the process of building a Web application based on ASP.NET three-layer framework, in which LINQ technology is used for access data .

Example 8-1 Building MyPetShop based on three-layer framework of ASP.NET

As is shown in Figure 8-2, MyPetShop based on three-layer framework of ASP.NET includes MyPetShop.Web, MyPetShop.BLL and MyPetShop.DAL.

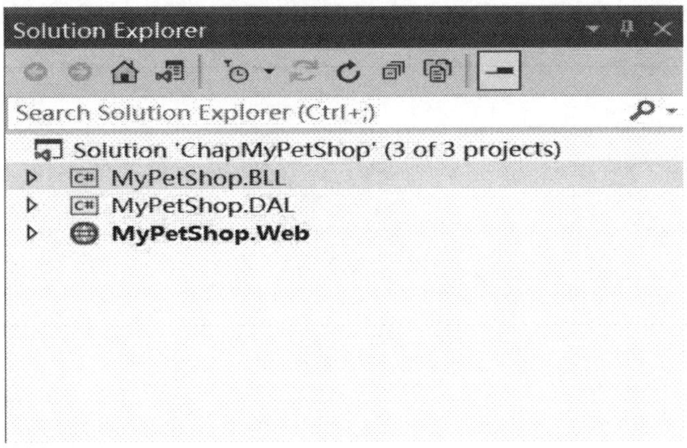

Figure 8-2 The Three-layer Framework of ASP.NET

Operating Steps:

(1) Creating ChapMyPetShop solution. New a ChapMyPetShop solution in C:\ASPNET folder, as is shown in Figure 8-3.

Figure 8-3 Newing ChapMyPetShop solution

(2) Adding MyPetShop.Web project. Adding MyPetShop.Web project in ChapMyPetShop solution

through selecting "ASP.NET empty site", as is shown in Figure 8-4.

Figure 8-4 Adding MyPetShop.Web Project

(3)Adding MyPetShop.BLL project.Right, clicking "Solution ChapMyPetShop" in "Solution Explorer" window, selecting "Add"→ "New Project" command in the pop-up shortcut menu, then selecting"Class Library(.NET Framework)" template in the rendered dialog, and entering name MyPetShop.BLL, as is shown in Figure 8-5. At last, clicking "Create" button, adding MyPetShop.BLL project.

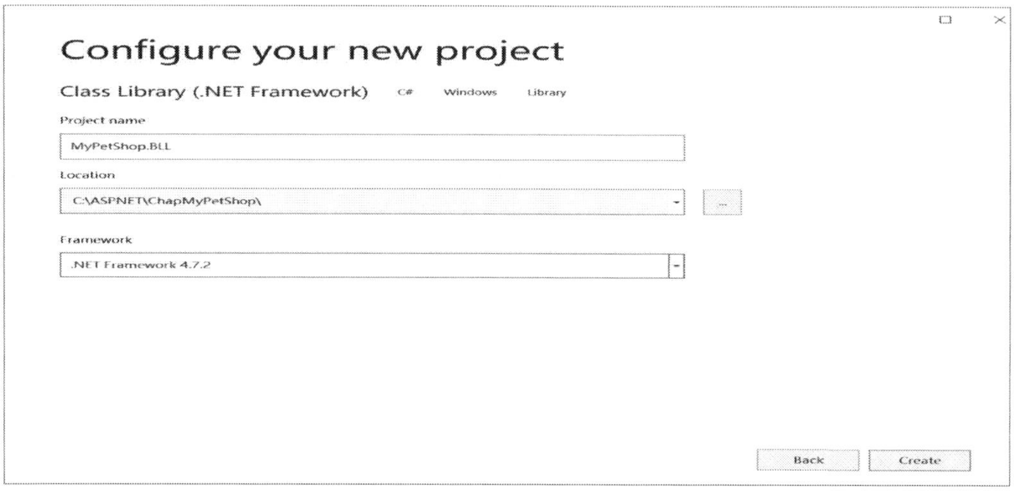

Figure 8-5 Adding MyPetShop.BLL Project

(4) Adding MyPetShop.DAL project. That is similar to the process of adding MyPetShop.BLL project, and changing the project name to be MyPetShop.DAL, as is shown in Figure 8-6, then clicking "Create" button, adding MyPetShop.DAL project in ChapMyPetShop solution.

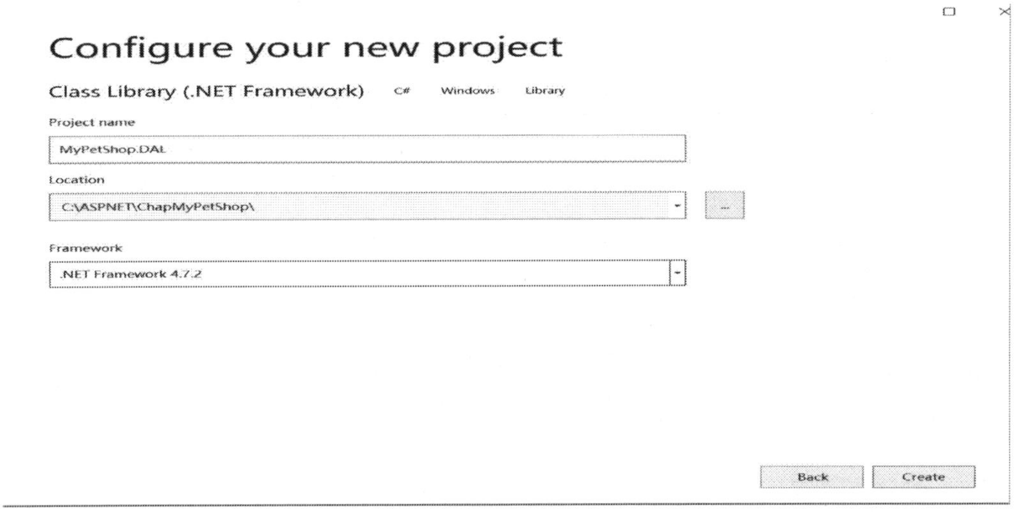

Figure 8-6 Adding MyPetShop.DAL Project

(5) Adding references at each level. According to the principle of three-layer framework of ASP. NET, MyPetShop.Web project in ChapMyPetShop solution need to reference MyPetShop.BLL project, while MyPetShop.BLL project need to reference MyPetShop.DAL project. The specific operations are as follows: For MyPetShop.Web project, right clicking MyPetShop.Web in Figure 8-2, selecting "Add"→ "Reference" command, selecting "Project"→MyPetShop.BLL in the rendered dialog, as is shown in Figure 8-7, then clicking "OK" button to establish the call relationship. For MyPetShop.BLL project, right clicking MyPetShop.BLL in Figure 8-2, selecting "Add"→ "Reference" command in the pop-up shortcut menu, selecting "Project"→MyPetShop.DAL in the rendered dialog, as is shown in Figure 8-8, then clicking "OK" button to establish the call relationship.

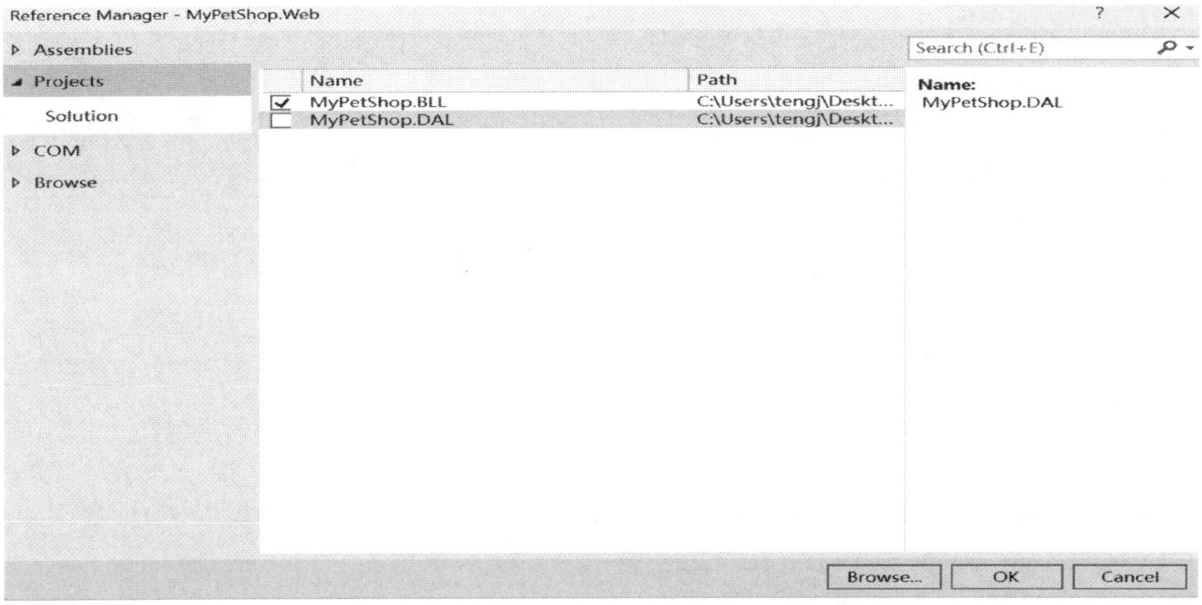

Figure 8-7 MyPetShop.Web Project Referencing MyPetShop.BLL Project

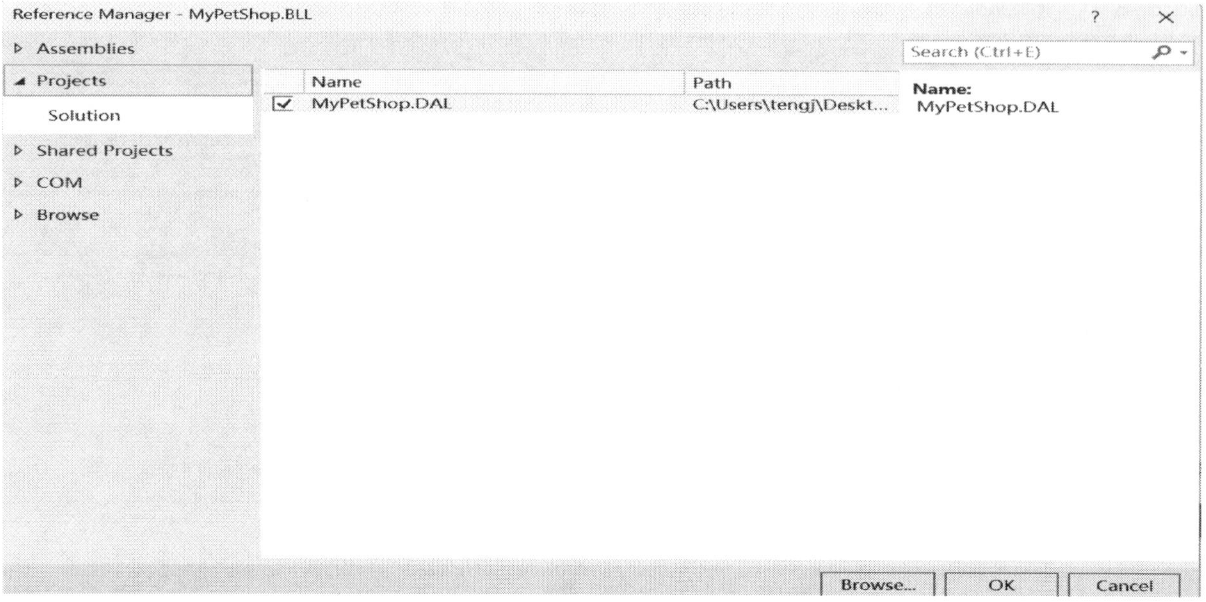

Figure 8-8 MyPetShop.BLL Project Referencing MyPetShop.DAL Project

8.3 User Management Based on Three-layer Framework of ASP.NET

User management is the function any Web application must include. This section will introduce the programming idea of three-layer framework of ASP.NET through User management.

8.3.1 User registration

A Web application usually provides the different functions according to the different users, so user registration is a prerequisite for normal usage of Web applications. The user registration needs to obtain the user name, email, password and other registration information from the presentation layer firstly, and then call the corresponding methods in the data access layer through the user name check, user addition and other methods in the business logic layer to realize the user name duplicate query, user record insertion and other operations in the database.

Example 8-2 Realizing the user registration of MyPetShop

As is shown in Figure 8-9, user name, email, password and confirmed password are required information. The email address entered must comply with the rules, and the password entered must be consistent with the confirmed password. After clicking the "Register Now" button, it will be checked whether the entered user name is the same as the user name contained in the MyPetShop database. If the name is the same, the message "The user name already exists!" will be displayed. Otherwise, a new user record will be inserted into the MyPetShop database. When you click the "I want to log in" link, you will jump to the user login page Login.aspx and pass the registered user name to Login.aspx.

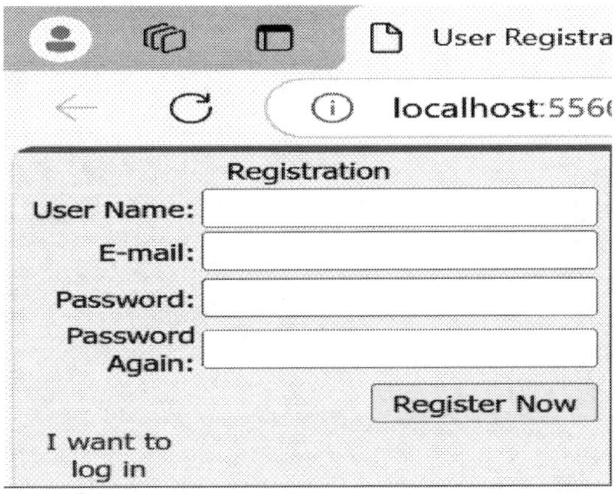

Figure 8-9 User Registration Interface of MyPetShop

Source Codes: CustomerService.cs

```
using MyPetShop.DAL;
using System.Collections.Generic;
using System.Linq;
namespace MyPetShop.BLL
{
 public class CustomerService
 {
  MyPetShopDataContext db = new MyPetShopDataContext();
  public int CheckLogin(string name, string password)
  {
    Customer customer = (from c in db.Customer
                   where c.Name == name && c.Password == password
                   select c).FirstOrDefault();
   if (customer != null)
   {
    return customer.CustomerId;
   }
   else
   {
    return 0;
   }
  }
  public void ChangePassword(int customerId, string password)
  {
   Customer customer = (from c in db.Customer
                   where c.CustomerId == customerId
                   select c).First();
   customer.Password = password;
   db.SubmitChanges();
  }
  public void ResetPassword(string name, string email)
```

```
    {
     Customer customer = (from c in db.Customer
                  where c.Name == name && c.Email == email
                  select c).First();
     customer.Password = name;
     db.SubmitChanges();
    }
    public bool IsNameExist(string name)
    {
     Customer customer = (from c in db.Customer
                  where c.Name == name
                  select c).FirstOrDefault();
     if (customer != null)
     {
      return true;
     }
     else
     {
      return false;
     }
    }
    public bool IsEmailExist(string name, string email)
    {
     Customer customer = (from c in db.Customer
                  where c.Name == name && c.Email == email
                  select c).FirstOrDefault();
     if (customer != null)
     {
      return true;
     }
     else
     {
      return false;
     }
    }
    public void Insert(string name, string password, string email)
    {
     Customer customer = new Customer
     {
      Name = name,
      Password = password,
      Email = email
     };
     db.Customer.InsertOnSubmit(customer);
     db.SubmitChanges();
    }
  }
}
```

Source Codes: NewUser.aspx

```
<%@ Page Language="C#" AutoEventWireup="true" CodeFile="NewUser.aspx.cs"
Inherits="NewUser" %>
<!DOCTYPE html>
<html xmlns="http://www.w3.org/1999/xhtml">
<head runat="server">
  <meta http-equiv="Content-Type" content="text/html; charset=utf-8" />
  <title>User Registration</title>
  <link href="~/Styles/Style.css" rel="stylesheet" type="text/css" />
</head>
<body>
  <form id="form1" runat="server">
    <div class="leftside">
      <table style="border-collapse: collapse;">
        <tr>
          <td class="tdcenter" colspan="2">Registration</td>
        </tr>
        <tr>
          <td class="tdright">User Name:</td>
          <td>
            <asp:TextBox ID="txtName" runat="server"></asp:TextBox></td>
          <td>
            <asp:RequiredFieldValidator ControlToValidate="txtName" Display="Dynamic"
ForeColor="Red" ID="rfvName" runat="server" ErrorMessage=" 必填
"></asp:RequiredFieldValidator>
          </td>
        </tr>
        <tr>
          <td class="tdright">Email:</td>
          <td>
            <asp:TextBox ID="txtEmail" runat="server"></asp:TextBox></td>
          <td>
            <asp:RequiredFieldValidator ControlToValidate="txtEmail" Display="Dynamic"
ForeColor="Red" ID="rfvEmail" runat="server" ErrorMessage=" 必填
"></asp:RequiredFieldValidator>
          </td>
        </tr>
        <tr>
          <td class="tdright" colspan="2">
            <asp:RegularExpressionValidator ID="revEmail" runat="server" ErrorMessage="Format is
Error!" ControlToValidate="txtEmail" Display="Dynamic" ForeColor="Red"
ValidationExpression="\w+([-+.']\w+)*@\w+([-.]\w+)*\.\w+([-.]\w+)*">
            </asp:RegularExpressionValidator>
          </td>
        </tr>
        <tr>
          <td class="tdright">Password:</td>
          <td>
```

```
            <asp:TextBox ID="txtPwd" runat="server" TextMode="Password"></asp:TextBox></td>
          <td>
            <asp:RequiredFieldValidator ControlToValidate="txtPwd" Display="Dynamic"
ForeColor="Red" ID="rfvPwd" runat="server" ErrorMessage=" 必填 "
></asp:RequiredFieldValidator>
          </td>
        </tr>
        <tr>
          <td class="tdright">Password again:</td>
          <td>
            <asp:TextBox ID="txtPwdAgain" runat="server"
 TextMode="Password"></asp:TextBox></td>
          <td>
            <asp:RequiredFieldValidator ControlToValidate="txtPwdAgain" Display="Dynamic"
ForeColor="Red" ID="rfvPwdAgain" runat="server" ErrorMessage=" 必填
></asp:RequiredFieldValidator>
          </td>
        </tr>
        <tr>
          <td class="tdright" colspan="2">
            <asp:CompareValidator ControlToValidate="txtPwdAgain" ControlToCompare="txtPwd"
                    Display="Dynamic" ForeColor="Red" ID="cvPwd" runat="server" ErrorMessage="2 密
              码不一致 "></asp:CompareValidator>
          </td>
        </tr>
        <tr>
          <td class="tdright" colspan="2">
           <asp:Button ID="btnReg" runat="server" Text="Register Now" OnClick="BtnReg_Click" />
          </td>
        </tr>
        <tr>
          <td><a href="Login.aspx">I want to login</a></td>
          <td>
            <asp:Label ID="lblMsg" runat="server" ForeColor="Red"></asp:Label></td>
        </tr>
      </table>
    </div>
  </form>
</body>
</html>
```

Source Codes: NewUser.aspx.cs

```
using MyPetShop.BLL;
using System;
using System.Web.UI;
public partial class NewUser : System.Web.UI.Page
```

```
{
 CustomerService customerSrv = new CustomerService();
 protected void BtnReg_Click(object sender, EventArgs e)
 {
  if (Page.IsValid)
  {
   if (customerSrv.IsNameExist(txtName.Text.Trim()))
   {
    lblMsg.Text = "User name has been exited!";
   }
   else
   {
    customerSrv.Insert(txtName.Text.Trim(), txtPwd.Text.Trim(), txtEmail.Text.Trim());
    Response.Redirect("Login.aspx?name=" + txtName.Text);
   }
  }
 }
}
```

Operating Steps:

(1) Because the ASP.NET validation is used, the implicit validation method that needs jQuery support referencing section 4.1 should be configured.

(2) Creating App_Data folder in MyPetShop.Web project, then adding MyPetShop database in this folder referencing section 6.2.

(3) Creating Styles folder in MyPetShop.Web project, then copying the Style.css file in MyPetShop\MyPetShop.Web \Styles folder into this folder.

(4) Creating MyPetShop.dbml file of LINQ to SQL class in MyPetShop.DAL project, then opening MyPetShop database, dragging all of data tables into the left window of object relationship designer of MyPetShop.dbml.

(5) As is shown in Figure 8-10, adding System.Data.Linq program set in MyPetShop.BLL project, then we can use LINQ to SQL to access MyPetShop database.

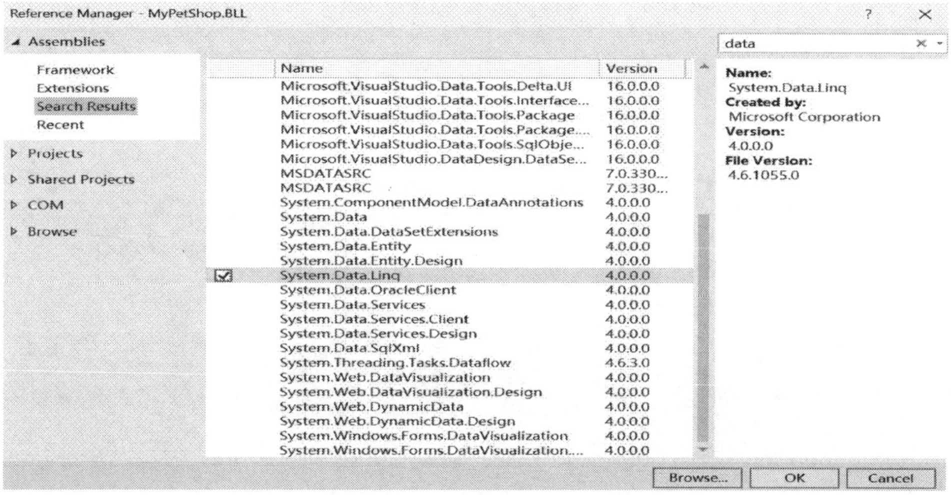

Figure 8-10 Adding System.Data.Linq program set in MyPetShop.BLL project

(6) Creating CustomerService.cs class file in MyPetShop.BLL project.

(7) Creating NewUser.aspx in MyPetShop.Web project, attaching Style.css style sheet under Styles folder referencing source codes, then adding <Table>element, every control and <a> element, setting <div>, <Table>, <a> elements and the attribute of each control.

(8) Creating NewUser.aspx.cs.

(9) Right clicking MyPetShop.Web project, selecting "Establishing Web Site" command, then compiling MyPetShop.Web project and MyPetShop.BLL project and MyPetShop.DAL project associated with it.

(10) Browsing NewUser.aspx and testing it.

8.3.2 User login

Usually, there are two situations for users to log in. One is that the user will be redirected from the user registration page to the user login page after successful registration; the other is that the user will access the user login page directly. The user name and password should be entered in the user login page at this time. User login needs to obtain the user name, password and other login information from the presentation layer firstly, and then call the corresponding methods in the data access layer to query the user login information in the database through the checking method of user name and password in the business logic layer.

Example 8-3 Realizing the user login of MyPetShop

When the user is successfully registered, clicking "I want to login" link in the Figure 8-9, the interface as is shown in Figure 8-11 is displayed; when the user accesses the login page directly, the interface as is shown in Figure 8-12 is displayed; when the user name or password is entered incorrectly, the interface as is shown in Figure 8-13 is displayed; when the administrator enters the user name and password correctly and then clicks "Login Now" button, the page will be jumped to ~/Admin/Default.aspx; when the average user enters the user name and password correctly and then clicks "Login Now" button, the page will be jumped to ~/Default.aspx; in addition, the user login interface also includes "I want to login!" and "Forget password!" link. After clicking them, the page will be jumped to NewUser.aspx and GetPwd.aspx.

Figure 8-11 User Login Interface After Registration is Successful

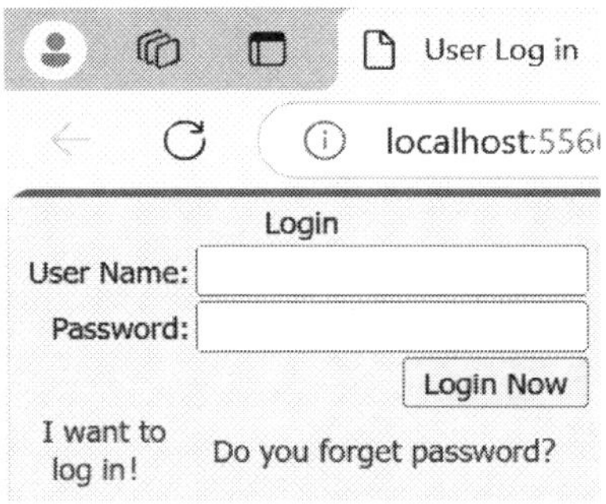

Figure8-12 User Login Interface That User Accesses Directly

Figure8-13 The Interface That User Name or Password is Error

Source Codes: CheckLogin() method of CustomerService.cs

```
public int CheckLogin(string name, string password)
   {
    Customer customer = (from c in db.Customer
                  where c.Name == name && c.Password == password
                  select c).FirstOrDefault();
    if (customer != null)
    {
     return customer.CustomerId;
    }
    else
    {
     return 0;
    }
   }
```

Source Codes: Login.aspx

```
 <%@ Page Language="C#" AutoEventWireup="true" CodeFile="Login.aspx.cs"
Inherits="Login" %>
<!DOCTYPE html>
<html xmlns="http://www.w3.org/1999/xhtml">
<head runat="server">
  <meta http-equiv="Content-Type" content="text/html; charset=utf-8" />
  <title>USer Login</title>
  <link href="~/Styles/Style.css" rel="stylesheet" type="text/css" />
</head>
<body>
  <form id="form1" runat="server">
   <div class="leftside">
    <table style="border-collapse: collapse;">
     <tr>
      <td class="tdcenter" colspan="2">Login</td>
     </tr>
     <tr>
      <td class="tdright">User Name:</td>
      <td>
       <asp:TextBox ID="txtName" runat="server"></asp:TextBox></td>
      <td>
       <asp:RequiredFieldValidator ControlToValidate="txtName" Display="Dynamic"
ForeColor="Red" ID="rfvName" runat="server" ErrorMessage=" 必填
"></asp:RequiredFieldValidator>
      </td>
     </tr>
     <tr>
      <td class="tdright">Password:</td>
      <td>
```

```
        <asp:TextBox ID="txtPwd" runat="server" TextMode="Password"></asp:TextBox></td>
       <td>
        <asp:RequiredFieldValidator ControlToValidate="txtPwd" Display="Dynamic"
ForeColor="Red" ID="rfvPwd" runat="server" ErrorMessage=" 必填
"></asp:RequiredFieldValidator>
       </td>
      </tr>
      <tr>
       <td colspan="2" class="tdright">
       <asp:Button ID="btnLogin" runat="server" Text="Login Now" OnClick="BtnLogin_Click"/>
       </td>
      </tr>
      <tr>
       <td><a href="NewUser.aspx">I want to register!</a></td>
       <td class="tdcenter"><a href="GetPwd.aspx">Forget Password ?  </a></td>
      </tr>
      <tr>
       <td colspan="2" class="tdright">
        <asp:Label ID="lblMsg" runat="server" ForeColor="Red"></asp:Label>
       </td>
      </tr>
     </table>
   </div>
  </form>
</body>
</html>
```

Source Codes: Login.aspx.cs

```
using MyPetShop.BLL;
using System;
using System.Web.UI;
public partial class Login : System.Web.UI.Page
{
 CustomerService customerSrv = new CustomerService();
 protected void Page_Load(object sender, EventArgs e)
 {
  if (!IsPostBack)
  {
   if (Request.QueryString["name"] != null)
   {
    txtName.Text = Request.QueryString["name"];
    lblMsg.Text = "Registration succeeded, please login!";
   }
  }
 }
 protected void BtnLogin_Click(object sender, EventArgs e)
 {
```

```
        if (Page.IsValid)
        {
          int customerId = customerSrv.CheckLogin(txtName.Text.Trim(), txtPwd.Text.Trim());
          if (customerId> 0)
          {
            Session.Clear();
            if (txtName.Text.Trim() == "admin")
            {
              Session["AdminId"] = customerId;
              Session["AdminName"] = txtName.Text;
              Response.Redirect("~/Admin/Default.aspx");
            }
            else
            {
              Session["CustomerId"] = customerId;
              Session["CustomerName"] = txtName.Text;
              Response.Redirect("~/Default.aspx");
            }
          }
          else
          {
            lblMsg.Text = "User Name or Password is error!";
          }
        }
      }
    }
```

Operating Steps:

(1) Adding CheckLogin() method in CustomerService.cs class file in MyPetShop.BLL project.

(2) Creating Login.aspx in MyPetShop.Web project, attaching Style.css style sheet under Styles folder referencing source codes, then adding <Table> element, every control and <a> element, and setting <div>, <Table>, <a> elements and the attributes of each control.

(3) Creating Login.aspx.cs.

(4) Right clicking MyPetShop.Web project, and executing "Establishing Web Site" command.

(5) Browsing NewUser.aspx and Login.aspx to test successful user login and direct access user login.

8.3.3 User login state and permission

In Web application, it is usually required to present different user login states and permissions according to anonymous users, general users and administrator users. If the user permission information is not saved in the database, you only need to obtain the user name information in the presentation layer, and then present the corresponding user login state and permission information.

Example 8-4 Presenting different user login states and permissions according to different users

When the user dosen't log in, the interface as is shown in Figure 8-14 is displayed; when the general user log in successfully, the interface as is shown in Figure 8-15 is displayed. Clicking "Password Change" and "Shopping Record" link buttons respectively, the page will be jumped to ~/ChangePwd. aspx, ~/OrderList.aspx; clicking "Exit Login" link button, Session variable is empty and the page is jumped to ~/Default.aspx. When the administrator user logs in successfully, the interface as is shown in Figure 8-16 is displayed. Clicking "System Administrator" link button, the page is jumped to ~/Admin/ Default.aspx; clicking "Exit Login" link button, the function the same as general user is executed.

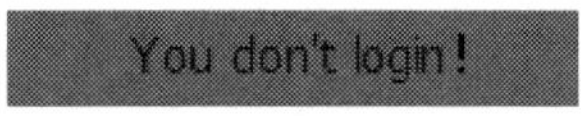

Figure 8-14
AnonymousUser Interface

Figure8-15
General User Interface

Figure8-16
Administrator User Interface

Source Codes: Default.aspx

```
<%@ Page Language="C#" AutoEventWireup="true" CodeFile="Default.aspx.cs" Inherits="_Default" %>
<!DOCTYPE html>
<html xmlns="http://www.w3.org/1999/xhtml">
<head runat="server">
  <meta http-equiv="Content-Type" content="text/html; charset=utf-8" />
  <title>User login state and permission</title>
  <link href="~/Styles/Style.css" rel="stylesheet" type="text/css" />
</head>
<body>
  <form id="form1" runat="server">
    <header class="header">
      <div class="status">
        <asp:Label ID="lblWelcome" runat="server" Text="You don't login!"></asp:Label>
        <asp:LinkButton ID="lnkbtnPwd" runat="server" ForeColor="White" Visible="false"
PostBackUrl="~/ChangePwd.aspx">Password Change</asp:LinkButton>
        <asp:LinkButton ID="lnkbtnManage" runat="server" ForeColor="White" Visible="false"
PostBackUrl="~/Admin/Default.aspx">System Management</asp:LinkButton>
        <asp:LinkButton ID="lnkbtnCart" runat="server" ForeColor="White" Visible="false"
PostBackUrl="~/OrderList.aspx">Shopping Record</asp:LinkButton>
        <asp:LinkButton ID="lnkbtnLogout" runat="server" ForeColor="White" Visible="false"
OnClick="LnkbtnLogout_Click">Exit Login</asp:LinkButton>
      </div>
    </header>
  </form>
</body>
</html>
```

Source Codes: Default.aspx.cs

```
using System;
public partial class _Default : System.Web.UI.Page
{
```

```
  protected void Page_Load(object sender, EventArgs e)

  {
   if (Session["AdminId"] != null || Session["CustomerId"] != null)
   {
    if (Session["AdminId"] != null)
    {
     lblWelcome.Text = "Hello, " + Session["AdminName"].ToString();
     lnkbtnManage.Visible = true;
    }
    else if (Session["CustomerId"] != null)
    {
     lblWelcome.Text = "Hello, " + Session["CustomerName"].ToString();
     lnkbtnPwd.Visible = true;
     lnkbtnCart.Visible = true;
    }
    lnkbtnLogout.Visible = true;
   }
  }
  protected void LnkbtnLogout_Click(object sender, EventArgs e)
  {
   Session.Clear();
   Response.Redirect("~/Default.aspx");
  }
}
```

Operating Steps:

(1) Creating Default.aspx in MyPetShop.Web project, attaching Style.css style sheet under Styles folder referencing source codes, then adding <Table> element, every control and <a> element, and setting <div>, <Table>, <a> elements and the attributes of each control.

(2) Creating Default.aspx.cs.

(3) Creating Admin folder in MyPetShop.Web project, and copying Default.aspx and Default.aspx.cs to Admin folder.

(4) For anonymous users, browsing the Default.aspx directly and testing it; for general users and administrator, browsing Login.aspx, entering the user name and password correctly, then clicking "Login Now" button and testing it.

8.3.4 User password changing

Usually, the function of user password changing can be provided after the user logs in successfully. Firstly, the original password, new password, confirming the new password and other information are obtained from the presentation layer, and then the corresponding methods in the data access layer are called through the methods in the business logic layer to implement the original password query in the database. If the original password entered is correct, then the corresponding methods in the data access layer are called through the methods in the business logic layer to implement the password changing in the database.

Example 8-5 Changing the password of the general users who have logged in

After the general user logs in successfully, clicking "Password Change" link button in the Figure 8-15, the function of password changing will be realized, the interface is shown as Figure 8-17.

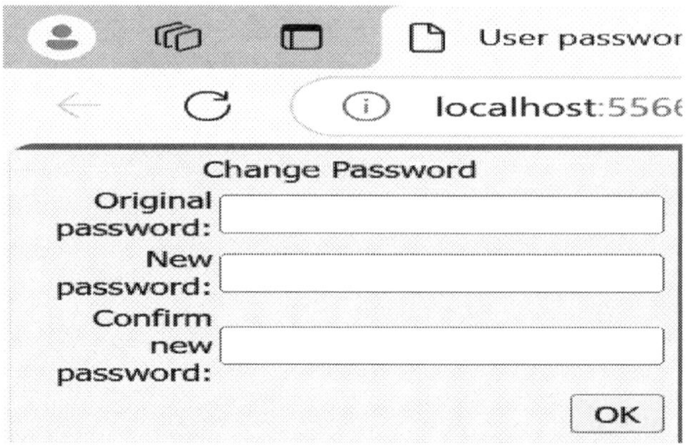

Figure8-17 Interface of User Password Changing

Source Codes: ChangePassword() method of CustomerService.cs

```
public void ChangePassword(int customerId, string password)
  {
   Customer customer = (from c in db.Customer
                 where c.CustomerId == customerId
                 select c).First();
   customer.Password = password;
   db.SubmitChanges();
  }
```

Source Codes: ChangePwd.aspx

```
<%@ Page Language="C#" AutoEventWireup="true" CodeFile="ChangePwd.aspx.cs"
Inherits="ChangePwd" %>
<!DOCTYPE html>
<html xmlns="http://www.w3.org/1999/xhtml">
<head runat="server">
 <meta http-equiv="Content-Type" content="text/html; charset=utf-8" />
 <title>User Password Changing</title>
 <link href="~/Styles/Style.css" rel="stylesheet" type="text/css" />
</head>
<body>
 <form id="form1" runat="server">
  <div class="leftside">
```

```
<table style="border-collapse: collapse;">
    <tr>
     <td class="tdcenter" colspan="2">Password Changing</td>
    </tr>
    <tr>
     <td class="tdright">Original Password:</td>
     <td>
      <asp:TextBox ID="txtOldPwd" runat="server" TextMode="Password"></asp:TextBox></td>
     <td>
       <asp:RequiredFieldValidator ControlToValidate="txtOldPwd" Display="Dynamic"
ForeColor="Red" ID="rfvOldPwd" runat="server" ErrorMessage=" 必填 ">
       </asp:RequiredFieldValidator>
     </td>
    </tr>
    <tr>
     <td class="tdright">New Password:</td>
     <td>
       <asp:TextBox ID="txtPwd" runat="server" TextMode="Password"></asp:TextBox></td>
     <td>
       <asp:RequiredFieldValidator ControlToValidate="txtPwd" Display="Dynamic"
ForeColor="Red" ID="rfvPwd" runat="server" ErrorMessage=" 必填 ">
       </asp:RequiredFieldValidator>
     </td>
    </tr>
    <tr>
     <td class="tdright">Confirming New Password:</td>
     <td>
    <asp:TextBox ID="txtPwdAgain" runat="server"
TextMode="Password"></asp:TextBox></td>
     <td>
       <asp:RequiredFieldValidator ControlToValidate="txtPwdAgain" Display="Dynamic"
ForeColor="Red" ID="rfvPwdAgain" runat="server" ErrorMessage=" 必填 ">
       </asp:RequiredFieldValidator>
     </td>
    </tr>
    <tr>
     <td class="tdright" colspan="2">
       <asp:CompareValidator ControlToValidate="txtPwdAgain" ControlToCompare="txtPwd"
    Display="Dynamic" ForeColor="Red" ID="cvPwd" runat="server" ErrorMessage="2 次新密
    码不一致 "></asp:CompareValidator>
     </td>
    </tr>
    <tr>
     <td class="tdright" colspan="2">
```

```
        <asp:Button ID="btnChangePwd" runat="server" Text="OK"
        OnClick="BtnChangePwd_Click" />
       </td>
      </tr>
      <tr>
       <td colspan="2">
        <asp:Label ID="lblMsg" runat="server" ForeColor="Red"></asp:Label></td>
      </tr>
     </table>
    </div>
   </form>
</body>
</html>
```

Source Codes: ChangePwd.aspx.cs

```
using MyPetShop.BLL;
using System;
using System.Web.UI;
public partial class ChangePwd : System.Web.UI.Page
{
 CustomerService customerSrv = new CustomerService();
 protected void Page_Load(object sender, EventArgs e)
 {
  if (Session["CustomerId"] == null)
  {
   Response.Redirect("~/Login.aspx");
  }
 }
 protected void BtnChangePwd_Click(object sender, EventArgs e)
 {
  if (Page.IsValid)
  {
   if (customerSrv.CheckLogin(Session["CustomerName"].ToString(), txtOldPwd.Text)> 0)
   {
    customerSrv.ChangePassword(Convert.ToInt32(Session["CustomerId"]), txtPwd.Text);
    lblMsg.Text = "Password Changing Successfully!";
   }
   else
   {
    lblMsg.Text = "The Original Password is incorrect!";
   }
  }
 }
}
```

Operating Steps:

(1) Adding ChangePassword() method in CustomerService.cs class file in MyPetShop.BLL project.

(2) Creating ChangePwd.aspx in MyPetShop.Web project, attaching Style.css style sheet under Styles folder referencing source codes, then adding <Table> element and every control, and setting <div>,<Table>elements and the attributes of each control.

(3) Creating ChangePwd.aspx.cs.

(4) Right clicking MyPetShop.Web project, and executing "Establishing Web Site" command.

(5) Browsing ChangePwd.aspx and testing it.

8.3.5 User password resetting

Firstly the user name, email and other information from the presentation layer are obtained, and then the corresponding methods in the data access layer are called through the methods in the business logic layer to realize the user name and email query operation in the database. If the user name and email entered are correct, the corresponding methods in the data access layer are called through the methods in the business logic layer to reset the user password in the database to be the corresponding user name, then the customized class in the presentation layer is called to send the password resetting email to the mailbox of the corresponding user. After receiving the password resetting email, users can obtain the reset password to log in.

Example 8-6 Resetting the user password

When the user forgets the password, clicking "Forget Pasword" link in Figure 8-11 or Figure 8-12, the page will be jumped to GetPwd.aspx, and the effect will be shown as in Figure 8-18. Entering the correct user name and email in Figure 8-18, clicking "Get Password" button, the window as is shown in Figure 8-19 is displayed.

Figure 8-18 Window of Resetting User ssword (1)

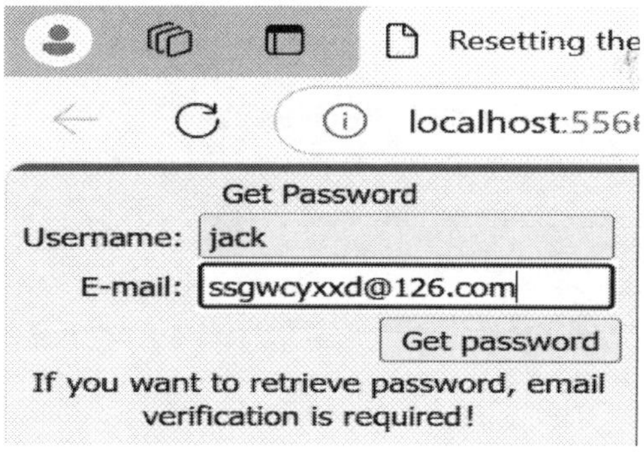

Figure 8-19 Window of Resetting User Password (2)

Source Codes: IsEmailExist() and ResetPassword() methods of CustomerService.cs

```
public bool IsEmailExist(string name, string email)
  {
   Customer customer = (from c in db.Customer
                  where c.Name == name && c.Email == email
                  select c).FirstOrDefault();
```

```
   if (customer != null)
   {
     return true;
   }
   else
   {
     return false;
   }
  public void ResetPassword(string name, string email)
  {
   Customer customer = (from c in db.Customer
                 where c.Name == name && c.Email == email
                 select c).First();
   customer.Password = name;
   db.SubmitChanges();
  }
```

Source Codes:<appSettings> in Web.config

```
<appSettings>
    <add key="MailFromAddress" value="3272344648@qq.com" />
  <add key="UseSsl" value="true" />
  <add key="UserName" value="3272344648" />
  <add key="Password" value="izjgffpdgniaiead" />
  <add key="ServerName" value="smtp.qq.com" />
  <add key="ServerPort" value="587" />
 </appSettings>
```

Source Codes: Custom EmailSender.cs

```
using System.Configuration;
using System.Net;
using System.Net.Mail;
public class EmailSender
{
  private string mailFromAddress = ConfigurationManager.AppSettings["MailFromAddress"];
  private bool useSsl = bool.Parse(ConfigurationManager.AppSettings["UseSsl"]);
  private string userName = ConfigurationManager.AppSettings["UserName"];
  private string password = ConfigurationManager.AppSettings["Password"];
  private string serverName = ConfigurationManager.AppSettings["ServerName"];
  private int serverPort = int.Parse(ConfigurationManager.AppSettings["ServerPort"]);
  private string findPassword;
  private string mailToAddress = "";

  public EmailSender(string address, string pwd)
  {
   mailToAddress = address;
```

```
  findPassword = pwd;
 }
 public void Send()
 {
  using (var smtpClient = new SmtpClient())
  {
   smtpClient.EnableSsl = useSsl;
   smtpClient.Host = serverName;
   smtpClient.Port = serverPort;
   smtpClient.Credentials = new NetworkCredential(userName, password);
   string body = "The password of MyPetShop has been reset: " + findPassword;
   MailMessage mailMessage = new MailMessage(
               mailFromAddress,
               mailToAddress,
               "MyPetShop User Password Reset",
               body);
   smtpClient.Send(mailMessage);
  }
 }
}
```

Source Codes: GetPwd.aspx

```
<%@ Page Language="C#" AutoEventWireup="true" CodeFile="GetPwd.aspx.cs"
Inherits="GetPwd" %>
<!DOCTYPE html>
<html xmlns="http://www.w3.org/1999/xhtml">
<head runat="server">
 <meta http-equiv="Content-Type" content="text/html; charset=utf-8" />
 <title>Reset User Password</title>
 <link href="~/Styles/Style.css" rel="stylesheet" type="text/css" />
</head>
<body>
 <form id="form1" runat="server">
  <div class="leftside">
   <table style="border-collapse: collapse;">
    <tr>
     <td class="tdcenter" colspan="2">Get Password</td>
    </tr>
    <tr>
     <td class="tdright">User Name:</td>
     <td>
      <asp:TextBox ID="txtName" runat="server"></asp:TextBox></td>
     <td>
      <asp:RequiredFieldValidator ControlToValidate="txtName" Display="Dynamic"
ForeColor="Red" ID="rfvName" runat="server" ErrorMessage=" 必填
"></asp:RequiredFieldValidator>
```

```
        </td>
      </tr>
      <tr>
        <td class="tdright">Email:</td>
        <td>
          <asp:TextBox ID="txtEmail" runat="server"></asp:TextBox></td>
        <td>
          <asp:RequiredFieldValidator ControlToValidate="txtEmail" Display="Dynamic"
ForeColor="Red" ID="rfvEmail" runat="server" ErrorMessage=" 必填
"></asp:RequiredFieldValidator>
        </td>
      </tr>
      <tr>
        <td class="tdright" colspan="2">
          <asp:RegularExpressionValidator ID="revEmail" runat="server"
            ErrorMessage="Format of mailbox is incorrect!" ControlToValidate="txtEmail"
Display="Dynamic" ForeColor="Red"
ValidationExpression="\w+([-+.']\w+)*@\w+([-.]\w+)*\.\w+([-.]\w+)*"></asp:Regular
ExpressionValidator>
        </td>
      </tr>
      <tr>
        <td class="tdright" colspan="2">
          <asp:Button ID="btnResetPwd" runat="server" Text="Get Password"
OnClick="BtnResetPwd_Click" />
        </td>
      </tr>
      <tr>
        <td colspan="2">If you want to get password, you need to varify your mailbox!</td>
      </tr>
      <tr>
        <td colspan="2">
          <asp:Label ID="lblMsg" runat="server" ForeColor="Red"></asp:Label></td>
      </tr>
    </table>
  </div>
 </form>
</body>
</html>
```

Source Codes: GetPwd.aspx.cs

```
using MyPetShop.BLL;
using System;
using System.Web.UI;
public partial class GetPwd : System.Web.UI.Page
{
```

```
CustomerService customerSrv = new CustomerService();
protected void BtnResetPwd_Click(object sender, EventArgs e)
{
 if (Page.IsValid)
 {
  if (!customerSrv.IsNameExist(txtName.Text.Trim()))
  {
   lblMsg.Text = "User name doesn't exit!";
  }
  else
  {
   if (!customerSrv.IsEmailExist(txtName.Text.Trim(), txtEmail.Text.Trim()))
   {
    lblMsg.Text = "Mailbox is not correct!";
   }
   else
   {
    customerSrv.ResetPassword(txtName.Text.Trim(), txtEmail.Text.Trim());
    EmailSender emailSender = new EmailSender(txtEmail.Text.Trim(), txtName.Text.Trim());
    emailSender.Send();
    lblMsg.Text = "Password has been sent your mailbox!";
   }
  }
 }
}
}
```

Operating Steps:

(1) Adding IsEmailExist() and ResetPassword() methods in the CustomerService.csin CustomerService.cs class file of MyPetShop.BLL project.

(2) Adding <appSettings> in <configuration> of Web.config.

(3) Adding App_Code of ASP.NET folder in MyPetShop.Web project, then establishing custom EmailSender.cs in this folder.

(4) Creating GetPwd.aspx in MyPetShop.Web project, attaching Style.css style sheet under Styles folder referencing source codes, then adding <Table> element and every control, and setting <div>,<Table>elements and the attributes of each control.

(6) Creating GetPwd.aspx.cs.

(7) Right clicking MyPetShop.Web project, and executing "Establishing Web Site" command.

(8) Browsing Login.aspx, then clicking "Forget Password" link and testing it.

8.4 Summary

➢ Three-layer framework of ASP.NET includes presentation layer, business logic layer and data access layer, which is one of the mainstream technologies for enterprises to develop Web applications. Therefore, it is very important to adapt commercial software development in the future through understanding and using three-layer framework of ASP.NET.

➢ User management usually includes user registration, user login, user state presentation, user password changing and resetting, etc. In the actual project development, the role based user authority management and other functions need to be further supplement.

8.5 Exercises

1. Fill- in- the- blank Questions

(1) ASP.NET three-tier architecture divides web applications into three layers______, ______, ______.

(2) In ASP.NET three-tier architecture, __________needs to reference; __________ , __________needs to reference____________.

(3) Firstly, users can get registration information such as user name from_______, then invoke the corresponding method in______through the username check method in______to perform operations such as querying usernames in the database.

2. True or False Questions

(1) Web layer is used to receive the input data from users, and also is used to display the processing results of BLL layer.(　　)

(2) BLL layer can access the database directly to complete some operations such as query, inserting, updating and deleting etc.(　　)

(3) When operating a database by using LINQ to SQL technology, the ASP.NET three-tier architecture can only consist of Web layer, DLL layer and DAL layer.(　　)

(4) The project of Web layer can reference the project of DAL layer directly.(　　)

(5) From the perspective of data accessing, user login only involves data query operations.(　　)

3.Programming Questions

(1) Create and debug all of the instances in this chapter.

(2) Add the verification code in example 8-2 and example 8-3.

(3) Add the user management function which include the ability to delete regular users in example 8-4.

(4) Modify example 8-6 by resetting the password to a 10-digit random number.

Chapter 9 Theme Master and Custom Controls

Points:

- Mastering the method of establishing and using the theme
- Understanding the master page and establishing the master page
- Mastering the method of creating a consistent layout by using master page
- Mastering the method of establishing and using the user controls

9.1 Theme

In Web applications, usually all pages have a uniform appearance and operating mode. ASP.NET usually provides a uniform appearance through applying the theme. The theme includes appearance, CSS files and image files, etc.

9.1.1 Summary of theme

Theme includes the attribute set that define the appearance of pages and controls. Theme can be seen as the expansion of the CSS. At least, the appearance files should be included in the theme. In addition, CSS files, image files and other resources can also be included. The theme usually corresponds to a folder when it is stored. You can select different themes to display different website styles.

Application theme is usually used, it is stored in App_Themes folder under the root folder of the website, that is, each subfolder in App_Themes folder corresponds to an application theme.

9.1.2 Custom theme

1. Theme and appearance file

A theme must include the appearance file. The operation steps are as follows:

(1) Creating Chap9Site Website.

(2) Right clicking Chap9Site Website and selecting "Add"→ "Add ASP.NET folder"→ "Theme" command in the pop-up shortcut menu, the App_Themes folder is established automatically under the root folder of VSC 2019, and the theme folder is established under this folder. Then the theme name is set to be Red.

(3) Right clicking Red folder, selecting "Add"→ "Appearance File" command, then entering the file name as Red.skin in the pop-up shortcut menu.

(4) Opening the Red.skin file, you can add appearance styles that define only appearance attributes

for different types of controls.

SkinID attribute can define multiple appearances for the same type of controls. If there is no SkinID, the controls are set the default appearance. If there is the SkinID, the appearance is called the named appearance. The duplicate SkinID values are not allowed for the same type of controls in the same theme.

The following example codes define three appearance styles for the Label control:

```
<asp:Label runat="server" ForeColor="#FF0000" Font-Size="X-Small"/>
<asp:Label runat="server" ForeColor="#00FF00" Font-Size="X-Small" SkinID="LabelGreen"/>
<asp:Label runat="server" ForeColor="#0000FF" Font-Size="X-Small" SkinID="LabelBlue"/>
```

When a variety of appearances are defined for the same type of controls, the theme used in a web page should be differentiated by the attribute SkinID of the controls. Such as:

```
<asp:Label ID="lblMsg" runat="server" ForeColor="#0000FF" Font-Size="X-Small" SkinID="LabelBlue"/>
```

2.Adding CSS to the theme

The appearance files only can define the style related to server controls. If you want to set the style of XHTML elements, you should add CSS file into the theme. You can do the following: right clicking the theme folder Red, then selecting "Add"→ "Style Sheet" command in the pop-up shortcut menu, then entering the file name as Red.css in the rendered dialog. Lastly, adding the style of XHTML elements in Red.css.

3.Adding image files to the theme

If you add image files in the theme, you can create the better control appearance. Usually the Images subfolder is established in the theme folder, then the suitable image files are added to the Images folder. If you want to use the files in Images folder, you can access them through the attribute URL of the controls which is used to link the image files.

9.1.3 Using theme

After customizing or downloading the theme from the web, you can use the theme in Web applications. You can use the theme in the single page, also can apply the theme in the part of the pages of the website or the whole website.

1.Applying the theme in a single page

If you want to apply the theme to a single page, you should use Theme or attribute StylesheetTheme of @Page directive. The sample codes are as follows:

```
<%@ Page Theme="ThemeName" %>
  <%@ Page StylesheetTheme="ThemeName" %>
```

The attribute StylesheetTheme indicates a dependent setting with a local control as the theme. That is to say, if you set the local attribute for some control, the attribute which is the same with the local attribute of this control in the theme will not work. If you use the attribute Theme, the local attribute will be covered by the attribute set in the theme.

2.Applying the theme to the website

You can apply the theme to the whole website by changing Web.config file of the website. The sample codes are as follows:

```
<configuration>
  <system.web>
    <pages theme="ThemeName"></pages>
  </system.web>
</configuration>
```

At this time, all of the pages of this website will apply the ThemeName theme.

If you want to apply the theme to a part of the pages of this website, one method is to put all of these pages into one folder, then establishing Web.config file in this folder to realize the configuration of this theme. The other method is to specify the subfolder through <location> element in Web.config file under the root folder. For example, the sample codes that are used to set the theme for SubDir folder are as follows:

```
<configuration>
  <location path="SubDir">
    <system.web>
      <pages theme="ThemeName"></pages>
    </system.web>
  </location>
```

3.Disable the theme

By default, the theme will rewrite the local setting of the pages and the appearance of the controls. If you want to predefine the appearance of some controls or the pages separately, you can disable the theme. When you want to do this, the attribute EnableTheming of the control and the page can be used. For example, the sample codes that are used to disable the theme in the page are as follows:

```
<%@ Page EnableTheming="False" %>
```

The sample codes that are used to disable the theme in the control are as follows:

```
<asp:Label ID="lblMsg" runat="server" EnableTheming="False"></asp:Label>
```

Example 9-1 Switching the theme dynamically

As is shown in Figure 9-1, when you select the different theme, the controls of the page will display the different appearance.

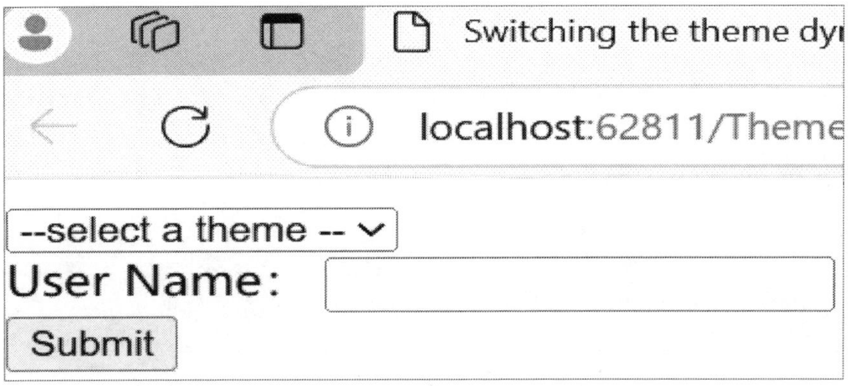

Figure 9-1 The Effect of Theme.aspx

Source Codes: Blue.skin

```
<asp:Label runat="server" ForeColor="Blue" />
<asp:TextBox runat="server" ForeColor="Blue" />
<asp:Button runat="server" ForeColor="Blue" />
```

Source Codes: Green.skin

```
<asp:Label runat="server" ForeColor="Green" />
<asp:TextBox runat="server" ForeColor="Green" />
<asp:Button runat="server" ForeColor="Green" />
```

Source Codes: Theme.aspx

```
<%@ Page Language="C#" AutoEventWireup="true" CodeFile="Theme.aspx.cs" Inherits="Theme" %>
<!DOCTYPE html>
<html xmlns="http://www.w3.org/1999/xhtml">
<head runat="server">
 <meta http-equiv="Content-Type" content="text/html; charset=utf-8" />
 <title>To switch the theme dynamically</title>
</head>
<body>
 <form id="form1" runat="server">
  <div>
   <asp:DropDownList ID="ddlThemes" runat="server" AutoPostBack="True">
    <asp:ListItem Value="0">--Selecting the theme--</asp:ListItem>
    <asp:ListItem>Blue</asp:ListItem>
    <asp:ListItem>Green</asp:ListItem>
   </asp:DropDownList><br />
   <asp:Label ID="lblName" runat="server" EnableTheming="True" Text="User Name: "></asp:Label>
   <asp:TextBox ID="txtName" runat="server" EnableTheming="True"></asp:TextBox><br />
   <asp:Button ID="btnSubmit" runat="server" EnableTheming="False" Text="OK" />
  </div>
 </form>
</body>
</html>
```

Source Codes: Theme.aspx.cs

```
using System;
using System.Web.UI;
public partial class Theme : System.Web.UI.Page
{
 protected void Page_PreInit(object sender, EventArgs e)
 {
  if (Request["ddlThemes"] != "0")
  {
   Page.Theme = Request["ddlThemes"];
  }
 }
}
```

Operating Steps:

(1) Creating Blue theme in Chap9Site website, then establishing Blue.skin file this theme.

(2) Creating Green theme in Chap9Site website, then establishing Green.skin file this theme.

(3) Creating Theme.aspx under the root folder of Chap9Site website, adding one DropDownLsit control, one Label control, one TextBox control, one Button control, and setting the attributes of each control referencing the source codes.

(4) Creating the Theme.aspx.cs and testing it.

Program description:

When setting the attribute Items of the ddlThemes control, the value of the attibute Value of the "-- Please select a theme --" item is set to be 0, so that you can easily determine whether "-- Please select a theme --" is selected in the program.

The setting of the attribute value of Page.Theme must be set in the processing codes of the Page. PreInit event. At this time, you can obtain the selected value in the ddlThemes control through Request ["ddlThemes"].

Because the value of the attribute EnableTheming of the btnSubmit control is False, the theme applied to the control is disabled, so that the color of the control will not change.

9.2 Master

Using the master page can establish a unified style of ASP.NET website quickly and conveniently, and easy to manage and maintain the website, improving the design efficiency.

9.2.1 Summary of master

Master page can establish a consistent layout for the page. When you use master page, it can define the appearance and the required behavior for the page, and then establish the content pages including the displaying content based on master page. When the user requests the content page, these pages will be merged with master page.

The advantages of master page are as follows:

(1) Using the master page can focus on common functions of a web page, that means if you want to modify the common functions of all of the pages, you just need to modify the master page.

(2) Using the master page can easily create a set of controls and codes, and the master page will be applied to a set of web pages.

(3) By controlling the presentation of placeholder controls, the master page can control the layout of the final page in detail.

The Master Page is recognized by the special @Master directive, and the directive replaces the @ Page directive which is used in the ordinary. aspx page. The master page also includes the other XHTML elements, such as <HTML>, <head> and <form>. In actual, the master page can use any XHTML elements and ASP.NET elements. Usually the company logo can be presented through a <img> element or the Image control in the master page, the static text can be used to declare the copyright and the server controls are used to create the web site navigation.

The master page can contain one or more placeholder controls ContentPlaceHolderl which can replace the content.

The extension of master page is .master. The content page specifies the file path of the master page through the MasterPageFile attribute. The content page contains the Content control, and the ContentPlaceHolderID attribute is used to associate it with the ContentPlaceHolder control in the master page.

9.2.2 Creating master page

The method of establishing the master page is the similar with the method of creating the web form.

Example 9-2 Creating the master page

This example will establish a master page Master.master. This page will use the common "top, middle and bottom" page layout.

Source Codes: MasterPage.master

```
<%@ Master Language="C#" AutoEventWireup="true" CodeFile="MasterPage.master.cs"
Inherits="MasterPage" %>
<!DOCTYPE html>
<html>
<head runat="server">
 <meta http-equiv="Content-Type" content="text/html; charset=utf-8" />
 <title>Master Page</title>
 <asp:ContentPlaceHolder ID="cphHead" runat="server">
 </asp:ContentPlaceHolder>
</head>
<body>
 <form id="form1" runat="server">
  <div>
   <header>
   Adding the information of web site logeo,search portal, login portal, site navigation bar ect.
   </header>
   <section>
    <asp:ContentPlaceHolder ID="cphSection" runat="server">
    </asp:ContentPlaceHolder>
   </section>
   <footer>
    Adding information such as copyright at the bottom of the page in the  master page.
   </footer>
  </div>
 </form>
</body>
</html>
```

Operating Steps:

(1) Right clicking Chap10Site web site, selecting "Add"→"Add new item" command in the pop-up shortcut menu, then selecting "Master Page" template in the rendered dialog, and entering the name of the master page as MasterPage.master. At this time, if the "Select Master Page" check box is selected, you can establish the master page based on the other master page. Clicking "Add" button to establish the file.

(2) Adding the XHTML element and the corresponding content referencing the source codes.

9.2.3 Creating content page

The master page provides a template for the unified layout, but if you want to display the content of the different pages, you should create the different content page. The content page only include the content that will be merged with the master page, you can add the text and controls that will be displayed when the user requests this page.

Example 9-3 Creating the content page

This example will create a content page based on the master page Master.master. Figure 9-2 provides the effect of the content page ContentPage.aspx.

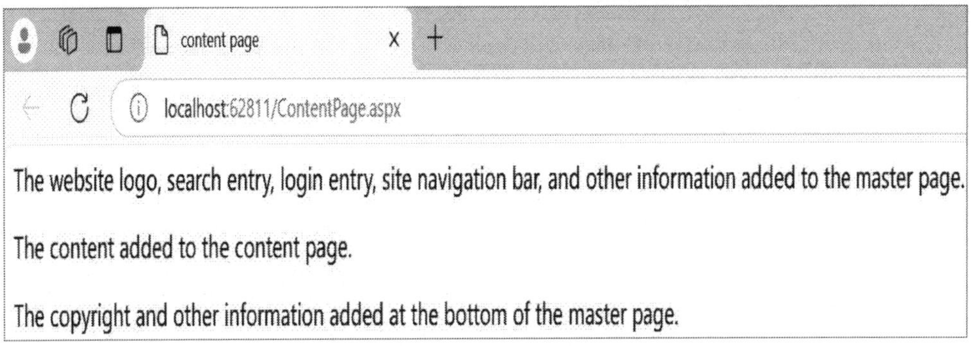

Figure 9-2 The Effect of ContentPage.aspx

Source Codes: ContentPage.aspx

```
<%@ Page Title="Content Page" Language="C#" MasterPageFile="~/Chap9/MasterPage.master"
AutoEventWireup="true" CodeFile="ContentPage.aspx.cs" Inherits="ContentPage" %>
<asp:Content ID="ContentHead" ContentPlaceHolderID="cphHead" runat="Server">
</asp:Content>
<asp:Content ID="ContentSection" runat="server" ContentPlaceHolderID="cphSection">
  <p>Adding the page content in the content page</p>
</asp:Content>
```

Operating Steps:

(1) Establishing MasterPage.master of example 9-2 in Chap9Site website.

(2) Establishing ContentPage.aspx in Chap9Site website. When you establish this page, you should select "Select Master Page" checkbox, and select MasterPage.master.

(3) According to the content that ContentPage.aspx will display, you should add text to the Content control ContentSection which corresponds to ContentPlaceHolder control cphSection. The information which is defined in MasterPage.master to unify the page layout will be gray, and can't be changed.

(4) Browsing the ContentPage.aspx and checking the effect.

9.3 User Control

In ASP.NET, in addition to using the Web server controls, you also can create the reusable custom controls according to your need, these controls are called user controls. User control is a kind of compound control, and the principle is very similar to the ASP.NET website. You can ask the user controls to add existing Web server controls, and define the attributes and methods of the controls. It is often used to unify the page display style in practical projects.

9.3.1 Summary of user control

When you design the Website, perhaps you want to realize some functions which can't be provided by the build-in server controls, and you want to extract the same user interface from the multiple pages to unify the page display style. Usually there are two methods to resolve these problems. One is that you can create the user controls, then define the attributes and methods. The other is that you can define custom controls, that means you can rewrite the derived class of Control or WebControl corresponding to the controls. By comparison, it is more convenient to create the user controls than creating the custom controls.

The corresponding file of the user control is similar with the .aspx file. It includes the user interface and method codes. So when you create the user control, you can take the similar method of creating the Web form, then add the controls you need into the file. Lastly, you can add the codes of the methods according your need.

The differences between the user control and the Web form are as follows:

(1) The extension name of user control is .ascx.

(2) There is not @Page directive in user control, but there is @Control directive.

(3) The user controls can not run as a separate file, and must be the same like other controls, which only can be used after adding them to the Web form.

(4) There are not <html>, <body> or <form> elements in the user control, and the elements must be in the host web pages. In addition, XHTML elements or the existing Web server controls can be added to user controls.

9.3.2 Establishing the user control

You can design a user control just like designing a Web form, or you can change a Web form to a user control.

1.Designing the user control

The steps of adding the user control to the web site are similar with the steps of adding Web form to the web site. The steps of creating a user control SearchUserControl.ascx under the root folder of the

Chap9Site website are as follows:

(1) Right clicking Chap9Site Website, selecting "Add"→ "Add New Item" command in the pop-up shortcut menu, then selecting "Web User Control"template in the rendered dialog, entering the name of the user control to be SearchUserControl.ascx, then clicking "Add" button to establish the file.

(2) Adding controls and the codes of the methods like the normal controls. In this example, one TextBox control and one Button control are added into the user control, and the method codes are written after the Page. Load event and btnSearch.Click event are triggered.

(3) If you need to interact with the other controls, you can add the public attributes for the user control. In this example, the public attribute Text is added into SearchUserControl class; the attribute value of Text of the Button control which is set in the Page_Load() method comes from the attribute value of Text of the user control; the attribute value of Text of the text box txtSearchKey is set in the codes of BtnSearch_Click() method.

Source Codes: SearchUserControl.ascx

```
<%@ Control Language="C#" AutoEventWireup="true"
CodeFile="SearchUserControl.ascx.cs" Inherits="SearchUserControl" %>
<asp:TextBox ID="txtSearchKey" runat="server"></asp:TextBox>
<asp:Button ID="btnSearch" runat="server" OnClick="BtnSearch_Click" Text="Search" />
```

Source Codes: SearchUserControl.ascx.cs

```
using System;
public partial class SearchUserControl : System.Web.UI.UserControl
{
 private string _Text;
 public string Text
 {
  get { return _Text; }
  set { _Text = value; }
 }
 protected void Page_Load(object sender, EventArgs e)
 {
  if (this.Text != "")
  {
   btnSearch.Text = this.Text;
  }
 }
 protected void BtnSearch_Click(object sender, EventArgs e)
 {
  txtSearchKey.Text = "Complete the searching";
 }
}
```

2.Converting the single page to the user control

The steps of converting a single page to the user control are as follows:

(1) Renaming the file extension name .aspx as .ascx.

(2) Removing <html>, <body> and <form> elements from the page; changing @ Page directive to @ Control directive. Removing all of the attributes of @ Control directive except for Language, AutoEventWireup, CodeFile and Inherits.

3.Converting code behind page to the user control

(1) Renaming the file extension name .aspx as .ascx.

(2) Renaming the file extension name .aspx.cs as .ascx.cs.

(3) Opening the. ascx.cs file and changing the inherited class from Page to UserControl.

(4) In the.ascx file, deleting <html>,<body> and<form>elements; changing @Page directive to @ Control directive; deleting all of the attributes except for Language, AutoEventWireup, CodeFile and Inherits in @ Control directive. In @Control directive, changing the attribute value of CodeFile to the renamed code behind file name.

9.3.3 Using the user control

If you want to use the user control, you should embody it in the Web form. In "Design" view of Web form, you can directly drag a user control file from the "Solution Explorer" window to the page to add the user control. In "Source" view, @ Register directives is added automatically, such as:

<%@ Register src="SearchUserControl.ascx" tagname="SearchUserControl" tagprefix="uc" %>

The attribute tagprefix specifies the prefix of the user control, which is similar with the asp prefix of Web server control. When you use the user control, you should add the prefix firstly, such as <uc:SearchUserControl...>. Attribute TagName specifies the name of the user control; attribute Src specifies the storage path of of the user control file.

Note: The user control can't be stored in the App_Code folder.

In <form> element of Web form, the example codes of the user control element which is automatically generated are as follows:

<uc:SearchUserControl ID="SearchUserControl1" runat="server" Text="Searching" />

Attribute Text is the public attribute of the user control SearchUserControl, the value of which can be set in "Attribute" window.

Example 9-4 Using the user control

This example adds the user control SearchUserControl to Web form. The effect is shown as Figure 9-3. Clicking "Searching" button, the browsing effect of Figure 9-4 will be displayed.

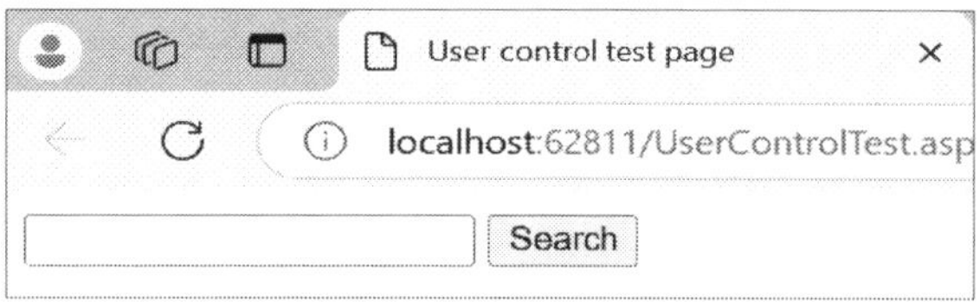

Figure 9-3 The Effect of UserControlTest.aspx (1)

Figure9-4 The Effect of UserControlTest.aspx (2)

Source Codes: UserControlTest.aspx

```
<%@ Page Language="C#" AutoEventWireup="true" CodeFile="UserControlTest.aspx.cs"
Inherits="UserControlTest" %>
<%@ Register Src="SearchUserControl.ascx" TagName="SearchUserControl" TagPrefix="uc" %>
<!DOCTYPE html>
<html xmlns="http://www.w3.org/1999/xhtml">
<head runat="server">
 <meta http-equiv="Content-Type" content="text/html; charset=utf-8" />
 <title>Test Page of The User Control</title>
</head>
<body>
 <form id="form1" runat="server">
  <div>
   <uc:SearchUserControl ID="SearchUserControl1" runat="server" Text="Searching" />
  </div>
 </form>
</body>
</html>
```

Operating Steps:

(1) Creating UserControlTest.aspx in the root folder of Chap9Site.

(2) In "Design" view, dragging SearchUserControl.ascx to the page, and setting the attribute Text of the control to "Searching".

(3) Browsing the effect of UserControlTest.aspx and testing the effect.

Program Description:

When the page is loaded into the user control, the Page.Load event which is defined in the user control is triggered to execute the codes of the Page_ Load() method which is defined in the user control, and the value of the attribute Text of the user control will be assigned to btnSearch.Text, so "Searching" is displayed on the button. When the "Searching" button is clicked, the Click event is triggered to execute method codes of btnSearch_ Click() which is defined in the user control, and "Complete Searching" in the text box txtSearchKey will be displayed. Of course, in practical projects, data searching often needs to be combined with the database.

9.4 Summary

- The skin file provides a consistent appearance for the server controls in the page.
- The theme corresponds to a theme folder and must be stored in the ASP.NET folder App_ Themes.
- The master page can be used to easily and quickly establish a unified style of ASP.NET website.
- User controls unify the page display style within the local scope of the page.
- The websites based on Web part enable the users to modify the content, appearance and behavior

of the page

directly from the browser, so as to realize the user personalization.

9.5 Exercises

1. True or False Questions

(1) The theme have a style sheet file at least. (   )

(2) The master page can only contain one ContentPlaceHolder control. (   )

(3) Each control type is only allowed to have one default control appearance within the same theme. (   )

(4) The SkinID value must be specified in the appearance of the control. (   )

(5) Duplicating SkinID is not allowed for a control type in the same theme. (   )

(6) The App_Code folder can contain user controls. (   )

(7) Properties can be defined in user controls. (   )

2. Multiple Choice Questions

(1) The theme does not include (   ).

A. Skin file   B. CSS file   C. Image file   D. config file

(2) A theme must include (   ).

A. Skin file   B. CSS file   C. Image file   D. config file

(3) The extension of the master page file is (   ).

A. .aspx   B. .master   C. .cs   D. .skin

(4) You can disable the theme by setting the (   ) property of controls and pages.

A. ProhibitTheming   B. StylesheetTheme   C. Theme   D. EnableTheming

3. Short-answer Questions

(1) How to convert single-file pages and code-behind pages into user controls?

(2) Describe the display principle of ASP.NET master pages during runtime briefly.

4. Programming Questions

(1) Create and debug all of the instances in this chapter.

(2) Design a master page and use it to establish a personal website.

(3) Design a theme and apply it to a message board system.

Chapter 10 The Web Site Navigation

Points:

- Understanding the implication of the navigation and implementation method
- Learning the structure of the site map file and properly establishing a site map
- Mastering the usage of the site navigation controls SiteMapPath, TreeView and Menu
- Mastering the usage of site navigation controls in the master page

10.1 The Site Map

In any websites with a large number of pages, the traditional navigation mode is that if you want to enable the user to switch between pages, you should scatter the hyperlinks on the page. This method requires a lot of maintenance. While site navigation in ASP.NET can create a centralized site map of the page, it can make the management of navigation simple.

10.1.1 The sitemap file

If you want to use site navigation in ASP.NET, you need to describe hierarchical structure of the pages of this website. The sitemap file is a XML file, and you can use <siteMapNode> element to describe the title, URL and other information of each page. When one or more sitemap files are used to describe the page hierarchy, one of the sitemap files must be stored under the root folder of the website and be named as Web.sitemap, and the other files can be stored in the other locations.

The codes of the default file of the website map are as follows:

```
<?xml version="1.0" encoding="utf-8" ?>
<siteMap xmlns="http://schemas.microsoft.com/AspNet/SiteMap-File-1.0">
  <siteMapNode url="" title=""  description="">
    <siteMapNode url="" title=""  description="" />
    <siteMapNode url="" title=""  description="" />
  </siteMapNode>
</siteMap>
```

Description: The root element <siteMap> contains the child element <siteMapNode>. All of the <siteMapNode> elements form the hierarchy of the website pages, and the first layer <siteMapNode> element is the home page of the website. The next layer <siteMapNode> element indicates the page below the first page.

The common attributes of <siteMapNode> element are shown in Table 10-1

Table 10-1 The common attribute table of <siteMapNode> element

Attribute	Description
description	Describe the effect of hyperlinks; when the mouse pointer points to a hyperlink, the prompt information will be given
siteMapFile	Reference the map file of another website
title	Display text which is used to represent the hyperlink
url	The URL address of the hyperlink target page

Example 10-1 Creating the site map

This example adds the site map to the ChapSite website, and the hierarchy of the pages included in the site map is shown in the Figure 10-1.

Figure 10-1 The Hierarchy Structure of The Page

Source Codes: Web.sitemap

```
<?xml version="1.0" encoding="utf-8" ?>
<siteMap xmlns="http://schemas.microsoft.com/AspNet/SiteMap-File-1.0">
 <siteMapNode url="~/Chap10/Home.aspx" title="Home Page" description="Home">
  <siteMapNode url="~/Chap10/Products.aspx" title="Products" description="All of The Products">
    <siteMapNode url="~/Chap10/Hardware.aspx" title="Hardware"
      description="Hardware" />
    <siteMapNode url="~/Chap10/Software.aspx" title="Software"
   description="Software" />
   </siteMapNode>
   <siteMapNode url="~/Chap10/Services.aspx" title="Services"
     description="After-sale Service">
    <siteMapNode url="~/Chap10/Training.aspx" title="Training"
      description="Training Service" />
    <siteMapNode url="~/Chap10/Consulting.aspx" title="Consulting"
      description="Consulting Service" />
```

```
      <siteMapNode url="~/Chap10/Support.aspx" title="Support"
        description="Technology Support" />
    </siteMapNode>
  </siteMapNode>
</siteMap>
```

Operating Steps:

Right clicking ChapSite website, selecting "Add"→ "Add New Item" command in the pop-up shortcut menu, then selecting "Site Map" template in the rendered dialog, clicking "Add" button to establish the sitemap file Web.sitemap, then entering the source codes.

10.1.2 Nested sitemap file

For the website with the complex pages, it is mixed to put all of the navigation information into a single Web.sitemap. So you can consider to use the nested sitemap file, that means you can scatter the information to multiple .sitemap files, then merge all of the .sitemap files into the Web.sitemap file under the root folder. At this time, you should use the attribute siteMapFile of <siteMapNode> element.

Example 10-2 Creating the nested site map

The function of this example is the same with the example 10-1, while it is realized by using nested site map. That means firstly, you should scatter the information describing the products and services to the Products.sitemap and Services.sitemap files, then set the value of attribute siteMapFile of <siteMapNode> element in Web1.sitemap to the included .sitemap file. Products. The Products.sitemap and Services.sitemap are stored under "chap10" folder, while the Web1.sitemap is stored under the root folder.

Source Codes: Web1.sitemap

```
<?xml version="1.0" encoding="utf-8" ?>
<siteMap xmlns="http://schemas.microsoft.com/AspNet/SiteMap-File-1.0">
  <siteMapNode url="~/Chap10/Home.aspx" title="Home" description="Home">
    <siteMapNode siteMapFile="~/Chap10/Products.sitemap" />
    <siteMapNode siteMapFile="~/Chap10/Services.sitemap" />
  </siteMapNode>
</siteMap>
```

Source Codes: Services.sitemap

```
<?xml version="1.0" encoding="utf-8" ?>
<siteMap xmlns="http://schemas.microsoft.com/AspNet/SiteMap-File-1.0">
  <siteMapNode url="~/Chap10/Services.aspx" title="Services" description="After-sale Service">
```

```
    <siteMapNode url="~/Chap10/Training.aspx" title="Training" description="Training Service" />
    <siteMapNode url="~/Chap10/Consulting.aspx" title="Consulting" description="Consulting Service"/>
    <siteMapNode url="~/Chap10/Support.aspx" title="Support" description="Technology Support"/>
  </siteMapNode>
</siteMap>
```

10.2 Displaying Navigation by Using SiteMapPath Control

In practice, the navigation where the current page is located on the current site hierarchy usually is added on the page. We call it breadcrumb function. The SiteMapPath control automatically implements the breadcrumb function. The SiteMapPath control can automatically bind the Web.sitemap file without the data source control. When you want to use the navigation, you only need to add the SiteMapPath control to the page. Of course, it is better to add the SiteMapPath control to the master page to achieve an unified website navigation interface.

The defined syntax format is as follows:

<asp:SiteMapPath ID="SiteMapPath1" runat="server"> </asp:SiteMapPath>

The common attributes of the SiteMapPath control are shown in Table 10-2

Table 10-2 The common attribute table of the SiteMapPath control

Attribute	Description
ParentLevelsDisplayed	Get or set the number of the parent node level relative to the current displayed node
PathDirection	Get or set the rendered order of the navigation path node
PathSeparator	Get or set a symbol to separate the navigation path of the website

Example 10-3 Displaying the navigation by using the SiteMapPath control

As is shown in Figure 10-2, the SiteMapPath control is used to display the site navigation.

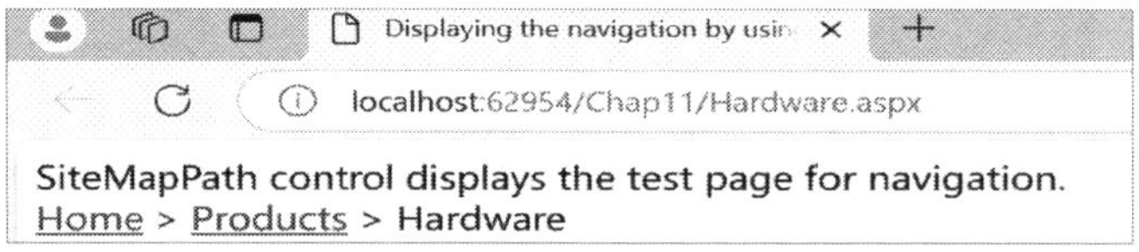

Figure 10-2 The Effect of Hardware.aspx

Source Codes: Hardware.aspx

```
<%@ Page Language="C#" AutoEventWireup="true" CodeFile="Hardware.aspx.cs"
Inherits="Chap10_Hardware" %>
<!DOCTYPE html>
<html xmlns="http://www.w3.org/1999/xhtml">
<head runat="server">
  <meta http-equiv="Content-Type" content="text/html; charset=utf-8" />
  <title>To display the navigation by using the SiteMapPath control</title>
</head>
<body>
<form id="form1" runat="server">
  <div>
```

```
    The test page of displaying the navigation by using the SiteMapPath control<br />
    <asp:SiteMapPath ID="SiteMapPath1" runat="server"></asp:SiteMapPath>
   </div>
  </form>
  </body>
  </html>
```

Operating Steps:

(1) Creating the sitemap file Web.sitemap which is the same with example 10-1.

(2) Creating Hardware.aspx in Chap10 folder. Adding one SiteMapPath control. At last, browsing Hardware.aspx and testing it.

10.3 Displaying Navigation by Using TreeView Control

TreeView control is usually used to display the hierarchical data in a tree structure. The site navigation can be realized by using the TreeView control, and the control can also be used to display the XML, table, or relational data.

10.3.1 TreeView control

Each item in a TreeView control is called a node, and each node is a TreeNode object. Nodes are divided into root node, parent node, child node and leaf node. The top of the nodes is the root node. There are multiple root nodes. The node without child nodes is the leaf node.

Syntax format is as follows:

`<asp:TreeView ID="TreeView1" runat="server"> </asp:TreeView>`

The common attributes of the TreeView control are shown in Table 10-3.

Table 10-3 The common attribute table of the TreeView control

Attribute	Description
Nodes	Get the set of all of the root nodes.
CollapseImageUrl	Display the URL of the image after the node is collapsed.
EnableClientScript	Whether to allow the expansion and collapse events to be handled on the client.
ExpandDepth	The number of the expanded series displayed at the first time.
ExpandImageUrl	Display the URL of the image after the node is expanded.
NoExpandImageUrl	Set the URL which is used to display the image corresponding to non collapsible nodes.
PathSeparator	Path separator between the nodes.
SelectedNode	The currently selected node.
SelectedValue	The vlaue of the currently selected.
ShowCheckBoxes	Whether to display the check box in front of the node.
ShowLines	Whether to show the connection between nodes.

Each node of TreeView control is the object of TreeNode class. When you build a TreeView, you often need to program the TreeNode object. The common attributes of the TreeNode control are shown in Table 10-4.

Table 10-4 The common attribute table of the TreeNode control

Attribute	Description
ChildNodes	Get the set of child nodes at the next level of the current node.
ImageUrl	Get or set the URL next to the node for displaying image.
NavigateUrl	Get or set the navigation URL when a node is clicked.
Parent	Get the parent node of the current node.

The node data of TreeView control can be added when you design the navigation. You also can dynamically add or modify the data by programming TreeNode objects. You can also bind data by using data source control. For example, you can fill the sitemap data into TreeView control by using SiteMapDataSource control, and get the filled data from XML file by using XmlDataSource control.

In addition, the nodes can be collapsed and expanded by using CollapseAll() and ExpandAll() methods of TreeView control, and can be added to the control by using Nodes. Add() method, and the specified nodes can be removed by using Nodes. Remove() method.

Example 10-4 Using TreeView control

The urban structure is shown by using TreeView control in this example, and the nodes can be dynamically added and removed, folded and unfolded. As is shown as Figure 10-3, after selecting "Jiaxing" node, entering "Haining" into the text box, then clicking "Add Node" button, the child node "Haining" is added under "Jiaxing" node.

Figure 10-3 The Effect of TreeView.aspx

Source Codes: TreeView.aspx

```
<%@ Page Language="C#" AutoEventWireup="true" CodeFile="TreeView.aspx.cs"
Inherits="Chap10_TreeView" %>
<!DOCTYPE html>
<html xmlns="http://www.w3.org/1999/xhtml">
<head runat="server">
 <meta http-equiv="Content-Type" content="text/html; charset=utf-8" />
```

```
  <title>To use TreeView control</title>
</head>
<body>
  <form id="form1" runat="server">
    <div>
      <table>
        <tr>
          <td style="width: 150px">
            <asp:TreeView ID="tvCity" runat="server" ShowLines="True">
              <SelectedNodeStyle BorderStyle="Solid" />
              <Nodes>
                <asp:TreeNode Text="Zhejiang" Value="zhejiang">
                  <asp:TreeNode Text="Hangzhou" Value="hangzhou"></asp:TreeNode>
                  <asp:TreeNode Text="Jiaxing" Value="jiaxing"></asp:TreeNode>
                  <asp:TreeNode Text="Ningbo" Value="ningbo"></asp:TreeNode>
                </asp:TreeNode>
              </Nodes>
            </asp:TreeView>
          </td>
          <td>
            <asp:TextBox ID="txtNode" runat="server" Width="105px"></asp:TextBox><br />
            <asp:Button ID="btnAddNode" runat="server" OnClick="BtnAddNode_Click" Text="Add
Node" Width="110px" /><br />
            <asp:Button ID="btnRemoveNode" runat="server" OnClick="BtnRemoveNode_Click"
Text="Remove the Current Node " Width="110px" /><br />
            <asp:Button ID="btnExpandAll" runat="server" OnClick="BtnExpandAll_Click"
Text="Expand All of the Nodes" Width="110px" /><br />
            <asp:Button ID="btnCollapseAll" runat="server" OnClick="BtnCollapseAll_Click"
Text="Collapse All of the Nodes" Width="110px" />
          </td>
        </tr>
      </table>
    </div>
  </form>
</body>
</html>
```

Source Codes: TreeView.aspx.cs

```
using System;
using System.Web.UI.WebControls;
public partial class Chap10_TreeView : System.Web.UI.Page
{
  protected void BtnRemoveNode_Click(object sender, EventArgs e)
  {
    if (tvCity.SelectedNode != null)
    {
      TreeNode parentNode = tvCity.SelectedNode.Parent;
      parentNode.ChildNodes.Remove(tvCity.SelectedNode);
    }
  }
  protected void BtnAddNode_Click(object sender, EventArgs e)
```

```
    {
     if (txtNode.Text.Trim().Length <1)
     {
      return;
     }
     TreeNode childNode = new TreeNode();
     childNode.Value = txtNode.Text.Trim();
     if (tvCity.SelectedNode != null)
     {
      tvCity.SelectedNode.ChildNodes.Add(childNode);
     }
     else
     {
      tvCity.Nodes.Add(childNode);
     }
     txtNode.Text = "";
    }
    protected void BtnCollapseAll_Click(object sender, EventArgs e)
    {
     tvCity.CollapseAll();
    }
    protected void BtnExpandAll_Click(object sender, EventArgs e)
    {
     tvCity.ExpandAll();
    }
   }
```

Operating Steps:

(1) Creating TreeView.aspx in the folder Chap10. Adding a one row two columns table for layout in "Design" view, and adding one TreeView, one TextBox control and four Button controls to the corresponding cell.

(2) Clicking the smart tag of TreeView, selecting "Edit Node" command, and adding the node in the dialog of "TreeView Node Editor" which is opened, as is shown in Figure 10-4.

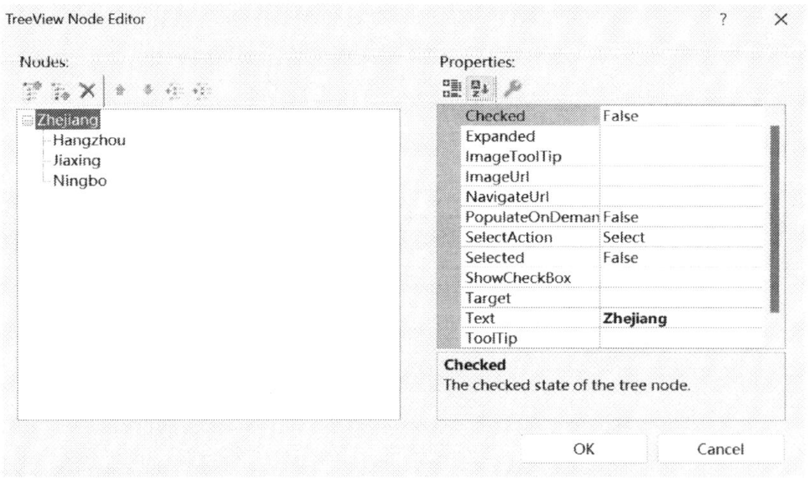

Figure 10-4 "TreeView Node Editor" Dialog

(3) Setting the attributes of the other controls referencing the source codes.

(4) Creating TreeView.aspx.cs, and at last, browsing the TreeView.aspx and testing it.

10.3.2 Realizing navigation by using TreeView control

There are two ways to populate data by using TreeView control to realize site navigation. Firstly, you can use the data source control SiteMapDataSource. At this time, the attribute value of DataSourceID of the TreeView control is set to the ID attribute value of the SiteMapDataSource control. The second is to use LINQ technology.

Example 10-5 Displaying navigation by using TreeView control

As is shown as Figure 10-5, the TreeView control displays the page structure diagram contained in the site map file in the form of the tree structure. The used site map file is the Web.sitemap created in example 10-1.

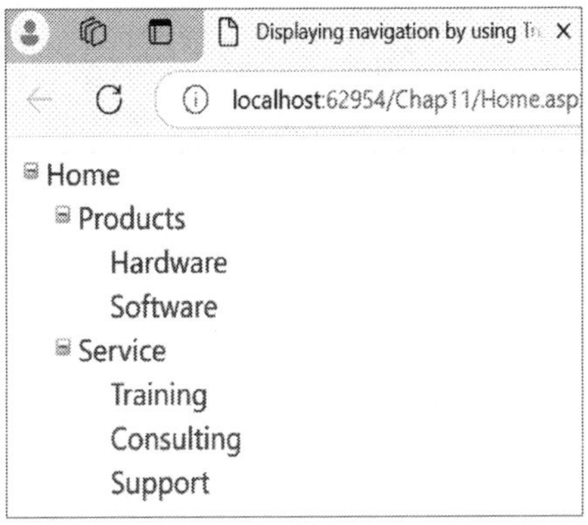

Figure 10-5 The Effect of Home.aspx

Source Codes: Home.aspx

```
<%@ Page Language="C#" AutoEventWireup="true" CodeFile="Home.aspx.cs"
Inherits="Chap10_Home" %>
<!DOCTYPE html>
<html xmlns="http://www.w3.org/1999/xhtml">
<head runat="server">
  <meta http-equiv="Content-Type" content="text/html; charset=utf-8" />
  <title>To display navigation by using TreeView control</title>
</head>
<body>
  <form id="form1" runat="server">
    <div>
    <asp:TreeView ID="tvSiteMap" runat="server" DataSourceID="smdsSiteMap"></asp:TreeView>
     <asp:SiteMapDataSource ID="smdsSiteMap" runat="server" />
    </div>
  </form>
</body>
</html>
```

Operating Steps:

Creating Home.aspx in the folder Chap10, adding the controls and setting the attributes referencing the source codes. At last, browsing the effect of Home.aspx.

Program Description:

The SiteMapDataSource control can automatically bind to Web.sitemap, and can display the navigation information in Web.sitemap on the page through the TreeView control.

10.4 Displaying Navigation by Using Menu Control

Menu control can display hierarchical data in a menu format. The control is similar with TreeView control, and it need to be supported by the data source control. For example, you can use the data source control SiteMapDataSource to realize the displaying effect of site navigation through Menu control. At this time, the attribute value of DataSourceID of the Menu control is set to the ID attribute value of the SiteMapDataSource control.

Orientation attribute of Menu control determines the arrangement of the menu. The value of Vertical indicates vertical arrangement, and the value of Horizontal indicates horizontal arrangement. The default value is Vertical.

Example 10-6 Displaying navigation by using Menu control

As is shown as Figure 10-6, the menu control can be used to render the site navigation in the form of the menu.

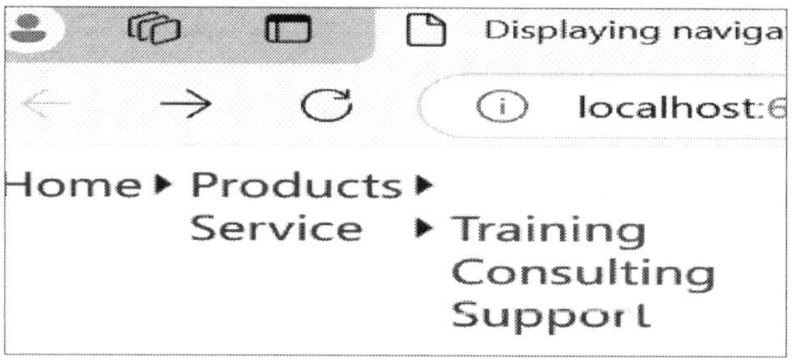

Figure 10-6 The Effect of Products.aspx

Source Codes: Products.aspx

```
<%@ Page Language="C#" AutoEventWireup="true" CodeFile="Products.aspx.cs"
Inherits="Chap10_Products" %>
<!DOCTYPE html>
<html xmlns="http://www.w3.org/1999/xhtml">
<head runat="server">
  <meta http-equiv="Content-Type" content="text/html; charset=utf-8" />
```

```
    <title>To display navigation by using Menu control</title>
  </head>
  <body>
    <form id="form1" runat="server">
     <div>
        <asp:Menu ID="mnuSiteMap" runat="server" DataSourceID="smdsSiteMap">
        </asp:Menu>
        <asp:SiteMapDataSource ID="smdsSiteMap" runat="server" />
      </div>
    </form>
  </body>
</html>
```

10.5 Using Site Navigation in Master Page

In ASP.NET, the site navigation control can be used in the master page, so the layout containing the navigation control can be created in the master page, then the master page is applied to all of the content pages. The steps of using site navigation based on the master page are as follows:

(1) Creating the master page which is used to navigate.

(2) Adding navigation control to the master page.

(3) Creating the content pages of the website, and associating the master page by using MasterPageFile attribute.

Example 10-7 Realizing site navigation based on the master page

As is shown as Figure 10-7, site navigation is realized through the master page, and the content page is associated with the master page, then entering some prompt information.

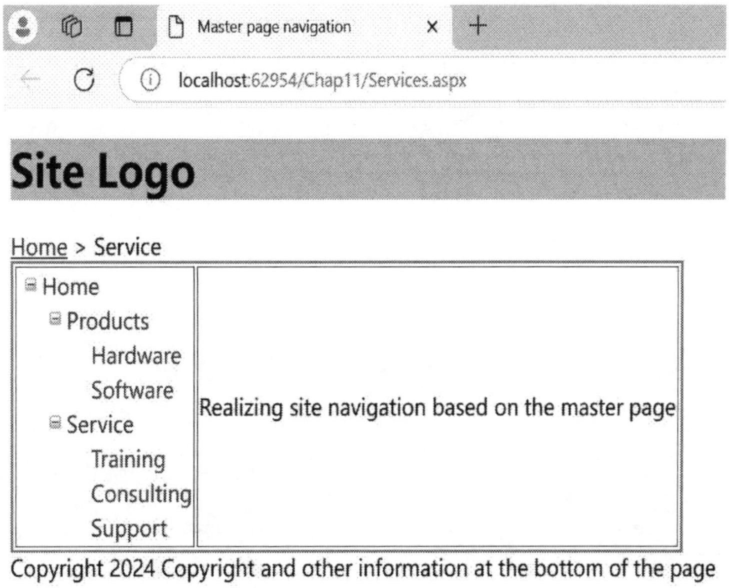

Figure 10-7 The Effect of Services.aspx

Source Codes: SiteMap.master

```
<%@ Master Language="C#" AutoEventWireup="true" CodeFile="SiteMap.master.cs"
Inherits="Chap10_SiteMap" %>
<!DOCTYPE html>
<html>
<head runat="server">
 <meta http-equiv="Content-Type" content="text/html; charset=utf-8" />
 <title></title>
 <asp:ContentPlaceHolder ID="head" runat="server">
 </asp:ContentPlaceHolder>
</head>
<body>
 <form id="form1" runat="server">
  <header>
   <h1 style="background-color: #C0C0C0">Site Logo</h1>
   <asp:SiteMapPath ID="SiteMapPath1" runat="server"></asp:SiteMapPath>
  </header>
  <section>
   <table style="border-style: solid">
    <tr>
     <td style="border-style: solid; border-width: thin;">
      <asp:TreeView ID="tvSiteMap" runat="server" DataSourceID="smdsSiteMap">
      </asp:TreeView>
      <asp:SiteMapDataSource ID="smdsSiteMap" runat="server" />
     </td>
     <td style="border-style: solid; border-width: thin;">
      <asp:ContentPlaceHolder ID="ContentPlaceHolder1" runat="server">
      </asp:ContentPlaceHolder>
     </td>
    </tr>
   </table>
  </section>
  <footer>Copyright 2018  </footer>
 </form>
</body>
</html>
```

Source Codes: Services.aspx

```
<%@ Page Title="Master Page Navigation" Language="C#" MasterPageFile="~/Chap10/SiteMap.master"
AutoEventWireup="true" CodeFile="Services.aspx.cs" Inherits="Chap10_Services" %>
<asp:Content ID="Content1" ContentPlaceHolderID="head" Runat="Server">
</asp:Content>
<asp:Content ID="Content2" ContentPlaceHolderID="ContentPlaceHolder1" Runat="Server">
 To realize site navigation by using the master page SiteMap.master
</asp:Content>
```

Operating Steps:

(1) Creating the master page SiteMap.maser in the folder Chap10, adding <header>, <section> and <footer> elements referencing the source codes, then adding controls and setting the attributes of each control and each element.

(2) Creating the content page Services.aspx associated with the master page in the folder Chap10, and entering the prompt information. At last, browsing the effect of Services.aspx. You can see the breadcrumb navigation at the bottom of "Site Logo" of this page, and the tree structure navigation on the left.

10.6 Summary

➢ ASP.NET provides a navigation system, which is used to describe the page structure of a website in an XML file (website map file).

➢ The SiteMapPath control is used to display breadcrumb navigation where the current page is located in the current website page hierarchy. The data source control is not required.

➢ The TreeView control displays the site map in a tree structure, which requires a data source control.

➢ The Menu control displays the site map in the form of a menu, which requires a data source control.

10.7 Exercises

1. Fill-in-blank Questions

(1) The extension of the site map file is__________.

(2) The URL attribute of the <siteMapNode> element represents__________.

(3) To utilize website navigation controls, the page structure of the website must be described in the __________file.

(4) The function of the PathDirection property of the SiteMapPath control is__________.

(5) The function of the Orientation property of the Menu control is__________.

2. True or False Questions

(1) A sitemap file can only contain one <siteMap> root element. (　　)

(2) Website navigation files can not be nested. (　　)

(3) Website navigation controls must access website map data through the SiteMapPath control. (　　)

(4) Navigation controls can not be added to the master page. (　　)

(5) Node data can be added to the TreeView control by using LINO technology.(　　)

3. Short-answer Questions

(1) Describe the basic format of the sitemap file.

(2) Give an example about how to utilize nesting to solve complex website navigation problems.

(3) How to implement website navigation functionality in the master page?

4. Programming Questions

(1) Create and debug all of the instances in this chapter.

(2) Analyze the page hierarchy of a website and establish a sitemap for that website.

(3) Create an XML file that describes the contents of this book and display this file by using the TreeView control.

(5) Populate a TreeView control with the website map data come from example 10-1 by using LINQ technology.

Chapter 11 ASP.NET Ajax

Points:

- Understanding the basic knowledge of Ajax
- Understanding the working principle of the Ajax.
- Understanding the ASP.NET Ajax technology
- Grasping the usage of the ASP.NET Ajax server controls
- Understanding the installation and control functions of AjaxControlToolkit

11.1 The Base of Ajax

Ajax is a technology that allows the client to exchange data with servers through asynchronous HTTP requests. The purpose is to build a Web application with good interactivity by using the mature technology. Usually, Ajax pages are referred to the Web pages without refreshing.

11.1.1 Summary of Ajax

It is well known that the desktop applications should have good interactivity. Web applications provide the services that the desktop applications can't provide, but because the Web applications need the Web server responds, waiting for the request to return, and generating a new page, so the program is less interactive than desktop applications. Ajax applies the interactivity of desktop applications to the Web applications to make the Web applications show dynamic and beautiful user interface.

The technologies of Ajax include as follows:

• The XMLHttpRequest object: The object allows the browser to communicate with the Web server, and the component can be used in above IE5.0 browser through the MSXML ActiveX.

• JavaScript codes: This is the core codes of running AJAX Web applications, and can be used to improve the communication with the server application.

• DHTML: The form can be updated dynamically by using the <div>, <span> and other dynamic HTML elements.

• Document object model DOM: It is used to process the HTML element and XML which is returned by the server through JavaScript codes.

Figure 11-1 provides the differences between traditional Web applications and Ajax Webapplications.

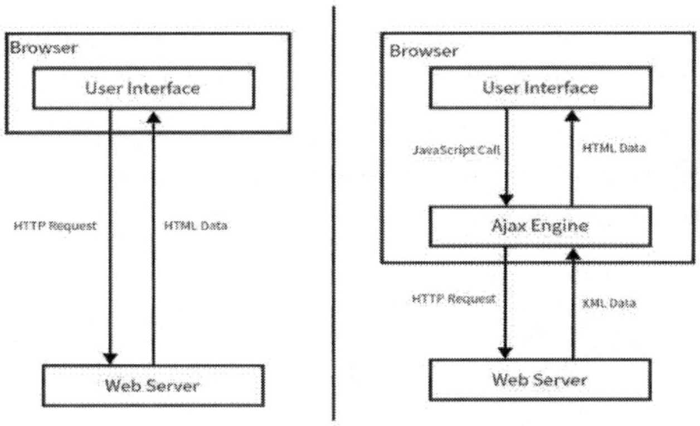

Figure 11-1 Differences between Traditional Web Applications and Ajax Web Applications

11.1.2 Technology of ASP.NET Ajax

ASP.NET Ajax is the Microsoft implementation method of Ajax. It is dedicated to ASP.NET pages. Ajax is used in the form of the control. The Ajax functions in ASP.NET can generate plentiful Web applications. Compared with the traditional Web application, Web applications based on the ASP.NET. Ajax have the following advantages:

- Refreshing a part of the page, that means only refreshing the part which has been changed of the page.
- Generating the proxy class automatically, that can simplify the process invoking the Web service method from client scripts.
- Supporting the most popular browsers.
- Because most of the work is executed in your browser, so the efficiency is greatly improved.

There are two methods to realize the Web applications based on ASP.NET Ajax: firstly "only client "solution, which uses the ASP.NET Ajax Library; secondly, "client and server" solution, which use both ASP.NET Ajax Library and ASP.NET server controls.

11.2 The Server Controls of ASP.NET Ajax

After the ASP.NET Ajax server control is added on the page of ASP.NET, the JavaScript will be sent to the browser to realize the function of Ajax automatically when you browse these pages.

11.2.1 ScriptManager control

ScriptManager control is the core of ASP.NET Ajax functions. It downloads the JavaScript of ASP. NET Ajax Library to the browser, and manages all of the ASP.NET Ajax resource on one page. Each page which realizes the Ajax function must include a ScriptManager control. The syntax format defined is as follows:

<asp:ScriptManager ID="ScriptManager1" runat="server" />

EnablePartialRendering attribute of ScriptManager control determines whether the page can be partially refreshed. The default value of this attribute is True.

1.Registering custom JavaScript in ScriptManager

The custom JavaScript file can be referenced through <script> element in ASP.NET page. But this method can't be used to partially refresh the page, and can't access some components of ASP.NET Ajax Library. If you want to let the custom JavaScript file support the Web applications based on ASP. NET Ajax, you must register this file in ScriptManager control of this page. The method is to add a ScriptReference object which points to the script file in the Scripts attribute set of the ScriptManager control. As is shown in Figure 11-2.

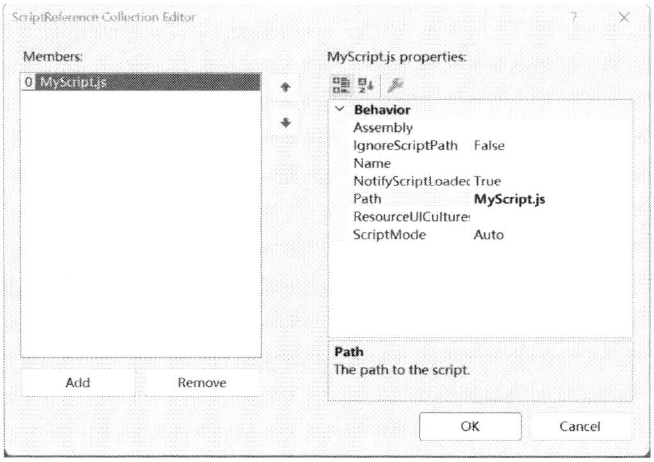

Figure 11-2 Setting Scripts Attribute of ScriptManager Control

The example codes are as follows:

```
<asp:ScriptManager ID=" ScriptManager1" runat="server">
  <Scripts>
    <asp:ScriptReference path="MyScript.js" />
  </Scripts>
</asp:ScriptManager>
```

The codes represent that the file MyScript.js of the curstom JavaScript is registered in the ScriptManager control ScriptManager1.

You also can use RegisterClientScriptBlock () method to directly register the curstom JavaScript in ScriptManager control. The example codes are as follows:

```
ScriptManager.RegisterClientScriptBlock(Button1, typeof(Button), DateTime.Now.ToString(),
"alert('welcome')", true);
```

2.Using ScriptManager in the master page

The ScriptManager control is added into the master page, then the other ASP.NET Ajax server controls is added into the content page. Only one ScriptManager control is allowed in ASP.NET Ajax page. So, if you have added a ScriptManager control in the master page, you can also add a ScriptManagerProxy control in the content page to execute the other functions of the ScriptManager control. ScriptManagerProxy control is dedicated to the content pages that use master pages. The example codes as follows represent that the file MyScript.js of the curstom JavaScript is registered in the content page by using ScriptManagerProxy control.

```
<%@ Page Language="C#" MasterPageFile="~/AjaxMasterPage.master" %>
<asp:Content ID="Content1" ContentPlaceHolderID="ContentPlaceHolder1" Runat="Server">
  <asp:ScriptManagerProxy ID="ScriptManagerProxy1" runat="server">
    <Scripts>
      <asp:ScriptReference Path="MyScript.js" />
    </Scripts>
  </asp:ScriptManagerProxy>
</asp:Content>
```

11.2.2 UpdatePanel control

The UpdatePanel control is a container control, and the control itself can't display any content on the page. The main function of this control is that it can partial refresh the control which is placed in it. Using the UpdatePanel control can reduce the screen flicker when the whole page is posted back, and can improve the interactivity of the pages and the user experience. At the same time, using this control can reduce the amount of data that are transferred between the client and the server.

You can place multiple UpdatePanel controls in one page. Each UpdatePanel control can specify the independent page region, and implement the independent local refreshing function. In practical, you should place the control that needs to be partially refreshed in the <ContentTemplate> child element inside the UpdatePanel control. You also can define the trigger by using <asp:AsyncPostBackTrigger> element within the <Triggers> element of the control. The example codes are as follows:

```
<asp:UpdatePanel ID="UpdatePanel1" runat="server">
   <ContentTemplate>
       ...... //Add need to refresh the control
   </ContentTemplate>
   <Triggers>
     <asp:AsyncPostBackTrigger ControlID="Button1" EventName="Click" />
   </Triggers>
</asp:UpdatePanel>
```

1.Refreshing UpdatePanel control by using the internal button included in UpdatePanel control

Example 11-1 Refreshing UpdatePanel control by using the internal button

As is shown in Figure 11-3 and Figure 11-4, clicking "Refresh" button will trigger the page back and forth, and the Label control included in UpdatePanel control will be refreshed, but the Label control outside UpdatePanel control isn't refreshed.

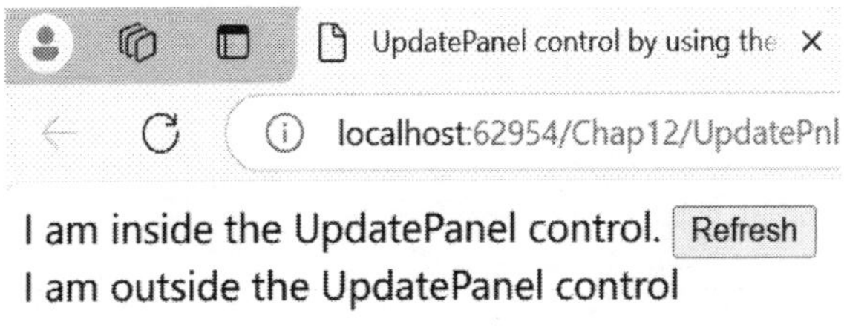

Figure 11-3 The Effect of UpdatePnlIn.aspx (1)

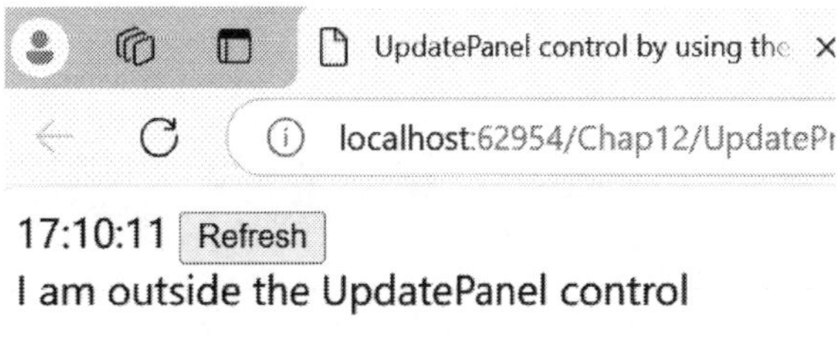

Figure 11-4 The Effect of UpdatePnlIn.aspx (2)

Source Codes: UpdatePnlIn.aspx

```
<%@ Page Language="C#" AutoEventWireup="true" CodeFile="UpdatePnlIn.aspx.cs"
Inherits="Chap11_UpdatePnlIn" %>
<!DOCTYPE html>
<html xmlns="http://www.w3.org/1999/xhtml">
<head runat="server">
 <meta http-equiv="Content-Type" content="text/html; charset=utf-8" />
 <title>Using the internal button to refresh the UpdatePanel control</title>
</head>
<body>
 <form id="form1" runat="server">
  <div>
   <asp:ScriptManager ID="ScriptManager1" runat="server" />
   <asp:UpdatePanel ID="UpdatePanel1" runat="server">
    <ContentTemplate>
     <asp:Label ID="lblInterior" runat="server"></asp:Label>
     <asp:Button ID="btnRefresh" runat="server" OnClick="BtnRefresh_Click" Text="Refresh" />
    </ContentTemplate>
   </asp:UpdatePanel>
   <asp:Label ID="lblExterior" runat="server"></asp:Label>
  </div>
 </form>
</body>
</html>
```

Source Codes: UpdatePnlIn.aspx.cs

```
using System;
public partial class Chap11_UpdatePnlIn : System.Web.UI.Page
{
 protected void Page_Load(object sender, EventArgs e)
 {
  lblInterior.Text = "I am in UpdatePanel control";
  lblExterior.Text = "I am outside UpdatePanel control";
 }
 protected void BtnRefresh_Click(object sender, EventArgs e)
 {
  lblInterior.Text = DateTime.Now.ToLongTimeString();
  lblExterior.Text = DateTime.Now.ToLongTimeString();
 }
}
```

Operating Steps:

(1) Creating UpdatePnlIn.aspx in the folder Chap11. Adding one ScriptManager control and one UpdatePanel control. The corresponding element of ScriptManager control must be placed the corresponding elements of the other controls.

(2) Adding one Lable control and one button control in UpdatePanel control, adding one Lable control outside the UpdatePanel control, and setting the attributes of each control referencing the source codes.

(3) Creating UpdatePnlIn.aspx.cs. At last, browsing the effect of UpdatePnlIn.aspx and testing the effect.

Program Description:

By default, any postback control within the UpdatePanel control (such as the Button control) will cause asynchronous postback and refresh the contents of the UpdatePanel. The Label control lblInterior is contained in the <ContentTemplate> child element of the UpdatePanel control UpdatePanel1. When you click the Refresh button, the page round-trip will be triggered, and the lblInterior on the page will be refreshed, but the lblExterior will not be refreshed.

In practical, other controls that can cause page round-trip are allowed to replace Button controls, such as DropDownList control whose attribute AutoPostBack is set to be true.

2.Refreshing UpdatePanel control by using the external button that isn't included in UpdatePanel control

If you want to refresh the partial page by using the external button, you should set the trigger in <Trigger> element of UpdatePanel control

Example 11-2 Refreshing UpdatePanel control by using the external button

As is shown in Figure 11-5 and Figure 11-6, clicking "Refresh" button will trigger the page back and forth, and the Label control on the page will be refreshed, but the Button control isn't refreshed.

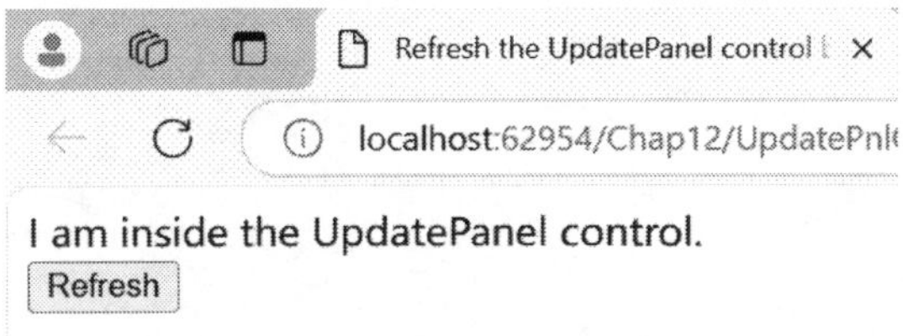

Figure 11-5 The Effect of UpdatePnlOut.aspx (1)

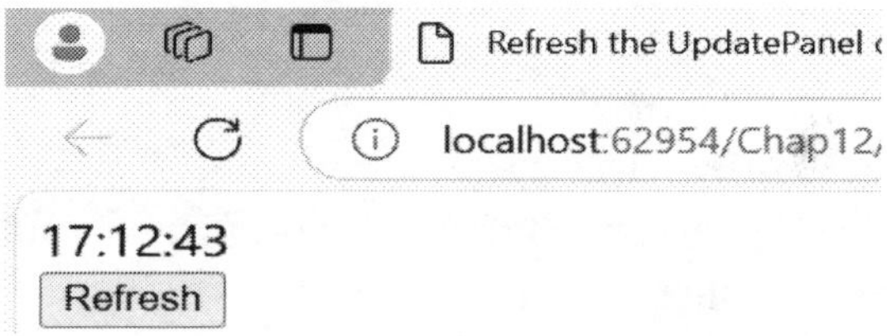

Figure 11-6 The Effect of UpdatePnlOut.aspx (2)

Source Codes: UpdatePnlOut.aspx

```
<%@ Page Language="C#" AutoEventWireup="true" CodeFile="UpdatePnlOut.aspx.cs"
Inherits="Chap11_UpdatePnlOut" %>
<!DOCTYPE html>
<html xmlns="http://www.w3.org/1999/xhtml">
<head runat="server">
 <meta http-equiv="Content-Type" content="text/html; charset=utf-8" />
 <title>To refresh UpdatePanel control by using the external button</title>
</head>
<body>
 <form id="form1" runat="server">
  <div>
```

```
        <asp:ScriptManager ID="ScriptManager1" runat="server" />
        <asp:UpdatePanel ID="UpdatePanel1" runat="server">
          <ContentTemplate>
            <asp:Label ID="lblInterior" runat="server"></asp:Label>
          </ContentTemplate>
          <Triggers>
            <asp:AsyncPostBackTrigger ControlID="btnRefresh" EventName="Click" />
          </Triggers>
        </asp:UpdatePanel>
        <asp:Button ID="btnRefresh" runat="server" OnClick="BtnRefresh_Click" Text="Refresh" />
      </div>
    </form>
  </body>
</html>
```

Source Codes: UpdatePnlOut.aspx.cs

```
using System;
public partial class Chap11_UpdatePnlOut : System.Web.UI.Page
{
  protected void Page_Load(object sender, EventArgs e)
  {
    lblInterior.Text = "I am in UpdatePanel control";
  }
  protected void BtnRefresh_Click(object sender, EventArgs e)
  {
    lblInterior.Text = DateTime.Now.ToLongTimeString();
  }
}
```

Operating Steps:

(1) Creating UpdatePnlOut.aspx in the folder Chap11. Adding one ScriptManager control and one UpdatePanel control.

(2) Adding one Lable control in UpdatePanel control, then adding one Button control outside UpdatePanel control. Specifying the trigger AsyncPostBack:btnRefresh.Click for UpdatePanel control UpdatePanel 1. As is shown in Figure 11-7.

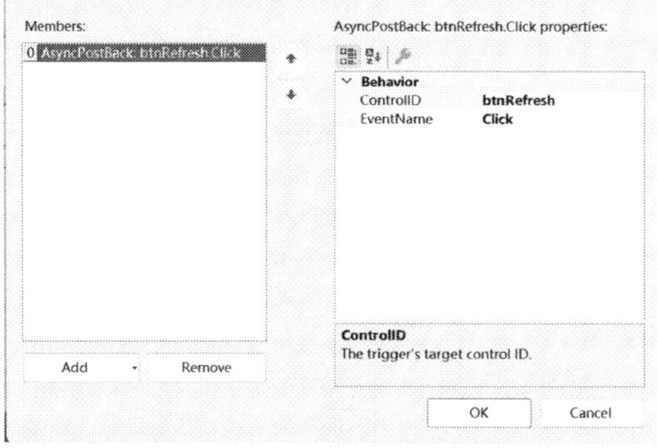

Figure 11-7 Setting the Trigger of UpdatePanel control

(3) Creating UpdatePnlOut.aspx.cs. At last, browsing the effect of UpdatePnlOut.aspx and testing the effect.

Program Description:

To avoid the unnecessary data echo, you can only place the control that needs to be updated in the corresponding <ContentTemplate> element of the UpdatePanel control, and place the control that triggers the echo event outside the UpdatePanel control, and set the trigger for the UpdatePanel control at the same time. In example 11-1, the loopback data related to the Button control needs to be returned, but this example does not need to return these loopback data. Therefore, a smaller asynchronous response will be returned.

3.Using multiple UpdatePanel controls in the same page

After the local page is refreshed, a synchronous postback can be executed to refresh the whole page, or an asynchronous postback can be executed to refresh the contents of one or more UpdatePanel controls. Whether the asynchronous postback is executed and the UpdatePanel control is refreshed will be determined according to the value of the attribute UpdateMode.

If the value of attribute UpdateMode of UpdatePanel control is set to Always, the content in the UpdatePanel control will be refreshed when the postback is executed.

If the value of attribute UpdateMode is set to Conditional, the contents of the UpdatePanel control will be refreshed in the following cases:

(1) When the Update() method of UpdatePanel control is explicitly called.

(2) When the UpdatePanel control is nested in another UpdatePanel control and the parent panel is refreshed.

(3) When a control that is defined as a trigger by using the attribute Triggers of the UpdatePanel control causes the postback.

(4) When the valude of the attribute ChildrenAsTriggers is set to True and the child control of the UpdatePanel control causes the postback.

Note: It is not allowed to set the value of the attribute ChildrenAsTriggers to False and the value of attribute UpdateMode to Always at the same time, otherwise an exception will be thrown.

Example 11-3 Using multiple UpdatePanel controls in the same page

As is shown in Figure 11-8 and Figure 11-9, there are two independent refreshing regions specified by UpdatePanel controls. In this example, clicking different buttons will refresh the different regions. When you click the "Refresh the first panel" button, the page round-trip will be triggered, and the lblUp1 control on the page will be refreshed. When you click the "Refresh the 2nd Panel" button, the page round-trip will be triggered, and the lblUp2 control on the page will be refreshed.

Figure 11-8 The Effect of MultiUpdatePanel.aspx (1)

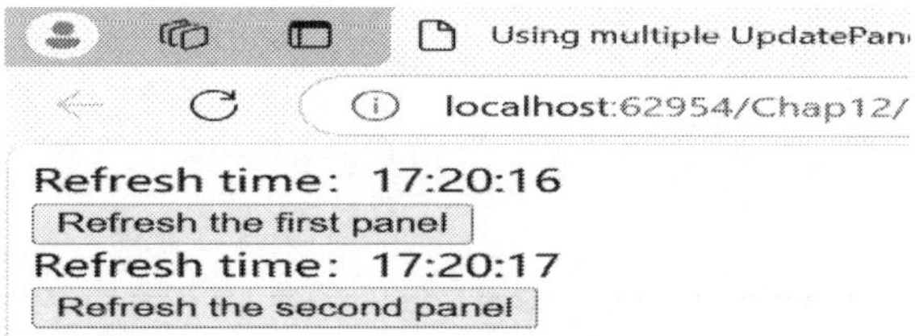

Figure 11-9 The Effect of MultiUpdatePanel.aspx (2)

Source Codes: MultiUpdatePanel.aspx

```
<%@ Page Language="C#" AutoEventWireup="true" CodeFile="MultiUpdatePanel.aspx.cs"
Inherits="Chap11_MultiUpdatePanel" %>
<!DOCTYPE html>
<html xmlns="http://www.w3.org/1999/xhtml">
<head runat="server">
  <meta http-equiv="Content-Type" content="text/html; charset=utf-8" />
  <title>To use multiple UpdatePanel controls in the same page</title>
</head>
<body>
  <form id="form1" runat="server">
    <div>
      <asp:ScriptManager ID="ScriptManager1" runat="server" />
      <asp:UpdatePanel ID="UpdatePanel1" runat="server" UpdateMode="Conditional">
        <ContentTemplate>
          <asp:Label ID="lblUp1" runat="server" Text="I am in the first panel"></asp:Label><br />
          <asp:Button ID="btnUp1" runat="server" OnClick="BtnUp1_Click" Text="Refresh the first
panel" />
        </ContentTemplate>
      </asp:UpdatePanel>
      <asp:UpdatePanel ID="UpdatePanel2" runat="server" UpdateMode="Conditional">
        <ContentTemplate>
          <asp:Label ID="lblUp2" runat="server" Text="I am in the 2nd panel"></asp:Label>
        </ContentTemplate>
        <Triggers>
          <asp:AsyncPostBackTrigger ControlID="btnUp2" EventName="Click" />
        </Triggers>
      </asp:UpdatePanel>
      <asp:Button ID="btnUp2" runat="server" OnClick="BtnUp2_Click" Text="Refresh the 2nd
panel" />
      <asp:UpdateProgress ID="UpdateProgress1" runat="server">
      </asp:UpdateProgress>
    </div>
  </form>
</body>
</html>
```

Source Codes: MultiUpdatePanel.aspx.cs

```
using System;
public partial class Chap11_MultiUpdatePanel : System.Web.UI.Page
{
  protected void BtnUp1_Click(object sender, EventArgs e)
  {
    lblUp1.Text = "Refresh Time: " + DateTime.Now.ToLongTimeString();
  }
  protected void BtnUp2_Click(object sender, EventArgs e)
  {
    lblUp2.Text = "Refresh Time: " + DateTime.Now.ToLongTimeString();
  }
}
```

Operating Steps:

(1) Creating MultiUpdatePanel.aspx in the folder Chap11. Adding one ScriptManager control and two UpdatePanel controls.

(2) Adding one Lable control and one Button control in UpdatePanel control UpdatePanel1.

(3) Adding one Lable control in UpdatePanel control UpdatePanel2, adding one Button control outside the two UpdatePanel controls, and setting the attributes of each control referencing the source codes.

(4) Creating MultiUpdatePanel.aspx.cs. At last, browsing the effect of MultiUpdatePanel.aspx and testing the effect.

11.2.3 Timer control

Timer control performs synchronous or asynchronous postbacks according to the defined intervals. When the contents of one or more UpdatePanel controls of the page needs to be regularly refreshed, the Timer control can be used.

Timer control will embed a JavaScript component into the page. After the time interval is defined by the attribute Interval, the Tick event of the Timer control will be triggered.

Attribute Interval can specify the frequency of the postback, while attribute Enabled can enable or disable the Timer control.

When you use Timer control, multiple Timer controls can be contained on the page, or you can use a Timer control as a trigger association control for multiple UpdatePanel controls on the page.

Example 11-4 Using Timer control

As is shown in Figure 11-10, in this example, the value of exchange rate on the page and the generation time of the exchange rate are periodically refreshed by using the Timer control. Initially, the Timer control triggers a page round trip every 5 seconds to update the content of the UpdatePanel. The user can choose to refresh the value of exchange rate every 5 seconds or every 60 seconds, or choose not to refresh the value.

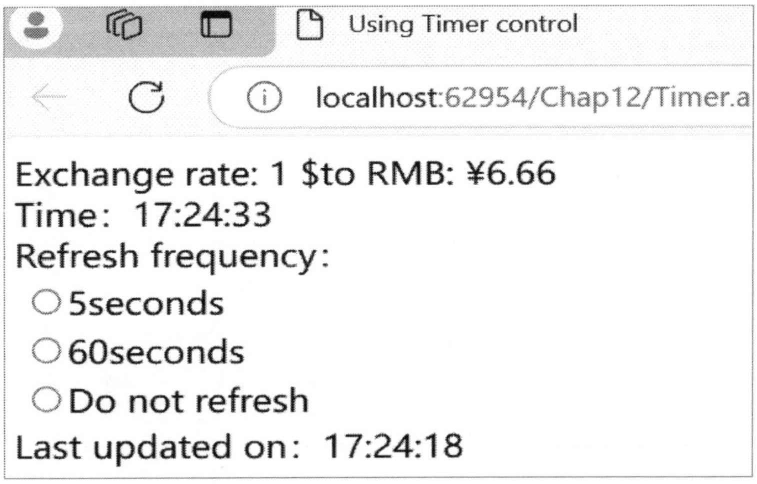

Figure 11-10 The Effect of Timer.aspx

Source Codes: Timer.aspx

```
<%@ Page Language="C#" AutoEventWireup="true" CodeFile="Timer.aspx.cs" Inherits="Chap11_Timer" %>
<!DOCTYPE html>
<html xmlns="http://www.w3.org/1999/xhtml">
<head runat="server">
 <meta http-equiv="Content-Type" content="text/html; charset=utf-8" />
 <title>To use Timer control</title>
</head>
<body>
 <form id="form1" runat="server">
  <div>
   <asp:ScriptManager ID="ScriptManager1" runat="server" />
   <asp:Timer ID="tmrStock" OnTick="TmrStock_Tick" runat="server" Interval="5000" />
   <asp:UpdatePanel ID="upStock" runat="server" UpdateMode="Conditional">
    <Triggers>
     <asp:AsyncPostBackTrigger ControlID="tmrStock" />
    </Triggers>
    <ContentTemplate>
     Exchange Rate: 1$ exchangeRMB <asp:Label ID="lblPrice"
         runat="server"></asp:Label><br />
     Time: <asp:Label ID="lblPriceTime" runat="server"></asp:Label>
    </ContentTemplate>
   </asp:UpdatePanel>
   Refresh Frequency: <br />
   <asp:RadioButtonList ID="rdoltFrequency" runat="server" AutoPostBack="True"
       OnSelectedIndexChanged="RdoltFrequency_SelectedIndexChanged">
    <asp:ListItem Value="5000">5 seconds</asp:ListItem>
    <asp:ListItem Value="60000">60 seconds</asp:ListItem>
    <asp:ListItem Value="0">No Refresh</asp:ListItem>
   </asp:RadioButtonList>
   The last refreshing time of the page:<asp:Label ID="lblPageTime" runat="server"></asp:Label>
  </div>
 </form>
</body>
</html>
```

Source Codes: Timer.aspx.cs

```
using System;
public partial class Chap11_Timer : System.Web.UI.Page
{
 protected void Page_Load(object sender, EventArgs e)
 {
```

```
        lblPageTime.Text = DateTime.Now.ToLongTimeString();
    }
    protected void TmrStock_Tick(object sender, EventArgs e)
    {
        lblPrice.Text = GetStockPrice();
        lblPriceTime.Text = DateTime.Now.ToLongTimeString();
    }
    private string GetStockPrice()
    {
        double randomStockPrice = 5.8 + new Random().NextDouble();
        return randomStockPrice.ToString("C");
    }
    protected void RdoltFrequency_SelectedIndexChanged(object sender, EventArgs e)
    {
        if (rdoltFrequency.SelectedValue == "0")
        {
            tmrStock.Enabled = false;
        }
        else
        {
            tmrStock.Enabled = true;
            tmrStock.Interval = int.Parse(rdoltFrequency.SelectedValue);
        }
    }
}
```

Operating Steps:

(1) Creating Timer.aspx in the folder Chap11. Adding one ScriptManager control, one Timer control, one UpdatePanel control and one RadioButtonList control. Adding two Label controls in UpdatePanel control, specifying the trigger, you can set Item attribute of the RadioButtonList control as is shown in Figure 11-11, setting the other attributes referencing the source codes.

(2) Creating Timer.aspx.cs. At last, browsing the Timer.aspx and testing it.

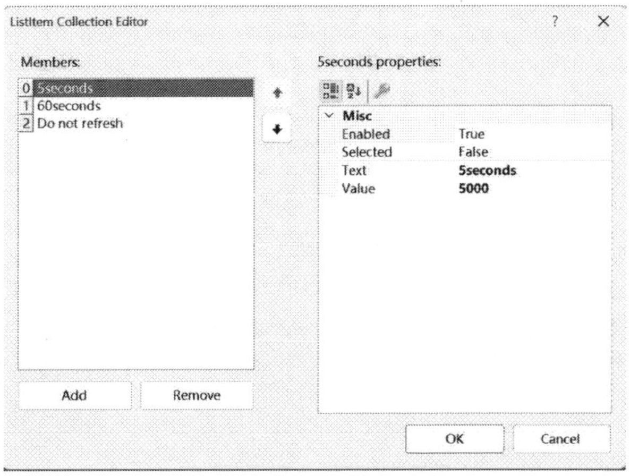

Figure 11-11 Setting the Items attribute of RadioButtonList control

Program Description:

When the value of attribute tmrStock.Enabled of tmrStock.Tick event is true, the time set by the tmrStock.Interval attribute is automatically triggered once, and the method codes of tmrStock_Tick() is executed. When the "5 seconds" or "60 seconds" is selected, the value of attribute tmrStock.Enabled is set to True, and the frequency of postback is set by modifying the value of attribute tmrStock.Interval. When the "Do not refresh" is selected, the value of attribute tmrStock.Enabled is set to False. At this time, the tmrStock.Tick event will not be triggered.

11.2.4 UpdateProgress control

When the web page contains one or more UpdatePanel controls that are used to refresh the partial page, UpdateProgress control can be used to design a more intuitive user interface (UI). If the partial page is refreshed slowly, UpdateProgress control can display the task completion.

In a web page, there can be multiple UpdateProgress controls, and every UpdateProgress control can be associated with a single UpdatePanel control by setting the attribute AssociatedUpdatePanelID of UpdateProgress control. You also can use the UpdateProgress control which is not associated with any particular UpdatePanel control. In this case, the control will show the progress messages of all of the UpdatePanel controls.

Example 11-5 Using UpdateProgress control

As is shown in Figure 11-12 and Figure 11-13, in this example, when you click the " Refresh" button, the progress bar information of the partial page refreshing is displayed.

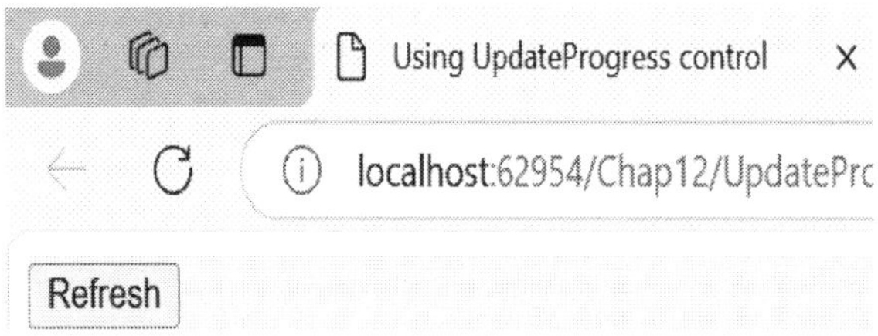

Figure 11-12 The Effect ofUpdateProgress.aspx (1)

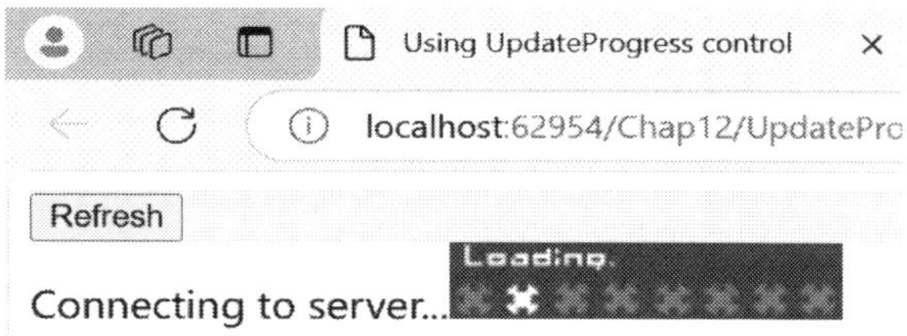

Figure 11-13 The Effect of UpdateProgress.aspx (2)

Source Codes: UpdateProgress.aspx

```
<%@ Page Language="C#" AutoEventWireup="true" CodeFile="UpdateProgress.aspx.cs"
Inherits="Chap11_UpdateProgress" %>
<!DOCTYPE html>
<html xmlns="http://www.w3.org/1999/xhtml">
<head runat="server">
  <meta http-equiv="Content-Type" content="text/html; charset=utf-8" />
  <title>To use UpdateProgress control</title>
</head>
<body>
  <form id="form1" runat="server">
```

```
    <div>
     <asp:ScriptManager ID="ScriptManager1" runat="server" />
     <asp:UpdatePanel ID="UpdatePanel1" runat="server">
      <ContentTemplate>
       <div style="background-color: #FFFFE0">
        <asp:Label ID="lblTime" runat="server"></asp:Label>
       <asp:Button ID="btnRefresh" runat="server" OnClick="BtnRefresh_Click" Text="Refresh"/>
       </div>
      </ContentTemplate>
     </asp:UpdatePanel>
     <asp:UpdateProgress runat="server" ID="UpdateProgress1">
      <ProgressTemplate>
      Connecting the server...<img src="wait.gif" alt="" />
      </ProgressTemplate>
     </asp:UpdateProgress>
    </div>
  </form>
</body>
</html>
```

Source Codes: UpdateProgress.aspx.cs

```
using System;
public partial class Chap11_UpdateProgress : System.Web.UI.Page
{
 protected void BtnRefresh_Click(object sender, EventArgs e)
 {
  System.Threading.Thread.Sleep(TimeSpan.FromSeconds(10));
  lblTime.Text = DateTime.Now.ToLongTimeString();
 }
}
```

Operating Steps:

(1) Creating UpdateProgress.aspx in the folder Chap11. Adding one ScriptManager control, one UpdateProgress control, and one UpdatePanel control. Adding one div layer in UpdatePanel control, and adding one Label control and one Button control in this layer. Entering "Connecting the server..." in the UpdateProgress control, adding a HTML control Image, and setting the attributes of each control referencing the source codes.

(2) Creating UpdateProgress.aspx.cs. At last, browsing the UpdateProgress.aspx and testing it.

Program Description:

In the codes of Click event processing of the btnRefresh button, in order to see the effect of the UpdateProgress control, you can use the Thread.Sleep () method to delay for 10 seconds, and then current time of the server will be returned to the server. In practical, the delay is often caused by large data traffic or server codes that take a long time to process, such as you will take a long time to query the complex database.

11.3 The AjaxControlToolkit Package

AjaxControlToolkit package is an open source project based on the ASP.NET Ajax framework. It provides an extended set of Ajax control tools, and the user can use the controls included in this set like using the other server controls of ASP.NET.

In VSC 2019, selecting "Web Site"→ "Manage NuGet Package" command to start the window of NuGet package, then searching AjaxControlToolkit and clicking "Install" button, NuGet can install the AjaxControlToolkit package into the site automatically. After installation, a new folder packages\AjaxControlToolkit.17.1.1.0 is added into the folder which is used to store the current storage solution file. The software version will be changed with the installation version.

The steps of using the controls included in AjaxControlToolkit package are as follows:

(1) Opening "ToolBox" window, right clicking the blank, selecting "Add Tab" in the pop-up shortcut menu command, and entering the tab name "AjaxControlToolkit".

(2) Right clicking "AjaxControlToolkit" tab, selecting "Choose Item" command in the pop-up shortcut menu, opening "Select Tool Box" dialog box, clicking "Browse" button, and selecting AjaxControlToolkit.dll file in the folder AjaxControlToolkit.17.1.1.0\lib\net40. At this time, VSC 2019 will selects all of the controls in the namespace AjaxControlToolkit, as is shown in Figure 11-14.

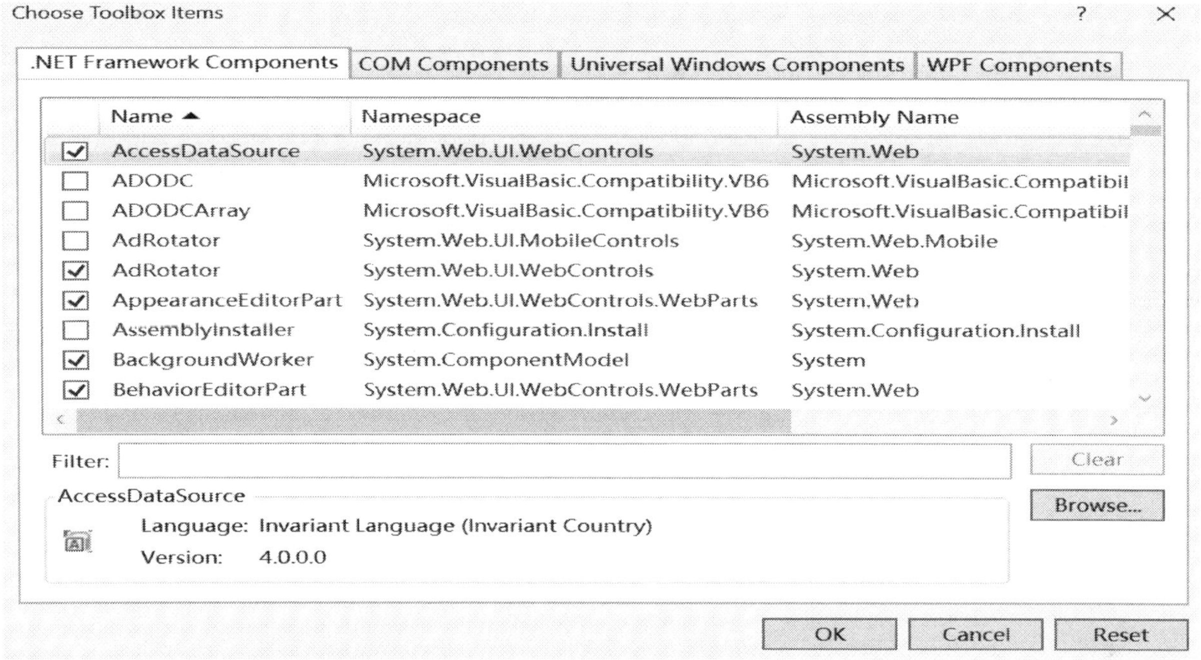

Figure 11-14 The Dialog Box of "Choose Tool Box Item"

(3) Clicking "OK" button in Figure 11-14, you can add Ajax controls.

Table 11-1 represents the common Ajax controls included in AjaxControlToolkit packages.

Table 11-1 The table of common Ajax controls included in AjaxControlToolkit packages

Controls	Descriptions
AlwaysVisibleControlExtender	The panel is suspended in a fixed position.
CollapsiblePanelExtender	The folding of the panel.
DropShadowExtender	Let the panel projected out of the shadows.
HoverMenuExtender	Display additional information panel.
ModalPopupExtender	Web page in the modal dialog box.
RoundedCornersExtender	Add the rounded effect for the panel.
TextBoxWatermarkExtender	The TextBox with watermark effect.
ToggleButtonExtender	Use pictures to instead of the CheckBox
SliderExtender	Web page slider.
DropDownExtender	SharePoint style drop-down menu.
ValidatorCalloutExtender	Even more striking the Validator.
ReorderList	Use the mouse to drag the change order entry.
Rating	Style rich rating function.
Accordion	The set of collapsible panels.
NoBot	Refused to robots.
CascadingDropDown	Realize linkage drop-down box.
ConfirmButtonExtender	With the function of confirm button.
DragPanelExtender	Can drag the window in the page.
DynamicPopulateExtender	Dynamic UpdatePanel.
FilteredTextBoxExtender	To prevent user input validation.
NumericUpDownExtender	Use the up and down arrows to adjust the value in the TextBox.
PagingBulletedListExtender	On the client side BulletedList index, paging and sorting.
PasswordStrength	The strength of the inspection password immediately.
PopupControlExtender	Help the user to input panel.
ResizableControlExtender	Drag and drop the frame to change the size of the panel.
AnimationExtender	Comparable to Flash the JavaScript animation.
UpdatePanelAnimationExtender	Let the UpdatePanel updates are no longer drab.
MutuallyExclusiveCheckBoxExtender	Allowed the selected radio button group.

Example 11-6 Using CalendarExtender control

The function of date inputting is widely used in the development of Web applications, and can be easily realized through the CalendarExtender control. As is shown in Figure 11-15, when the text box gets the focus, the calender dialog will pop up, after clicking the date. The date is displayed on the text box. After clicking the start time and end time, clicking "Search" button, the prompt message will be displayed as is shown in Figure 11-16.

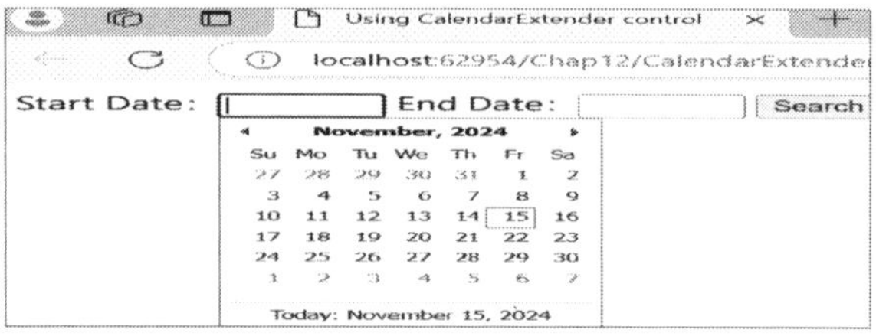

Figure 11-15 The Effect of CalendarExtender.aspx (1)

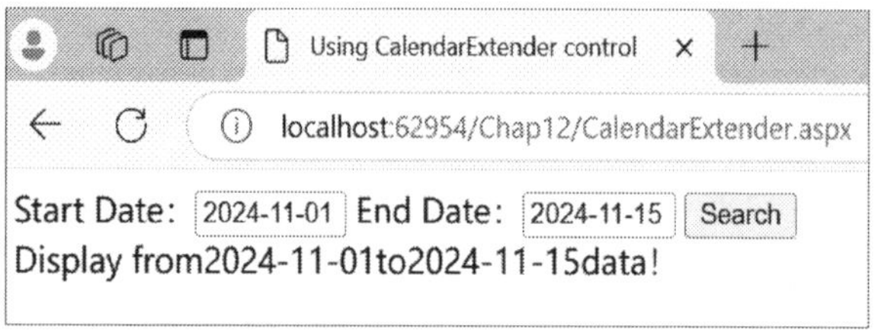

Figure 11-16 The Effect of CalendarExtender.aspx (2)

Source Codes: CalendarExtender.aspx

```
<%@ Page Language="C#" AutoEventWireup="true" CodeFile="c.aspx.cs"
Inherits="Chap11_CalendarExtender" %>
<!DOCTYPE html>
<html xmlns="http://www.w3.org/1999/xhtml">
<head runat="server">
  <meta http-equiv="Content-Type" content="text/html; charset=utf-8" />
  <title>To use CalendarExtender control</title>
</head>
<body>
  <form id="form1" runat="server">
    <div>
      <asp:ScriptManager ID="ScriptManager1" runat="server">
      </asp:ScriptManager>
      Start Time: <asp:TextBox ID="txtStartTime" runat="server" Width="70px"></asp:TextBox>
      <ajaxToolkit:CalendarExtender ID="txtStartTime_cldE" runat="server"
TargetControlID="txtStartTime" Format="yyyy-MM-dd" />
      End Time: <asp:TextBox ID="txtEndTime" runat="server" Width="70px"></asp:TextBox>
      <ajaxToolkit:CalendarExtender ID="txtEndTime_cldE" runat="server"
TargetControlID="txtEndTime" Format="yyyy-MM-dd" />
    <asp:Button ID="btnSearch" runat="server" Text="Search" OnClick="BtnSearch_Click" /><br />
      <asp:Label ID="lblDisplay" runat="server"></asp:Label>
    </div>
  </form>
</body>
</html>
```

Source Codes: CalendarExtender.aspx.cs

```
using System;
public partial class Chap11_CalendarExtender : System.Web.UI.Page
{
  protected void BtnSearch_Click(object sender, EventArgs e)
  {
    lblDisplay.Text = "Display from" + txtStartTime.Text + "to " + txtEndTime.Text + "data!";
  }
}
```

Operating Steps:

(1) Installing AjaxControlToolkit package through "Web Site"→ "Manage NuGet Package" command.

(2) Creating CalendarExtender.aspx in folder Chap11, adding one ScriptManager control, two TextBox controls, two CalendarExtender controls, and one Button control, entering "Start Time" and "End Time" at the proper location, and setting the attributes of each control referencing the source codes.

(3) Creating CalendarExtender.aspx.cs. At last, browsing the CalendarExtender.aspx and testing it.

Program Description:

CalendarExtender control establishes an association with the corresponding text box through the attribute TargetControlID. Setting the display format of the date through the Format attribute, where the year, month and date are represented by yyyy, MM and dd respectively, and should be case-sensitive.

Example 11-7 Using PasswordStrength control

In order to effectively prevent the violent password cracking, it is often necessary to detect the strength of the password entered by the user when the user registers the web site. In this example, two different password strength prompt modes are given. As is shown in Figure 11-17, when you enter the passwords in the password text box with the different strength, the information of "Strength: weak", "Strength: medium" and "Strength: strong" will be prompted respectively. As is shown in Figure 11-18, when you enter the passwords with the different strength in the "Confirm Password" text box, the bar with red, blue, and green will be displayed respectively.

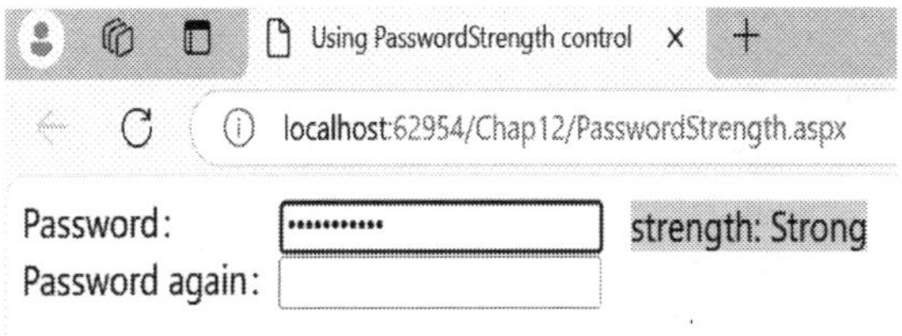

Figure 11-17 The Effect of PasswordStrength.aspx (1)

Figure 11-18 The Effect of PasswordStrength.aspx (2)

Source Codes: PasswordStrength.aspx

```
<%@ Page Language="C#" AutoEventWireup="true" CodeFile="PasswordStrength.aspx.cs"
Inherits="Chap11_PasswordStrength" %>
<!DOCTYPE html>
<html xmlns="http://www.w3.org/1999/xhtml">
<head runat="server">
  <meta http-equiv="Content-Type" content="text/html; charset=utf-8" />
  <title>To use PasswordStrength  control</title>
  <style type="text/css">
    .BarWeak { color: Red; background-color: Red; }
    .BarAverage { color: Blue; background-color: Blue; }
    .BarGood { color: Green; background-color: Green; }
    .BarBorder { width: 100px; }
```

```
        .table { width: 98%; }
        .div { width: 338px; }
        .td { width: 80px; text-align: right; }
    </style>
</head>
<body>
    <form id="form1" runat="server">
      <div class="div">
        <asp:ScriptManager ID="ScriptManager1" runat="server">
        </asp:ScriptManager>
        <table class="table">
          <tr>
            <td class="td">Password:
            </td>
            <td>
              <asp:TextBox ID="txtPwd" runat="server" TextMode="Password"></asp:TextBox>
              <ajaxToolkit:PasswordStrength ID="txtPwd_PasswordStrength" runat="server"
TargetControlID="txtPwd" PrefixText="Strength: " TextStrengthDescriptions="weak; medium; strong" />
            </td>
          </tr>
          <tr>
            <td class="td">Confirm Password:
            </td>
            <td>
              <asp:TextBox ID="txtPwdCfm" runat="server" TextMode="Password"></asp:TextBox>
              <ajaxToolkit:PasswordStrength ID="txtPwdCfm_PasswordStrength" runat="server"
TargetControlID="txtPwdCfm" BarBorderCssClass="BarBorder" StrengthIndicatorType="BarIndic
ator" StrengthStyles="BarWeak; BarAverage; BarGood" />
            </td>
          </tr>
        </table>
      </div>
    </form>
</body>
</html>
```

Operating Steps:

(1) Installing AjaxControlToolkit package through "Web Site"→ "Manage NuGet Package" command.

(2) Creating PasswordStrength.aspx in folder Chap11, adding one ScriptManager control, two TextBox controls, and two PasswordStrength controls, entering "Password" and "Confirm Password" at the proper location, and setting the attributes of each control referencing the source codes. At last, browsing the CalendarExtender.aspx and testing it.

Program Description:

PasswordStrength control prompts the password strength in text method by default. If you want to prompt the password strength in progress bar, you need to set the attribute StrengthIndicatorType="Bar Indicator". When the password strength is prompted in text method, you can set the different password strength information through the attribute TextStrengthDescriptions; when the password strength is prompted by the progress bar, the progress bar border style and the progress bar information of the different color are set through the attributeBarBorderCssClass and StrengthStyles attributes, where the different color are distinguished by different styles. For example, in this example, the three levels of password strength "weak", "medium" and "strong" correspond to "red", "blue" and "green" respectively, and are represented by the styles BarWeek, BarAverage and BarGood respectively.

PasswordStrength control also includes the other common attributes, such as MinimumLowerCase CharactersMinimumNumericCharacters, MinimumSymbolCharacters, MinimumUpperCaseCharacters, and RequiresUpperAndLowerCaseCharacters.

11.4 Summary

➢ ScriptManager control is the core of ASP.NET Ajax, and every Ajax page must contain ScriptManager control.

➢ UpdatePanel control defines the region of the page that is refreshed by using asynchronous postback.

➢ UpdateProgress control provides information about the state of the UpdatePanel when it partially refreshes the page.

➢ Timer control performs the page postback by defining a fixed time interval.

➢ AjaxControlToolkit extends the functions of server controls.

11.5 Exercises

1. Fill-in-blank Questions

(1)________page is often referred to as a refresh-free web page.

(2) The technologies used by Ajax applications include________, ________, ________.

(3)________control is the core of ASP.NET Ajax function.

(4) To use the UpdatePanel control, ________control must be added firstly.

2. True or False Questions

(1) Two UpdatePanel controls can be placed on a page at most.(　　)

(2) The usage of the ScriptManager control is the same with the ScriptManagerProxy control.(　　)

(3) The EnablePartialRendering property of the ScriptManager control determines whether a page can be partially refreshed. By default, the value of the EnablePartialRendering property is True.(　　)

(4) The AjaxControlToolkit package is installed by default in VSC 2019.(　　)

(5) The value of Interval property of the Timer control is defined in seconds, with a default value of 60 seconds.(　　)

(6) In ASP.NET Ajax, except for ASP.NET Ajax Library, custom JavaScript code can also be used.(　　)

(7) After setting up, clicking the button anywhere on the page can refresh the content within the pdatePanel control.(　　)

3. Multiple-choice questions

(1)Among the following technologies, (　　) is not necessary for Ajax applications?

A.ASP.NET　　B. JavaScript　　C. XML　　D. XMLHttpRequest object

(2)Among the following controls, (　　) is required for ASP.NET Ajax pages?

A.Timer　　B. UpdatePanel　　C. UpdateProgress　　D. ScriptManager

(3)(　　) is correct regarding the number of UpdatePanel controls that can be used on a page?

A. One　　B. At most one　　C. Multiple　　D. At least one

(4)(　　) can not be used to extend the TextBox control?

A.BalloonPopupExtender　　B. UpdatePanelAnimationExtender　　C. AutoCompleteExtender

D. CalendarExtender

4. Programming Questions

(1) Create and debug all of the instances in this chapter.

(2) Design and implement a page that automatically displays the next product.

(3) Design and implement a page for local data query refresh, with the following requirements:

① After selecting a product name from the dropdown list box, display the query results in the GridView, without refreshing other parts of the page.

② Use controls to display the completion status of tasks.

(4) Design and implement a guestbook based on ASP.NET Ajax.

Chapter 12 Web Service

Points:

- Understanding the function of Web service
- Creating Web service
- Mastering how to call Web service

12.1 Web Service

In practical applications, especially in the large enterprise, the data often come from the different platforms and systems. In this case, Web service integration provides a convenient way. The data in the different systems can be accessed by accessing and using the remote Web service.

Web applications not only can share data but also can use the data generated by the other application through the Web service, and don't worry about how other applications generate this data.

Note: It is the important characteristic of the Web service that the information which is returned is the data rather than the page.

Web services need to implement a series of agreements. In the network communication, HTTP protocol is used as the basis of network transmission, and other transmission protocols such as SMTP and FTP can also be used. In the message processing, the simple object access protocol SOAP is used as the message delivery standard.

Web service also needs the support of the Web Service Description Language WSDL and the "Unified Description Discovery Integration" protocol UDDI. WSDL is based on XML format, which is used to describe the Web service information. UDDI is used to store Web service information and publish Web service, and can provide the function of searching Web service.

The actual application process of a Web service is shown in Figure 12-1.

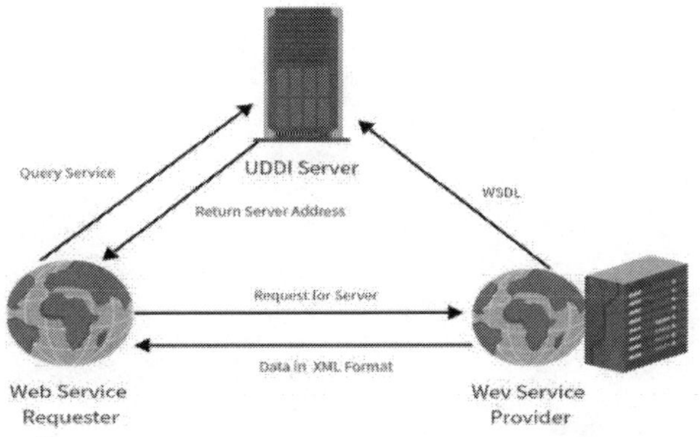

Figure 12-1 The Actual Aapplication of The Web Service

12.1.2 Creating ASP.NET Web service

The essence of creating Web service is to establish one or more methods in the class that supports SOAP communication. You can establish a custom Web service through ASP.NET. The generated Web service meets the industry standards of SOAP, XML and WSDL. So the clients from other platforms are allowed to interact with ASP.NET Web services. As long as the client can send SOAP messages that meet the standards, the client can call ASP.NET Web services, regardless of the platform of the client.

In actual operation, you need to create a service file with a file extension as .asmx, and then declare the Web service in the file. At the same time, you need to create a class file in the APP_Code folder to define the Web service method.

Note: The Web window files and corresponding class files are stored in the same folder, while the class files corresponding to the Web service are stored in the APP_Code folder.

Example 12-1 Creating ASP.NET Web service

The ASP.NET Web service created in this example contains a HelloWorld() method, which returns "I am the data returned by calling the Web service!". The browsing effect of Web service is shown as Figure 12-2. In Figure 12-2, clicking "Service Description" link will display the WDSL description of Web service, as is shown in Figure 12-3; clicking HelloWorld() method can test the created Web service, as is shown in Figure 12-4. In Figure 12-4, clicking "Call" button will call HelloWorld() method, and the XML information including "I am the data returned by calling the Web service!" will be returned.

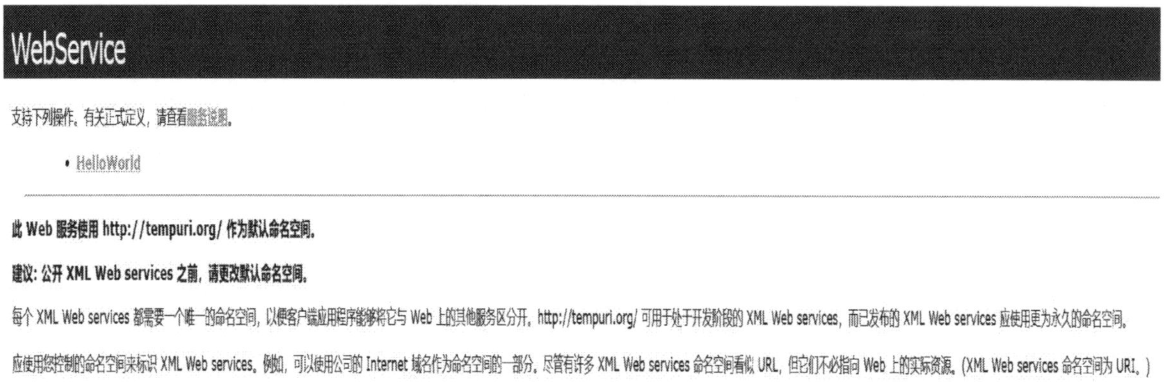

Figure 12-2 The Effect of WebService.asmx

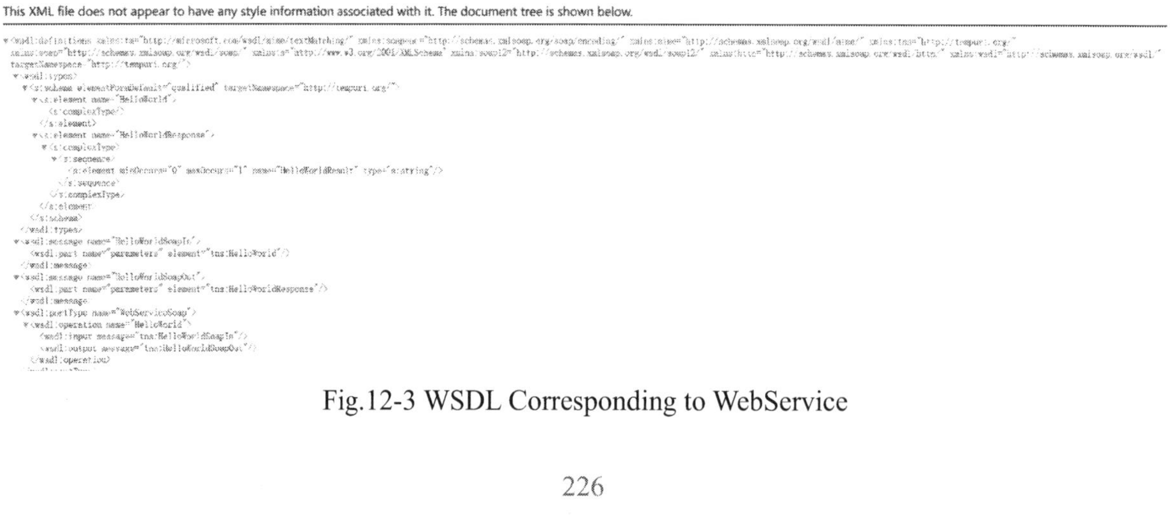

Fig.12-3 WSDL Corresponding to WebService

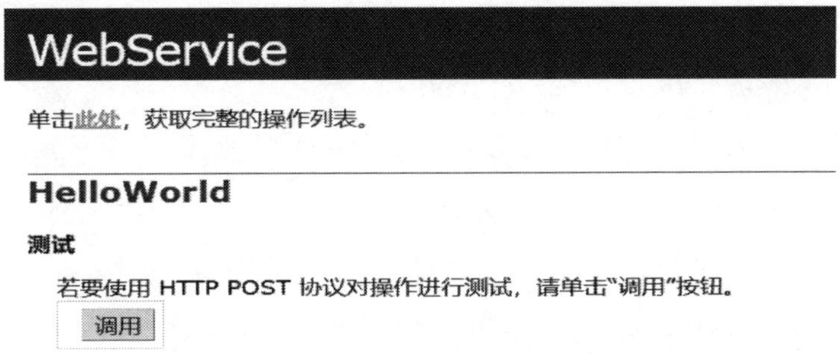

Figure 12-4 The Effect of WebService Test

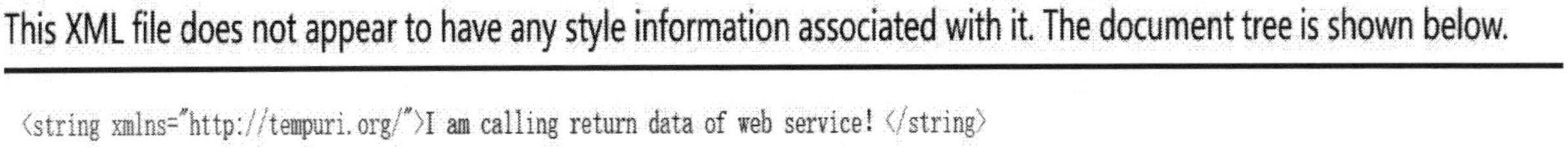

Fig.12-5 The XML Data Returned by HelloWorld() Method in WebService

Source Codes: WebService.asmx

```
<%@ WebService Language="C#" CodeBehind="~/App_Code/WebService.cs"
Class="WebService" %>
```

Source Codes: WebService.cs

```
using System;
using System.Web.Services;
/// <summary>
/// </summary>
[WebService(Namespace = "http://tempuri.org/")]
[WebServiceBinding(ConformsTo = WsiProfiles.BasicProfile1_1)]
public class WebService : System.Web.Services.WebService
{
 public WebService()
 {
  //InitializeComponent();
 }

 [WebMethod]
 public string HelloWorld()
 {
  return "I am the data returned by calling the Web service!";
 }
}
```

Operating Steps:

(1) Creating Chap12Site website in Book Solution.

(2) Right clicking Chap12Site website, selecting "Add"→ "Add New Item" command in the pop-up shortcut menu, then selecting "Web service(ASMX)" template in the rendered dialog box, entering the file name of Web service as WebService.asmx, and clicking "Add" button to establish the file.

(3) Opening WebService.cs in App_Code folder, and entering the content in the shadow part. At last, browsing WebService.asmx and testing it.

Program Description:

In WebService.cs, [WebService (Namespace=" http://tempuri.org/ ")] represents the namespace of this service.

[WebServiceBinding (ConformisTo=WsiProfiles. BasicProfile1_1)] indicates that the specification of Web service is "WS-I Basic Specification Version 1.1".

The essence of creating a Web service is to create a subclass of System.Web.Services.WebService. Before creating a class method, you must add [WebMethod]. If [WebMethod] is not used for declaration, the defined method can only be called inside the service.

12.1.3 Calling ASP.NET Web service

ASP.NET Web service can be used in Web applications, Windows form, mobile Web applications and applications that are edited by using the other program language. In this section, we mainly introduce how to use Web service in the Web applications based on ASP.NET. When you use Web service, in order to allow Microsoft Ajax to call ASP.NET Web service from script libraries, you need to declare [System. Web. Script. Services. ScriptService] before the defined class of Web service.

If you want to use some ASP.NET Web service, you need to add the Web service to the website in the form of "service reference", and then call the service by creating an instance of the service.

Example 12-2 Calling ASP.NET Web service

As shown as Figure 12-6 and Figure 12-7, clicking "Test Web Service" button will call the HelloWorld() method of Web service which is created in example 12-1, and "I am the data returned by calling the Web service!" will be returned.

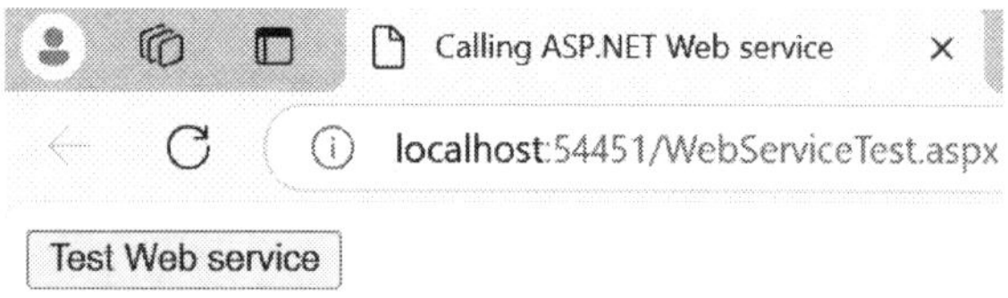

Figure 12-6 The Effect of WebServiceTest.aspx (1)

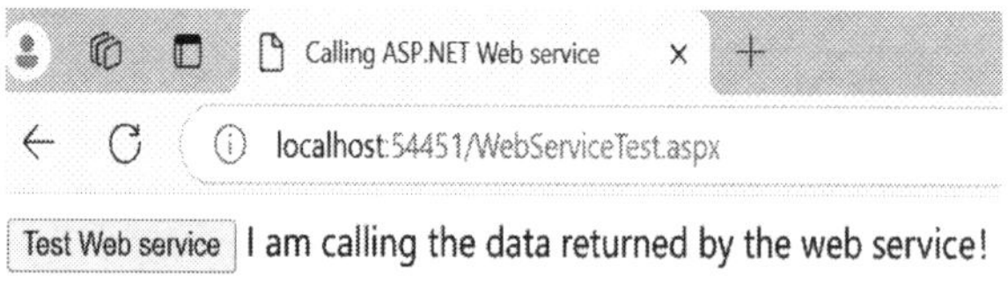

Figure 12-7 The Effect of WebServiceTest.aspx (2)

Source Codes: WebServiceTest.aspx

```
<%@ Page Language="C#" AutoEventWireup="true" CodeFile="WebServiceTest.aspx.cs"
Inherits="WebServiceTest" %>
<!DOCTYPE html>
<html xmlns="http://www.w3.org/1999/xhtml">
<head runat="server">
 <meta http-equiv="Content-Type" content="text/html; charset=utf-8" />


<title>To call ASP.NET Web Service</title>
</head>
<body>
 <form id="form1" runat="server">
  <div>
   <asp:Button ID="btnTest" runat="server" OnClick="BtnTest_Click" Text="Test Web Service" />
    <asp:Label ID="lblMsg" runat="server"></asp:Label>
  </div>
 </form>
</body>
</html>
```

Source Codes: WebServiceTest.aspx.cs

```
using System;
public partial class WebServiceTest : System.Web.UI.Page
{
 protected void BtnTest_Click(object sender, EventArgs e)
 {
ServiceRefWeb.WebServiceSoapClient soapClient = new ServiceRefWeb. WebServiceSoapClient();
  lblMsg.Text = soapClient.HelloWorld();
 }
}
```

Operating Steps:

(1) Adding the Service Reference. Right clicking Chap12Site website, and selecting "Add"→ "Service Reference" command in the pop-up shortcut menu. "Add Service Reference", clicking "Discover" button, all of the services in the solution of the current web site will be added into the "Service" list box automatically. Selecting WebService.asmx and entering namespace ServiceRefWeb, the interface is shown as Figure 12-8. Clicking "Add" button, the service reference is added. At this time, ServiceRefWeb subfolder which is used to describe the WebService information of ASP.NET Web service is created in App_WebReferences folder automatically.

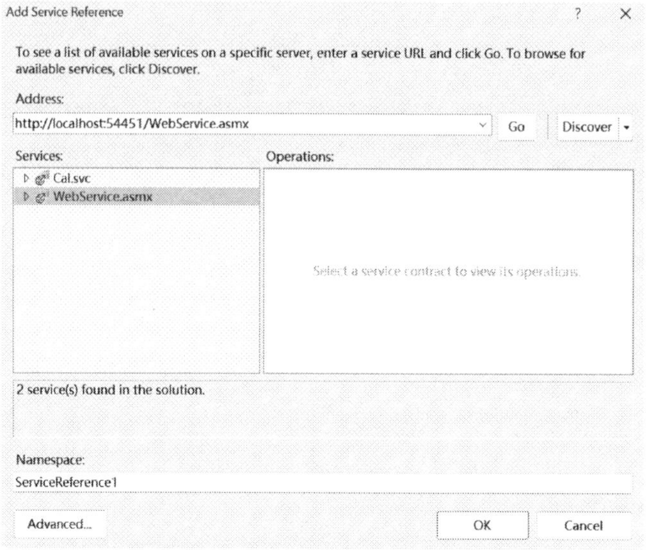

Figure 12-8 "Add Service Reference" Dialog

(2) Creating Web form file and calling WebService.New WebServiceTest.aspx under root folder in Chap12Site website, adding one Button control and one Label control, and setting the attributes of each control referencing the source codes. Establishing WebServiceTest.aspx.cs. At last, browsing WebServiceTest.aspx and testing it.

Program Description:

When you click the "Test Web Service" button, firstly, the instance soapClient of WebServiceSoapClient is created, and then the HelloWorld() method is called to return the data and the data will be displayed on lblMsg.

Example 12-3 Using AutoCompleteExtender control based on Web service

As is shown in Figure 12-9 ~Figure 12-11, in this example, when you enter the character a (or other content) in the text box, a list of product name containing the character a will be automatically displayed. Selecting the product name Ant, and clicking the "Search" button, the information related to the product will be displayed.

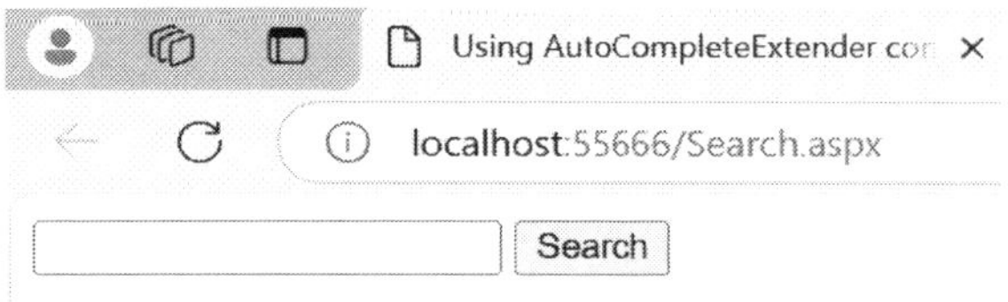

Figure 12-9 The Effect of Search.aspx (1)

Figure 12-10 The Effect of Search.aspx (2)

Figure 12-11 The Effect of Search.aspx (3)

Source Codes: ProductService.cs

```
using MyPetShop.DAL;
using System.Collections.Generic;
using System.Data.Linq.SqlClient;
using System.Linq;
namespace MyPetShop.BLL
{
 public class ProductService
 {
  MyPetShopDataContext db = new MyPetShopDataContext();
  public List<Product> GetProductBySearchText(string searchText)
  {
   return (from p in db.Product
        where SqlMethods.Like(p.Name, "%" + searchText + "%")
        select p).ToList();
  }
 }
}
```

Source Codes: SearchService.asmx

```
<%@ WebService Language="C#" CodeBehind="~/App_Code/SearchServicecs"Class="SearchService" %>
```

Source Codes: SearchService.cs

```
using MyPetShop.BLL;
using System;
using System.Collections.Generic;
using System.Web.Services;
[WebService(Namespace = "http://tempuri.org/")]
[WebServiceBinding(ConformsTo = WsiProfiles.BasicProfile1_1)]
[System.Web.Script.Services.ScriptService]
public class SearchService : System.Web.Services.WebService
{
 public SearchService()
 {
  //InitializeComponent();
 }
 [WebMethod]
 public string[] GetStrings(string prefixText)
 {
  ProductService productSrv = new ProductService();
  var products = productSrv.GetProductBySearchText(prefixText);
  List<String> list = new List<String>();
  foreach (var product in products)
  {
   list.Add(product.Name);
  }
  return list.ToArray();
 }
}
```

Source Codes: Search.aspx

```
<%@ Page Language="C#" AutoEventWireup="true" CodeFile="Search.aspx.cs" Inherits="Search" %>
<%@ Register Assembly="AjaxControlToolkit" Namespace="AjaxControlToolkit"
 TagPrefix="ajaxToolkit" %>
<!DOCTYPE html>
<html xmlns="http://www.w3.org/1999/xhtml">
<head runat="server">
  <meta http-equiv="Content-Type" content="text/html; charset=utf-8" />
  <title>To use AutoCompleteExtender control based on Web service</title>
</head>
<body>
<form id="form1" runat="server">
  <div>
    <asp:ScriptManager ID="ScriptManager1" runat="server"></asp:ScriptManager>
    <asp:TextBox ID="txtSearch" runat="server"></asp:TextBox>
    <ajaxToolkit:AutoCompleteExtender ID="txtSearch_AutoCompleteExtender" runat="server"
MinimumPrefixLength="1" ServiceMethod="GetStrings" ServicePath="SearchService.asmx"
TargetControlID="txtSearch">
    </ajaxToolkit:AutoCompleteExtender>
    <asp:Button ID="btnSearch" runat="server" OnClick="BtnSearch_Click" Text="Search" />
    <asp:GridView ID="gvProduct" runat="server">
    </asp:GridView>
  </div>
</form>
</body>
</html>
```

Source Codes: Search.aspx.cs

```
using MyPetShop.BLL;
using System;
public partial class Search : System.Web.UI.Page
{
  ProductService productSrv = new ProductService();
  protected void BtnSearch_Click(object sender, EventArgs e)
  {
    gvProduct.DataSource = productSrv.GetProductBySearchText(txtSearch.Text);
    gvProduct.DataBind();
  }
}
```

Operating Steps:

(1) In this example, because the database should be accessed, so we create this instance by using

the ChapMyPetShop solution of three-layer framework. Opening ChapMyPetShop solution, new ProductService.cs file in MyPetShop.BLL layer project.

(2) New SearchService.asmx and SearchService.cs files corresponding to Web service SearchService in MyPetShop.Web layer project.

(3) Installing AjaxControlToolKit in MyPetShop.Web layer project by using NuGet package manager, and establishing "Ajax Control Toolkit " option in "Tool Box" window referencing section 11.3.

(4) Creating Search.aspx in MyPetShop.Web layer project, adding one ScriptManager control, one TextBox control, one AutoCompleteExtender control, one Button Control and one GridView control, and setting the attributes of each control referencing the source codes.

(5) Creating Search.aspx.cs. At last, browsing Search.aspx and testing it.

(6) Right clicking Chap12Site website, selecting "Add"→ "Add New Item" command in the pop-up shortcut menu, then selecting "Web service(ASMX)" template in the rendered dialog box, entering the file name of Web service as WebService.asmx, and clicking "Add" button to establish the file.

(7) Opening WebService.cs in App_Code folder, and entering the content in the shadow part. At last, browsing WebService.asmx and testing it.

Program Description:

Because the established Web service will be called by the Ajax control AutoCompleteExtender, you must declare [System. Web. Script. Services. ScriptService] before defining the Web service class SearchService in Search.cs.

12.2 Summary

This chapter introduces the basic working principles of web services and how to establish and invoke ASP.NET web services. The web services are used to reuse data and software, that provides convenience for establishing distributed systems. Implementing web services needs the support of protocols such as HTTP, SMTP, SOAP, WSDL, and UDDI. The web service template provided by Visual Studio Code (VSC2O19) offers a convenient approach for creating and invoking ASP.NET web services. When invoking ASP.NET web services, it is necessary to add a service reference firstly and then apply it to the web form.

12.3 Exercises

1. Fill in the blank questions

(1) ASP.NETWeb services are created based on________.

(2) ASP. The extension of the NET web service file is .asmx, and its back-end encoding file is located in the________folder.

(3) ASP. The NET Web service file uses the________directive to replace @ Page directive.

(4) The difference between ASP.NET Web service classes and regular classes is that________needs to be added before the method.

(5) To call ASP NET Web services from ASP NET Ajax script, ________need to be added before the class.

2. True or False Questions

(1) Web services can only be used in ASP.NET web application. (　　)

(2) Method overloading dose not be allowed by ASP.NET Web services. (　　)

(3) The class files corresponding to web services are usually stored in ASP_Code folders. (　　)

3.Multiple-choice questions

(1) The communication protocol of web services does not include (　　).

A. HTTP　　B. XML　　C. SOAP　　D. TCP/IP

(2) If you want to use ASP.NET Web services in a website, you must add (　　) to the website.

A. Service reference　　B. Reference　　C. XML reference　　D. Web site

(3) Which of the following statements is incorrect (　　)?

A. The essence of establishing ASP.NET Web services is to establish an inherited class from System.Web.Services.WebService.

B. Adding [WebMethod] before an ASP.NET Web service class method defines a method that can only be called internally within the service.

C. ASP.NET Web services can be called by systems developed in other languages after they are established. D. ASP.NET Web services comply with the SOAP industry standard.

4. Short-answer questions

(1) Why you use web services?

(2) What commands are included in the .asmx file for ASP.NET Web services? What attributes does this instruction include?

5. Programming Questions

(1) Create and debug all of the instances in this chapter.

(2) Design an ASP.NET Web service that retrieves the city based on its zip code and test the service.

(3) WebXML.com.cn offers a Web service for weather forecasting, accessible at http://www.webxml.com.cn/WebServices/WeatherWebService.asmx. Please develop an application that utilizes this service to implement the weather forecast query function.

Chapter 13 File Processing

Points:

- Mastering the operation of drives and folders on the Web server
- Mastering the operations of creating, moving, copying and deleting files on the Web server
- Mastering the method of reading and writing files on the Web server
- Be familiar with file upload operation

13.1 Drives Folders and File Processing

In Web applications, the operation of drives, folders and files on Web servers is very extensive, such as the increasingly popular network hard disk. When you want to use them, you need to import the System.IO namespace to handle the basic operations of drives, folders and files.

13.1.1 Getting the drive information

DriveInfo class can realize the accessing to the specified driver information. The DriveInfo class can be used to easily obtain the name, type, size and state information of each drive on the Web server. The common attributes and methods are shown as Table 13-1.

Table 13-1 The table of attributes and methods of DriveInfo class

Attribute and Method	Description
AvailableFreeSpace attribute	Get available free capacity of drive
DriveFormat attribute	Get the name of the file system, such as NTFS or FAT32
IsReady attribute	Logical value indicating whether a specific drive is ready
Name attribute	Get the name of the drive
RootDirectory attribute	Get the root folder of the drive
TotalSize attribute	Get the total storage capacity of the drive
VolumeLabel attribute	Get or set the volume label of the drive
GetDrives() method	Get the names of all logical drives on the Web server

Example 13-1 Displaying all of the drive information on the Web service

As is shown in Figure 13-1, when the page is loaded, the information of all drives in the current system is obtained, and each drive is displayed in the TreeView control as a node.

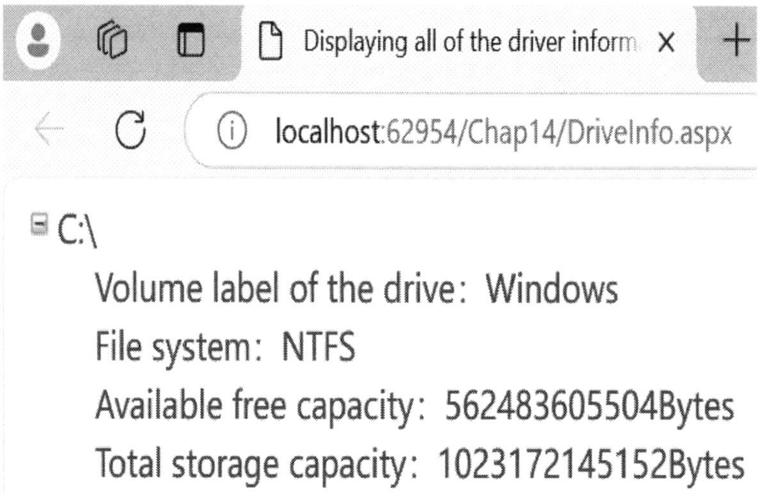

Figure 13-1 Effect of DriveInfo.aspx

Source Codes: DriveInfo.aspx

```
<%@ Page Language="C#" AutoEventWireup="true" CodeFile="DriveInfo.aspx.cs"
Inherits="Chap13_DriveInfo" %>
<!DOCTYPE html>
<html xmlns="http://www.w3.org/1999/xhtml">
<head runat="server">
  <meta http-equiv="Content-Type" content="text/html; charset=utf-8" />
  <title>To display the information of all of the drives on the Web service</title>
</head>
<body>
  <form id="form1" runat="server">
    <div>
      <asp:TreeView ID="tvDrive" runat="server"></asp:TreeView>
    </div>
  </form>
</body>
</html>
```

Source Codes: DriveInfo.aspx.cs

```
using System;
using System.IO;
using System.Web.UI;
using System.Web.UI.WebControls;
public partial class Chap13_DriveInfo : System.Web.UI.Page
{
  protected void Page_Load(object sender, EventArgs e)
```

```
{
 if (!Page.IsPostBack)
 {
  DriveInfo[] allDrives = DriveInfo.GetDrives();
  foreach (DriveInfo driveInfo in allDrives)
  {
   if (driveInfo.IsReady == true)
   {
    TreeNode treeNode = new TreeNode();
    treeNode.Value = driveInfo.Name;
    tvDrive.Nodes.Add(treeNode);
    TreeNode childNode = new TreeNode();
    childNode.Value = "Volume label of the drive: " + driveInfo.VolumeLabel;
    treeNode.ChildNodes.Add(childNode);
    childNode = new TreeNode();
    childNode.Value = "File system: " + driveInfo.DriveFormat;
    treeNode.ChildNodes.Add(childNode);
    childNode = new TreeNode();
    childNode.Value = "Available idle capacity: " + driveInfo.AvailableFreeSpace + "Bytes";
    treeNode.ChildNodes.Add(childNode)
    childNode = new TreeNode();
    childNode.Value = "Total storage capacity: " + driveInfo.TotalSize + "Bytes";
    treeNode.ChildNodes.Add(childNode);
   }
   else
   {
    TreeNode nodeNotUse = new TreeNode();
    nodeNotUse.Value = driveInfo.Name + "(drive not ready)";
    tvDrive.Nodes.Add(nodeNotUse);
   }
  }
 }
}
}
```

Operating Steps:

(1) Creating DriveInfo.aspx in the folder Chap12, adding one TreeView control, and setting ID attribute value of the control.

(2) Creating DriveInfo.aspx.cs. At last, browsing the effect of MultiUpdatePanel.aspx and testing the effect.

Program Description:

The namespace System.IO needs to be imported to implement the file operation. The program uses DriveInfo. GetDrives() to obtain all the drive collection objects allDrives, and then uses the foreach statement to traverse allDrives, adding the drive information to the TreeView control in the form of nodes.

13.1.2 Folder operation

If you want to operate the folders in Web service, you should use Directory class and DirectoryInfo class in namespace System.IO. When you use the methods provided by the Directory class and DirectoryInfo class, you can create and delete folders, copy, move and rename folders, traverse folders, and set or obtain folder information. The common methods of Directory class are shown as Table 13-2, and the common methods of DirectoryInfo class are shown as Table 13-3.

Table 13-2 The table of common methods of Directory class

Method	Description
CreateDirectory()	Create a folder in the specified path
Delete()	Delete the specified folder
Exists()	Determine if the folder path exists
GetCurrentDirectory()	Get the current folder of the application.
GetDirectories()	Get a collection of all subfolder names in the specified folder
GetFiles()	Return the collection of all files in the specified folder.
GetFileSystemEntries()	Return the name collection of all files and subfolders in the specified folder.
GetLogicalDrives()	Retrieve the name of the logical drive in the format "<drive letter>: ".
GetParent()	Retrieve the parent folder of the specified path, including absolute path and relative path.
Move()	Move the file or folder and its contents to a new location.
SetCurrentDirectory()	Set current folder

Table 13-3 The table of common methods of DirectoryInfo class

Method	Description
Create()	Create a folder
CreateSubdirectory ()	Create one or more subfolders in the specified path
Delete()	Delete the current folder
GetDirectories()	Return the subfolders of the current folder
GetFiles()	Return the collection of all files in the current folder
MoveTo()	Move the current folder to the new location
ToString()	Return the original path passed by the user

All methods of the Directory class are static, that means that all of these methods can be called directly, and all methods will be subject to security checks during they are executed. The method of the DirectoryInfo class is an instance method. An instance of the DirectoryInfo class must be created before it is used.

In the operation of folders and files, the most error prone is the path processing. .NET Framework provides the Path class which is used to process path. The common methods of Path class are shown as Table 13-4

Table 13-4 The table of common methods of Path class

Method	Description
ChangeExtension()	Change the extension of the path string
Combine()	Merge two path strings
GetDirectoryName()	Return the folder information of the specified path string
GetExtension()	Return the extension of the specified path string
GetFileName()	Return the file name and extension of the specified path string
GetFileNameWithoutExtension()	Return the file name without an extension
GetFullPath()	Return the absolute path of the specified path string.
GetPathRoot()	Get the root folder information of the specified path
GetRandomFileName()	Return a random folder name or file name.

Example 13-2 Counting the size of specified folder

As is shown in Figure 13-2, after entering the folder path in the text box, clicking Calculate to traverse all subfolders and files under the folder and counting the size, then the folder structure in a tree is displayed.

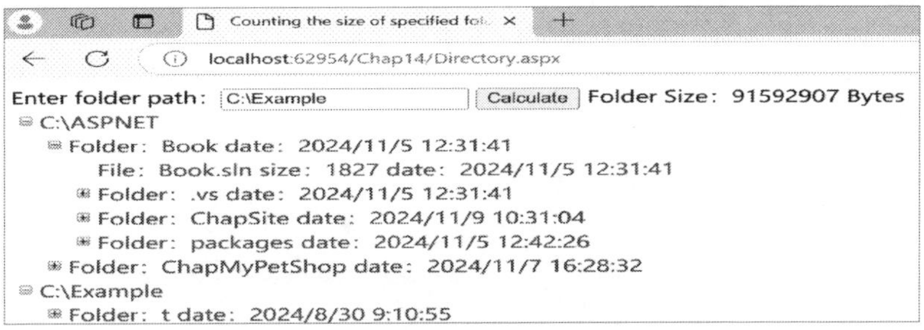

Figure 13-2 Effect of Directory.aspx

Source Codes: Directory.aspx

```
<%@ Page Language="C#" AutoEventWireup="true" CodeFile="Directory.aspx.cs"
Inherits="Chap13_Directory" %>
<!DOCTYPE html>
<html xmlns="http://www.w3.org/1999/xhtml">
<head runat="server">
  <meta http-equiv="Content-Type" content="text/html; charset=utf-8" />
  <title>To count the size of specified folder</title>
</head>
<body>
 <form id="form1" runat="server">
   <div>
     Enter Folder Path: <asp:TextBox ID="txtInput" runat="server"></asp:TextBox>
     <asp:Button ID="btnCompute" runat="server" OnClick="BtnCompute_Click" Text="Count" />
```

```
        <asp:Label ID="lblMsg" runat="server"></asp:Label>
        <asp:TreeView ID="tvDir" runat="server"></asp:TreeView>
      </div>
    </form>
</body>
</html>
```

Source Codes: Directory.aspx.cs

```
using System;
using System.IO;
using System.Web.UI.WebControls;
public partial class Chap13_Directory : System.Web.UI.Page
{
 protected void BtnCompute_Click(object sender, EventArgs e)
 {
  string path = txtInput.Text;
  if (Directory.Exists(path))
  {
   DirectoryInfo dirInfo = new DirectoryInfo(path);
   TreeNode node = new TreeNode(path);
   lblMsg.Text = "Folder Size: " + DirSize(dirInfo, node).ToString() + " Bytes";
   tvDir.Nodes.Add(node);
  }
  else
  {
   lblMsg.Text = "Folder you enter doesn't exit!";
  }
 }
  public static long DirSize(DirectoryInfo dirInfo, TreeNode parent)
 {
  long size = 0;
  FileInfo[] fis = dirInfo.GetFiles();
foreach (FileInfo fi in fis)
  {
   TreeNode node = new TreeNode();
   node.Value = "File: " + fi.Name + " Size: " + fi.Length + " Date: " + fi.CreationTime;
   parent.ChildNodes.Add(node);
   size += fi.Length;
  }
DirectoryInfo[] dis = dirInfo.GetDirectories();
  foreach (DirectoryInfo di in dis)
  {
   TreeNode nodeDir = new TreeNode();
   nodeDir.Value = di.Name;
   nodeDir.Text = "Folder: " + di.Name + " Date: " + di.CreationTime;
   parent.ChildNodes.Add(nodeDir);
   size += DirSize(di, nodeDir);
  }
  return (size);
 }
}
```

Operating Steps:

(1) Creating Directory.aspx in the folder Chap13, adding one TreeView control, one TextBox control, one Button control, one Label control, and setting the attributes of each control.

(2) Creating Directory.aspx.cs. At last, browsing the effect of Directory.aspx and testing the effect.

Program Description:

The custom static method DirSize() is divided into two parts:

(1) For the files under the folder, using the statement "FileInfo [] fis=dirInfo. GetFiles();" to return the collection of FileInfo objects, and then accumulate all file sizes.

(2) For the subfolders under the folder, using the statement "DirectoryInfo [] dis=dirInfo. GetDirectories();" to return the collection of DirectoryInfo objects, and then using the recursive to call DirSize() method to calculate the sum of all file sizes under the subfolder.

In addition, using the statements "parent. ChildNodes. Add (node);" and "parent. ChildNodes. Add (nodeDir);" to add files and folders to the TreeView control to form a directory tree.

13.1.3 File operation

The File and FileInfo classes of ASP.NET provide the methods for creating, copying, deleting, moving, and opening files. The common methods of File class are shown as Table 13-5. The common methods of FileInfo class are shown as Table 13-6. Some functions of File class and FileInfo class are the same, but the methods in the File class are static methods. The methods in the FileInfo class are all instance methods.

Table 13-5 The table of common methods of File class

Method	Description
AppendAllText()	Append the specified string to the file. If the file does not exist, create the file
AppendText()	Create a StreamWriter and append UTF-8 encoded text to the existing file
Copy()	Copy file
Create()	Create a file in the specified path
CreateText()	Create or open a text file for writing UTF-8 encoding
Delete()	Delete file
Exists()	Determine whether the file exists
GetCreationTime()	Return the date and time the file or folder was created
GetLastAccessTime()	Return the date and time when the file or folder was last accessed
GetLastWriteTime()	Return the date and time when the file or folder was last written
Move()	Move file
Open()	Open FileStream on the specified path
OpenRead()	Open an existing file for reading
OpenText()	Open an existing UTF-8 encoded text file for reading
OpenWrite()	Open an existing file to write
ReadAllText()	Open a text file, read all lines of the file into a string, and then close the file
Replace()	Replace the contents of the specified file with the contents of another file. This process will delete the original file and create a backup of the replaced file
SetCreationTime()	Set the creation date and time of the file
SetLastAccessTime()	Set the date and time when the file was last accessed
SetLastWriteTime()	Set the date and time when the file was last written
WriteAllText()	Create a new file, write contents in the file, and then close the file. If the target file already exists, it will be overwritten

Table 13-6 The table of common methods of FileInfo class

Method	Description
AppendText()	Create a StreamWriter and append text to the file
CopyTo()	Copy file
Create()	Create file
CreateText()	Create a StreamWriter to write to a new text file.
Delete()	Delete file
MoveTo ()	Move the specified file to a new location and provide the option to specify a new file name
Open()	Open the file with various read/write access rights and sharing privileges.
OpenRead()	Create a read-only FileStream
OpenText()	Create a StreamReader that uses UTF-8 encoding and reads from an existing text file
OpenWrite()	Create write-only FileStream
Replace()	Replace the contents of the specified file with the current file, delete the original file, and create a backup of the replaced file
ToString()	Return path as string
WriteAllText()	Create a new file, write contents in the file, and then close the file. If the target file already exists, it will be overwritten

Example 13-3 Creating, copying, deleting and moving the file

As is shown in Figure 13-3~Figure 13-5, in this example, the file creation, copy, deletion and move operations according to the input source file and target file path will be implemented, and the corresponding operation information prompt is given.

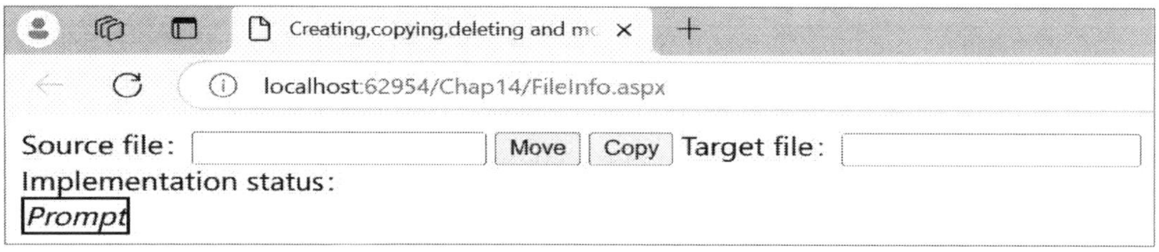

Figure 13-3 Effect of FileInfo.aspx

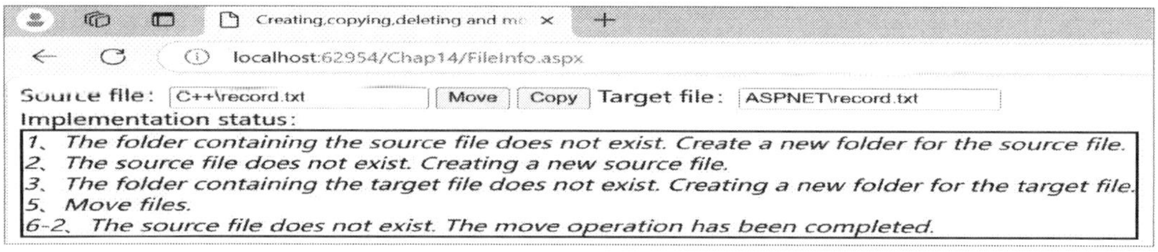

Figure 13-4 Effect of Moving the File

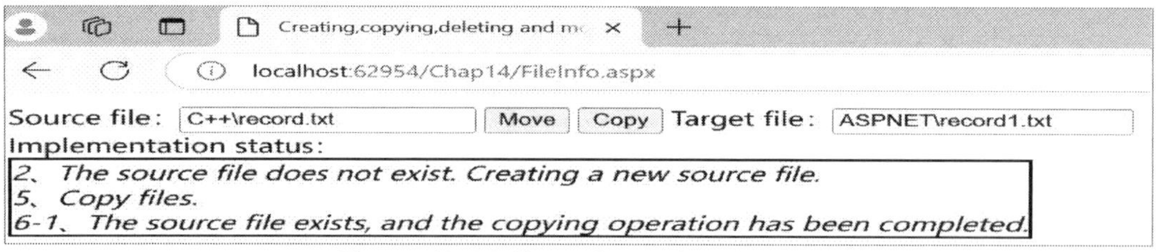

Figure 13-5 Effect of Copying the File

Source Codes: FileInfo.aspx

```
<%@ Page Language="C#" AutoEventWireup="true" CodeFile="FileInfo.aspx.cs"
Inherits="Chap13_FileInfo" %>
<!DOCTYPE html>
<html xmlns="http://www.w3.org/1999/xhtml">
<head runat="server">
  <meta http-equiv="Content-Type" content="text/html; charset=utf-8" />
  <title>To create,copy,delete and move the file</title>
</head>
<body>
  <form id="form1" runat="server">
    <div>
      Source File: <asp:TextBox ID="txtSource" runat="server"></asp:TextBox>
      <asp:Button ID="btnMove" runat="server" OnClick="BtnMove_Click" Text="Move" />
      <asp:Button ID="btnCopy" runat="server" OnClick="BtnCopy_Click" Text="Copy" />
      Target File: <asp:TextBox ID="txtTarget" runat="server"></asp:TextBox><br />
      Implementation: <br />
      <asp:Label ID="lblMsg" runat="server" BorderWidth="2px" Font-Italic="True" Text="Prompt
Information"></asp:Label>
    </div>
  </form>
</body>
</html>
```

Source Codes: FileInfo.aspx.cs

```
using System;
using System.IO;
public partial class Chap13_FileInfo : System.Web.UI.Page
{
  protected void BtnMove_Click(object sender, EventArgs e)
  {
    string pathSouce = txtSource.Text.Trim();
    string pathTarget = txtTarget.Text.Trim();
    if ((pathSouce.Length> 0) && (pathTarget.Length> 0))
    {
      lblMsg.Text = MoveCopyFile(pathSouce, pathTarget, false);
    }
  }
  protected void BtnCopy_Click(object sender, EventArgs e)
  {
    string pathSouce = txtSource.Text.Trim();
    string pathTarget = txtTarget.Text.Trim();
```

```
  if ((pathSouce.Length> 0) && (pathTarget.Length> 0))
  {
   lblMsg.Text = MoveCopyFile(pathSouce, pathTarget, true);
  }
}
private string MoveCopyFile(string pathSource, string pathTarget, bool act)
{
  String resMsg = "";
  string pathRoot = Server.MapPath("");
  pathSource = Path.Combine(pathRoot, pathSource);
  pathTarget = Path.Combine(pathRoot, pathTarget);
  try
  {
   string directoryName = Path.GetDirectoryName(pathSource);
   if (!Directory.Exists(directoryName))
   {
    Directory.CreateDirectory(directoryName);
    resMsg = resMsg + "1, The folder where the source file is located does not exist. Create a new folder where
the source file is located. <br />";
   }
   if (!File.Exists(pathSource))
   {
    using (FileStream fs = File.Create(pathSource)) { }
    resMsg = resMsg + "2, The source file does not exist. Create a new source file. <br />";
   }
   directoryName = Path.GetDirectoryName(pathTarget);
   if (!Directory.Exists(directoryName))
   {
    Directory.CreateDirectory(directoryName);
    resMsg = resMsg + "3, The folder where the target file is located does not exist. The folder where the new
target file is located. <br />";
   }
   if (act) //若 act 为 true,
   {
    File.Copy(pathSource, pathTarget, true);
    resMsg = resMsg + "5, Copy file. <br />";
   }
   else
   {
    if (File.Exists(pathTarget))
    {
     File.Delete(pathTarget);
     resMsg = resMsg + "4, The target file exists, delete the target file. <br />";
    }
```

```
            File.Move(pathSource, pathTarget);
            resMsg = resMsg + "5, Move file. <br />";
          }
          if (File.Exists(pathSource))
          {
            resMsg = resMsg + "6-1, Source file exists, copy operation completed. <br />";
          }
          else
          {
            resMsg = resMsg + "6-2, Source file does not exist, move operation completed. <br />";
          }
        }
        catch (Exception e)
        {
          resMsg = resMsg + "7, Program execution exception. error message: " + e.ToString();
        }
        return resMsg;
      }
    }
```

Operating Steps:

(1) Creating FileInfo.aspx in the folder Chap13, adding controls and setting the attributes of each control referencing the source codes.

(2) Creating FileInfo.aspx.cs. At last, browsing the effect of FileInfo.aspx and testing the effect.

Program Description:

If the source folder does not exist, the statement "Directory. CreateDirectory (directoryName);" will create the folder. If the file does not exist, the statement "using (FileStream fs=File. Create (pathSource)) {}" will create an empty file, and then the fs object will be closed automatically.

In addition, you can also use the CreationTime attribute of the FileInfo class to obtain the file creation time, and the Length attribute to obtain the file size and other information.

13.2 Reading and Writing the File

Reading and writing files is an important operation in Web applications. You need to read and write files to save program data, dynamically generate pages, or modify application configuration information. In .NET Framework, the general model for reading and writing I/O data based on Stream class and Reader/Writer class is adopted.

13.2.1 Stream class

In .NET, reading and writing data are implemented in the form of data streams. Stream class provides the basic function for I/O, but stream class is an abstract class, so in order to complete the operation of different data streams, its derived class must be used. Such as, the memory operation is implemented by using MemoryStream class, and the file operation is implemented through FileStream class Taking the common FileStream class as an example:

The FileStream class can read, write, open and close files, and can operate the other file-related operating system handles. Reading and writing operations can be specified as synchronous or asynchronous operations. By default, the file is opened synchronously.

The common attributes of FileStream class are shown as Table 13-7.

Table 13-7 The table of the common attributes of FileStream class

Attribute	**Description**
CanRead	Whether the current data stream supports reading
CanWrite	Whether the current data stream supports writing
Length	Data stream length (in bytes)
Name	Get the name of the FileStream passed to the constructor
ReadTimeout	Get or set a value (in milliseconds) to determine the reading time that the data stream before timeout
WriteTimeout	Get or set a value (in milliseconds) to determine the write time of the data stream before timeout

The common methods of FileStream class are shown as Table 13-8.

Table 13-8 The table of the common attributes of FileStream class

Method	**Description**
BeginRead()	Start asynchronous reading
BeginWrite()	Start asynchronous writing
Close()	Close the current data flow and release all resources associated with it
EndRead()	Complete asynchronous reading
EndWrite()	Complete asynchronous writing
Flush()	Write the data of data stream in the buffer into a file, and then clear the data in the buffer
Lock()	Allow reading access while preventing other processes from changing FileStream.
Read()	Read a byte block from the data stream and write the data to the specified buffer.
ReadByte()	Read a byte from the file and offset the reading position by one byte
Unlock()	Allow other processes to access all or part of a previously locked file.
Write()	Write the data read from the buffer to the data stream.
WriteByte()	Write a byte to the current location of the file stream.

Note: Read() and Write() can read and write the file synchronously while BeginRead(), EndRead(), BeginWrite(), and EndWrite() methods can read and write the file asynchronously. When you write files asynchronously, you need to use the Lock() and UnLock() methods to resolve the file sharing conflict.

After the data flow is used, the Close () method of the data flow should be called to close the data flow. In addition, using can be used to ensure that the data stream is closed after you use the data stream.

Example 13-4 Reading and writing the file by using FileStream class

In this example, you firstly should determine whether the file Test.txt exists in the Chap13 folder under the root folder of the website. If it does not exist, create a new Test.txt file and write "The First Line!"; if it exists, you can open and read the file, as is shown in Figure 13-6. Clicking the "Add" button to add the content entered in the text box to the end of the file, and then read the file content and display it on the page, as is shown in Figure 13-7.

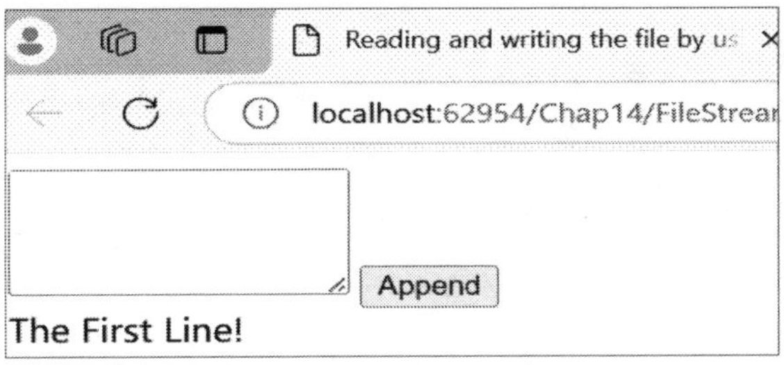

Figure 13-6 The Effect FileStream Class Read File

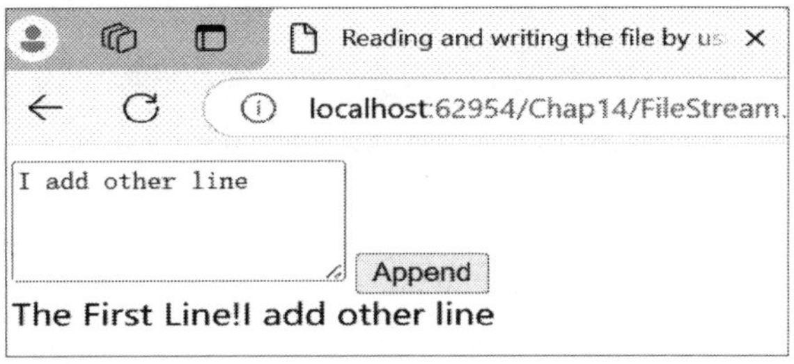

Figure 13-7 The Effect FileStream Class Write File

Source Codes: FileStream.aspx

```
<%@ Page Language="C#" AutoEventWireup="true" CodeFile="FileStream.aspx.cs"
Inherits="Chap13_FileStream" %>
<!DOCTYPE html>
<html xmlns="http://www.w3.org/1999/xhtml">
<head runat="server">
 <meta http-equiv="Content-Type" content="text/html; charset=utf-8" />
 <title>To read and write the file by using FileStream class</title>
</head>
<body>
 <form id="form1" runat="server">
  <div>
<asp:TextBox ID="txtAppend" runat="server" Height="58px" TextMode="MultiLine"></asp:TextBox>
  <asp:Button ID="btnAppend" runat="server" Text="Add" OnClick="BtnAppend_Click" /><br />
   <asp:Label ID="lblShow" runat="server"></asp:Label>
  </div>
 </form>
</body>
</html>
```

Source Codes: FileStream.aspx.cs

```
using System;
using System.IO;
using System.Text;
public partial class Chap13_FileStream : System.Web.UI.Page
```

```
{
    protected void Page_Load(object sender, EventArgs e)
    {
        string fileName = Path.Combine(Request.PhysicalApplicationPath, @"Chap13\Test.txt");
        if (File.Exists(fileName))
        {
            lblShow.Text = ReadText();
        }
        else
        {
            AppendText("The First Line!");
            lblShow.Text = "The First Line!";
        }
    }
    protected void BtnAppend_Click(object sender, EventArgs e)
    {
        string appStr = txtAppend.Text.Trim();
        if (appStr.Length> 0)
        {
            AppendText(appStr);
            lblShow.Text = ReadText();
        }
    }
    private string ReadText()
    {
        string fileName = Path.Combine(Request.PhysicalApplicationPath, @"Chap13\Test.txt");
        FileStream fs = File.Open(fileName, FileMode.Open, FileAccess.Read, FileShare.Read);
        byte[] data = new byte[fs.Length];
        fs.Read(data, 0, (int)fs.Length);
        fs.Close();
        return Encoding.UTF8.GetString(data);
    }
    private void AppendText(string addText)
    {
        string fileName = Path.Combine(Request.PhysicalApplicationPath, @"Chap13\Test.txt");
        FileStream fs = File.Open(fileName, FileMode.Append, FileAccess.Write, FileShare.None);
        byte[] data = Encoding.UTF8.GetBytes(addText);
        fs.Write(data, 0, data.Length);
        fs.Flush();
        fs.Close();
    }
}
```

Operating Steps:

(1)Creating FileStream.aspx in the folder Chap13, adding controls and setting the attributes of each control referencing the source codes.

(2)Creating FileStream.aspx.cs. At last, browsing the effect of FileStream.aspx and testing the effect.

Program Description:

At first, there is no Test.txt file in the Chap13 folder under the root folder of the website. At this time, calling "AppendText (" The First Line! ");" to execute the file writing operation. When you click the "Append" button, calling "AppendText (appStr);" to add the content entered in the text box to the end of the file, and then executing the "lblShow. Text=ReadText();" statement to read the contents of the Test. txt file and displaying it on the lblShow control.

The Request.PhysicalApplicationPath attribute gets the root folder of the website. The Path. Combine() method combines the two paths into a path string.

Encoding.UTF8 means that UTF-8 encoding is adopted for encoding. At this time, Chinese is supported to be written into the file. If the other encoding methods are used, garbled codes will appear when writing Chinese in the file. In addition, in order to use the Encoding class, you need to import the namespace System.Text.

13.2.2 Reader and Writer classes

Different from the Stream class, Reader and Writer classes can complete operations such as reading and writing bytes in the data stream. .NET Framework provides the different Reader and Writer classes according to the different types of data stream. Table 13-9 and Table13-10 list separately Reader and Writer classes.

Table 13-9 The corresponding table of Reader class

Reader Class	Description
System.IO.BinaryReader	Read data from the data stream as a binary value
System.IO.StreamReader	Read characters from byte data stream, which is derived from TextReader
System.IO.StringReader	Read text as a series of memory strings, which is derived from TextReader
System.IO.TextReader	An abstract class that reads a series of characters

Table 13-10 The corresponding table of Writer class

Writer Class	Description
System.IO.BinaryWriter	Write binary basic data to the data stream
System.IO.StreamWriter	Write characters into the data stream, which is derived from TextWriter
System.IO.StringWriter	Write text into a memory string, which is derived from TextWriter.
System.IO.TextWriter	An abstract class that writes a series of characters
System.IO.TextReader	An abstract class that reads a series of characters

1.TextReader class and TextWriter class

As abstract classes, TextReader and TextWriter classes are used to read and write content of text types. When you use them, the object instances of their derived class should be established.

The common methods of TextReader class are shown as Table 13-11. The common methods of

TextWriter class are shown as Table 13-12.

Table 13-11 The table of the common methods of TextReader class

Method	Description
Close()	Close TextReader and release all of the system resources associated with it
Peek()	Read the next character without using it. When the end of the file is read, the returned value - 1 can be used to determine whether the end of the file has been reached
Read()	Read data from the input data stream
ReadBlock()	Read the characters with the maximum count value from the current data stream, and then write the data which start from the index value to the buffer
ReadLine()	Read a line of characters from the current data stream and return the data as a string
ReadToEnd()	Read all of the characters from the current position to the end and return them as a string

Table 13-12 The table of the common methods of TextWriter class

Method	Description
Close()	Close the current writer and release any system resources associated with the writer
Flush()	Write the buffer data to a file, and then clear the contents of the buffer. If this method is not used, the data in the buffer will be written to the file when the file is closed
Write()	Write the given data into the text data stream without the newline characters
WriteLine()	Write a line and add a newline character

Example 13-5 Reading and writing the text file by using StreamReader and StreamWriter

In Figure 13-8, if you click the "Write Text File" button, a text file Txt.txt will be created under the Temp folder of the current folder, and a line of text "Li Ming 23" will be written; if you click the "Read Text File" button, the contents of the Txt.txt file will be read and displayed in the Label control, as is shown in Figure 13-9.

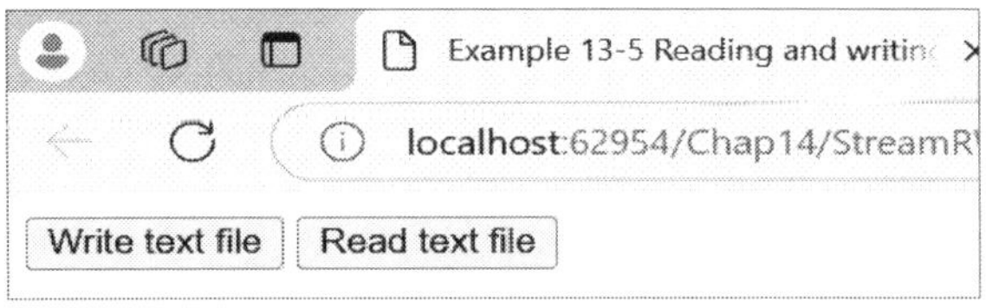

Figure 13-8 The Effect of StreamRW.aspx (1)

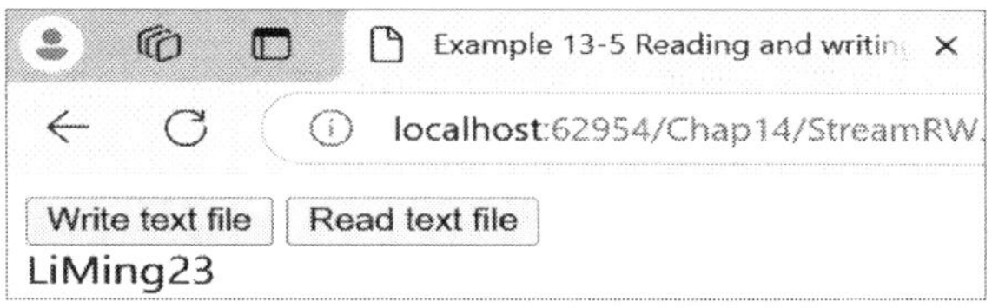

Figure 13-9 The Effect of StreamRW.aspx (2)

Source Codes: StreamRW.aspx

```
<%@ Page Language="C#" AutoEventWireup="true" CodeFile="StreamRW.aspx.cs"
Inherits="Chap13_StreamRW" %>
<!DOCTYPE html>
<html xmlns="http://www.w3.org/1999/xhtml">
```

```
<head runat="server">
  <meta http-equiv="Content-Type" content="text/html; charset=utf-8" />
  <title> To read and write the text file by using StreamReader and StreamWriter classes</title>
</head>
<body>
  <form id="form1" runat="server">
    <div>
    <asp:Button ID="btnWrite" runat="server" OnClick="BtnWrite_Click" Text="Write Text File" />
 <asp:Button ID="btnRead" runat="server" OnClick="BtnRead_Click" Text="Read Text File" /><br />
      <asp:Label ID="lblShow" runat="server"></asp:Label>
    </div>
  </form>
</body>
</html>
```

Source Codes: StreamRW.aspx.cs

```
using System;
using System.IO;
public partial class Chap13_StreamRW : System.Web.UI.Page
{
  protected void BtnWrite_Click(object sender, EventArgs e)
  {
    string bootDir = Server.MapPath("");
    string fileName = Path.Combine(bootDir, @"Temp\Txt.txt");
    TextWriter sw = new StreamWriter(fileName);
    sw.Write("Li Ming");
    sw.WriteLine(23);
    sw.Flush();
    sw.Close();
  }
  protected void BtnRead_Click(object sender, EventArgs e)
  {
    string bootDir = Server.MapPath("");
    string fileName = Path.Combine(bootDir, @"Temp\Txt.txt");
    TextReader sr = new StreamReader(fileName);
    string tmpStr = sr.ReadToEnd();
    sr.Close();
  }
}
```

Operating Steps:

(1) Creating StreamRW.aspx in the folder Chap13, adding controls and setting the attributes of each

control referencing the source codes.

(2) Creating StreamRW.aspx.cs. At last, browsing the effect of StreamRW.aspx and testing the effect.

Program Description:

When you click the "Write Text File" button, if the Temp\Txt.txt under the current folder does not exist, you should reate a new file. Otherwise, opening the file and writing the file contents in an overwriting way. If you want to add the content to the file, you need to modify the statement "TextWriter sw=new StreamWriter (fileName);" to:

TextWriter sw = new StreamWriter(fileName, true);

The parameter true indicates the adding mode, and then the Write() method is called to add the data to the text data stream.

2.BinaryReader class and BinaryWriter class

BinaryReader and BinaryWriter classes are used to read and write the binary data file. BinaryWriter class can write data to a file in its internal format, so when you read the data, the different Read method can be used. Such as, ReadString() can be used to read the character, and ReadInt32() can be used to read the integer.

Example 13-6 Reading and writing the binary file by using BinaryReader and BinaryWriter

In Figure 13-10, if you click the "Write Binary File" button, a binary file Bin.bin will be created under the Temp folder of the current folder, and the string "Li Ming " and integer 23 will be written; if you click the "Read Binary File" button, the contents of the Bin.bin file will be read and displayed in the Label control, as is shown in Figure 13-11.

Figure 13-10 The Effect of BinaryRW.aspx (1)

Figure 13-11 The Effect of BinaryRW.aspx (2)

Source Codes: BinaryRW.aspx

```
<%@ Page Language="C#" AutoEventWireup="true" CodeFile="BinaryRW.aspx.cs"
Inherits="Chap13_BinaryRW" %>
<!DOCTYPE html>
<html xmlns="http://www.w3.org/1999/xhtml">
<head runat="server">
  <meta http-equiv="Content-Type" content="text/html; charset=utf-8" />
  <title>Read and Write Binary File</title>
</head>
<body>
  <form id="form1" runat="server">
    <div>
```

```
<asp:Button ID="btnWrite" runat="server" OnClick="BtnWrite_Click" Text="Write Binary File" />
    <asp:Button ID="btnRead" runat="server" OnClick="BtnRead_Click" Text="Read Binary File" /><br />
    <asp:Label ID="lblShow" runat="server"></asp:Label>
  </div>
 </form>
</body>
</html>
```

Source Codes: BinaryRW.aspx.cs

```
using System;
using System.IO;
public partial class Chap13_BinaryRW : System.Web.UI.Page
{
  protected void BtnWrite_Click(object sender, EventArgs e)
  {
string bootDir = Server.MapPath("");
    string fileName = Path.Combine(bootDir, @"Temp\Bin.bin");
    BinaryWriter bw = new BinaryWriter(File.OpenWrite(fileName));
    string name = "Li Ming";
    int age = 23;
    bw.Write(name);
    bw.Write(age);
    bw.Flush();
    bw.Close();
  }
  protected void BtnRead_Click(object sender, EventArgs e)
  {
    string bootDir = Server.MapPath("");
    string fileName = Path.Combine(bootDir, @"Temp\Bin.bin");
    BinaryReader br = new BinaryReader(File.OpenRead(fileName));
    string name;
    int age;
    name = br.ReadString();
    age = br.ReadInt32();
    br.Close();
    lblShow.Text = "Name: " + name + " Age: " + age.ToString();
  }
}
```

Operating Steps:

(1) Creating BinaryRW.aspx in the folder Chap13, adding controls and setting the attributes of each control referencing the source codes.

(2) Creating BinaryRW.aspx.cs. At last, browsing the effect of BinaryRW.aspx and testing the effect.

Program Description:

The name value which is written is the string type, and the age value is the integer type, so the ReadString() and ReadInt32() methods are used correspondingly when reading data.

13.3 File Uploading

The FileUpload control provides a convenient way for users to upload files to the Web server. When you upload the file, you can limit the size of the file, or check its attributes before saving the uploaded file. The FileUpload control is displayed as a text box and a Browse button on the page. When the user has selected the file to upload and submitted the page, the file will be uploaded as a part of the HTTP request.

PostedFile attribute of FileUpload control can get the file HttpPostedFile object which is uploaded by using the FileUpload control. You can use this object to access the other attributes of the uploaded file. For example, the ContentLength attribute can obtain the length of the uploaded file; The ContentType attribute can obtain the MIME content type of the uploaded file; The FileName attribute can get the file name of the uploaded file. You also can use SaveAs() method to save the uploaded file to the Web server.

Example 13-7 Uploading the file by using FileUpload

In Figure 13-12, if you click the "Browse" button, the " Select File to Load" dialog box is displayed, selecting the file, and then clicking the "Upload File" button to upload the file to the Uploads folder under the root folder of the website, and the prompt message is displayed, as is shown in Figure 13-13. At the same time, the size of the uploaded file must not exceed 200KB, and the file extension must be bmp, jpg, or gif image file.

Figure 13-12 The Effect of FileUpload.aspx (1)

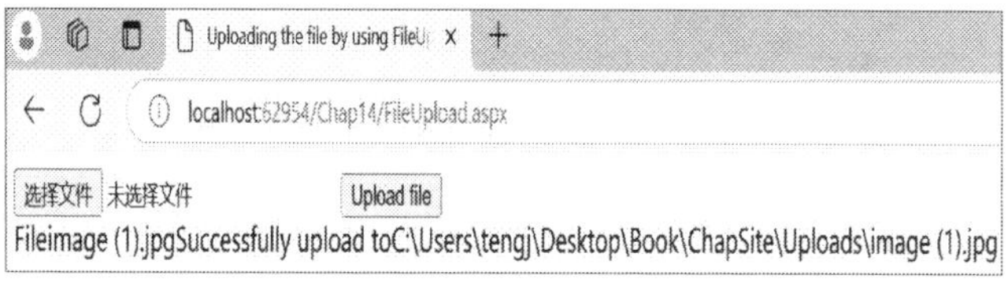

Figure 13-13 The Effect of FileUpload.aspx (2)

Source Codes: FileUpload.aspx

```
<%@ Page Language="C#" AutoEventWireup="true" CodeFile="FileUpload.aspx.cs"
Inherits="Chap13_FileUpload" %>
<!DOCTYPE html>
<html xmlns="http://www.w3.org/1999/xhtml">
<head runat="server">
  <meta http-equiv="Content-Type" content="text/html; charset=utf-8" />
  <title>To upload the file by using FileUpload</title>
</head>
```

```
<body>
 <form id="form1" runat="server">
  <div>
   <asp:FileUpload ID="fupImg" runat="server" />
<asp:Button ID="btnUpload" runat="server" OnClick="BtnUpload_Click" Text="Upload File" /><br />
   <asp:Label ID="lblMsg" runat="server"></asp:Label>
  </div>
 </form>
</body>
</html>
```

Source Codes: FileUpload.aspx.cs

```
using System;
using System.IO;
public partial class Chap13_FileUpload : System.Web.UI.Page
{
 private string uploadDir;
 protected void Page_Load(object sender, EventArgs e)
 {
  uploadDir = Path.Combine(Request.PhysicalApplicationPath, "Uploads");
 }
 protected void BtnUpload_Click(object sender, EventArgs e)
 {
  if (fupImg.PostedFile.FileName == "")
  {
   lblMsg.Text = "No file upload!";
  }
  else
  {
   if (fupImg.PostedFile.ContentLength> 204800)
   {
    lblMsg.Text = "File size cannot exceed 200KB!";
   }
   else // 文件大小未超过 200KB
   {
    string extension = Path.GetExtension(fupImg.PostedFile.FileName);
    switch (extension.ToLower())
    {
     case ".bmp":
     case ".gif":
     case ".jpg":
      break;
     default:
      lblMsg.Text = "The extension must be bmp, gif 或 jpg!";
      return;
    }
```

```
            string fileName = Path.GetFileName(fupImg.PostedFile.FileName)
            string fullPath = Path.Combine(uploadDir, fileName);
            try
            {
             fupImg.PostedFile.SaveAs(fullPath);
             lblMsg.Text = "File" + fileName + "Successfully uploaded to" + fullPath;
            }
            catch (Exception ee)
            {
             lblMsg.Text = ee.Message;
            }
          }
        }
      }
    }
```

Operating Steps:

(1) Creating Uploads folder under the root folder of ChapSite website.

(2) Creating FileUpload.aspx in the folder Chap13, adding controls and setting the attributes of each control referencing the source codes.

(3) Creating FileUpload.aspx.cs. At last, browsing the effect of FileUpload.aspx and testing the effect.

13.4 Summary

➢ In order to implement folder and file operations on the Web server, you need DriveInfo, Directory, DirectoryInfo, File, FileInfo and Path classes in the System.IO namespace.

➢ A general model for reading and writing I/O data is implemented based on Stream class and Reader/Writer class.

➢ The FileUpload control can be used to upload files to the Web server.

13.5 Exercises

1. Fill in the blank questions

(1) To manage the file system on the web server, the namespace that needs to be imported is_______.

(2) The name of the drive can be obtained through the_______property of the DriveInfo class.

(3) The_______method of the HttpPosterdFile object can upload files to a web server.

(4) You can call the_______method to return the extension of the uploaded file.

(5) The_______method of the File class can be used to determine whether the specified file exists.

(6) The function of the SetCurrentDirectory method of the Directory class is_______.

2. True or False Questions

(l) The DirectoryInfo class can be used in web applications to manage client file systems. (   )

(2) The TextReader class is derived from the StreamReader class. (   )

(3) The code snippets included in the using statement will automatically close the data stream that is opened after execution. (   )

(4) Using UTF-8 encoding can write Chinese into text files. (   )

3. Multiple-choice questions

(1) The_______property of the DriveInfo class can retrieve the total storage capacity on the drive.

A. AvailableFreeSpace B. TotalFreeSpace C. TotalSize D. Size

(2) The_________method of the Directory class can retrieve the current working folder of the web application.

A. GetCurrentDirectory B. GetDirectories C. GetDirectoryRoot D. GetLogicalDrives

(3) Among the methods provided by the FileStream class for manipulating data streams,_______can synchronize file operations.

A. BeginWrite B. Write C. EndRead D. BeginRead

(4) The operation that cannot be completed by using the PostedFile property of the FileUpload control is (   ).

A. Uploading a file B. Obtaining the type of the uploaded file

C. Obtaining the size of the uploaded file D. Downloading a file

4. Short-answer questions

(1) What is the difference and connection between files and data streams?

(2) What folder management functions does the Directory class have? What methods are used to achieve them?

(3) What are the functions of the FileStream, StreamReader, and StreamWriter classes, and what is the connections between them?

5. Programming Questions

(1) Create and debug all of the instances in this chapter.

(2) Design a simple message book. Require that the messages should include the title, content, message sender, and message time. Each message is saved separately as a text file and a suitable file name is selected for saving (to solve the problem of duplicate file names).

(3) Write a comprehensive web application that utilizes the Directory class. Request that firstly you should confirm whether the specified folder exists, and if it exists, you should delete the folder; If it does not exist, you should establish the folder. Then, you should move this folder to a new location.

(4) Develop a web application that offers back-end folder and file management functionalities. The requirements are as follows:

① Set the website root folder as the current folder, displaying all subfolder names in the left list box and all file names in the right list box.

② When clicking a subfolder name in the left list box, update the current folder and refresh the page.

③ When clicking the "Return to Previous Folder" button, should also update the current folder and refresh the page.

④ When clicking the "Create New Folder" button, a new folder should be created within the current folder.

⑤ When clicking the "Delete Current Folder" button, the current folder should be deleted.

⑥ When clicking the "Upload Files to Current Folder" button, should upload the selected files to the current folder.

Chapter 14 MyPetShop Application

Points:

- Understanding the overall design architecture of MyPetShop application
- Imitating the database in the MyPetShop application and designing the MyPetShop database
- Imitating the user controls in the MyPetShop application, and designing and applying user controls
- Imitating the front-end functional modules in MyPetShop application, and designing and implementing front-end functional modules
- Imitating the shopping cart module in MyPetShop application, and designing and implementing the shopping cart module
- Imitating the order processing module in MyPetShop application, and designing and implementing the order processing module
- Imitating the back-end function management module in MyPetShop application, and designing and implementing the back-end function management module
- Imitating ASP. in MyPetShop application NET three-tier architecture, and be proficient in using ASP NET three-tier architecture

14.1 Overall Design of The System

The overall design includes system function module design, user control design, overall design of system database, configuration file design for Web. Config, and the overall idea of developing MyPetShop application based on VSC 2019.

14.1.1 System function module design

1. Front-end product browsing module

In this module, users can search and browse all of the product's information according to various conditions, as is shown in Figure 14-1.

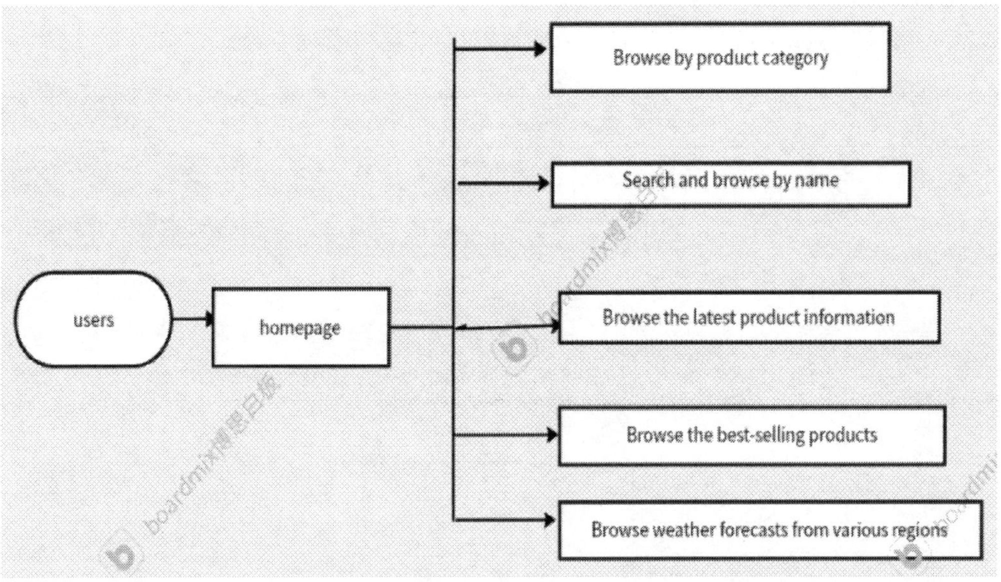

Figure 14-1 The Flow Chart of Front-end Product Browsing Module

2.User registration and login module

After registering, users can be called members, and they can only achieve product settlement after successfully logging in. Registered users also have the function of changing and retrieving passwords. The process is shown in the Figure 14-2.

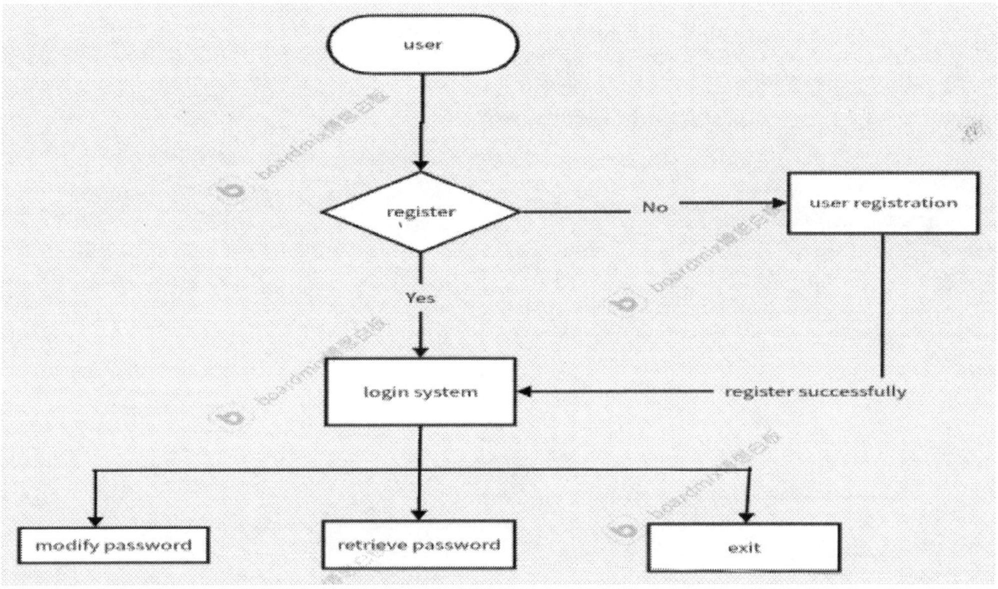

Figure 14-2 The Flow Chart of User Rregistration and Login Module

3.Shopping cart module

The shopping cart contains all of the product information that the user intends to purchase, including product number, product name, product price, purchase quantity, and total price payed by the user. When users browse product details, if they decide to purchase, they can add the product to their shopping cart and continue browsing other products. The process is shown in the Figure 14-3.

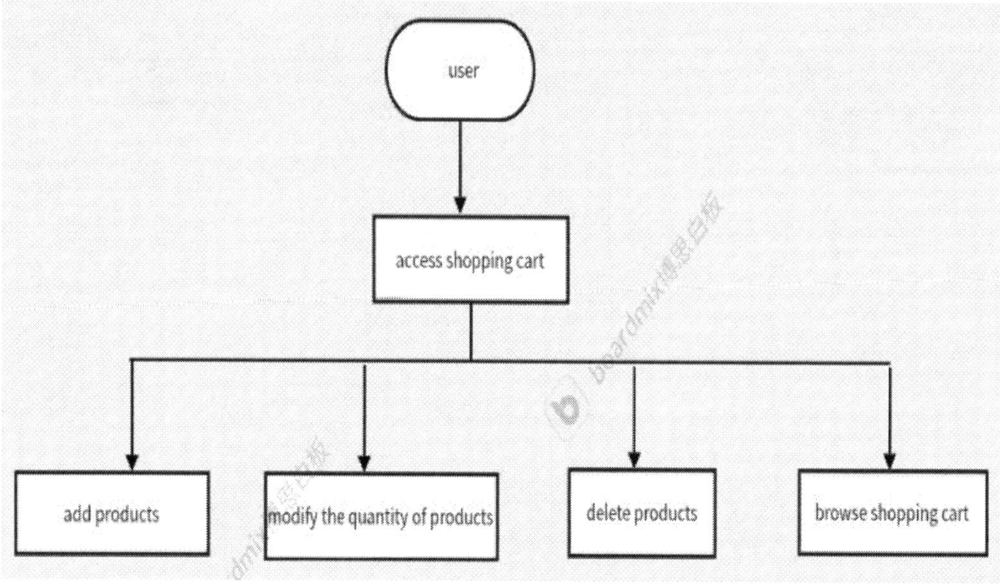

Figure 14-3 The Flow Chart of Shopping Cart Module

4.Order settlement module

After completing the shopping, the user can enter the settlement center, where the system calculates the price of the purchased products and quantity, and finally generates the amount payed by the user. Then the user places an order with the system and provides information such as delivery address and payment method. The process is shown in Figure 14-4.

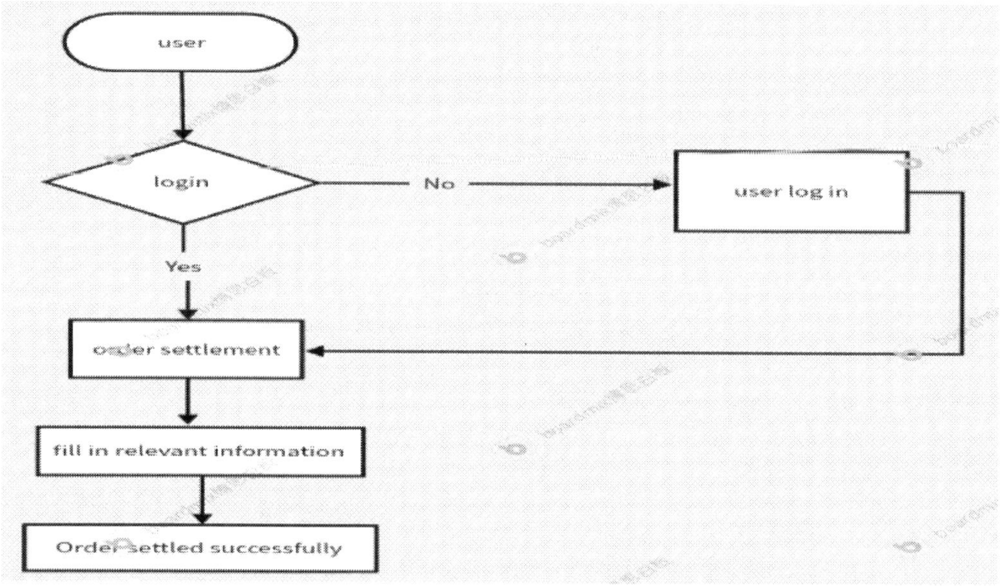

Figure 14-4 The Flow Chart of Order Settlement Module

5.Back-end management module

The back-end management module is a back-end management platform designed according to the requirements of system data maintenance. Only the administrator can access the back-end functional modules to complete system maintenance and management. The process is shown in Figure 14-5.

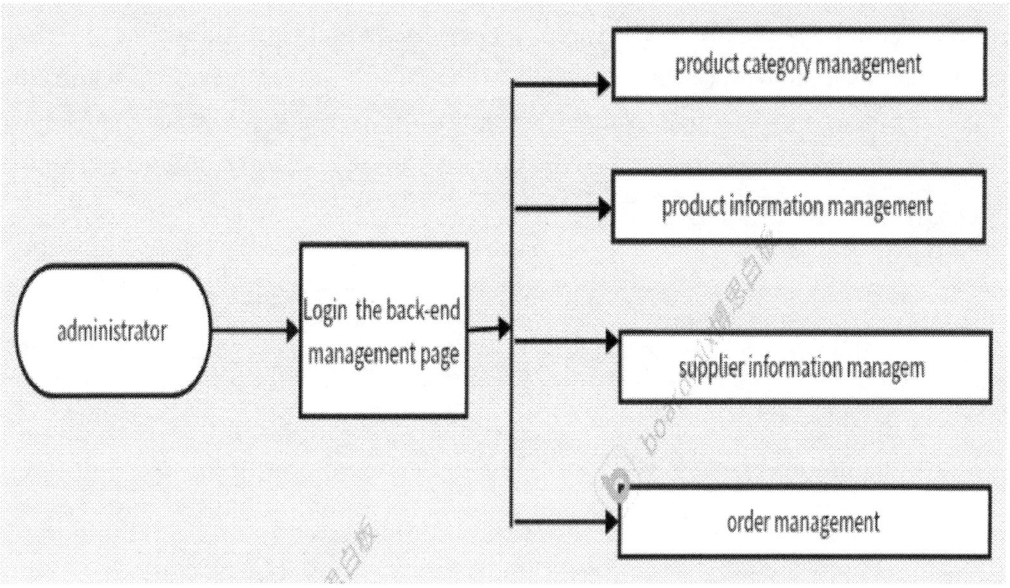

Figure 14-5 The Flow Chart of Back-end Management Module

14.1.2 User control design

The user controls in the MyPetShop application are mainly designed to unify the page style, and the seven user controls are designed according to specific functional needs.

- AutoShow user control: It implements automatic scheduled refresh function for popular products.
- Category user control: It implements the function of displaying product categories.
- The NewProduct user control: It implements the display function of the latest products.
- PetTree user control: It implements product classification and navigation functions including products.
- SiteMap user control: It implements website navigation function based on the website map.
- UserStatus user control: It displays different login statuses and permission information for different users·
- Weather user control: It implements the weather forecast function for major cities in all provinces across the country.

14.1.3 Overall design of system database

MyPetShop application is developed by using SQLServerExpressLocalDB and the database which is used is MyPetShop.mdf.

MyPetShop.mdf database was established by developers and consists of seven tables: CartItem, Category, Customer, Order, OrderItem, Product, and Supplier. Among them, the CartItem table stores detail information about shopping carts; the Category table stores product category information; the

Customer table stores user information; the Order table stores order information, the OrderItem table stores order detail information; the Product table stores product information; and the Supplier table stores supplier information.

14.1.4 Web.config file

The Web. config file in the MyPetShop application is used to set database connection strings, define Ajax Control Toolkit tag prefixes, set calls to weather forecast web services, set email sender information, and more. Among them, the definition of the AjaxControl Toolkit tag prefix is automatically completed when you install the AjaxControl Toolkit package through NuGet, and the setting for calling the weather forecast web service is automatically completed when you add a weather forecast web service reference.

Source Codes: the partial codes of Web.config

```
<configuration>
  <connectionStrings>
  <add name="MyPetShop.DAL.Properties.Settings.MyPetShopConnectionString"
connectionString="Data
Source=(LocalDB)\MSSQLLocalDB;AttachDbFilename=|DataDirectory|\MyPetShop.mdf;Integrated
Security=True" providerName="System.Data.SqlClient" />
 </connectionStrings>

 <system.web>
  <compilation debug="true" targetFramework="4.6.1" />
  <httpRuntime targetFramework="4.6.1" />

  <pages>
   <!-- 定义 AjaxControlToolkit 标记前缀，对应页面中的 @ Register 指令 -->
   <controls>
 <add tagPrefix="ajaxToolkit" assembly="AjaxControlToolkit" namespace="AjaxControlToolkit" />
   </controls>
  </pages>
 </system.web>
 <system.serviceModel>
  <bindings />
  <client />
 </system.serviceModel>

 <appSettings>
    <add key="WeatherServiceRef.WeatherWebService"
 value="http://www.webxml.com.cn/WebServices/WeatherWebService.asmx" />
   <add key="MailFromAddress" value="3272344648@qq.com" />
   <add key="UseSsl" value="true" />
   <add key="Username" value="3272344648" />
```

```
    <add key="Password" value="srzwlgkfypxddaga" />
    <add key="ServerName" value="smtp.qq.com" />
    <add key="ServerPort" value="587" />
  </appSettings>

  <system.codedom>
    <compilers>
      <compiler language="c#;cs;csharp" extension=".cs"
type="Microsoft.CodeDom.Providers.DotNetCompilerPlatform.CSharpCodeProvider,
Microsoft.CodeDom.Providers.DotNetCompilerPlatform, Version=1.0.7.0, Culture=neutral,
PublicKeyToken=31bf3856ad364e35"warningLevel="4"compilerOptions="/langversion:default /
/nowarn:1659;1699;1701" />
      <compiler language="vb;vbs;visualbasic;vbscript" extension=".vb"
type="Microsoft.CodeDom.Providers.DotNetCompilerPlatform.VBCodeProvider,
Microsoft.CodeDom.Providers.DotNetCompilerPlatform, Version=1.0.7.0, Culture=neutral,
PublicKeyToken=31bf3856ad364e35" warningLevel="4" compilerOptions="/langversion:default //
/nowarn:41008 /define:_MYTYPE=\&quot;Web\&quot; /optionInfer+" />
    </compilers>
  </system.codedom>
</configuration>
```

14.1.5 The overall idea of developing MyPetShop application based on VSC 2019

MyPetShop application is based on the Entity Framework and utilizes LINQ technology to access data. It is built by using the three-tier architecture of ASP.NET, including MyPetShop.Web presentation layer project, MyPetSho. BLL business logic layer project, and MyPetShop.DAL data access layer project. The overall development strategy is as follows.

(1) Creating a new MyPetShop solution.

(2) Adding MyPetShop.Web presentation layer project.

(3) Adding MyPetShop. BLL business logic layer project.

(4) Adding MyPetShop. DAL data access Layer Project.

(5) Adding references between projects at different levels.

(6) Downloading the source code package of this book, then extracting the MyPetShop source code package, and copying folders such as Images, Prod_Images, Scripts (containing official jQuery script files), Styles (containing official Bootstrap style files and custom Style.cs and Weather.cs files), SQL (containing custom MyPetShop database script files), etc.

(7) Installing AjaxControl Toolkit.

(8) Creating new folders such as Admin, App_Cde, App_Sata, UserControl, etc.

(9) Establishing MyPetShop.mdf database.

(10) Establishing the "ADO. NET entity data model"- MyPetShop .edmx file.

(11) Modifying the Web.config file.

(12) Createing a new Global.asax file.

(13) Adding files such as CartItemService.cs, CategorizeService. cs, Customer Service. cs, OrderService. cs, ProductService. cs, and SupplyService. cs at MyPetShop The BLL business logic layer .

(14) Creating the master page MasterPage.master, and then taking it as the basis to create various pages under the root folder and Admin sub-folders.

(15) Generating website command.

(16) Starting from Default. aspx and conducting an overall test of the MyPetShop application.

14.2 MyPetShop.mdf DataBase Design

MyPetShop.mdf data base stores information such as shopping cart, product categories, users, orders, products, suppliers, etc.

14.2.1 Database design

1. Shopping cart information table

The table is named CartItem, which includes carItem id, customer id, product id, product name, list price and quantity. The information is shown in table14-1:

Table 14-1 CartItem

Field	Type	Notes
CarItemId	int	Primary key, increment automatically
CustomerId	int	Foreign key, Not Null
ProId	int	Foreign key, Not Null
ProName	nvarchar(80)	Not Null
ListPrice	decimal(20)	Not Null
Qty	int	Not Null

3.Shopping cart information table

The table is named Category, which includes category id, category name, and category description. The information is shown in table14-2:

Table 14-2 Category

Field	Type	Notes
CategoryId	int	Primary key, increment automatically
Name	nvarchar(80)	Not Null
Descn	nvarchar(255)	Not Null

4.Customer information table

The table is named Customer, which includes customer id, customer name, password and Emain. The information is shown in table14-3:

Table 14-3 Customer

Field	Type	Notes
CustomerId	int	Primary key, increment automatically
Name	nvarchar(80)	Not Null
Password	nvarchar(80)	Not Null
Email	nvarchar(80)	Not Null

5. Order information table

The table is named Order, which includes order id, customer id, user name, order date, customer address, the city where customer is located, the state where customer is located, the city zip of customer, customer phone, and order status. The information is shown in table14-4:

Table 14-4 Order

Field	Type	Notes
OrederId	int	Primary key, increment automatically
CustomerId	int	Foreign key. Not Null
UserName	nvarchar(80)	Not Null
OrderDate	datetime	Not Null
Addr1	nvarchar(80)	Null
Addr2	nvarchar(80)	Null
City	nvarchar(80)	Null
State	nvarchar(80)	Null
Zip	nvarchar(6)	Null
Phone	nvarchar(40)	Null
Status	nvarchar(10)	Null

5.Oder detail information table

The table is named OrderItem, which includes order item id, order id, product name, list price, quantity and total price. The information is shown in table14-5:

Table 14-5 OderItem

Field	Type	Notes
ItemId	int	Primary key, increment automatically
OrderId	int	Foreign key. Not Null
ProName	nvarchar(80)	Null
ListPrice	decimal(10,2)	Null
Qty	int	Not Null
TotalPrice	decimal(10,2)	Null

6.Product information table

The table is named Product, which includes product id, product category id, list price, unit cost, supplier id,product name, product description, product image and quantity. The information is shown in table14-6:

Table 14-6 Product

Field	Type	Notes
ProductId	int	Primary key, increment automatically
CategoryId	int	Foreign key. Not Null
ListPrice	decimal(10,2)	Null
UnitCost	decimal(10,2)	Null
SuppId	int	Foreign key
Name	nvarchar(80)	Null
Descn	nvarchar(255)	Null
Image	nvarchar(80)	Image path
Qty	int	Not Null

7.Supplier information table

The table is named Supplier, which includes supplier id, supplier name, supplier address, the city where supplier is located, state where supplier is located, the city zip and phone of supplier. The information is shown in table14-7:

Table 14-7 Supplier

Field	Type	Notes
SuppId	int	Primary key, increment automatically
Name	int	Null
Addr1	nvarchar(80)	Null
Addr2	nvarchar(80)	Null
City	nvarchar(80)	Null
State	nvarchar(80)	Null
Zip	nvarchar(6)	Null
Phone	nvarchar(40)	Null

14.2.2 Data table connection design

To provide data support for the required functions of the system and consider the requirement for referential integrity between data, the relationship between each data table in the MyPetShop.mdf database is shown in Figure 14-6.

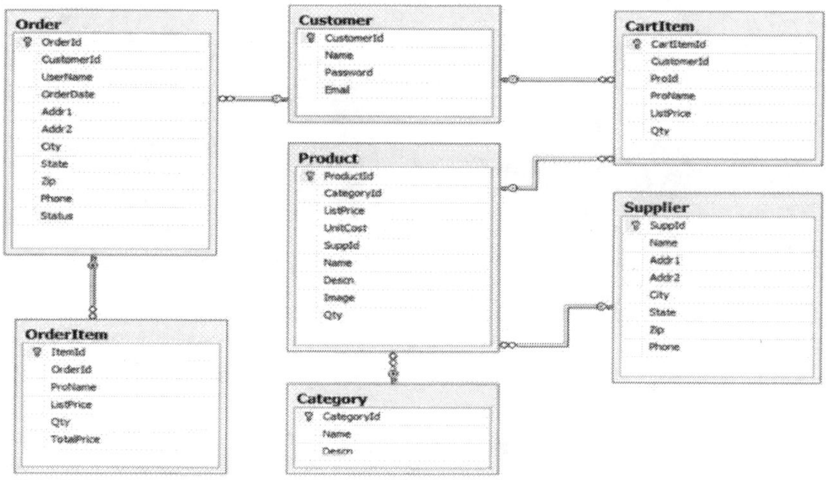

Figure 14-6 The Relationship Chat Between Data Tables

14.3 Custom Controls Design

14.3.1 "Time Refreshing Automatically of Hot Selling Products" user control

This control is implemented by AutoShow. ascx, which mainly includes a Markdown control and multiple "AJAX Extension" server controls (Updating Panel, Updating Progress, and Timer controls). It is used to automatically refresh hot selling product information at scheduled times. The operate effect is shown in Figure 14-7.

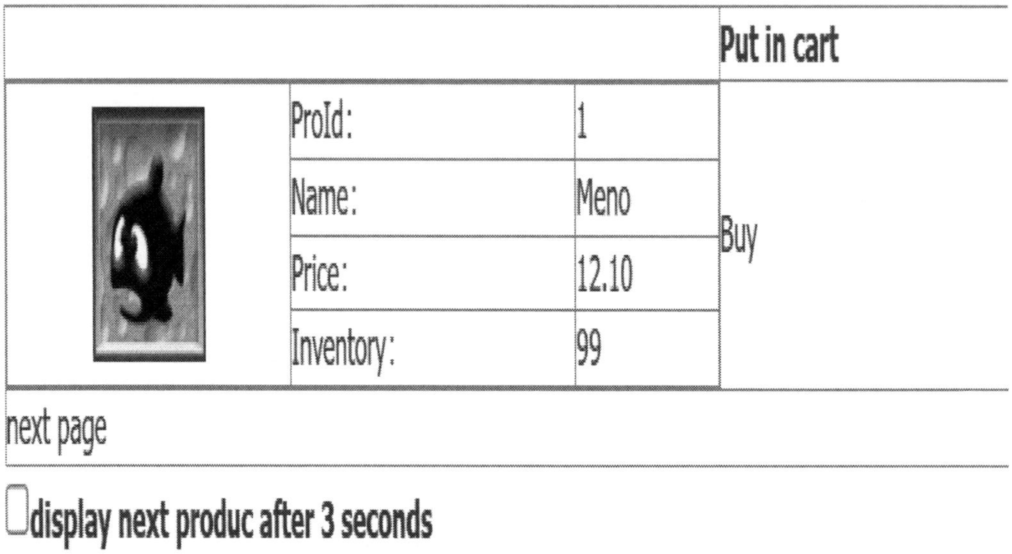

Figure 14-7 The Effect of "Time refreshing automatically of hot selling products" User Control

14.3.2 "Product Category List" user control

This control is implemented by Categorize.ascx. It mainly includes a Markdown control which is used to display product categories and the number of products contained in that category. The product category name is displayed as a hyperlink, and if you click the product category name, you can enter the product list page of that category. The operate effect is shown in Figure 14-8.

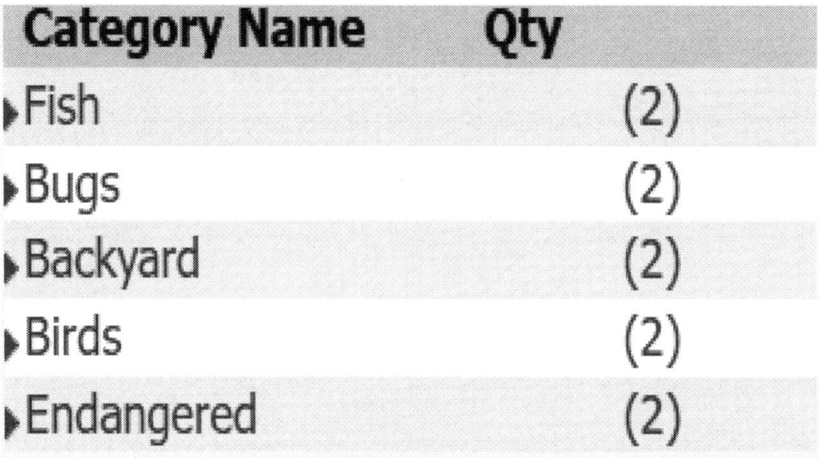

Figure 14-8 The Effect of "Product category list" User Control

14.3.3 "New Product List" user control

This control is implemented by NewProduct. ascx and mainly includes a Markdown control, which is used to display the newest product information, including product names and price information. If you clicking the product name, you will be taken to the product details page. The operate effect is shown in Figure 14-9.

Name	ListPrice
Pointy	¥35.50
Panda	¥47.70
Flowerloving	¥25.20
Domestic	¥45.50
Zebra	¥40.40
Cat	¥38.50
Butterfly	¥24.70

Figure 14-9 The Effect of "New product list" User Control

14.3.4 "Product Category and Navigation" user control

This control is implemented by PetTree.acx. It mainly includes a TreeView control, which is used to implement product category and the navigation function of all products in the corresponding category. The operate effect is shown in Figure 14-10.

Figure 14-10 The Effect of "Product category and navigation" User Control

14.3.5 "Website Navigation" user control

This control is implemented by SiteMap.acx and mainly includes a SiteMapPath control to implement website navigation function. You should note that before implementing website navigation function, you should create a sitemap file Web.sitemap firstly. The operate effect of the user control is shown in Figure 14-11.

Figure 14-11 The Effect of "Website navigation" User Control

14.3.6 "User Status" user control

This control is used to display different user login status information and operate functions. When the user do not log in, it will display the status message "You haven't logged in yet!". When a regular user (using the username Jack as an example) logs in, the status message "username" is displayed with three action link buttons for password modification, shopping history, and log out. When the administrator user (using the username admin as an example) logs in, it displays "admin". The operate effect of the "User Status" user control is shown in Figures 14-12 to 14-14.

Figure 14-12 The Effect of "User status" User Control Without User Login

Figure 14-13 The Effect of "User status" User Control of General User Login

Figure 14-14 The Effect of "User status" User Control of Administrator Login

14.3.7 "Weather Forecast" user control

This control is implemented by Weather.ascx, which is used to display weather conditions by calling a Web service. In order to realize the function of weather forecast, you must take two key steps. Firstly, you should add Web service of weather forecast by using "add service references" command; secondly, you can display the information of weather forecast by calling the corresponding methods of Web service of weather forecast, such as GetC;ityWeather (string cityCode) method.

Note: Because weather forecast web service is sourced from the Internet, it is necessary to connect to the Internet when adding service references and testing.

14.4 Front-end Page Design

14.4.1 Master page

MyPetShop application integrates website, navigation bar, website navigation, copyright and product search function together by using master technology. Simultaneously, it applies ASP.NET Ajax technology and Bootstrap. css style sheets provided by the Bootstrap framework.

There are two key steps when you design the master page:

(1) User controls are added to the master page. Among them, the "User Status" user control and the "Website Navigation" user control are used.

(2) Product search function is implemented by using ASP.NET Ajax technology.

The master page is designed in Figure 15-15.

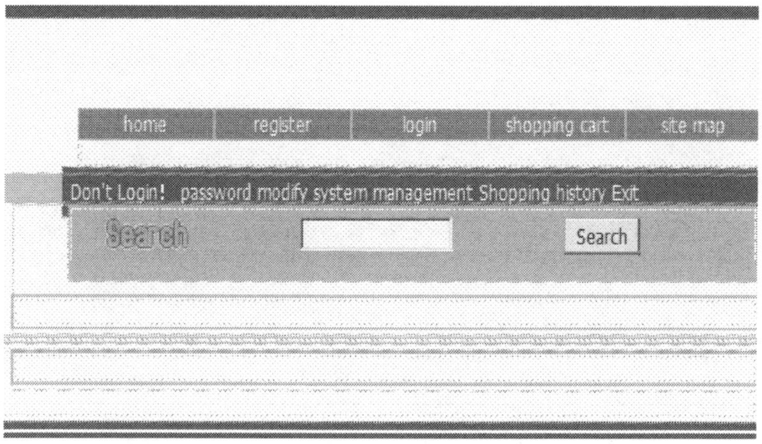

Figure 15-15 The Interface Design of Master Page

14.4.2 Home page

The home page of MyPetShop application is implemented on Default.aspx. Except for displaying the master page, home page displays the information of newest products, hot selling products, product category and weather forecast etc.

Home page design mainly involves three aspects:

(1) Using ASP.NET Ajax technology.

(2) Adding custom user controls. Four user controls are mainly used. They are the "Time Refreshing Automatically of Hot Selling Products" user control, the "Newest Product List" user control, the "Product Category List" user control, and the "Weather Forecast" user control. The page is designed in Figure 14-16.

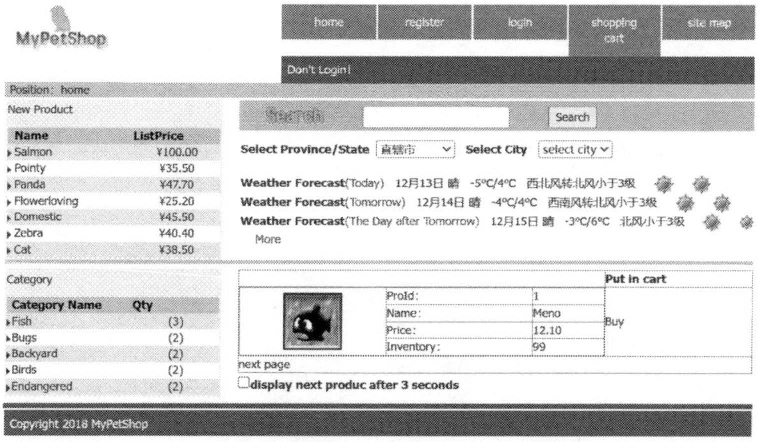

Figure 14-16 The Design of Home Page

14.4.3 Product detail page

Product detail page is implemented on ProShow.aspx. You can browse all of the product information according to the category, and you also can browse the information of some special products. This page includes two parts:

(1) Adding "Product Category and Navigation" user control.

(2) Creating a GridView control which is used to display product information in a list format. This control also provides pagination display function and "purchase" link.

The page is designed in Figure 14-17.

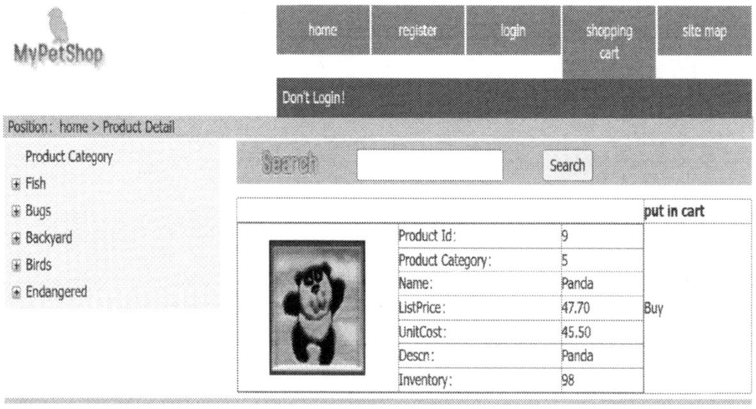

Figure 14-17 The Design of Product Detail Page

14.4.4 Product search page

Product search page is implemented on Search.aspx. The main function is to implement fuzzy search and display product detail information.

(3) Search.aspx design is similar with ProShow.aspx. Apart from referencing master page, this page only adds one "Product Category and Navigation" user control and one GridView control. The GridView control is used to display product information in a list format, and provide pagination display function and "purchase" link. GridView control can display detail information of four products in one page. Users can add products to their cart by clicking the "Purchase" link, which passes the product ID as a parameter to the shopping cart page.

The page is designed in Figure 14-18.

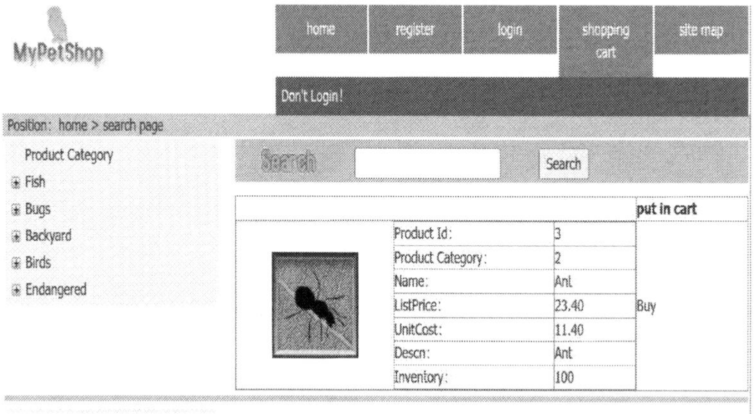

Figure 14-18 The Design of Product Search Page

14.5 Design of User Login and Registration Module

This module offers users the following functions: registering new users, logging into the system, changing user passwords, retrieving lost passwords, and logging out of the system.

14.5.1 Registering new users

The function of registering new users is implemented on the NewUser.aspx page, which mainly involves controls such as text boxes, buttons, and validation controls. The validation controls primarily utilize the RequiredFieldValidator, CompareValidator and RegularExpressionValidator.

The page is designed in Figure 14-19.

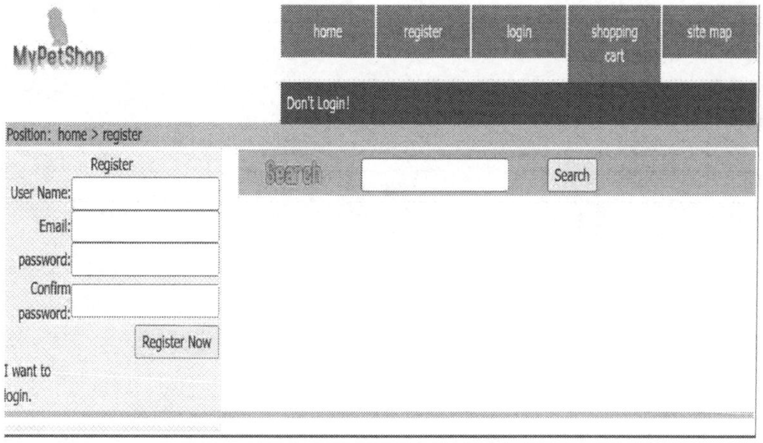

Figure 14-19 The Design of Registering New Users Page

14.5.2 User login

User login is implemented through the Login.aspx page, which mainly involves controls such as text boxes, buttons, and validation controls. The validation control mainly uses Required FieldValidator.

The page is designed in Figure 14-20.

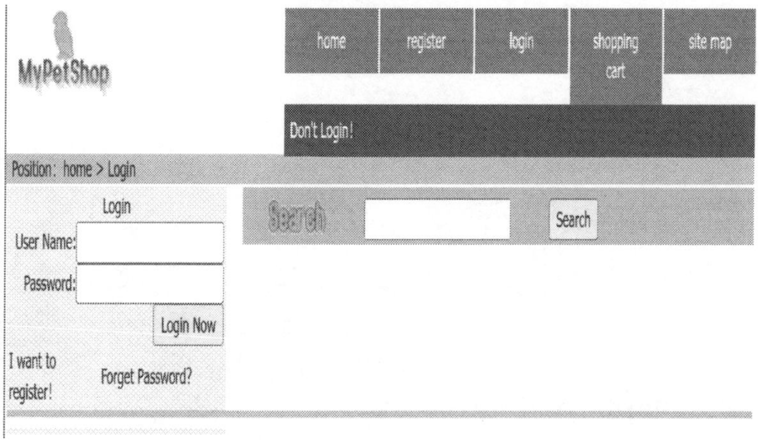

Figure 14-20 The Design of User Login Page

14.5.3 Changing user password

Changing user password is implemented through the ChangePwd.aspx page, which mainly involves controls such as text boxes, buttons, and validation controls. The validation control mainly uses RequiredFieldValidator and CompareValidator.

The page is designed in Figure 14-21.

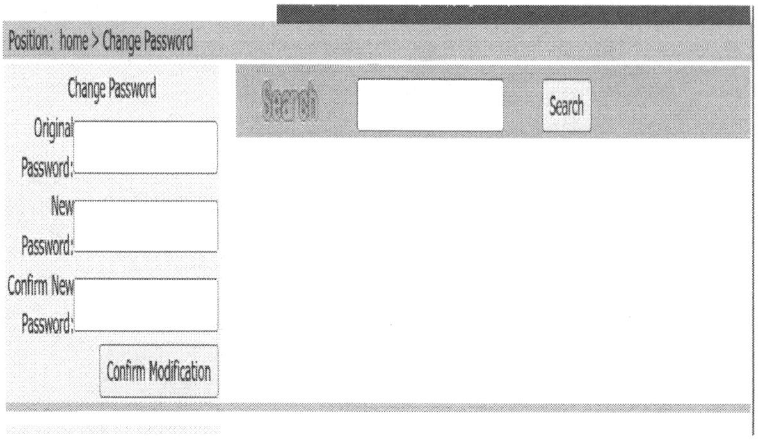

Figure 14-21 The Design of Change User Password

14.5.4 Getting user password

Getting user password is implemented through the GetPwd.aspx page, which mainly involves controls such as text boxes, buttons, and validation controls. The validation control mainly uses RequiredFieldValidator and RegularExpressionValidator.

The page is designed in Figure 14-22.

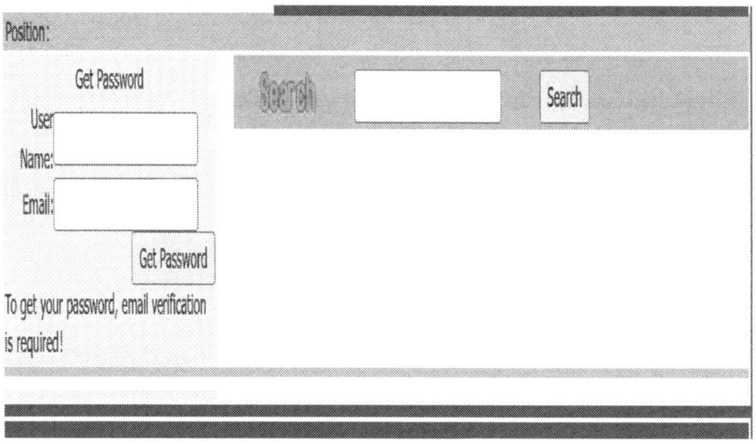

Figure 14-22 The Design of Get User Password

14.6 Design of Shopping Cart Module

The shopping cart module primarily provides functions for designing, viewing, and managing shopping carts. These include the design of shopping cart storage, adding products to the cart, viewing products in the cart, and modifying products in the cart. The shopping cart module is implemented through the ShopCart.aspx page.

14.6.1 Design and implementation of shopping cart storage

The shopping cart is designed and implemented by using database storage technology. A CartItem information table is established in the database to store the contents of users' shopping carts. The detail contents of different users' shopping carts are distinguished based on their user IDs. Therefore, users can only interact with the shopping cart after successfully logging in.

14.6.2 Design of shopping cart page

The ShopCart.aspx page implements all the functions of the shopping cart, including deleting items from the cart, modifying purchase quantities, and clearing the cart. In the design interface of the shopping cart page, there is a GridView control for displaying all items in the shopping cart, four Button controls for implementing shopping cart related operations, and four Label controls for displaying different prompt information.

14.6.3 Design and implementation of shopping cart

The shopping cart function primarily encompasses several features, including adding items to the cart, deleting items from the cart, adjusting the quantity of items in the cart, clearing the cart, and redirecting to the settlement page.

1.Adding items to shopping cart

When browsing the detail product information page, clicking the "Purchase" link button will redirect the user to the ShopCart.aspx page. At the same time, the product number of the item will also be passed as a query string to the page. This will be used in the Page.Load event handling code of the ShopCart.aspx page to complete the functionality of adding and displaying shopping cart items.

The browsing effect is shown in Figure 14-23.

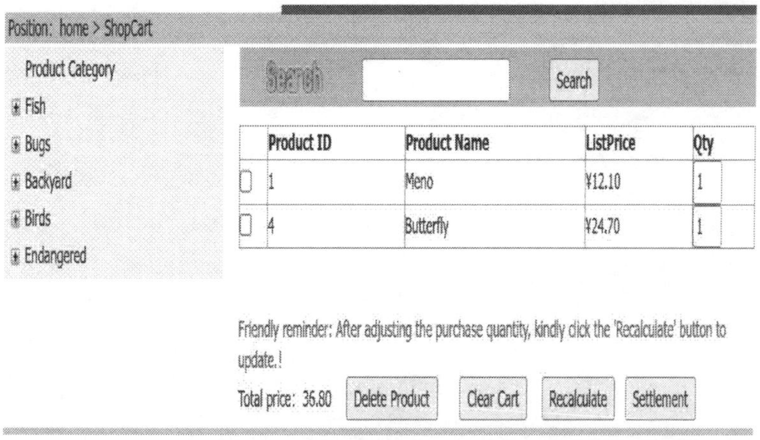

Figure 14-23 Browse Effect after Adding Products

2.Deleting items from shopping cart

In Figure 14-23, if the user does not wish to purchase a specific product, he can first check the checkbox next to the corresponding product, and then click the "Delete Product" button to delete the product from the shopping cart.

3.Modifying the quantity of items in the shopping cart

When a user adds a product to his shopping cart and wishes to purchase additional identical products, he can modify the quantity of the product in the shopping cart. To do so, the user simply needs to adjust the value in the text box located in the "Purchase Quantity" column for the corresponding product as shown in Figure 14-23, and then click the "Recalculate" button to recalculate the total price of the purchased items.

4.Clearing the items in the shopping cart

After adding products to the shopping cart, if the user does not want to purchase all the added products, they can click the "Clear Cart" button to delete all the product records in the shopping cart. After clearing the shopping cart, the user will be redirected to the homepage Default.aspx.

5.Settling all items in the shopping cart

After selecting the product, the user can click the "Settlement" button to redirect the page to the order settlement page SubmitCart.aspx for product settlement. Of course, in practical applications, settlement also needs to be associated with electronic payments, etc.

14.7 Design of Order Processing Module

Order processing primarily facilitates order management functions, encompassing order creation and browsing, which is realized through the SubmitCart.aspx and OrderList.aspx pages, respectively.

Accessing to the order processing page is restricted to logged-in users, and each logged-in user can solely browse their own order details. If a user is not logged in or registered, accessing the order processing page will redirect them to the user login page Login.aspx. They can only proceed to access the order processing page after registering and logging in.

14.7.1 Creating an Order

When clicking the "Settlement" button on the shopping cart page, the logged-in user (using username Jack as an example) will be redirected to the order creation page SubmitCart.aspx. This page mainly comprises text input and data validation controls, in order to collect the address of user delivery and invoice shipping. The browsing interface is shown in Figure 14-24.

Figure 14-24 Browse Effect of Creating the Order

After confirming that the address is correct, the user can click the "Submit" button to place the order, and a prompt message indicating successful order placement will appear.

14.7.2 Viewing the order

The viewing order function enables users (taking username Jack as an example) to view all of their order information, which is implemented on the OrderList.aspx page. Upon successful purchase of a product, a corresponding order is generated. Users can redirect to the order viewing page by clicking the "Shopping Records" link within the "User Status" user control to access all of their shopping records. The order viewing page primarily consists of a GridView control, which is used to display all of the user's order information. The browsing effect is shown in Figure 14-25.

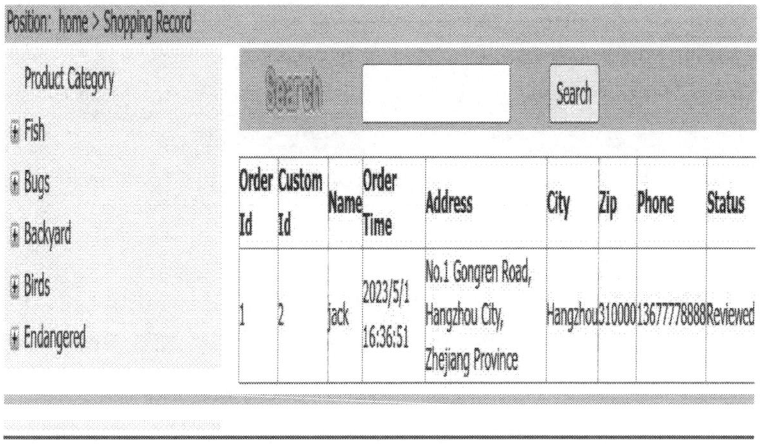

Figure 14-25 Browse Effect of Viewing the Order

14.8 Design of Back-end Management Module

The back-end management module primarily serves the function of data management, encompassing four key areas: product category management, supplier information management, product management, and order management. All implementation pages are stored in the Admin folder of the MePetShop application.

The back-end management module can only be accessed and operated after the administrator logs in. The administrator account for this system is "admin" with a password of "12345".

Note: The MyPetShop application does not support user registration, modification, deletion, and other related functions for administrators, which need to be improved in practical engineering applications.

14.8.1 Product category management

The product category management is implemented by the CategoryMaster.aspx page, primarily utilizing the Repeater control to manage product category information. The Repeater control displays product catetgory information, and clicking the "Edit", "Delete", and "New" links allows for the modification, deletion, and addition of product category information, respectively. The browsing effect of the product category management page (using the administrator username admin as an example) is shown in Figure 14-26.

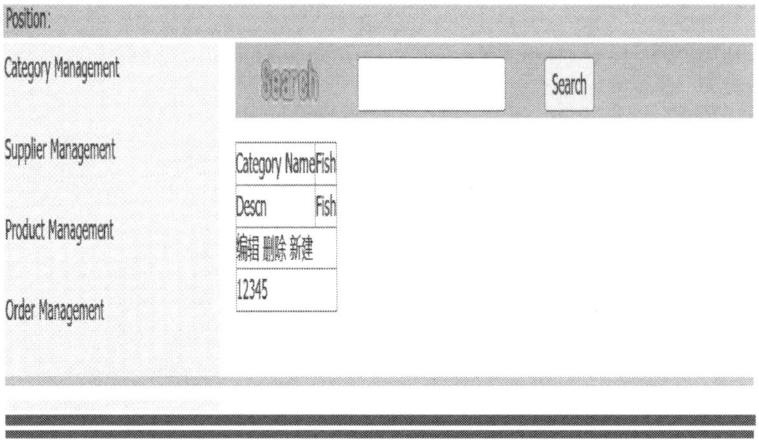

Figure 14-26 Browse Effect of Product Category Management

14.8.2 Supplier management

Supplier management is implemented through the SupplierMaster.aspx page, primarily utilizing the Repeater control to achieve the supplier information management function. The Repeater control displays supplier information, and clicking the "Edit", "Delete", and "New" links can respectively achieve the functions of modifying, deleting, and adding supplier information. The browsing effect of the supplier management page (using the administrator username admin as an example) is shown in Figure 14-27.

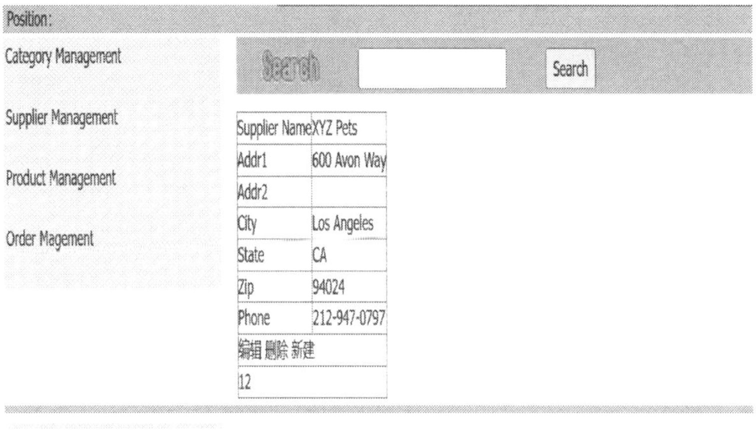

Figure 14-27 Browse Effect of Supplier Management

14.8.3 Product management

Product management is implemented through the ProductMaster.aspx page, primarily utilizing the ObjectDataShow and GridView controls to realize product management. The GridView control displays product information in a paginated format. The browsing effect of the Product management page (using the administrator username admin as an example) is shown in Figure 14-28.

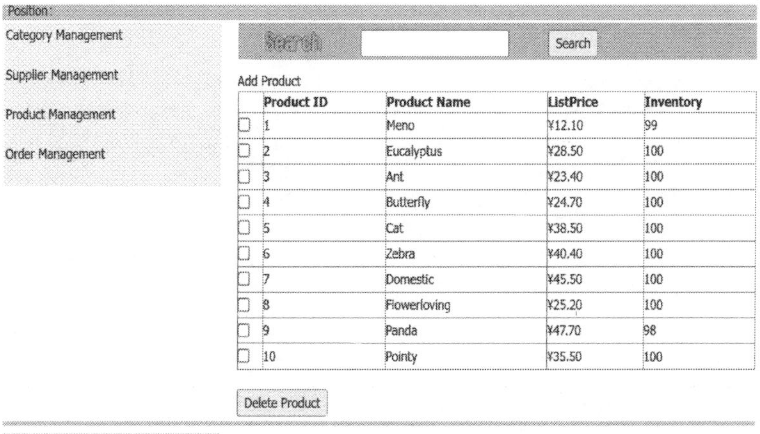

Figure 14-28 Browse Effect of Product Management

1.Adding product information

Adding product information is implemented through the AddPro.aspx page. When the "Add Product" link button is clicked on the product information management page, the page is redirected to AddPro.aspx. On the AddPro.aspx page, various server controls and data validation controls are used for entering product information. After entering the correct product information, the administrator user (using the admin username as an example) clicks the "Add Product" button to add the product information. The browsing effect (taking adding product Salmon as an example) is shown in Figure 14-29.

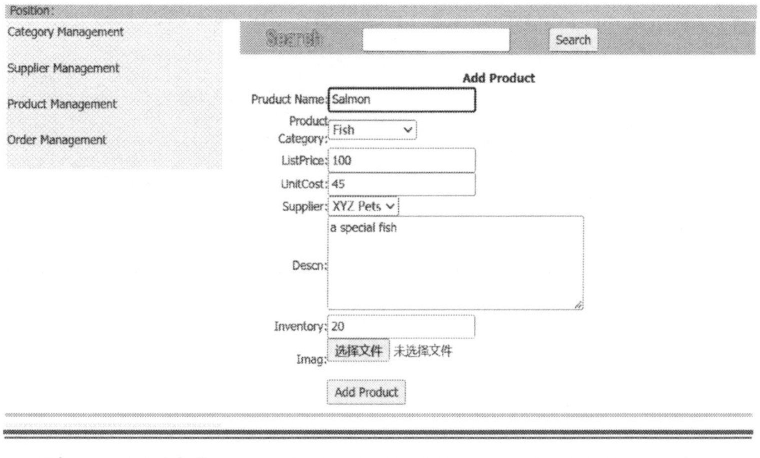

Figure 14-29 Browse Effect of Adding Product Information

2.Modifying product information

The modification of product information is implemented on the ProductSub.aspx page. When you click on the product name (presented as a hyperlink) in the product information management page, the page is redirected to ProductSub.aspx, and the product number is passed as a QueryString parameter to ProductSub.aspx. The ProductSub.aspx page uses various server controls and data validation controls to display corresponding product information based on the passed product number. When the administrator user (using the administrator username admin as an example) modifies the product information, clicking the "Modify Product" button will save the modified product information to MyPetShop.mdf. The browsing effect of ProductSub.aspx (taking modifying product Cat as an example) is shown in Figure 14-30.

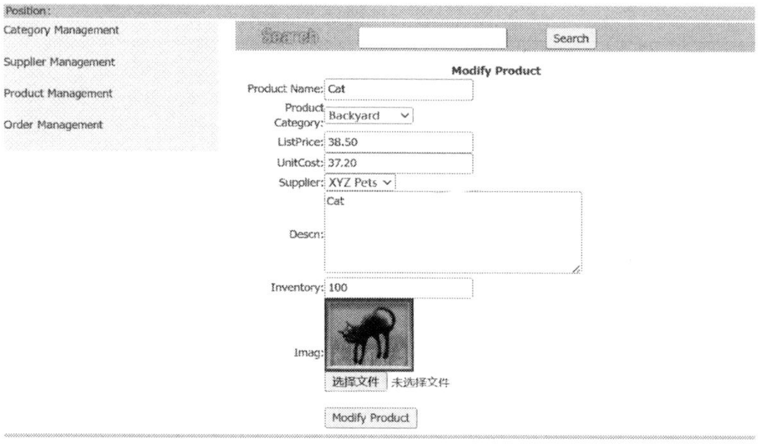

Figure 14-30 Browse Effect of Modifying Product Information

3.Deleting product information

In the Figure 15-28, selecting the checkbox next to the corresponding product and clicking the "Delete Product" button to perform the deletion of the product.

14.8.4 Order management

Order management is implemented through OrderMaster.aspx page, which realizes order management function by using GridView control. The browsing effect is shown in Figure 14-31.

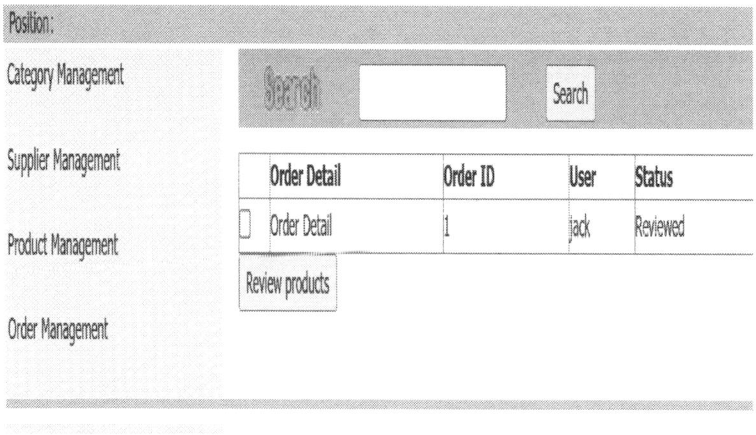

Figure 14-31 Browse Effect of Order Management

1.Viewing order details

Viewing order details is implemented by OrderSub.aspx. Each order contains one or more products. When the administrator wants to view the order details, they can click the "Order Details" link in Figure 15-31, and the page will be redirected to OrderSub.aspx. At the same time, the order number will be passed as a QueryString parameter to OrderSub.aspx. The OrderSub.aspx page displays detail information about the corresponding order based on the obtained order number, including the purchase details and address information that make up the order. The browsing effect (using the administrator username admin as an example) is shown in Figure 14-32.

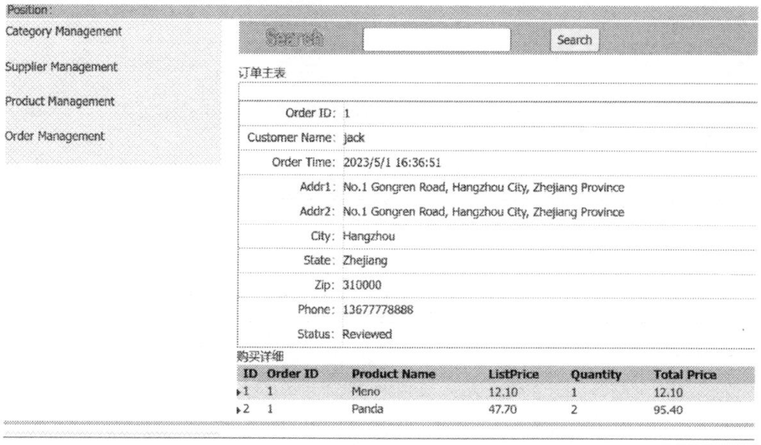

Figure 14-32 Browse Effect of Order Detail Page

2.Reviewing orders

On the order management page, selecting the checkbox next to the corresponding order information in the order list. Click the "Review Product" button to approve the corresponding order, and the order status will change to "Approved". The browsing effect (taking the example of administrator user admin reviewing user Jack's order) is shown in Figure 14-33.

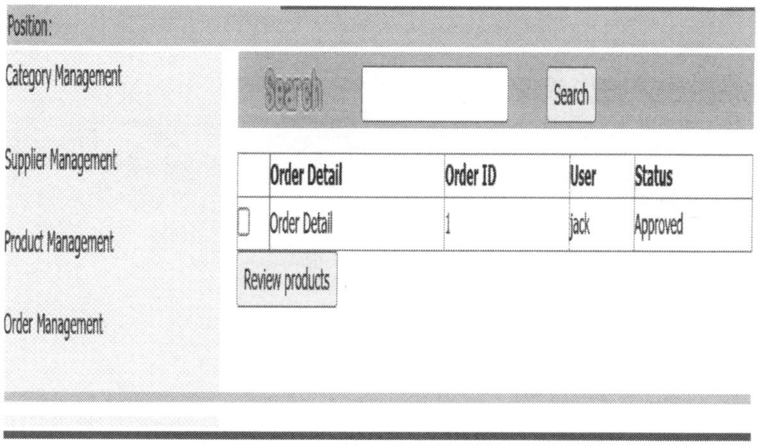

Figure 14-33 Browse Effect of Reviewing Order

14.9 Summary

The development process of the comprehensive MyPetShop instance encompasses overall system design and development strategy, database design, user control design, front-end page design, user registration and login modules, shopping cart module design, order processing module design, and back-end management module design. This instance utilizes the VSC 2019 to develop platform and integrate the entire process of developing web applications based on the ASP.NET three-tier architecture. It provides us with an excellent learning template. Through studying the MyPetShop application, you can comprehend its design philosophy and subsequently familiarize yourself with and master the methods of developing web applications by using the ASP.NET three-tier architecture.

14.10 Exercises

1. Analyze and debug the MyPetShop application.
2. Create a Web application by yourself according to your interests.

Made in the USA
Monee, IL
05 November 2026

67968827R00164